Women and the Colonial Gaze

Edited by

Tamara L. Hunt

and

Micheline R. Lessard

NEW YORK UNIVERSITY PRESS
Washington Square, New York

First published in the U.S.A. in 2002 by
NEW YORK UNIVERSITY PRESS
Washington Square
New York, N.Y. 10003

This book is printed on paper suitable for recycling and made from fully managed and sustained forest sources.

Library of Congress Cataloging-in-Publication Data

Women and the colonial gaze / edited by Tamara L. Hunt and Micheline R. Lessard.
p. cm.
Includes bibliographical references and index.
ISBN 0–8147–3646–7 (cloth : alk. paper) — ISBN 0–8147–3647–5 (pbk. : alk. paper)
1. Women—Colonization. 2. Indigenous women—Social conditions. 3. Imperialism—Social aspects. I. Hunt, Tamara L. II. Lessard, Micheline R.

HQ1122 .W624 2002
305.42—dc21 2001051201

Printed and bound in Great Britain by
Antony Rowe Ltd, Chippenham, Wiltshire

Contents

Acknowledgements

This book grew out of a panel organized by Micheline Lessard for the 1996 Berkshire Conference on Women's History which was held at Chapel Hill, NC. Our thanks go to Dr Karen Ray who commented on the panel and ultimately wrote and essay for the collection, and Dr Ann Taylor Allen who chaired the panel and connected us with Jennifer Hammer of New York University Press who first proposed the idea for the collection. Dr Susan Rabe was helpful in identifying potential contributors for the volume. Patricia Wiltshire and Luciana O'Flaherty of Palgrave Publishing have been both patient and helpful as we guided the book towards completion. Ruth Willats provided invaluable editorial guidance and support. Finally, Dr Scott Hughes Myerly provided substantial editorial input and compiled the initial index for the volume.

Notes on the Contributors

Margaret Zoller Booth is an assistant professor in the Program of Educational Foundations and Inquiry at Bowling Green State University in Ohio. She received her PhD in Curriculum and Instruction with a specialization in Educational Psychology and International/Comparative Education from Ohio University in 1991. She is the author of several articles in such journals as *Comparative Education* and *Comparative Education Review* and has presented a number of scholarly papers in the United States and in Africa.

Nupur Chaudhuri is an assistant professor at Texas Southern University. She received her PhD from Kansas State University in 1974, and is the author of numerous articles and reviews. She was the co-editor of *Western Women and Imperialism: Complicity and Resistance* (Indiana, 1992) and is currently working on a manuscript entitled "Life in a Gilded Cage: Memsahibs in Nineteenth-Century India."

Jane Crawford is Professor and Chair of the Classics and Archeology Department and Director of the Humanities Program at Loyola Marymount University. She received her PhD from the University of California at Los Angeles. Her publications include *M.T. Cicero: The Lost and Unpublished Speeches* (1984) and *M.T. Cicero: The Fragmentary Speeches* (1994).

Carmen Ramos-Escandon holds a PhD from SUNY at Stony Brook in Latin American History and two Masters degrees from the University of Texas at Austin in Latin American Studies and Latin American Literature. She has published two readers on gender, *Genero y Historia* (1991) and *El genero en perspectiva Mexico* (1992), and her *Presencia y Transparencia* (1987) is a reader on women in Mexico. She has contributed to a number of collected volumes on gender and women, and has published in major historical journals. Currently, she is a national researcher at CIESAS and teaches at the postgraduate History program at UNA in Mexico City.

Anna Fernyhough is a graduate of the University of London and holds an MA in Anthropology from the University of Illinois. Her expertise lies in archaeology and human osteology, in which areas she has published reports and articles. She has also published previously on women in Ethiopia, where she has lived and worked with her husband, Tim. A qualified school teacher, her current post is at a school in Northamptonshire, England.

Timothy Fernyhough received his PhD in African History from the University of Illinois in Urbana-Champaign. At one time Assistant Director of the Center for African Studies at the University of Florida, he is currently Director of Studies and Senior Tutor in History, Department of American Studies and History, Brunel University, England. He is the author of articles and book chapters on Ethiopian social history.

Laura Fishman is director of the Women's Studies program and assistant professor of history at York College, of the City University of New York, where she teaches courses in European history, colonialism, and women's history. She received her PhD in European history from the City University of New York, where her doctoral dissertation was a comparative study of English and French attitudes towards Native Americans in the early modern era. She is also the author of several published articles and conference papers that focus on early French colonial ventures in Florida and Brazil. Current research interests include analysis of missionary goals and strategies, and the role of the colonial experience in redefining contemporary European attitudes towards work.

Katherine E. Fleming is an assistant professor of history at New York University. She received her PhD in History from the University of California at Berkeley in 1995. A former Mellon research fellow, she has published several articles and book reviews on Ottoman history, and a book, *Ali Pasha of Ioannina: a Study in Cultural Representation* (1999). She is currently the review editor of the *South East European Monitor.*

Ruth Wallis Herndon is an associate professor of history at the University of Toledo. She received her PhD from the American University in 1992. She is the author of a number of journal essays and book chapters. Her essay, coauthored with Narragansett elder Ella Sekatau, "The Right to a Name: Narragansett People and Rhode Island Officials in the Revolutionary Era" in *Ethnohistory*, won the 1998 Heizer prize. Her most recent publication is *Unwelcome Americans: Living on the Margin in Early New England* (2001). She is currently working on a book on orphan apprenticeship in early America, a project which is supported by a major grant from the Spencer Foundation.

Tamara L. Hunt is an associate professor of history at Loyola Marymount University in Los Angeles. She received a PhD in history from the University of Illinois and has been the recipient of a number of grants and awards, including an NEH Fellowship and an ACLS grant. She is the author of articles that have appeared in essay collections and in journals such as *Albion* and *Victorian Periodicals Review*, as well as a monograph, *Defining John Bull: Caricature and National Identity in Late Georgian England* (2001). She is currently working on a monograph on eighteenth-century women in the London publishing trades.

Micheline R. Lessard is assistant professor of Asian history at the University of Ottawa. She obtained her PhD in Southeast Asian History from Cornell University, as well as a BA and MA in Asian history from Concordia University in Montreal. She is the recipient of numerous grants including the Social Science and Humanities Research Council of Canada, Social Science Research Council, Mellon Dissertation Fellowship, and Luce Fellowship. She has published several articles, including "Curious Relations: Jesuit Perceptions of the Vietnamese" in *Essays into Vietnamese Pasts*, published by Southeast Asia Press of Cornell University.

Luis Martínez-Fernández is currently an Associate Professor and Chair of the Department of Puerto Rican and Hispanic Caribbean Studies at Rutgers University. He received his PhD from Duke University in 1990 and is the author of *Fighting Slavery in the Caribbean: The Life and Times of a British Family in Nineteenth-Century Havana* (1998), as well as numerous articles on nineteenth- and twentieth-century Caribbean history. His monograph *Protestantism and Political Conflict in the Nineteenth-Century Hispanic Caribbean* will be published in 2002.

Isabel Bonet O'Connor is an assistant professor of history at Southern Indiana University, having received her PhD at UCLA. The recipient of a number of scholarly fellowships and grants, including several Del Amo Foundation fellowships, and a grant from the American Academy of Research Historians of Medieval Spain, she has published several articles in scholarly journals on the conflict between Christians and Muslims in fourteenth-century Spain.

Karen A. Ray is Professor of Humanities at Marianopolis College. She has published numerous articles on Government of India policy toward the Indian diaspora and has been a consultant on the history of the diaspora for both textbooks and official publications. Her research has been funded over several years by the Social Science and Humanities Research Council of Canada, and she has three times been senior fellow of the Shastri Indo-Canadian Institute. The volume *East and West Indies: the Abolition of Indentured Emigration and the Politics of Colonial Rule* is in progress.

Jiweon Shin is currently finishing her dissertation in Sociology at Harvard University and teaching in the Social Studies program at Harvard. She recently completed a two-year appointment as a fellow-in-residence at the Center for the Study of World Religions at Harvard University, and has received a Dissertation Research Fellowship from the Social Science Research Council. Her research interests include cultural/religious change in East Asia, and she has published several articles on Korean popular culture in the global context and on modern women's identity in Korea.

Verónica Vázquez Garcia received her PhD from Carleton University in 1995 where her dissertation was awarded a Senate Medal for oustanding academic achievement. She presently teaches at the Colegio de Postraguados en Ciencias Agricolas, Texcoco, Mexico. Her research focuses on gender and natural resource management in southern Veracruz. She has been awarded a Leadership Grant from the MacArthur Foundation to conduct an action-research project in this region. Her publications have appeared in various edited books and several journals, including the *International Journal of Canadian Studies*, the *Canadian Journal of Development Studies, Revista Mexicana de Ciencias Politicas y Sociales*, and *Cuadernos Agrarios*, among others.

Introduction

Tamara L. Hunt

When colonial powers considered their subject peoples, they often employed what could be called the "colonial gaze": that is, they saw the colonies through eyes that were blurred by misinformation, misconceptions, and stereotypes. Since the 1970s, scholars such as Edward Said have cast this in terms of the imperialist viewing the "Other," arguing that colonial powers construct conceptualizations of subject peoples that serve the interests of those who rule.[1] But the use of the "Other" to refer to women pre-dates Said's work, and women's studies scholars have used the term ever since Simone de Beauvoir set forth her theory of "Woman, the Other" in *The Second Sex* in 1949.[2] The essays in the present volume suggest that there is a distinct juncture between these two views of the "Other," and that imperialism and gender were closely linked in a number of ways. Because imperialistic nations typically have patriarchal social structures, the fact that women in subject lands often did not conform to the gender constructs of the dominant imperial culture was used to explain the "uncivilized" nature of their society. Similarly, conquering countries often attributed "feminine" characteristics to all subject peoples as a means of explaining characteristics that from the colonial point of view were unfamiliar and undesirable. This tends to throw into high relief the notion that the "masculine" characteristics of the conquering nation are naturally dominant, thereby legitimizing colonial rule as a reflection of male superiority which was seen as "natural" in society.

Thus, this work contributes to the recent literature on colonialism in a number of ways. For example, some scholars have shown that the colonialist mentality tended to portray subject countries and their citizens as effeminate, weak, submissive, and irrational – and thus in need of protection and guidance from masculine imperial authority. This is one of the themes in *Imagining India* (1990), in which Ronald Inden posits that the development of Orientalist European ideologies during the Enlightenment ultimately excluded Indians and their institutions from playing an active role in the development of their own history.[3] Complicating this issue, however, are questions of complicity, resistance, and adaptation, all of which have been raised by a number of scholars, including Mrinalini Sinha in *Colonial Masculinity* (1995), who suggests that middle-class Bengali men (often portrayed as "effeminate" and thus different from the "masculine" Englishman) ultimately shared so many assumptions with their British overlords that their nationalistic campaign actually "brought them into closer harmony with colonial rule."[4]

However, using gendered symbols to depict the colonies did not always convey negative messages and, as Dominic David Alessio has shown, female figures used to represent the white settlement colonies were viewed favorably by potential emigrants. Nevertheless, this reinforced an imperial ethos, as emigrant women were increasingly seen as imperial agents for upholding racial and moral standards in the colonies.[5] Reina Lewis's *Gendering Orientalism* (1996) similarly argues that the gendered ideology that surrounded the imperial endeavor allowed and even encouraged white women to expand their influence as cultural agents and producers, in this case through painting and writing. Another persuasive case for the close relationship between gender and imperialism is found in Anne McClintock's *Imperial Leather* (1995), which demonstrated the relationship between feminized domesticity and imperial mastery in the nineteenth century within the context of a much broader analysis of race, gender, sexuality, and imperialism. Such views influenced and shaped relations between colonizers and colonized, and this interplay was an important element in the evolution of colonial policies.[6]

One important way in which ideas about imperial territories reached the home country was through travel accounts, and as recent scholarship shows, these seemingly straightforward descriptive works are often important, albeit subtle, agents of imperialism. For example, Mary Louise Pratt's *Imperial Eyes: Travel Writing and Transculturation* (1992) deftly sketches the ways in which travel writing fostered a process of "Euroimperialism," arguing that such writings and explorations have "produced Europe's differentiated conceptions of itself in relation to something it became possible to call 'the rest of the world'." However, Pratt rejects a simply binary view of colonialism (e.g. self/Other) to argue that the colonial encounter was a matter of transculturation, a "contact zone [in which] disparate cultures meet, clash, and grapple with each other, often in highly asymmetrical relations of domination and subordination."[7] Similarly, in her study of Victorian women's travel writing about Southeast Asia (*Place Matters*, 1996), Susan Morgan demonstrates the elusive and complex nature of Victorian attitudes toward the colonies. She emphasizes the fact that the gender of the viewer, as well as a host of other factors, could shape and define the colonial gaze and, like Pratt, rejects the idea that there was a uniform imperial ideology that applied to all foreign territories at all times. Further, Morgan stresses that the gender of the travel writer substantially influenced the colonial view found in travel accounts and, even when female Victorian travel writers applied patriarchal or masculine values to the colonial scene, they did more than "mouth the party lines." Yet at the same time, the political and social variables of each individual situation meant that these women did not create an identifiable "female imperial rhetoric," thus emphasizing the complex and diverse nature of imperial ideology.[8] Similarly, Susan L. Blake and Cheryl McEwan have shown that the gender of travel writers on Africa significantly impacted the ways in which foreign territories, landscapes, and societies were presented to domestic audiences.[9]

A few recent works, such as the special issue of the *Journal of Women's History* (1990),[10] have taken a multinational approach to the study of gender within a colonial context. Some, such as the collection of essays *Nation, Empire and Colony* (ed. Ruth Roach Pierson and Nupur Chaudhuri, 1998), have examined the power relations between the colonies and their metropoles through the prism of class, race, and sexuality.[11] Others, while also multinational in scope, have analyzed gender relations within the specific context of a given imperial power, thereby bringing together, within an interpretive framework, the notions of gender and empire. In studies such as *Gender and Imperialism* (ed. Clare Midgely, 1998), gender is at the center of the interplay between men and women of the colonies and men and women of the imperial nation.[12] Yet other studies, particularly those that have appeared in special issues of scholarly journals such as *Gender and History*, have taken a more continental approach, such as analyzing gender relations within colonized nations, and demonstrating the multiplicity of layers and the complexity of power relations at play in numerous colonial contexts.[13] Finally, gender and gender relations have been at the center of studies examining the concepts and the historical processes of nations, nation-building, and nationalism. These studies, including *Gendered Nations* (ed. Ida Blom, Karen Hagemann, and Catherine Hall, 2000) are also multinational in approach and highlight the broad spectrum within which operate gender relations.[14]

The essays in the present volume, most of which were written for this volume and appear in print for the first time, also reflect a multinational approach to issues of gender and colonialism.[15] However, the principal focus is on the "gaze," the lens through which the "Other" is interpreted and subsequently depicted. The representations and the composition of the interpretive lens reflect multiple layers of power relations that are more nuanced than simple relations between the colonizer and the colonized. While these representations of the "Other" at times resulted in specific and concrete colonial policies, often these policies were a reaction to power relations within the colonies, to struggles and political tensions operating on a number of levels. In this book, the concept of the "colonial" is taken more broadly than in most anthologies of colonialism and imperialism. It covers a longer time-frame and a broader geographical spectrum. The essays are therefore presented in a way that highlights these temporal and geographical locations. This work is divided into three geographical divisions – Europe, the Americas, and Asia and Africa – and within each of these parts, the essays appear in chronological order based on their subject matter, ranging from the pre-common era to the twentieth century. A number of methodologies are reflected in this compilation, including literary representations, dissection of legal documents, examination of specific colonial policies, and historiographical analysis. The content, presentation, and methodologies used in this collection of essays therefore provide a rich tapestry of colonial experiences. They illustrate the complexity of the lens through which others are examined and depicted.

While this geographical and chronological division has been adopted for reasons of clarity, it should not be forgotten that the essays provide a comparative context for understanding the intersection of gender and colonialism as it occurred across time and over diverse regions. Thus, the following discussion of the essays serves to highlight the themes they touch upon and to provide a more comprehensive overview of the overall work. Several essays in this collection show how colonial perceptions of women were used and manipulated. According to Laura Fishman,[16] sixteenth-century missionaries and explorers gathered detailed information about the Tupinamba people of Brazil, but drew conclusions that actually focused on their own culture. Some praised the modesty and chastity of Tupi women – despite the fact that the culture was polygynous and matrilocal – in order to condemn the morals and manners of European women. Thus, Fishman suggests that native women were romanticized to serve a quite different agenda.

K.E. Fleming[17] shows how such romanticism was also used to simulate control over lands not formally colonized. She argues that Philhellenism and the Hellenic ideal embraced by intellectuals from Britain and Western Europe were forms of surrogate colonialism in which the history and ideology of Greece were annexed instead of the country itself. Yet when travelers from Britain visited Greece, which they viewed as the land of their cultural forebears, they were disappointed because they perceived the Greek people to be "ignorant peasants," and not the heroic, idealized figures of the distant classical past. Consequently, to preserve their illusions, Westerners developed an image of Greece as a noble, heroic woman in chains, surrounded by the degradation of contemporary Greek culture, and therefore in need of a western "knight" to come to her rescue, and preserve a past which Western society viewed as actually belonging to itself rather than to contemporary Greeks.

A similar manipulation of history is the subject of Carmen Ramos-Escandón's essay[18] on Concepción Gimeno de Flaquer, a late nineteenth-century Spanish feminist and author. A resident of Mexico for more than a decade, Gimeno's speeches and writings formed a cultural link between Spain and the former colony. This is especially true in her depictions of the Aztecs, most notably in her portrayal of Malintzin, the Aztec woman who served as Hernan Cortes's interpreter as he conquered her people. Although Gimeno argued that Aztec society gave women greater power and influence than did European society, she nevertheless endowed her heroines with European characteristics and even depicted Malintzin with classical Greek features and dress.

In addition, Gimeno describes Malintzin as a devout Catholic who was anxious to help her people by actively seeking to convert them to Christianity and the superior benefits of Western culture. Thus, while Gimeno's colonialist ethos is reflected in her portrayal of Malintzin as a willing collaborator, a feminist ideology also emerges in her depiction of Aztec women as strong-willed characters who voiced their own opinions and asserted themselves.

Such manipulation of history was not new in the nineteenth-century colonial world; as Jane Crawford[19] shows, imperial Roman historians approached the subject of colonial women with a variety of such agendas. Tacitus portrayed Cartimandua and Boudicca, two British queens, in radically different ways to suit different purposes. His account of Cartimandua's reign emphasized her immorality and unsavory character, which both reflected his distrust of women who engaged in politics and commented on contemporary Roman affairs. This view is echoed by Dio, another Roman historian, whose approach reflects another way observers used their perceptions of colonized women to highlight the supposedly savage – and inferior – nature of subject peoples. According to Crawford, both Tacitus and Dio suggested that it was "unnatural" for any society to have a female monarch, and the fact that the British tribes were ruled by queens was thus evidence of their barbarity. Tacitus' portrayal of another British queen, Boudicca, also served as a foil to critique Rome, but his goal in writing about her, and thus his assessment of her actions, was different. He does not praise her as a political leader, but as a wronged wife and mother who sought to protect her family. This reflected the idealized virtues of a Roman matron. Further, he initially praised her and her people for rebelling, thus recalling the virtuous citizens of the early Roman republic who threw off oppressive tyrants. Only when the victorious Britons turned to revenge-killing and looting did he condemn them as uncouth barbarians.

Centuries later, when the British themselves had become a colonial power, British travelers used descriptions of native women as a means of conveying politically significant messages about various peoples of the empire. As Nupur Chaudhuri[20] shows in her analysis of the writings of two British women travelers to India, the tenor of their works generally mirrored the colonial situation. Eliza Fay traveled to India in the late eighteenth century, when much of the subcontinent was still under the control of local rulers and was thus considered remote and exotic by most Britons. Yet when the anonymous female author known as "A.U." wrote a century later, most of India was under British control, and improved transportation and communication had made Britons more familiar with Indian culture. Although both women focused on Indian culture and private life, their approaches were different. Fay portrayed Bengali women of Calcutta as the "Other" by stressing the difference between their customs and those of her readers; Indian women to her were a curiosity whose exotic nature needed to be described and explained. A century later, A.U. also portrayed the Indian women of Calcutta as the "Other," but she viewed them as inferior, subject peoples who needed to be guided by the British toward civilization. As in the cases described by Ramos-Escandón and Crawford, A.U. supported the ideals of imperialism through her descriptions of native women by denigrating them for their supposed failure to act in a "civilized" fashion – that is, for not acting like their conquerors.

Yet this attitude was not reserved solely for "exotic" peoples of distant colonies; as Tamara Hunt[21] shows, the English held strikingly similar attitudes about the Irish. By the eighteenth century, war and property confiscation had placed the vast majority of Irish Gaelic Catholic peasants under the control of a relatively small group of English and lowland Scots Protestant landlords. To maintain and justify their dominance over the Irish majority, English stereotypes of the Irish emerged, portraying them as wild, crude, and barbaric. But after Ireland joined the United Kingdom in 1801 – supposedly as an equal partner – this image changed. Just as Fleming's essay shows that Greece was envisioned as a woman in need of a British knight to save her, so Ireland came to be depicted in the nineteenth century as a woman who needed to be controlled and guided by a civilized, masculine England.

In the colonial context, however, such views not only shaped perceptions about colonized people, they also influenced colonial policies. Hunt shows that English officials enforced the poor laws and distributed famine relief based on accepted English Victorian gender roles where men were the breadwinners and women were housewives who had no separate income, thereby ignoring the fact that most Irish peasant women made substantial monetary contributions to their family economies. Thus, when such policies failed to meet their goals, officials often attempted to change women's behavior to suit official plans rather than adapt their strategies to meet existing needs.

Thus in Ireland, as in India, the emphasis placed on gender roles among subject peoples was used as a means of further controlling colonial societies by erecting or maintaining rigid gender, race, and class distinctions between rulers and their subjects, and this is reflected in the essays by Isabel O'Connor,[22] Luis Martínez-Fernández,[23] and Ruth Herndon[24] as well. O'Connor argues that in late medieval Spain, officials of ruling Christian states often failed to punish Christian men for having sexual relations with Muslim women, even though the law strictly forbade such contact and the Muslim women were supposed to be severely punished or sold into slavery. Instead, these states encouraged Muslim women to become prostitutes to service the male Christian population. This seeming paradox reflected an effort by the Spanish rulers to emphasize the inferior position of the Muslim subject population by allowing men from the ruling society to have sexual access to subject women. Thus, this legal ambiguity was more about wielding power than about maintaining sexual morality, and strict Islamic laws requiring women to be chaste and virtuous only made the insult to the Muslim community more blatant.

Controlling access to women was also a hallmark of the highly stratified colonial society of nineteenth-century Cuba. As in the case of medieval Spain,

Cuban women of color, whether slave or free, generally were more sexually accessible to men of the ruling class than were white women, but because whites made up only a tiny fraction of the Cuban population and were overwhelmingly outnumbered by slaves, the women of the ruling class became a central symbol for demarcating ruler and subject. As Martínez-Fernández shows, an extremely restrictive code of behavior emerged for Spanish women which was directly related to these class, racial, and gender imbalances and restrictions. Ladies in Cuba literally lived behind bars, and even when they ventured out to go shopping or visiting, custom forbade them from leaving their specially built, high-wheeled carriages for as much as an instant while in the streets. This rule was so rigid that shops developed an early form of drive-by shopping – the clerks brought the goods to each carriage, where they were inspected or tried on within the secluded interior.

Martínez-Fernández points out that cultures which severely restrict the behavior of ruling-class women usually emerge where the dominant class is greatly outnumbered by a large slave population, such as in the antebellum American South. But in other places in America where European settlers quickly came to outnumber and/or dominate native peoples, officials who attempted to enforce European gender roles as part of a process of "civilizing" indigenous peoples generally directed their efforts toward making native women conform to European ideals. Herndon shows that in colonial Rhode Island, Indian women who lived on the fringes of white society came to symbolize disorder because they did not conform to English notions of community and patriarchal family structure. During the eighteenth century, colonial officials used residence laws and access to public financial support as a means to control women whose lifestyles seemed to challenge colonial patriarchy, such as in cases where they and their children lived without a resident male head of household, groups of adult women lived together, or women with children had no fixed residence. Town officials tried to make such women conform in several ways: they, or their children, might be forced into indentured servitude, thereby placing them under the control of a "respectable" white man; or they might be "warned out," whereby officials tried to get rid of them by ejecting them permanently from the town. This attempt to subordinate or banish women ultimately led to their obliteration as individuals in the public record, reducing them to anonymous "squaws" or "mustees" and ceasing to differentiate between them and black women.

Women could also become "invisible" when their people were coerced or bribed to adopt European-style economic and social customs. Verónica Vázquez Garcia's comparative analysis of land ownership in colonial Mexico and Canada[25] shows that despite the differences in the two cases, the end result of European conquest for native women was remarkably similar. In Mexico, pre-conquest inheritance customs stressed lateral ties across sibling groups rather than lineal bequests from parents to children. In this system, women regularly inherited and bequeathed land, including rights to communal land. However, as part of the Spanish conquest, officials began enforcing a patriarchal social structure through religious and legal sanctions, which in turn emphasized lineal inheritance through the male line. This trend continued even after independence, as nineteenth-century liberals used legislation to undercut those remaining communities that had collective land ownership in order to integrate indigenous people more fully into Western society and thereby make them "useful citizens." Yet even in the collectives that survived into the twentieth century, women ultimately lost their individual rights; legislation gave them custodial membership, holding land in trust for their children, but no inherent land rights as individuals.

Although British authorities faced different circumstances in Canada and used a different colonial approach than the Spanish did in Mexico, Vázquez Garcia shows that the results for native women there were similar. Neither Iroquois nor Algonkian society fitted the British model – the former was matrilineal and matrilocal, with women controlling land use and distribution, the latter were a migratory people whose men and women had complementary roles. Although the French and British did not conquer and control these peoples outright in the first centuries of European contact, they nevertheless had a significant impact on these societies, undermining women's position through propagation of patriarchal religion and by changing the economic basis of society by placing a high economic value on fur trapping by Indian men, so undermining the economic activities of women. Once the British consolidated control, however, they adopted policies whose intent was similar to those described by Herndon in Rhode Island – forcing the Indians to adopt British customs and values. Both the Iroquois and the Algonkian peoples were urged to learn English, adopt English social customs, and take up English-style farming. It was clear that the British intended this offer to encourage a patriarchal family structure by granting land only to men and on the condition that they conformed. Further, as was the case in Mexico and Rhode Island, Indian women in Canada lost their identity under a patriarchal colonial government, for the Indian Act of 1876 defined Indians as male persons of a particular band. Women who married non-Indians ceased to be considered Indians and lost virtually all the rights guaranteed to Indians by treaty, and even those few that remained could be taken away for "immoral" behavior.

In all these instances, it is clear that colonial officials believed that controlling the behavior of native women was an important component of successful rule. By the later nineteenth century, however, the development of highly stratified gender roles in European society also began to influence colonial policy. In Britain and France in particular, society envisioned women as guardians of the home and morality, and the moral lynchpin that held civilized society together.

It is thus hardly surprising that colonial administrators came to view native women as a central element in "civilizing" indigenous society. British administrators in Swaziland clearly had this goal, as Margaret Booth[26] shows in her analysis of colonial educational policy for Swazi girls. Although the general educational goal in Swaziland was to train and "civilize" workers, education for girls was clearly intended to teach them to be good wives and mothers in the Western mold, not prepare them for jobs. Moreover, educational policy documents from the first decades of the twentieth century make it clear that British administrators equated girls' training in cooking, sewing, arts and crafts, and hygiene with civilization. Thus, missionary and colonial aims merged, as administrators sought to promote a civilized Christian culture built around women who were trained to fulfill their domestic duties – and raise their children – in accordance with Western ideals of domesticity and patriarchy.

Late nineteenth-century French administrators viewed the women in their colonies in a similar way. As Micheline Lessard[27] shows, educational policy in colonial Vietnam sought to transform Vietnamese women into good Frenchwomen. Educators envisioned Vietnamese mothers teaching French language and culture to their children, who would thus learn to love their French "mother" (i.e., France) from infancy. Clearly, a goal of this policy was to promote Vietnamese loyalty to France, but it also reflected fears rooted in French domestic concerns, which were in turn projected on the colonies. In France itself, officials worried about a declining domestic population and the supposed moral degeneration of the working classes, both of which, it was feared, would reduce France's standing as a great world power. These concerns also came to figure in colonial policy toward women. Ignoring the brutal colonial economic conditions that kept most Vietnamese in poverty, colonial officials asserted that the high infant mortality rate was the result of women's lack of an adequate education, which resulted in poor maternal skills and a failure to maintain adequate hygiene. Officials also worried about the "degenerate" nature of the Vietnamese; on the one hand, they feared it would infect Frenchmen who lived in the country for an extended period, yet on the other, they worried that the Vietnamese people would adopt the degenerate culture of the French working classes. In either case, teaching young women "proper" conduct was a major element in the remedy.

Such efforts to indoctrinate the women of a conquered country with the cultural values of the oppressor was not limited to the colonies of Western nations, as is shown in Jiweon Shin's essay[28] on Korean women. Japanese aggression in Asia in the early twentieth century led Korean intellectuals to begin promoting women's education for the first time in their history, in the belief that educated mothers would be better able to prepare the next generation for the struggles to maintain independence that lay ahead. Even greater changes occurred after Japan fully conquered Korea, and the image of the "New Woman" appeared; this further undermined traditional culture by stressing that women's right to education and employment opportunities was as important as that given to men, and even superseded women's traditional obligations to home and family. Yet while this movement quickly fell from favor, new educational goals for Korean women emerged in the 1930s, when Japan demanded that Korea make greater contributions to Japanese military mobilization and instituted educational policies intended to mold Koreans into "good Japanese." In response, Korean nationalists countered by promoting the idea of "glorified motherhood," which stressed the need for women to learn all aspects of Korean culture in order to enable them to raise a new generation of patriotic Koreans to oppose the cultural colonialism of Japan.

Shin's essay not only shows that women's place in society was viewed as a crucial one in transforming colonial culture, it also clearly shows that men in this colonized country attempted to shape women's roles to help achieve political goals. This is a major point of Karen Ray's essay[29] on indentured women in colonial India. The end of slavery in the British empire in 1833 was not matched by a decline in the need for labor, so cash-crop plantations throughout the imperial territories turned to long-term indentured servitude to supply their labor needs, drawing heavily on India for labor world-wide. Conditions for indentured servants were abysmal, often mirroring those of slavery: individuals might be tricked or forced into service and sent far away from their homes to undertake backbreaking labor. Women were especially vulnerable to abuse from male overseers, and the shortage of women on the plantations, or "coolie lines," made rape, prostitution, or forced marriage common. The initial attack on indentured servitude by male Indian nationalists focused on the image of the vulnerable and victimized Indian woman. In this ideology, these women personified the nation, suffering at the hands of the foreign oppressor, who robbed them of their dignity and identity. Since the campaign to end indentured servitude emerged at the very beginning of nationalist struggles in India, its rhetoric and ideology were incorporated into the later political struggle. This led to a view that Ray calls "victimology," an ideology that viewed women as helpless, perpetual victims – or potential victims – as a basic component of the nationalist program. Yet as Ray points out, this image overlooked the fact that, for many Indian women, indentured service (despite its dangers and problems) offered them opportunities for employment and independence that were not readily found in caste-bound India, with its child marriages and restrictions on women. Thus, she raises questions about the nature of empowerment; can this term be applied to liberation movements that demand that women continuously live the role of victim?

Other essays in this volume touch upon this question, showing that colonized women's images and roles are often circumscribed by their own men for their own purposes. O'Connor shows in her essay on medieval Spain that even though Muslim women were often pursued by Christian men who considered them fair game, Muslim men were less tolerant of their illicit sexual behavior and often passed sentences of stoning or whipping on women who were thought to have dishonored their families. While this emphasis on female chastity was part of Islamic beliefs, it is clear that Muslim men also saw this as a means of safeguarding their community from further subversion by the ruling

Christian community. Somewhat paradoxically, it was this aim that led Muslim men to rescue some women who had been convicted of sexual misconduct and sentenced to slavery in a Christian household. Even though the women would be outcasts in the Muslim community as punishment for their transgressions, Islamic leaders nevertheless saw this as a way of protecting their community from further abuse. In either case, women and sexual access to them were a vital part of community identity, but men, not women, determined that identity.

Women were doubly colonized – by nationality and by gender – in other colonial contexts. For example, Hunt shows in her study of Irish women, that in the late nineteenth century the male leader of Ireland's nationalist Land League adopted English attitudes toward women in politics. After forming the Ladies' Land League to symbolically continue the fight against unfair rents for Irish peasants while the male Land League leaders were in gaol, these same men were dismayed to discover on their release that instead of being a mere figurehead organization, the Ladies' Land League had actively pursued their assignment and had proved to be far more efficient than the men, thus carrying on the long tradition of female involvement in public and political affairs. This was more than embarrassing for the men, since they were planning a constitutional campaign in the British Parliament to persuade England and the world that the Irish were sufficiently "civilized" to be entrusted with a greater degree of self-rule. But since the Western world equated civilization with patriarchy, women had to be removed from the political process. In consequence, male Irish politicians adopted this ideology and began telling Irish women that their patriotic duty consisted solely in being good wives, sisters, and mothers who supported their men by maintaining true Irish households that embraced Irish culture.

In a similar way, Lessard shows that male Vietnamese nationalists created for themselves the image of women as the teachers and guardians of the nation's culture and identity. Anti-colonialists called upon women to be the "mothers of the nation" who would inculcate Vietnamese culture in their children, despite the heavy promotion of French culture by the colonial administration. Yet ironically, the French emphasis on educating women solely for a domestic role had one consequence that both Vietnamese and French leaders could agree upon; by limiting technical and academic education to men, women were unable to compete for skilled jobs. Vietnamese men approved, since they were more likely to be able to secure better-paying positions, while French leaders viewed this as a welcome means of keeping down the number of unemployed and disgruntled.

A similar unity of colonial and indigenous purpose was evident in the educational policies of Swaziland, but in this case, the colonial administration accommodated local concerns as part of Britain's policy of indirect rule. Precolonial Swazi education had been age- and gender-specific; consequently, the idea of giving women equal access to education and employment met with resistance from Swazi leaders. They claimed that this taught women to despise Swazi customs; while educated women did not have as many employment opportunities as men, they nevertheless became more independent. This view came to dominate post-World War II British educational policies, not only because the nineteenth-century colonial goal of educating women to "civilize" their households still lingered, but also because the British administration wanted to secure the friendship of the Swazi monarchy, through which it intended to rule the country indirectly. Thus, even though some administrators expressed a desire to advance women's economic opportunities, neither the colonial administration nor the local power hierarchy saw this as beneficial to Swazi men, and the policies instead reproduced the patriarchy which supported the political goals of men.

Clearly, material benefits for men in colonial territories could motivate them to adopt the ideology of their rulers at the expense of women, and this has had consequences that linger to the present day. Nowhere was this indicated more clearly than in the case of land ownership as described by Vázquez Garcia. Although the Mexican revolution of the early twentieth century was a popular uprising that united rural and urban poor with the rising class of capitalists, the land reforms that followed it clearly embraced the lineal, patriarchal views of land ownership first promoted by Spanish overlords centuries before. An Act of 1927, which defined landholders of communal property as male, gave widows only custodial rights to land, holding it in trust for her late husband's (male) minor children. By the time women were given individual right to communal land in 1971, most of the land had been distributed and, with the passive contrivance of the Mexican government, local leaders simply ignored women's claims. In 1992, new legislation stripped widows and children of their limited inheritance rights, declaring that land could be willed away at the discretion of the male owner, without provision for his wife or children.

Similarly, Canadian governments encouraged patriarchy by giving land to men who conformed to English customs, and women's identity as Indians was gutted by the Indian Act of 1876 which declared that if an Indian woman married a non-Indian, she ceased to be an Indian. Indian activism in the first half of the twentieth century brought about renewed discussion of the status of native Americans, but the restrictions on women who married outside the Indian community were strengthened in 1951, subjecting them to involuntary eviction from reserves and loss of their rights as Indians. Although world pressure in the 1980s forced Canada to dramatically change these laws and reclassify women as Indians who had been summarily stripped of their identity, the male-dominated leadership of local bands resisted attempts to grant band membership to these women and their children. Since only band members have a right to live on reserves, participate in its politics, and share the resources, this resistance is as much a matter of economics as it is of identity. Nevertheless, men – whether Indians or whites – determined a native woman's identity and place in the social structure.

Even scholars could be guilty of attempting to create identities for non-Western women in order to fit established anthropological or cultural models, as shown in the essays by Laura Fishman and Timothy and Anna Fernyhough.[30] Although Fishman examines the Tupinamba of Brazil and the Fernyhoughs study Ethiopian women, both note that twentieth-century scholarship has reflected the West's patriarchal society, as anthropologists have projected the gender patterns of their own culture onto that of their subjects. Fishman also points out that native peoples were persuaded or forced over time to adopt European social structures, which in turn may have obscured the existence of a more egalitarian or even matriarchal pre-colonial society. Some scholars even preferred to see such altered societies as evidence for the universal nature of patriarchy. These views have led scholars to give more weight to men's activities, often assuming that native women's work was never highly valued or that it was confined solely to domestic affairs.

Studies that made such assumptions could present a seriously flawed view of women's role and status, as the Fernyhoughs reveal in their essay on Ethiopian women. Even though Ethiopia was never successfully colonized by a Western power, its history and scholarly views of its women in particular have undergone a type of historiographical and anthropological colonization by scholars in the first wave of African studies in the mid-twentieth century. In some ways, this is comparable to the eighteenth- and nineteenth-century travelers to Greece described in Fleming's study (Chapter 3), for the Fernyhoughs show that many Western scholars approached Ethiopian history with established models of how women fit into that history. Thus, Ethiopian women often were viewed with a scholarly, yet nevertheless colonial, gaze. For example, in the 1960s, male scholars applied unilineal inheritance models developed by such major anthropological figures as E. Evans-Pritchard and A.R. Radcliffe-Brown to describe the various cultures of Ethiopia, even though more broadly-based descent groups were found among the Amhara, one of the major ethnic groups. In some respects, this recalls the ideology in colonial Mexico highlighted by Vázquez-Garcia, in which colonial administrators sought to replace sibling inheritance with strict lineal descent. Although scholars were not literally imposing such social structures on the Amhara, applying such a model to Ethiopian women inherently undervalued their historic role in society since unilineal descent groups tend to emphasize men's claims to land, status, and power.

In a related context, the Fernyhoughs note that such an emphasis on unilineal descent exacerbates the tendency of male scholars to view Ethiopian society from a patriarchal perspective – that is, they view women solely in terms of their relationships to men, as mothers, wives, and daughters. This approach is misleading, as the Fernyhoughs show through an examination of recent scholarship on Ethiopian women's history. Aristocratic women could be powerful rulers and landowners in their own right, and some individual rights were enjoyed by all free women, including the commonly used right to seek a divorce and receive a half-share of the household possessions. However, all this took place within the context of a male social framework, and men frequently denigrated women in surviving documents. The Fernyhoughs rightly caution against taking these male views as representing the society as a whole, but they also warn against over-emphasizing women's role to compensate for any potential misogyny in the sources.

This essay on Ethiopian women serves as a reminder of the potential difficulties that exist in the union of gender and colonial history. For instance, it is very easy to view women as passive actors in colonial affairs, subject solely to the whims of men. However, a number of the essays in this collection remind us that women sometimes took affairs into their own hands. For example, Herdon shows that some Indian women were able to maintain their independence by using the English system to their advantage. In a similar way, Hunt shows that Irish women manipulated the English poor laws as part of a larger survival strategy. Vázquez Garcia shows that in the twentieth century, both Mexican women and Canadian women joined groups who agitated for the return of their identities as citizens and landowners, while Shin shows that in the 1920s, Korean women openly campaigned for greater individual freedoms as part of the "New Woman" ideology.

Sources, too, need to be examined with great care. Fishman and the Fernyhoughs point out that even eminent scholars can be guilty of unintentional bias so substantial as to create a false view of the past. In the case of ancient Roman historians, Crawford shows that such distortion was intentional, although Fleming's essay on eighteenth-century Greece shows that scholars could also be self-delusional. Women as well as men could espouse a gendered imperial ethos, as shown by Chaudhuri's essay on British women's writings on India and Ramos-Escandón's study of Concepción Gimeno's views of the Aztecs. Gimeno's use of the media to propagate her interpretation of Aztec history serves as a reminder that newspapers and journals could often be made to serve the aims of empire, especially when it came to promoting a particular type of identity for women, as Shin shows was also the case in Korea. Such publications, as well as diaries, letters, and even official reports, show that native men could also take up the gendered attitudes of their rulers, as shown in Hunt's essay on Ireland, Lessard's study of Vietnam, and Booth's analysis of education in Swaziland. Vázquez Garcia's comparative approach to Mexico and Canada reflects a similar situation, and it suggests that laws could reflect gendered views of society, a point also made by O'Connor's analysis of medieval Spain and Herdon's study of colonial Rhode Island.

In sum, colonial perceptions of gender – and, more specifically, of women's social, political, and economic role – were such an important element of colonial ideology, actions, and policy that colonial studies and women's studies both need to examine this issue in greater detail in order to develop a more complete understanding of the nature of the colonial ethos. This collection, through its broad geographical and chronological scope, attempts to reflect the pervasive and enduring nature of the gendered colonial gaze, and is an effort to contribute to our understanding of the complexities and interrelationships of gender and colonialism in their many guises.

Part I

Colonialism within Europe

1

Cartimandua, Boudicca, and Rebellion: British Queens and Roman Colonial Views

Jane Crawford

From a tiny village on the banks of the Tiber, the city of Rome grew to encompass a huge empire, including millions of inhabitants in the Mediterranean world and beyond. The conquest and subjugation of this vast territory, which took place over the course of several centuries, was the responsibility of the armies of the republic and the emperors; the administration of it fell first to the Senate and then to imperial appointees. As areas of the Empire were conquered, they were organized into provinces and the process of Romanization began. The adoption of Roman law and customs, obligations and amenities occurred at varying rates and with a greater or lesser degree of completeness, depending on the indigenous culture of the conquered peoples. But in virtually no case was a territory subdued and pacified without difficulties, setbacks, and conflicts, often including outright rebellion. Stephen Dyson's important articles demonstrate clearly the patterns of native revolt in the Roman Empire and present cogent reasons for these rebellions. It is my intention in this essay to examine the role of women in native unrest and revolts in Britain, focusing on identified leaders who not only worked behind the scenes, using their marital or religious status to influence native resistance to Rome, but also took active roles in rebellion. After a discussion of the events shaped by their participation, I will analyze the way in which the Roman historians reporting on these issues present them, and discuss how their attitudes reflect on the status of non-Roman women in the Roman Empire.

Native rebellions, according to Dyson, are "one of the most persistent phenomena related to the extension of Roman conquest and control in the Western Empire."[1] Generally they occur fairly early in the process of Romanization and often involve substantial areas of the province or territory. The leaders of such revolts are sometimes from the ruling class of the tribes in rebellion, but sometimes not; the relationships of the tribe and its leaders to the Roman conquerors also varies in nature. Dyson points out several areas which are of concern in a discussion of native rebellions: the structure of the indigenous society and the effect on it of subjugation and Romanization; the leadership during the rebellion; the unity (or lack of it) among the rebels; causes of the revolt; religion; and the reaction of the Romans in the face of the revolt and its impact.[2]

Although native unrest and uprisings occurred all over the Roman world, I will concentrate on two in Britain. Both of these centered upon a woman as leader; Cartimandua, a client-queen of the Romans, was involved in episodes of unrest and dissent in AD 51, 58 and 69. Boudicca led a major uprising in AD 60/61,[3] which had serious consequences for Roman rule in Britain. I will discuss the general topics adduced by Dyson, as well as the specific circumstances informing these women's roles. In examining the primary sources, I will show how the actions of Cartimandua and Boudicca are portrayed by the Roman historians who tell their stories, and how they are characterized as barbarian, non-Roman women by the authors. Finally, I will analyze the picture(s) of the barbarians and draw some conclusions on their validity and on their resonance for Roman culture.

There are certainly other women – queens and commoners – who inspired rebellion and led troops against the Roman Empire. Prominent among these are, of course, Cleopatra of Egypt and Zenobia of Palmyra (Syria). These women, however fascinating and important they may be, fall outside the scope of this essay because they both ruled in sophisticated realms which had been under Roman influence for many years, and whose culture was far more developed, Romanized, and above all, stable. My interest lies in the analysis of the Roman attitude toward the truly Other; the woman outside the respectable Greco-Rome pale; the uncivilized barbarian.

The first of the barbarian women of influence that I will consider is Cartimandua, Queen of the Brigantes, a loose federation of people who occupied the Pennines, Yorkshire, and Lancashire.[4] The Brigantian tribes formed a client kingdom along the northern frontier of the area governed by Aulus Plautius in the years immediately following the Claudian invasion of AD 43. One of the Romans' tried-and-true methods of controlling conquered peoples was to establish sympathetic native rulers as clients of the Emperor, who took on the king or ruler in a patron–client relationship, assuming thereby that the subjects of the ruler would in turn be bound to him by the same dependency. This was an inexpensive and nearly effortless way to secure the outer borders of a territory.[5] Cartimandua was just such a client, "acceptable to all these diverse peoples as she was probably a member of one of the leading families,"[6] or, more likely in my view, she may have been imposed by the Romans for their own reasons. She also made a dynastic marriage to Venutius, a leader from a tribe to the north, and remained loyal to Rome for at least the next two decades. With her help, Rome thus secured a volatile and vulnerable border.[7]

Cartimandua's role in peace and war in Britain is told by Tacitus in the *Histories* and the *Annales*. She makes her first appearance in the portion of the *Histories* covering the events of the year AD 51, when she handed over to the Romans a British leader named Caratacus, who had rebelled against the newly arrived propraetor P. Ostorius Scapula. Despite having put up a strong challenge to Scapula, Caratacus failed to win the day and his family was taken prisoner in the final battle (Tac. *Ann.* 12.35.7). According to Tacitus, Caratacus hoped to carry on guerrilla warfare against the Romans, and tried to find refuge with the queen: *cum fidem Cartimanduae reginae Brigantum petivisset, vinctus ac victoribus traditus est*: "although he had sought the protection of the Brigantian queen Cartimandua, he was bound and handed over to the victors" (Tac. *Ann.* 12.36.1).[8]

This move was certainly pro-Roman on Cartimandua's part and may have caused her some difficulties among her people. After all, the Brigantes had been involved in unrest a few years earlier (Tac. *Ann.* 12.32.3: *discordia apud Brigantas*), which, although quickly settled, had been worrisome enough to recall Ostorius Scapula from an expedition to the west (Tac. *Ann.* 12.32.4). In acting now so openly in favor of the Romans, what was Cartimandua doing?

The answer is clear: she was protecting herself and her interests. When Rome acknowledged her position as queen of the Brigantes, both sides gained from the relationship. Cartimandua received powerful support; Rome protected its frontiers. As a client-queen, Cartimandua could help Rome, and in fact was obligated to do so by their agreement. Moreover, it was important to her to clear up the negative impression left by the recent unrest among her tribesmen.[9] Tacitus neatly summarizes her position and her actions: *Cartimandua Brigantibus imperitabat, pollens nobilitate; et auxerat potentiam postquam capto per dolum rege Carataco instruxuisse triumphum Claudii Caesaris videbatur*: "Cartimandua, powerful because of her high birth, was ruling over the Brigantes, and she afterwards had increased her power, when she was credited with having captured King Caratacus by trickery and so provided an adornment for the triumph of Claudius Caesar" (Tac. *Hist.* 3.45.1). The key words here are *auxerat potentiam* – she had increased her power. By her cooperation with Rome she had solidified her position as ruler – an important consideration in view of the apparent volatility of her people.

A few years later, in AD 57,[10] Cartimandua's service to Rome stood her in good stead. Tacitus tells us of a quarrel between the queen and her consort Venutius, which she tried to settle by getting Venutius' brother and other male relatives in her power through deception (*callidis artibus*: Tac. *Ann.* 12.40.4). This ploy failed, not surprisingly in my view, for the obvious reason that her (male) opponents were furious at her actions: *inde accensi hostes, stimulante ignominia, ne feminae imperio subdurentur*: "[they were] incensed, and driven by the ignominy of having to submit to the rule of a woman" (Tac. *Ann.* 12.40.5). As we shall see, the idea of being outsmarted by a woman and made subservient to her was utterly loathsome to the Roman men. So angry were they that the men in question then revolted against Cartimandua, led, no doubt, by her estranged husband. And the queen's allies, the Romans, intervened in her behalf, having foreseen her difficulties: *missae auxilio cohortes acre proelium fecere, cuius initio ambiguo finis laetior fuit*: "the cohorts sent to the rescue fought a fierce battle, whose outcome was doubtful at first, but whose end was happier" (Tac. *Ann.* 12.40.6). Cartimandua's policies paid off. Her power was reaffirmed and there seems to have been a reconciliation with Venutius. Rome had gone to considerable trouble to keep Cartimandua in power, even intervening openly in the affairs of the Brigantes, and the reward came a few years later; the Brigantes did not take part in the rebellion of Boudicca (Tac. *Agricola* 31.4).[11]

We next hear of Cartimandua in AD 69, when her kingdom was again rocked by dissent. This time, however, Cartimandua appeared to be the instigator. According to Tacitus, she replaced her husband Venutius, whom she had come to despise, with another man: *spreto Venutio (is fuit maritus) armigerum eius Vellocatum in matrimonium regnumque accepit*: "having spurned Venutius (he was her husband), she took his armor bearer Vellocatus in marriage and in rule" (Tac. *Hist.* 3.45.1). This insult – a scandalous act in Tacitus' words (*flagitio*) – aroused immediate and widespread distress among her subjects, who supported the spurned husband. Some of the Brigantes revolted with Venutius, who also called in aid from outside the kingdom. Cartimandua, now in a precarious position, asked the Romans for help. They sent cavalry and foot soldiers, who finally rescued the queen but left Venutius in charge of the kingdom: *regnum Venutio, bellum nobis relictum*.

It should be noted that the similarity of Tacitus' accounts of the events of the fifties (*Ann.* 12.40) and of 69 (*Hist.* 3.45) has led some scholars to infer that the two passages relate the same events.[12] However, Braund, in a convincing argument, has shown that Tacitus does in fact refer to two different episodes in Cartimandua's career. After explaining away the similarities, Braund points out the differences between the passages, which are indeed significant:

> In the Annals Cartimandua captures Venutius' relatives; in the Histories these relatives are not mentioned, but Vellocatus appears, who is not mentioned in the Annals. In the Annals, Venutius' attack is launched from outside the kingdom (albeit with Brigantes other than Venutius himself); in the Histories it is combined with an internal uprising. Again, while Roman forces were involved on both occasions, the details are very different. In the Annals they had anticipated Venutius' attack, while in the Histories Cartimandua requested them after Venutius' invasion. Moreover, the forces involved are different. In the Annals there were a legion and cohorts, but in the Histories there were only cohorts and cavalry. Nor is it particularly remarkable that Cartimandua, having benefited from Roman military support against Venutius in the fifties, should call upon it again for the same purpose in A. D. 69. Finally, of course, the outcome of the two affairs was different: in the fifties Venutius was repelled, but in A. D. 69 it was Cartimandua who had to flee, leaving the kingdom to Venutius.[13]

Cartimandua survived, but Rome's policy of using the Brigantes as a buffer state to protect its northern frontier had to be abandoned. It is clear that this queen, and her kingdom, were important to the Romans' long-term strategy for Britain and so it is understandable that they continued to support her for many years.

Cartimandua's influence in British affairs was great and that is why Tacitus reports on her doings three times in his works. Yet Tacitus' presentation of Cartimandua is a study in insinuation and allusion aimed at undermining her character and denouncing her morals. The historian's hidden agenda was to explicate and comment upon the political situation at Rome, of necessity using the same terminology to analyze Rome and Britain, yet "in writing about 'the other,' Tacitus was also writing about 'the self'."[14] In his writing, Tacitus creates an image which resonates with both "self" and "Other," and clearly, this image can be manipulated to make his point(s) about power and identity. This is what Tacitus does with the image of Cartimandua. We must keep in mind his agenda when discussing the queen, for "in writing Britain [he is] also writing Rome."[15]

What does this mean for Tacitus' narrative of Cartimandua? Let us look at his presentation of the queen and her actions. First, in the *Annales*, Tacitus reports that Cartimandua gave up Caratacus to the Romans; although he had relied on her *fides*, she had betrayed him, handing him over in chains. This was degrading to a prince such as Caratacus, since chains are meant for the servile. Here Cartimandua is meant to appear as morally corrupt; while Caratacus is portrayed as the noble enemy fighting for *libertas*, his betrayer acts as a treacherous friend, showing her subservience to the Romans. To Tacitus' readers, Caratacus seems admirable and Cartimandua despicable.

In our second meeting with Cartimandua, Tacitus again portrays her in a negative light, recounting how 'with cunning arts' she captured Venutius' male relatives. This use of trickery is unfair and results in undeserved disgrace for those who must submit to female rule. Here, Cartimandua has acted in a base manner by cheating. Tacitus' implication is that this is a feminine trait, and all the more unacceptable.

In the *Histories*, Cartimandua is definitively portrayed as evil. She not only surrenders Caratacus, but captures him by trickery to boot (*per dolum*). When Venutius rebels, it is because he hates her as well as Rome, because she has shamed him by taking a lover.[16] She commits adultery; he is the wronged husband. She alienates the citizenry; he gains their support. She is saved by the Romans; her kingdom is lost. In Tacitus' judgement, presented in this moralizing way, Cartimandua comes out very badly indeed.

All of this reflects Tacitus' (and his readers') distrust of and hostility to queens and female rulers in general, which in turn resonates with the uneasy political climate in Rome and in the imperial household, where slaves, freedmen and women might at any time attempt to take over imperial power, and thus overturn the existing social and political order.[17] Tacitus' portrayal of Cartimandua represents these fears and alerts his readers, in veiled language, to be always on guard against such threats.

After AD 69 we hear no more of Cartimandua. She may have lived out her years under Roman protection in Britain, or perhaps in Italy[18] as did Carapaces before her.[19] Cartimandua had been an important and powerful client-queen, and her fate was closely tied to Rome's strategic interests in Britain. Tacitus' portrayal of her as a clever and dangerous barbarian queen, even though an ally of Rome, both reflects these facts and reveals his feelings about female rulers at home and abroad.

More famous than Cartimandua in Romano-British history, or perhaps more infamous, is Boudicca, the leader of the great revolt of AD 60/61, less than twenty years after the conquest of south-eastern Britain in AD 43. Although Julius Caesar had made contact with the peoples of this area in 53 and 54 BC, and strong trade relations between the two cultures had been established, nearly a century elapsed before Roman armies returned to subjugate the territory.[20] The rebellion is well documented by Tacitus, in the *Annales* and the *Agricola* (written *c.* AD 98), and in Dio Caesius' *Roman History*, written about a century after Tacitus' account.[21] Although Dio was a Greek, he lived and wrote in Rome for many years and his viewpoint is wholly Roman. There is also considerable archaeological evidence for the revolt, which adds support to and vivifies the literary narrative.

Under the Emperor Claudius, Britain was invaded again in AD 43. Sutorius tells us that Claudius spent little time in Britain: *Expeditionem unam omnino suscepit eamque modicam . . . sine ullo proelio aut sanguine intra paucissimos dies parte insulae in deditionem recepta, sexto quam profectus erat mense Roman rediit triumphavitque maximo apparatu*: "he undertook only one campaign and it was modest . . . without any battle or bloodshed, when a part of the island had surrendered within a very few days, after six months he returned to Rome and celebrated a magnificent triumph" (*Life of Claudius*, 17, 1–2).

After his brief visit, Claudius left Britain in the hands of a series of appointed commanders. In AD 47, the propraeter Publius Ostorius Scapula was in charge, and he immediately faced resistance from some who thought that, as a new commander, he would be vulnerable. After an initial victory, he sought to disarm the natives and thus avoid "a hostile and disloyal peace" (*infensaque et infida pax*: Tac. *Ann.* 12.31.1). Principal among the resistance were the Iceni, described by Tacitus as *valida gens nec proeliis contusi, quia societatem nostram volentes accesserant*: "a strong people, not yet beaten in battle, since they had entered into alliance with us voluntarily" (Tac. *Ann.* 12.31.3). Despite a temporary coalition of tribes, the Iceni were defeated (Tac. *Ann.* 12.32.1), followed by the Ceanigi, the Brigantes, and, temporarily, the Silures. A colony of Roman veterans was then established at Camulodunum (Colchester) on conquered ground: *subsidium adversus rebelles et inbuendis sociis ad officia legum*: "as a protection against the rebels and to accustom the friendly tribes to the duties of the law." In other words, to promote Romanization.

Romanization is the process of acculturation by which native peoples adopt, more or less willingly, certain accoutrements of Roman civilization.

The degree to which this phenomenon was imposed upon the native culture and the depth to which it penetrated such areas of native life as religion, tribal structure, the legal system and the economy varied greatly.[22] It was certainly aided by trade contact, the importation of Roman goods, and the spread of Roman customs, yet it was always a deliberate policy of Roman rule and frequently caused tensions and friction, which led to misunderstanding, distrust, and even outright war. High on this list was the overbearing presence of the Romans and their often insensitive treatment of the native population.

An example of this insensitivity occurred just prior to the revolt led by Boudicca, when the Roman Governor Sutorius Paulinus attacked the island of Mona (Anglesey) in the west. This area was a stronghold of the Druids, whom the Romans considered dangerous instigators of rebellion and insurrection. The extent of Druid influence on British affairs at this time has been debated, although some believe that the Druids wanted to maintain and even strengthen hostility to Rome because they knew that under Roman rule their influence would be lessened. To avoid this, they tried to keep the native tribesmen free from the influences of Romanization and out of the Romans' control.[23] Although it has been speculated that the Druids used their influence to urge other tribes to join Boudicca's rebellion, there is no mention of this in either Tacitus or Dio.[24] Dyson discounts the power of the Druids to inspire opposition to the Romans;[25] however, since the Druidical priesthood was chosen mainly from the nobles among the Celtic peoples,[26] I think that it is hardly likely that they did not have considerable influence among the chieftains. With this background in mind, it is not surprising that when Paulinus marched against Anglesey, there was outrage at the attack on the center of the Druidic religion, since it was such an important factor in Celtic culture.

Leaving the "subdued" part of Britain, with its garrison of veterans at Camulodunum, Paulinus led his forces against the people of Anglesey. Of the battle there, Tacitus writes: *Stabat pro litore diversa acies, densa armis virisque, intercursantibus feminis; in modum Furiarum veste ferali, crinibus deiectis faces praeferebant, Druidaeque circum, preces diras. sublatis ad caelum manibus fundentes, novitate aspectus perculere militem. . . . Dein cohortationibus ducis et se ipsi stimulantes, ne muliebre et fanaticum agmen pavescerent, inferent signa sternuntque obvios*: "There stood on the shore a varied battle line, thick with arms and men, with women interspersed, in dark clothes like Furies and with their hair flowing loose they brandished torches. And the Druids in a circle, raising their hands to the heavens and shouting dire curses terrified the [Roman] soldiers with the shocking spectacle . . . then at the urging of the leader and inspiring themselves not to be afraid of a band of fanatics and females, they attacked and cut down all whom they encountered" (Tac. *Ann.* 12.30.1–2). Tacitus goes on to say that the victorious Romans established a garrison and cut down the Druids' sacred groves. Such cavalier treatment of their native religious beliefs certainly should have inflamed the Britons.

Meanwhile, in the south-eastern part of Britain, the Iceni and others were chafing under Roman rule. The veterans at Camulodunum treated them contemptuously: *acerrimo in veteranos odio. Quippe in coloniam Camulodunum recens deducti quasi cunctam regionem muneri accepissent, pellebant domibus, exturbabant agris, captivos, servos appellando*: "there was very bitter hatred against the veterans. Recently having been settled at Camulodunum, they took the whole region as if it were a gift; they were driving the people from their homes and expelling them from their lands, while calling them 'slaves' and 'captives' " (Tac. *Ann.* 14.31.4–7). In addition, the huge Roman temple built and dedicated to the Divine Claudius in Camulodunum[27] loomed over them "as if a citadel of eternal domination" (*quasi arx aeternae dominationis*).[28] The colony, established as a stronghold against rebellion and to promote Romanization (Tac. *Ann.* 12.32.4), had failed in both goals. Instead of winning over the people, the veterans had enraged them; instead of a distinction, the temple of the imperial cult was a hated burden.[29]

There were economic reasons behind the revolt as well; according to Dio (*Roman History* 62.2), under Claudius monies had been granted to the leading Britons; these were, in the Britons' eyes, gifts, but the procurator Decianus Catus demanded their repayment. Moreover, Seneca (the Roman author and former tutor to the Emperor Nero) had lent the Britons 40,000,000 sesterces, and now called in the loan all at once. Of course, the conquered people paid taxes and indemnities, and when Catus increased these, bitterness grew. Tacitus adds to the Britons' list of grievances: *Namque absentia legati remoto metu Britanni agitare inter se mala servitudinis, conferre iniurias et interpretando accendere: nihil profici patientia nisi ut graviora tamquam ex facili tolerantibus impereatur. Singulos sibi olim reges fuisse, nunc binos imponi, e quibus legatus in sanguinem, procurator in bona saeviret. Aeque discordiam praepositorum, aeque concordiam subiectis exitiosam. Alterius manus centuriones, alterius servos vim et contumelias miscere. Nihil iam cupiditati, nihil libidini exceptum*: "For since fear was taken away by the absence of the legate, the Britons discussed the evils of servitude among themselves, and compared injuries, exaggerating them in the interpretation. Their patience was no use to them except to be ruled more harshly as they submitted easily. Before there were single kings, now two were imposed, of whom the governor ravaged their life-blood, the procurator, their goods. The agreement or discord of those in charge was equally deadly to their subjects, the tools of the one, the centurions, of the other, his slaves, combined insults. Nothing was exempt from their greed, nothing from their lust" (Tac. *Agricola* 15.1–2).

It is these two evils, greed and lust, which define the proximate cause of Boudicca's revolt. Prior to his death, Prasutagus, the chief of the Iceni and husband of Boudicca, had been a loyal and long-standing client-king of the Romans, and had prospered under them (Tacitus [*Ann.* 14.31.1] describes him as *longa opulentia clarus*: "famous for his long prosperity"). In his will (he died in AD 59) he bequeathed half of his wealth to the Emperor Nero, and the rest to his two daughters.[30] Tacitus writes: *tali obsequio ratus regnumque et domum suam procul iniuria fore*: "thinking that with such deference he might place his kingdom and his household far from danger" (Tac. *Ann.* 14.31.1).[31] But his hopes were not fulfilled; instead, the Romans decided to incorporate the kingdom directly into the administrative structure of the province,[32] and they did so with astonishing cruelty and insensitivity: *Quod contra vertit, adeo ut regnum per centuriones, domus per servos velut capta vastarentur. Iam primum uxor eius Boudicca verberibus adfecta et filiae stupro violatae sunt; praecipui quique Icenorum avitis bonis exuuntur, et propinqui regis inter mancipia habebantur. Qua contumelia et metu graviorum, quando in formam provinciae cesserant, rapiunt arma, commotis ad rebellationem Trinovantibus et qui alii nondum servitio fracti resumere libertatem occultis coniurationibus pepigerant*: "This turned out the opposite, so that his kingdom was ravaged by centurions and his household by slaves, as if they were prizes of war. First his wife Boudicca was lashed, then his daughters were raped. The chiefs of the Iceni were deprived of their ancestral goods, and close relatives of the king were held as slaves. Because of this outrage and through fear of worse things, since they had been changed into the form of a province (i.e., their status as allies was no more), they took up arms, and incited the Trinovantes to rebellion and others who, not yet broken by servitude, had sworn in secret gatherings to regain their liberty" (Tac. *Ann.* 14.31.2–4).

All the elements necessary for rebellion were at hand: increased taxation, economic stress, confiscation of land and wealth, religious affronts, loss of status, and finally hideous personal outrage. Moreover, as Sutorius Paulinus and most of the Roman troops were far away in Wales, there was opportunity. Now all that was needed was a leader.

Dio (*Roman History* 62.2.2) tells us that "the person who was chiefly instrumental in rousing the natives and persuading them to fight the Romans, the person who was thought worthy to be their leader and who directed the conduct of the entire war, was Boudicca, a Briton woman of the royal family and possessed of greater intelligence than often belongs to women."[33] Note that she is not referred to here as a queen, nor does Tacitus give her that title; in the *Agricola* (16.1) she is described as *generis regii femina duce* – a woman leader of royal rank. She did not, it seems, lead by virtue of being the widow of King Prasutagus. In introducing her as the *dux* of the Britons, Tacitus notes that they did not distinguish between sexes in military command (*Agricola* 16.1).[34] But in fact, the reasons why she held such a dominant leadership position are unclear, although "as the outraged wife and mother, she did assume a tremendous symbolic role in the rebellion."[35] But what can we say about Boudicca's leadership, and about the leadership of women in general? What do our sources contribute to our understanding of this issue in the Roman Empire?

The fact that the British would accede to a woman ruler marks them as different from the Romans. Indeed, Tacitus makes Boudicca herself say, "it was customary with Britons to fight under female captaincy" (Tac. *Ann.* 14.35.1), but such a thing was unheard of for the Romans. In Greco-Roman ideology the idea of the *dux femina* is one that signals disgrace for males, and the theme is widely found in the literature. Women who have power and use it are foreign – not members of normal Greek or Roman society. If a man is subject to a queen – a *dux femina* – he is disgraced and the only way to erase this shame is to conquer her.[36] As we have seen above, Tacitus' opinion that to show cowardice "before a band of females and fanatics" (a telling juxtaposition of terms) was the worst sort of behavior (*Ann.* 14.30.2). It is no wonder that Dio writes that "a terrible disaster occurred in Britain: two cities were sacked, 80,000 of the Romans and of their allies perished, and the island was lost to Rome. Moreover, all this ruin was brought upon the Romans by a woman, a fact which in itself caused them the greatest shame" (*Roman History* 62.1.1).

It is interesting to compare Tacitus' presentation of Boudicca in the *Agricola* and the *Annales* with Dio's version, and it is important to keep in mind the historians' goals and intentions in writing their accounts of the rebellion. Certainly in Tacitus, imperial Roman politics lurk close to the surface of his narrative, and both authors use Boudicca to illustrate various points about political and cultural aspects of the Roman cultural construct.

Tacitus' account of Boudicca's rebellion and his characterization of her in the *Annales* is the most sympathetic; she is presented not as a queen (which, like "king," has negative connotations for the Romans), but as a wronged widow and mother. Boudicca is presented as the type of woman who sets an example for men as she resists oppression and fights for liberty.[37] How does Tacitus arrive at this view of Boudicca? After all, she is a barbarian and barbarians are clearly not Romans.

To begin with, Tacitus has set the stage for the reader to consider her not as a barbarian by emphasizing the Romanness of Prasutagus in making a will. Boudicca is presented as a woman of the upper class – the kind of woman, who, if she were a Roman, would be considered decent according to traditional Roman values.[38] Thus the abuse she and her daughters suffer at the hands of the Romans – specifically identified as slaves by Tacitus – is all the more outrageous. The Romans had deep-seated fears of the power of slaves and their potential to subvert the social order by rebellion and/or violence against their masters,[39] and Tacitus uses that fear to arouse sympathy for Boudicca. Moreover, Tacitus extends this sympathy to the British rebels, by making their fight against *contumelia et metu graviorem* appear to be noble. Although they are barbarians and they are fighting against Rome, we are to think that this is the way Romans would act in a similar situation. These are Roman values, not irrational barbarian impulses, and their resistance is seen as moral and even just.[40]

The villain in the piece is the procurator, Decianus Catus, and after the initial successes of the Britons (the fall of Camulodunum and the rout of the ninth legion), he flees to Gaul. Now, the Roman governor Sutorius Paulinus, who has been away fighting at Anglesey, returns to prominence in the narrative, displaying the typical Roman virtues of rationality and remarkable steadiness (*mira constantia*: *Ann.* 14.33.1). The British rampage destroys Londinum (London) and Verulamium (St. Albans). Tacitus reports that after London was ransacked and burned, "there was a similar catastrophe in Verulamium; as the barbarians, taking delight in plunder and at the same time being lazy, left aside the forts and garrisons, and went for the richest plunder. . . . It is established that nearly 70,000 Roman citizens and allies perished in these places, for the natives did not take captives nor sell anyone into slavery, but they hastened to the slaughter, seeking revenge in the meantime" (Tac. *Ann.* 14.33.4–6).[41] Their behavior resonates with barbarian lack of control and violence as opposed to the Romans' disciplined, virtuous strength. The roles have been re-reversed, and the Romans and their leader now reclaim moral high ground, while the barbarians have sunk to their level and to that of the evil Roman Catus.[42]

Because Boudicca has been absent from the story since her introduction, she "has not been directly implicated in the British descent into barbarism and retains her personal moral superiority."[43] Before the final battle, Tacitus has her address her army:

> Boudicca, riding in a chariot with her daughters, approached clan after clan and spoke. "It was customary, she knew, with the Britons to fight under female captaincy; but now she was not seeking revenge, as a queen of famous ancestry, for her stolen realm and power. Rather, as a woman of the people, she wished to avenge seeking her lost liberty, her body tortured by whipping, and the damaged honor of her daughters. Roman greed had gone so far that their very bodies, old age itself, or maidenhood, were not left unpolluted. Yet the gods were on the side of their righteous revenge: one legion that had dared to fight them, had perished; the rest were hiding in their camps, or looking for a way to escape. They would never face even the din and roar of those many thousands, much less their attack and their weapons! If they themselves thought about the forces under arms and the causes of the war, on the field they must either conquer or die. This a woman has resolved – the men might live and be slaves."
>
> (Tac. *Ann.* 14.35.1–5)

Her speech recounts the causes of the rebellion and underlines what is at stake, while at the same time urging and rallying her troops. But her great bravery is not rational – it is based only on emotion and passion – a great stirring of sentiment without any discipline. By putting this speech in Boudicca's mouth, Tacitus makes it clear that the British are doomed to fail, even with this worthy woman as their leader. And here we see "the interrelated issues of gender and freedom: this woman, for all her shortcomings, stands for freedom or death, where men may prefer life and slavery."[44]

Dio's picture of Boudicca is quite different; she is presented, not as a wife and mother, not as a victim of injustice, but as a queen, and a ferocious one at that. In Dio's view, Boudicca is an instigator of the rebellion, which he sees as the result of financial, not personal injustices. He provides us with a description of her formidable presence:

> This woman assembled her army, to the number of some 120,000, and then ascended a tribunal that had been constructed of earth in the Roman fashion. In stature she was very tall, in appearance most terrifying, in the glance of her eye most fierce, and her voice was harsh; a great mass of the tawniest hair fell to her hips; around her neck was a golden necklace, and she wore a tunic of diverse colours over which a thick mantle was fastened with a brooch. This was her invariable attire. She now grasped a spear to aid her in terrifying all beholders.
>
> (*Roman History*, 62.2)[45]

Clearly this picture is not one of a Roman woman – her hair, her clothes, her spear all label her as the Other – the barbarian. And in Dio's account, Boudicca's long speech is capped by her use of a strange rite of divination, calling upon a British goddess, Adraste: "I call upon you as woman speaking to woman." Although she asserts her womanhood, Dio's portrait masculinizes her – she is not seen as wife and mother, but as a type of Amazon, with the size and voice of a man, and with a man's weapons. In her speech she lists female rulers (Semiramis, Nitocris, Messalina, Aggripina), culminating with Nero, whom she calls *domina* – mistress – and contrasts herself and British masculinity to Nero's femininity and Roman (and Eastern) softness. It is a bold speech, but flawed in its reasoning. Dio's Boudicca, like Tacitus', is mistaken in her analysis of the Romans' power and determination.

In the end, the British are defeated and Boudicca dies. Tacitus reports that she, proud and dignified, took poison; Dio attributes her death to an unexpected illness, asserting that she would have gone on fighting. In his view the revolt is really Boudicca's; she is the inspiration and the leader, and it is only with her death and burial that the Britons are truly defeated.

In contrast to both these pictures is the portrait of Boudicca in the *Agricola*, which was written twenty years earlier than the *Annales*. Here the causes of the revolt are more generalized and widespread, focusing on the loss of *libertas*. Boudicca is introduced as a royal female leader, but not as a queen (Tac. *Agricola* 16.1), and nothing is said about the outrages she and her family suffered. Tacitus' version of the actual events of the revolt is somewhat different here as well. However, this account should not be dismissed as inaccurate; rather it reflects a different "authorial strategy" on the part of Tacitus.[46]

It is clear that Tacitus and Dio use both Cartimandua and Boudicca to illustrate parts of their agenda in writing history. In their portrayals of these women and their actions, the *Annales*, the *Histories*, the *Agricola*, and the *Roman Histories* go beyond the historical report of a revolt in Britain; beneath the accounts of these events lies a layer of commentary on and criticism of Roman imperial politics. It is veiled and allusive, but it is clearly there. Tacitus and Dio have painted their pictures of Boudicca and Cartimandua in a way that reveals not only the Roman view of barbarian women, but also of Roman rulers and their rule in Rome itself.

2

Between Whipping and Slavery: Double Jeopardy against *Mudejar* Women in Medieval Spain

Isabel Bonet O'Connor

Medieval Spain was a multicultural and multi-religious society. From the late eleventh to the thirteenth centuries, the Christian kingdoms of Spain embarked on an extensive military campaign which resulted in the conquest of most of the Iberian peninsula, except for the kingdom of Granada, in the southernmost part of Spain. As a consequence of this campaign, the Christian kingdoms acquired large geographical areas. After the territorial expansion, the Christian kingdoms faced the need for the settlement and economic exploitation of the conquered areas. Thus, in a manner similar to the Islamic *dhimma*, the Christians allowed the conquered Muslims, or *Mudejars*, to remain *in situ* to ensure the economic development of the newly acquired territory.[1] In order to avoid religious contamination, however, *Mudejars*, Christians, and Jews were not supposed to have contact with each other. Consequently, medieval Spain included within its main society alternative societies in which *Mudejars* and Jews could, at least in theory, practice their religion, own property, and be governed by their own laws and by members of their own community.

Mudejars and Jews formed semi-autonomous societies and were not allowed to hold positions of power within Christian Spain. Learning about this alternative society is not an easy task, since the greatest majority of the sources comes from Christian archives and thus inform us about *Mudejars* and Jews through the distorted eyes of the Christian conquerors. If learning about *Mudejars* in general is difficult, learning about *Mudejar* women is even harder. *Mudejar* women do not appear in Christian documents as often as *Mudejar* men for two reasons: not only were they members of a conquered religious minority, but also within that group they played a very limited role in the public sphere. The majority of *Mudejar* women who appear in Christian sources are those who lived at the margins of their own community, namely prostitutes and slaves. Marginalized by both the *Mudejar* and Christian societies, *Mudejar* prostitutes and slaves became the most powerless members of medieval Spanish society. Despite the principle of separation of the three different religious groups, *Mudejar* prostitutes, slaves, and *Mudejar* women in general became easy prey, especially for Christian men, the most powerful members of medieval Spanish society.

In the aftermath of the Christian conquest, the different medieval Spanish kingdoms highly valued *Mudejar* women as settlers. In 1287, for example, after the *moreria* or *Mudejar* quarter of Xàtiva was left almost depopulated after a Granadan attack and a Christian assault on it, the crown specified that the *Mudejar* men and women who wanted to settle there were not to be harmed or disturbed in any manner.[2] The fact that the document specified "Sarracenos et Sarracenas" is not merely formulaic. The crown, as well as the *Mudejar* community, was well aware of the importance of the reproductive ability of *Mudejar* women, which guaranteed the presence of enough *Mudejar* population and in turn the stability of the different morerias and the kingdoms in general.

The same principle applied to the *Mudejar* community. As a separate entity within the Christian society, the *Mudejar* community needed to remain strong to fight acculturation to the Christian way of life. With their reproductive power, *Mudejar* women ensured a supply of population and ultimately the survival of the *Mudejar* community. To do so, however, it was essential to ensure that the offspring was *Mudejar* and that the honor of the woman and her family was preserved. This was especially the case when the legitimacy of the children was questionable. This concern resulted in specific regulations which both Christians and *Mudejars* agreed to include in some of the surrender treaties that followed the Christian military conquest. In 1252, for example, the king of Aragon granted the *Mudejars* of Xàtiva a charter that spelled out their rights as well as their obligations to the crown. The charter specified that if an unmarried *Mudejar* woman was found pregnant, she had to pay the crown five sous. Moreover, if a *Mudejar* man denied paternity of a child, and the mother was able to prove that the child was his, the *Mudejar* man in question had to pay the crown twenty sous.[3]

As the regulations included in the surrender treaty of Xàtiva indicate, *Mudejar* society valued very highly the honor of its women. A *Mudejar* woman who had illicit sexual relations stained the honor of her family. Christian documents referred to any type of sexual misconduct among unmarried partners as adultery. In true cases of adultery, however, "adultery in both religious and secular law came to signify only the action of a married woman with no similar popular meaning for the married man. Though she and her lover would in theory be equally culpable, she would have the harder test of innocence and earn the greater punishment if guilty."[4]

In most cases of adultery, the accusation against the *Mudejar* woman was based on circumstantial evidence and simple suspicion. In Xàtiva, for example, in 1320, Ali Abenhahamet, nephew of Ali Abenhabib, went to the *çalmedina* (or police official) of the *moreria* to report that he had seen Fatima, his uncle Ali's wife, and another *Mudejar* man from Xàtiva, Muhammad Giber, coming out of a house "one after the other."[5] The manner in which the couple left the house made Ali suspect that an illicit sexual act had taken place. The *çalmedina* accused Muhammad and Fatima before the *qadi* (or Muslim judge) of Xàtiva of committing adultery. Muhammad, however, refused to admit to the crime, so the *qadi* sentenced Muhammad and Fatima to a year in captivity. Muhammad appealed the *qadi*'s sentence to the king on the grounds that it contradicted the Sunna (or Islamic law). The king ordered the *qadi* to hand over the case to the *qadi* general of the kingdom of Valencia, who was to determine whether the penalty imposed on Muhammad had been decided on the basis of personal animosity between him and the *qadi* of Xàtiva.[6] Indeed, Islamic law "prescribed 100 lashes for fornication, and stoning for adultery, albeit the rules of evidence made proof of adultery practically impossible without a confession."[7] Both Muhammad and Fatima were to be stoned in this case.[8] The fact that Muhammad refused to confess to the crime and appealed the decision of the *qadi* to the king illustrates how much easier it was for a *Mudejar* man to combat accusations of adultery than for a *Mudejar* woman. Indeed, the king's positive response to Muhammad's request for judicial review did not include a revision of her case.

Moreover, Fatima's case illustrates not only how simple it was to accuse a woman of sexual misconduct, but also how such accusations were often brought about by her relatives. Most often, since the sexual misconduct of the *Mudejar* woman stained the honor of her own family, her agnate relatives brought about the accusation against her. In any case, other *Mudejars* were always willing to accuse *Mudejar* women of sexual misconduct, since the accuser received half the proceedings from the sale of the *Mudejar* woman who became a slave because of a sexual crime.[9]

If illicit sexual contact among members of the *Mudejar* community was highly punishable, especially for the woman, it was even more so when it was committed between a Christian and a *Mudejar*. Such cases were seen as a violation of the principle of separation of the three religious groups, which was the theoretical foundation of Spain's medieval society. Sexual contact across religious lines endangered the spiritual well-being of the Christian community. The penalties prescribed in these cases, however, varied depending on the religious affiliation of the female partner involved. Christian women were considered out of reach of *Mudejar* men, who in theory at least were severely punished for having sex with Christian women. In 1326, for example, the king of Aragon established that the *Mudejars* who left the kingdom of Valencia for Granada either on a temporary or permanent basis should be able to do so after paying the crown the mandatory sum of money. This, however, did not apply to those *Mudejars* who committed what the crown considered the most serious offenses, namely those *Mudejar* men who had sex with a Christian woman, sodomites, and those who counterfeited money.[10] Indeed, the *Furs* (law code) of the kingdom of Valencia prescribed the death penalty for both the *Mudejar* man and the Christian woman involved.[11]

In reality, however, most *Mudejar* males escaped the death penalty by fleeing their town and it is not clear what punishment Christian women suffered.[12] In May 1312, for example, after having been whipped, a Christian woman who had accused several *Mudejars* of Xàtiva, including a son of Giber, of having had sex with her disappeared. The local Christian officials wanted to find her to ask her which one of the two sons of Giber had sex with her. Giber had two sons; one was 18 or 19 years old, and the other was 15 or 16. They had both left the *moreria* of Xàtiva. The king informed the Christian officials that he wanted the guilty son to remain in hiding and the innocent one to return to the *moreria* of Xàtiva, where he was to be exonerated of the crime.[13] In 1313, when interrogated by the bailiff general of the kingdom of Valencia, the Christian woman who had made the accusation against one of the sons of Giber retracted her confession. She confessed that she had not had sexual contact with any *Mudejar* man, but that she had said so at the instigation of other people. Thus, the king absolved Abdullah, the oldest son of Giber, and allowed him to return to Xàtiva.[14]

The crown was also willing to grant pardons for such crimes to *Mudejar* men of high social status within the *Mudejar* community. In 1318, for example, the king of Aragon absolved Ali Ray, a *Mudejar* of Xàtiva, of having had sexual relations with a Christian woman. The document absolved Ali of all criminal and civil charges against him. It also stated that the other people involved in the crime were Don Giber, Don Sabba, Don Roig and Don Ali Almisserai.[15] As the use of Don indicates, the accused were prominent members of the *Mudejar* community of Xàtiva. Indeed, they were the masters of the paper manufacturing industry. Their gender and social status was an important factor in granting them immunity from prosecution.

The crown, however, was less willing to grant pardons to *Mudejar* women who had sex with Christian men. Unlike Christian women, *Mudejar* women were considered fair game. Law codes prescribed lighter punishment for Christian males who had sex with *Mudejar* women than for *Mudejar* men who had sex with Christian women. According to the *Furs* of Valencia, Christian men who were "caught with Muslim women were to be whipped naked through the streets together with their partner in crime."[16] In reality, however, even a recent male convert to Christianity, a former Muslim, and thus not considered the equal of a Christian, was absolved in 1312 of the crime of having had sex with Axux, a *Mudejar* woman.[17] Sex with the female members of a conquered community reinforced the inferior status of that population and re-enacted its conquest. According to Louise Mirrer, *Mudejar* and Jewish women, "possessed by Christian men signify male Muslim and Jewish defeat."[18] Moreover, contemporary literary texts, such as Pártese el moro Alicante, use the "stereotype of the Muslim woman who invites, legitimates and satisfies Christian desire."[19]

The stricter punishment prescribed for *Mudejar* women was not unilaterally imposed on them by the Christian society in which they lived, but was also the product of the *Mudejar* community's emphasis on preserving the honor of *Mudejar* females. Thus, *Mudejar* women "committed two crimes when they had sex with Christians; they violated Christian laws against miscegenation, and they violated Muslim legal prohibitions on sexual intercourse outside of marriage."[20] *Mudejar qadis*, following Islamic law, often prescribed stoning or whipping for the *Mudejar* woman. The punishment imposed was particularly severe when the woman was an adulteress.[21] Thus, many *Mudejar* women accused of having sex with Christian men chose slavery over the punishment imposed on them by Islamic law. These women, often in the prime of their life, were valuable slaves. *Mudejar* women who chose to become slaves of the crown rather than physical punishment were granted as prizes to members of the royal household or to other important figures in medieval Spain. The king of Aragon often granted *Mudejar* slave women to a Christian to pay off a debt or a favor. In 1293, for example, King Jaume II of Aragon granted a *Mudejar* slave woman to the knight Arnau de Mataró.[22] In 1320, King Jaume II granted a *Mudejar* slave woman to his chamberlain. For some unspecified reason, the royal chamberlain was unable to receive the *Mudejar* slave woman in question, so the king assigned him 500 sous of Barcelona instead.[23] The large amount of money indicates that *Mudejar* slave women were a highly priced and valued commodity.

While slavery seemed a better solution than enduring physical punishment, the fate of such slave women was not always clear. In some cases, the Christian owner maintained sexual relations with the *Mudejar* slave woman. In other cases, *Mudejar* slave women were redeemed. Some *Mudejar* slave women purchased a license from the crown, which allowed them to beg for alms in the *morerias* of the kingdom to collect enough money for their redemption. However, after redemption, *Mudejar* slave women were at risk of being enslaved again.

Some *Mudejar* slave women were freed by their co-religionists. This was the case of Nuça, a *Mudejar* slave woman from Xàtiva. In December 1315, Berenguer de Fluvià, a Christian from Xàtiva, accused several *Mudejars* of the same town of taking the *Mudejar* slave woman Nuça from his house, hiding her in the *moreria* of Xàtiva and helping her flee to Castile to escape slavery. As a result, Berenguer had suffered great damage.[24] Indeed, to remedy his loss, Berenguer took the law into his hands and broke into the *moreria* of Xàtiva with a group of Christians not only at night, but also during the day, and caused great damage.[25] The king ordered the lieutenant procurator of the kingdom of Valencia to investigate the crime and to provide the appropriate compensation to the *Mudejars* of Xàtiva.

In January 1316, however, the *Mudejar* community of Xàtiva again complained to the lieutenant procurator of the kingdom of Valencia. This time, Berenguer accused not only several *Mudejar* men and women from Xàtiva of extracting Nuça from his house at night, but the entire *Mudejar* community of Xàtiva of assisting Nuça. The *Mudejars* of Xàtiva complained that Berenguer's latest accusation contradicted the Sunna and the original privileges granted them by the crown of Aragon.[26]

The case dragged on in the courts for several more years. On February 4, 1317, the lieutenant procurator of the kingdom of Valencia wrote once again to the king regarding Nuça's case. According to the Christian official, the *Mudejars* of Xàtiva who had been accused in the case had offered to pay the crown 2,000 sous in return for their absolution.[27] It is not clear why Nuça had become a slave of Berenguer de Fluvià in the first place. However, considering the fact that many *Mudejar* women became slaves as a result of adultery, it is likely that those circumstances applied to her also. Moreover, Nuça must have been a *Mudejar* woman from the *moreria* of Xàtiva, since several local *Mudejars* helped her escape. *Mudejar* assistance to *Mudejar* slave women represents the two tendencies that were at work in the *Mudejar* community. Although *Mudejar* women accused of sexual crimes who became slaves were social outcasts within the *Mudejar* community, *Mudejars* were aware of the need to protect their community against Christian abuse. Indeed, as a result of the case, the *Mudejars* of Xàtiva were forced to pay a much higher sum of money to the crown. In January 1318, the leaders of the *Mudejar* community of Xàtiva complained that the property of those who had assisted Nuça did not suffice to pay the 14,000 sous that they owed the crown.[28] To cover the entire sum, the *Mudejar* leaders of Xàtiva were allowed to impose an internal tax on the community.

Berenguer's insistence on punishing the *Mudejars* of Xàtiva who assisted Nuça and the length of the trial illustrate Nuça's value to Berenguer.[29] Indeed, the *Mudejar* community of Xàtiva was not the only one that received punishment for assisting Nuça in her journey to Castile. In December 1317, the *Mudejars* of Aiora, near Xàtiva, were forced to pay an unspecified fine to the crown for helping her escape.[30] In January of the next year, at the request of the noble Jaspert, viscount of Castellnou, the crown re-examined the sentence applied to two *Mudejar* women from Canals who had been condemned for assisting Nuça to escape. One woman had been sentenced to death and the other to the amputation of an ear. After reconsideration, the woman condemned to the amputation of her ear was pardoned, while the one condemned to death was to suffer the amputation of her ear. The latter sentence was also pardoned by the crown. Interestingly, in 1318, the two *Mudejar* women had already been sold into slavery. The king ordered the two women be freed and the money from their sale be returned to their buyers.[31]

Mudejar women accused of committing crimes attempted to escape punishment in different ways. In Xàtiva, for example, the *Mudejar* bailiff of the *moreria*, whose daughter was the jailkeeper of the same *moreria*, fled to Granada and took with him two *Mudejar* women who were being held in the jail accused of committing an unspecified crime, very likely of a sexual nature.[32] As for many other *Mudejars*, Granada provided a safe haven for these two *Mudejar* women.

Conversion to Christianity also provided an escape route to *Mudejar* women accused of having sex with Christian men. By converting to Christianity, *Mudejar* women sought to avoid slavery. Indeed, among such converts, *Mudejar* women represented the largest number. Conversion to Christianity, was also a welcome alternative for the *Mudejar* woman when her relationship with a Christian or Jewish man was based on true love. In 1310, for example, Doménec Carbonell, a Christian of Xàtiva, induced a *Mudejar* woman to convert to Christianity by marrying her.[33] While the relationship between Doménec and the unnamed *Mudejar* woman ended happily, that was not the case for the woman's young brother. After her wedding, the *Mudejar* woman sent her brother at night into the *moreria* of Xàtiva to collect her personal belongings. The boy was discovered entering the *moreria* and was sentenced by the *qadi* to slavery, since the *Mudejars* of Xàtiva suspected him of wanting to convert to Christianity also. After being enslaved, he did convert.[34] The fact that the *Mudejar* slave woman sent her brother at night to collect her movable property indicates that she left the *moreria* in a hurry and that she feared a hostile reception by her former co-religionists, and the treatment her brother received indicates that her fears were well grounded.[35] In general, converts to Christianity were not well received by either the Christian or the *Mudejar* community, which saw in the neophytes a source of religious contamination. Moreover, the *Mudejar* woman in question may have feared being accused of having sex with a Christian man by her own relatives or by the *Mudejar* community.

Some *Mudejar* women, especially those who lacked the support of their relatives or of the *Mudejar* community, turned to prostitution. Like their Christian counterparts, *Mudejar* prostitutes purchased a license from the crown to practice their trade. The licensing of *Mudejar* prostitutes was a lucrative business for the crown, which had great interest in regulating and taxing prostitution. Indeed, those *Mudejar* prostitutes who did not buy a license from the crown were enslaved. Prostitutes provided a valuable service to society, since "they were believed to divert males from more serious sins of homosexuality, incest, adultery, and prostituting honest women."[36] Once more, however, the attitude towards *Mudejar* prostitutes differed from that toward Christian prostitutes. While the prostitution of Christian women was tolerated, the prostitution of *Mudejar* women was encouraged. Since *Mudejar* women were Muslim and therefore already damned, the crown did not need to preoccupy itself with the moral well-being of *Mudejar* prostitutes. The crown was not alone in its exploitation of *Mudejar* prostitutes. Many owners of *Mudejar* slave women put them to work in the brothels and kept their wages.[37]

Prostitution was concentrated in the taverns, baths, and *funduqs* (inns) of the *morerias*. Despite prohibitions of inter-faith sex, *Mudejar* prostitutes had many Christian clients. Indeed, urban changes beginning at the end the thirteenth century created an atmosphere that propitiated contact between Mudejar prostitutes and Christian males. Increasingly at this time, and due to Christian population growth which could not be accommodated in the Christian sector of town, a number of Christians moved outside the walls near the *morerias*. This was a source of concern for Christian officials, since both taverns and brothels incited sex and violence between the two communities. In 1269, for example, the justiciar records of Cocentaina indicate that a penalty of 10 sous was to be imposed on Christian men who went to the brothel located in the *moreria* after dark.[38]

Sexual contact between *Mudejar* women and Christian men also took the form of rape. As in the other types of inter-faith sex, *Mudejar* women suffered the greatest consequences. In 1295, in Cocentaina, Hale, wife of Muhammad Ralli, accused R. de Turballos, a Christian from the nearby hamlet of the same name, of forcing her daughter Muhdia to have sex with him.[39] It was probably because the *Mudejar* woman suffered greater consequences in sexual encounters with Christian men, including rape, that Hale demanded justice from the Christian justiciar of Cocentaina. Moreover, the Christian males involved in such cases often attempted to escape punishment by accusing the *Mudejar* woman of being a prostitute. Hale had an additional concern, since "the violation of a daughter's chastity, committed with the consent of the daughter or not, constituted an assault on the family's honor."[40]

Illicit sexual encounters were not limited to cases between Christians and *Mudejars* or Jews. The members of the two religious minorities present in medieval Spain also came in contact through sex. Although *Mudejars* and Jews lived in separate quarters in medieval Spanish towns, and in theory were to be ruled by their own leaders and laws, these two groups came in contact mainly through economic activities. In many cases, *Mudejar* slave women worked in Jewish households or acted as wet nurses for Jewish children. While living in the same house, many *Mudejar* females engaged in sexual affairs with their Jewish owners or employers and became their concubines. However, since both Jews and *Mudejars* were already condemned for their religious beliefs, the crown placed less emphasis on punishing such cases. In 1298, for example, Jaume de Xàrica, the procurator of the kingdoms of Valencia and Murcia held captive Abulfacem, a Jew from Mula, and Axone, his *Mudejar* concubine, and confiscated their property, ostensibly because they were living in concubinage, although the procurator's intervention in the case actually was motivated by financial gain.[41] However, under the law Abulfacem and Axone were to be judged by the proper Jewish and *Mudejar* officials, and in this case the king instructed the procurator that "since the abovementioned people are alien to our law," he should not intervene in the case, but should release them and return their property.[42] The king's instructions, however, are highly surprising, especially at a time when the royal registers report abundant cases of fiscal and legal abuse of *Mudejars* and Jews at the hands of Christian royal officials. The crown's interest in this case obviously did not stem from the illicit sexual relationship between two non-Christians; since the crime did not represent a danger to Christian morality, the crown showed no interest in punishing Abulfacem and Axone.[43] Rather, it seems the procurator's corruption and disregard for the law motivated royal action. As Boswell points out, the crown displayed "disregard for Muslim marriage and morality in general: a Muslim woman who bought pardon for adultery was given permission to remarry, though her first husband was known to be living, and the children of illegitimate unions between Muslims were ordered to be hanged – a startling provision for a Catholic monarchy." [44]

The protective boundaries that medieval Spain established around the three religious groups that lived within it were easily transgressed in daily life. A great deal of contact among conquerors and conquered occurred through sex. *Mudejar* women suffered double jeopardy in their sexual contact with Christians. They were cut off from positions of power by virtue of their conquered status and gender. As the least powerful members of medieval Spanish society, *Mudejar* women endured the worst penalties for having sex across religious lines, even when they were raped, while their Christian partners were released after paying a monetary penalty to the crown. Convicted of having sex with a Christian man, *Mudejar* women became outcasts within the *Mudejar* community for bringing shame to their family. Most of these women became slaves of the crown in order to escape the physical punishment prescribed by Islamic law. A life of slavery, however, did not guarantee them any protection. Indeed, many *Mudejar* slave women turned to prostitution. As prostitutes, *Mudejar* women brought money to the royal coffers and, by attracting the attention of Christian males, saved honest Christian women from a life of prostitution.

Thus, both the conquered Muslim and dominant Christian communities viewed women's sexuality as a type of colonial boundary. On the one hand, Muslim communities in post-conquest Spain sought to maintain their religious and cultural identity by restricting Muslim women's procreative activity solely within the legitmate boundaries of marriage to co-religionists. On the other hand, however, Christians viewed Muslim women through the eyes of foreign conquerors and colonizers whose religion taught them that they were superior to heretical Muslims. For them, maintaining sexual access to Muslim women was both an expression of Christian domination of the Muslim community and a sexual outlet for Christian men who might otherwise sin by debauching fellow Christians, men or women. In either case, the Christian conquest of Spain and the subsequent reduction of Muslims to a colonial people placed *Mudejar* women squarely in the middle of the colonial context, with the result that they were rendered virtually powerless by both Muslim and Christian societies.

3

Greece in Chains: Philhellenism to the Rescue of a Damsel in Distress

Katherine E. Fleming

> *Your nostalgia has created*
> *A non-existent country, with laws*
> *Alien to earth and man.*
>
> George Seferis
> (trans. Edmund Keeley and Philip Sherrard)

In 1979, Edward Said proposed in *Orientalism* that Western or "Occidental" views of "the Orient" were based on and reflected the ideas, beliefs, and prejudices that Western observers brought to their colonial experiences, and thus were a means of domesticating these territories.[1] Although Said's thesis has inspired much debate and controversy, it has also led to a re-examination of the contemporary accounts and attitudes found in colonial literature.[2] As much scholarship of the last decade has demonstrated, one of the primary preoccupations of Western colonial discourse of the early modern and modern periods has been the description and definition of colonized women. In the present volume, several authors show that the colonialist writings of curious travelers, bureaucrats, and missionaries alike evince a fascination with women, their role in the preservation (or destruction) of cultural mores, their connection (or lack thereof) to the broader society around them, and their simultaneously "pristine" and "contaminated" nature.[3] Building on scholarship concerned with such depictions, other studies have focused not just on women as the described object of colonialist writings, but on women as the authorial subject. Elsewhere in this volume, Carmen Ramos-Escandon and Nupur Chaudhuri focus on women authors who served as interpreters of indigeous colonial culture for public audiences in Europe.[4] These add to the scholarship on women as colonial interpreters, such as Sara Mills' *Discourses of Difference: Women's Travel Writing and Colonialism* and Susan Morgan's *Place Matters: Gendered Geography in Victorian Women's Travel Books about Southeast Asia.*[5] Such works give attention to the ways in which colonialist women's travel writing constitutes a distinctive genre in its own right. They argue that there are distinct and readily identifiable differences between travel narratives penned by men and those authored by women.

Branching out from such interpretive concerns, other studies have gone further still, by contending that colonialist discourse is an inherently gendered genre, in which depictions of colonized territories have provided a means of bolstering Western colonial control over those territories. That is to say, such studies show that the role of gender in the construction of travel narratives runs far deeper than might be suggested by analyses concerned simply with whether a given narrative was penned by a man or a woman. So, for instance, we see in the works of such scholars as Ronald Inden that in travel writings on colonized lands, those places themselves are understood in gendered terms and are typically portrayed as female, in juxtaposition to the presumed masculinity of the colonizer's homeland. Thus, as Inden argues, India itself – not just its inhabitants – during the British colonial period came to be understood as a fundamentally female entity. Writing of British colonial descriptions of Hinduism, for example, Inden observes that they convey the notion that "Hinduism is a female presence who is able, through her very amorphousness and absorptive powers, to baffle and perhaps even threaten Western rationality, clearly a male in this encounter. European reason penetrates the womb of Indian unreason but always at the risk of being engulfed by her."[6] Through the literary inscribing of colonized territories as female (weak, submissive, penetrated, illogical, and chaotic), colonialist power thus emerges as male – dominant, penetrative, logical, and ordered; and a number of studies have amply underscored Inden's point.[7]

Such works, most building on Said (as does Inden himself), demonstrate the ways in which colonialist discourse often has relied on the rhetoric of otherness and difference in the effort to articulate, define, and justify the dominance of the colonizer over the colonized. And difference of gender is, of course, a fundamental form of otherness, one that, conveniently to colonialist purposes, bears with it the implications of male strength, rationality, and consequent ability to dominate, in opposition to the presumption of female weakness, illogicality, and a consequent need to be dominated.

Yet, despite the overwhelming body of work focusing on the interplay of gender, colonialism, and travel produced over the decades, there is some further room for discussion. What, for instance, are we to make of territories that never came under official colonial rule, but that nevertheless have been described in terms often strikingly similar to those we now associate with colonial control? It is the aim of this chapter to suggest that, in certain cases, the rhetorical devices of colonialism were deployed as a means of simulating control over other lands and a means whereby those lands were made to seem familiar, less threatening, and somehow beneath the penumbra of European colonialism. And just as more traditionally colonized lands were understood and described through the gendered rhetoric of colonialism, so too were these lands of "simulated colonialism," but with some distinctive and telling differences.

Whereas so-called Orientalist (a term I here use exclusively in its Saidian sense) discourse has most frequently had as its backdrop colonialism and western imperialism, such mechanisms of Western political control were absent in the preponderance of the lands of the Ottoman Empire and are completely absent from the southern Balkans. Rather, in the territories with which this chapter is concerned the backdrop for discourse is not colonialism but travel – specifically, travel to "classical Greece." This travel was thus not merely a matter of covering geographical space, but more importantly of covering chronological distance as well.

To go to Greece in the eighteenth and nineteenth centuries was no matter of pseudo-anthropology; the basic goal was to come face to face with Greece's classical past, not to visit the country's modern-day inhabitants. Thus most Western travelers had virtually no interest in its contemporary residents, and if travelers studied the modern-day Greeks at all, it was only because they hoped to find in them the vestigial, living traces of ancient Hellas and the ancient Hellenes. Similarly, places were of interest solely, or at the very least largely, because of their possible centrality and importance in antiquity. Travel, most literally a matter of movement through space, thus became a form of movement through time. Many scholars of early modern and modern Greece have identified this sense of movement back through time as a distinctive feature of travel writing about Greece. Artemis Leontis, for example, in her recent *Topographies of Hellenism* writes of Greece's classical sites:

> As elsewhere in the Mediterranean basin, here [European travelers] seemed to travel back in time as they moved southeast around the globe. Here they could reflect on their present condition even as they developed a passion for their past. . . . Here, facing breathtaking ruins, architectural marvels such as the Parthenon, they sometimes overcame the fatigue of their modern world, although they also frequently pined away for northern convenience.[8]

Such a vision, not surprisingly, tends not only to romanticize the past, but also to devalue the present, and many eighteenth- and nineteenth-century travel accounts reflect this development. In one example, J.P. Mahaffy, in his *Rambles and Studies in Greece*, declares with offhanded (and dubious) authority that "Everywhere the modern Greek town is a mere survival of the old."[9] Of an innkeeper in Tripoli he similarly laments that the man "turned out a disgraceful villain, in fact quite up to the mark of the innkeepers of whom Plato in his day complained."[10] Women were also viewed as reflections of Greece's glorious past; in the early nineteenth century, Edward Giffard, in his *Short Visit to the Ionian Islands, Athens, and the Morea*, describes a beautiful young woman he met at a party as "the Helen of the evening";[11] meanwhile, other visitors wax lyrical about the aquiline noses and classical bone structure of the Greek women. Everywhere, it seems, what lay in the past was of greater interest than what appeared before the viewer's eyes.

Over and over again, we see the romantic vision of Greece's classical past being used as the interpretive lens for all aspects of Greece's present. This romantic sentiment is a form of nostalgia – as distinct from "memory" – a filtered recollection, not of a past as it actually was, but rather as these travelers would have it be. The Greece with which they were confronted was thus but a smoky semblance of the nostalgic Greece which they "remembered" from their study of classical Greek language, literature, philosophy, and culture.

The desire to have an eyewitness experience of the supposed founts of Western civilization had, by the last decades of the seventeenth century, become so widespread that travel to Italy was at that time a virtually institutionalized feature of the education of gentlemen of the higher classes. Indeed, by the end of the seventeenth century, this circuit had become so standard that it was given its own name; "The Grand Tour" had become a requisite chapter in an Englishman's education.[12] During the eighteenth century unprecedented numbers of travelers, most with tutors in tow, set off for Italy and the surrounding lands.

By the century's end, however, Greece came to supplant Italy as the most desirable destination for such scholar-travelers. When the French Revolutionary and Napoleonic Wars (1792–1815) brought about an abrupt halt to all travel in France and soon after in Italy, Greece presented itself as a logical, if also a dauntingly exotic, alternative. Quite aside from the political problems forcing such a change in itinerary, Greece already had impressed itself upon the minds of many as the "true" land in which to seek an education. By the eighteenth century many travelers – who might best be termed the "Grand Tourists" – were already beginning to feel that Italy was a bit hackneyed as a travel destination, that it had been overdone and was not exotic enough or far enough off the beaten track to provide them with the required sense of adventure and apprehension of otherness. There was also an increased interest in the classical civilization specifically of Greece and the growing sense that Italy was but a poor imitation of the real thing. As Gustave Flaubert wrote after his first visit to Greece, "The Parthenon spoiled Roman art for me: it seems lumpish and trivial in comparison. Greece is so beautiful."

Such comments (most famous among them, perhaps, being Shelley's breathless exclamation that "We are all Greeks"[13]) have consistently been classified simply as paradigms of romanticist philhellenism (the romantic love of Greece) and the Hellenic Ideal – the belief (literal or metaphoric) that Greece was the wellspring of Western civilization and culture in virtually all its forms. For example, in his preface to *Hellas*, Shelley explains that:

> Our laws, our literature, our religion, our arts have their root in Greece. But for Greece – Rome, the instructor, the conqueror, or the metropolis of our ancestors, would have spread no illumination with her arms, and we might still have been savages and idolators; or, what is worse, might have arrived at such a stagnant and miserable state of social institution as China and Japan possess.[14]

Yet implicit in such statements is a form of surrogate colonialism, a proprietary sense that Greece, or at least the Greek past, was the rightful possession of Western Europe. Despite the fact that the backdrop for travel literature written on Greece is not one of colonialism and imperial control, but rather of this philhellenism and the Hellenic Ideal, it is clear that the "love" these travelers had for Greece bore strong overtones of a presumed superiority, control, and familiarity.

The European travelers likewise felt themselves to be familiar with the Greek past – to know it, indeed, better than the contemporary Greeks did themselves. For example, William Martin Leake's 1835 account of the evolution of the Greek language clearly shows that he believes himself to be a better judge of the purity of the Greek language than the Greeks themselves. Of a specific northern dialect he writes:

> The Greek spoken at Ioannina is of a more polished kind than is usually heard. . . . its phrases are more Hellenic, and its construction more grammatical . . . some words . . . are of pure Hellenic derivation; they . . . have been preserved in the same manner as in every country ancient forms are sometimes employed by rustics which have long been obsolete in cities . . . [15]

Leake's narrative goes on to provide a lengthy list of all the words extant in the region's dialect that he had identified as being of Homeric origin. Leake and others felt themselves to be perfectly qualified to judge the Greek spoken by the Greeks whom they encountered; indeed, they felt that their knowledge of Greek was better even than that of the Greeks. This knowledge constituted a form of control that was based on the European visitors' sense of themselves as the proper arbiters of "greekness," in regard to how this concept was evidenced in the language, religion, and culture of Greece's present-day inhabitants.

The fact that it was Greece's classical past that was used as the yardstick against which that present was measured allowed Europeans to retain their sense of superior knowledge. It was European culture, after all, which had for centuries fetishized the Greek classical past and enshrined that fetish as the centerpiece of the Western academy. The Greeks, whose own knowledge of the classical past was by the eighteenth century patchy, to say the least, were in any case far more interested in their Byzantine past, redolent as it was with Imperial success and Orthodox Christian theocracy – the two features of Greek life most fully eradicated by the experience of Ottoman rule. The Europeans, in short, had defined the terms of Greek cultural "success" as being linked to a supposed continuity with the classical past, had deemed themselves the only appropriate judges as to whether continuity had been attained, and had condemned the Greeks for failing to measure up to an ideal with which the Greeks themselves were hardly familiar, and which until the late eighteenth century, they were arguably little interested.[16]

I would suggest, then, that this backdrop of philhellenism and the cultural ethos of the Hellenic Ideal are best viewed as surrogate forms of colonialism and that the travelers who were propelled to Greece by philhellenic impulses are in some sense best understood as pseudo-colonialists. The philhellenic impulse underlying the Grand Tour can be seen as representative of a different form of colonialism, cultural rather than political, by means of which the history and ideology, rather than territory, were claimed, invaded, and annexed. And just as travel became a matter not so much of geography as of chronology, the terrain of conquest became not a literal, physical landscape, but rather a historical and discursive one, an interest that I identity as a form of "surrogate" colonialism in Greece.

The peculiarly "metaphoric" circumstances of the colonial relationship between Western Europe and Greece account both for the striking similarity of rhetoric used in descriptions of both Greece and of those lands which lay under literal colonial domination, and specifically in certain, key distinctions. On the one hand, rhetorical devices typical of colonialist writing were used in regard to Greece, despite the fact that the Greek lands were never a direct colony of the West, because the cultural assumptions upon which philhellenism and the Hellenic Ideal were based allowed these ideologies to function as a surrogate colonialism. On the other hand, the premise of the Hellenic Ideal – that there was an intimate and direct link between Greece and Western civilization, of which England in the nineteenth century was thought to be the paradigm – presumed that Greece, unlike India or Egypt, was not wholly "Other." That is, the peculiar circumstances attendant upon a form of colonialism that sprang from an ideology not of otherness but rather of sameness give a very distinctive quality to "colonial" writings on Greece vis-à-vis those which addressed other, differently colonized, territories.

Greece, then, was not a country of otherness but of sameness for the philhellenes, which meant that the West could find its own origins in Greece. The problem for these travelers who visited Greece, however, was that all too frequently Greeks themselves defied the Hellenic Ideal, by presenting visitors not with a tableau of romanticist familiarity but rather with one of shocking otherness. The people, their language, their cultural habits – none measured up to the romantic ideals of the philhellenes. Even whilst Western visitors exclaimed upon the vestigial similarities between the classical Greeks and their modern progeny, one can trace throughout the travel writings of the period a sense of disappointment that the Greeks with whom Western travelers came in contact were not really up to the idealized standards which shone from the venerable tomes of Greek antiquity. These travelers were hard-pressed to describe what they believed to be the degenerate state of the Greeks, most of whom bore no clear resemblance to the lofty Ancients of whom they were thought to be the direct descendants.

This frustration, clearly, was a product of the assumptions of the Hellenic Ideal, with its insistence that the modern Greeks, like the Western Europeans themselves, were the inheritors of the classical age of Perikles. It also was a product of philhellenism, with its imperative that Greece and all things Greek were uniformly to be embraced. What were Western European travelers to make of the evidence that so manifestly seemed to contradict these ideologies? The tensions inherent in such a position account in large part for some peculiar notions that appeared within the colonialist rhetoric of travel writings on Greece.

Greece and the Greeks had clearly fallen on hard times. Many philhellenes were shocked by the fact that the Greeks they found in Greece bore little resemblance to what they had read in the course of their study of the classics. We clearly can see in their writings the struggle to make sense of the discrepancy between what was hoped for and what in actuality was found. In his *Travels*, for instance, Thomas Watkins, who visited Greece in the late 1780s, wrote of Elis, close to the site of the classical Olympic Games:

> As I gazed upon [it] . . . the melancholy reflection of its departed glory succeeded the joy I at first felt. I looked steadfastly upon it, my remembrance made my sorrow insupportable, and I burst into tears. No man ever knew the Greeks who did not admire them above all other people: how then could I behold their country without lamenting the loss of such inhabitants?[17]

Watkins, convinced as he is that he "[knows] the Greeks," had no choice but to declare them a vanished race when confronted with the reality that the modern-day Greeks bore little, if any, resemblance to their supposed forebears.

Intent as such European philhellenes were to view the Greeks as the noble descendants of the classical Hellenes, they needed an explanation for the numerous differences between what they had expected to find and what they actually did find. The easiest explanation, of course, was that the Greeks had been brought to their reduced state through the evil interventions of the Turks. This strategy was almost universally deployed by philhellene visitors to Greece during the Ottoman period, among them Choiseul-Gouffier, who wrote in his letters that "Travelers, who have made observations on the character of the Greeks under the Ottoman yoke, justly reproach them with hypocrisy, perfidy, and meanness. These vices are not inherent in their nature, but are the consequence of the servitude in which they live."[18]

A favorite theme for such travelers was that of the harem, a topos (erroneously) understood as both decidedly restrictive and Oriental, and thus rich with symbolism bearing on the plight of Greece as a whole. (The sequestering of women was not, in fact, adopted by Greeks from the Turks, but rather the other way around, of which few travelers were aware.) The harem, like the Ottoman

Empire, was viewed as oppressive and alien. Just as Greece's degeneration as a whole was attributable to Turkish oppression, so also was the degeneration of Greek women the result of Turkish cultural impositions. In 1809 William Martin Leake, somewhat bluntly, gave this assessment of the women of a harem in northern Greece:

> There, indifferently clothed, fed, and lodged, confined to latticed apartments, without amusement or exercise, in a situation where the air in summer and autumn is unhealthy, they cannot but soon lose their health and attractions. . . . As few women, even of the higher classes . . . possess either elegance or beauty, it cannot be supposed that these peasant girls can have much to recommend them after the first glow of health is worn off in their sickly confinement.[19]

Other travelers report that Greek women, so long under the control of foreign dominators, have in some way lost their true femininity; that under the Turkish yoke they have become constrained, awkward, and lacking in grace and expression. A popular theme in this regard is that of dancing, an activity at which Greek women were thought to have excelled during the classical period, but which in modern times they had all but abandoned. Lamenting the fact that Greek women were no longer free to dance, Robert Pashley in his *Travels in Crete* referred to no less an authority than Socrates in explaining that Greek women should, on the basis of historical precedent, be permitted to dance. Pashley states that:

> In the Symposium of Xenophon, the great Athenian sage, who is said by Cicero to have brought down philosophy to the earth, to arbitrate on the ordinary social relations and affairs of mankind, is described as having made the varied and agile motions of a dancing-girl the basis of a philosophical lesson, which he bestowed on his disciples.[20]

Again, however, historical circumstances have put Greek women in a situation of constraint, and their true, free nature has been suppressed.

It was but a short step from explaining the pitiful state of modern Greek women as the result of Turkish depravity to asserting that Greece had suffered a similar decay for the same reasons. Most dramatic of all the effects this peculiar, surrogate form of colonialism exerted on eighteenth- and nineteenth-century depictions of Greece was the way in which it affected the gendered element in such depictions. Just as were India and other colonial territories and peoples, Greece – the land itself, not just the inhabitants – was understood as a fundamentally female entity. But here the connotations of femininity connected not so much to the qualities of mysteriousness, whimsy, danger, and illogicality (the primary gender attributes in feminized depictions of India), as to those of valor, dignity, beauty, and faithfulness. In short, Greece was understood as a noble woman, a princess, the idealized woman of classical Greek literature, and if she had been brought to her current degenerate state through intervention of the Ottoman Turks, only a second intervention by the gallant, gentlemanly, civilized, colonial, Western European male could set her free.

This image was turned into literal reality in 1782 in Choiseul-Gouffier's *Voyage Pittoresque de la Grèce*, a book that went on to enjoy huge popularity in the West. Its frontispiece bore an engraving entitled "Greece in Chains," in which the allegorized Greece, an imperious and beautiful but manacled woman, reclines upon a tomb in a graveyard full of classical ruins dotted with monuments to such great men of antiquity as Lycurgus, Miltiades, and Themistocles. Noble and graceful, the woman is nevertheless clearly in a reduced state and has, one concludes, seen happier times. The image, then, is simultaneously one of defiance and pathos, and carries a tension that is typical of Choiseul-Gouffier's text itself, which also bears echoes of this simultaneous evocation of glory and defeat. As the modern scholar Terence Spencer observes:

> In spite of the enthusiasm which the author feels for the classic land, there succeeds a more dolorous sentiment, caused by the excessive contempt and humiliation into which the descendants of men so celebrated has fallen. In the midst of the degradation before his eyes, he seeks to disentangle some hereditary traits of the character of the Greeks, as one seeks the imprint of an ancient medal beneath the rust which covers it and is devouring it.[21]

Greece, this noble lady in respose, chained but nevertheless valiant, is, as Spencer suggests, surrounded by "degradation" that has not diminished the fundamental nobility of the Hellene but which obscures it. To the observer who describes her thus, it is not a far step to view Greece as desperately in need of the gentlemanly interference of some benevolent, more powerful (and, one might suspect, manly) outside power. The woman that is Greece is, in short, a damsel in distress, a woman who cries out for help, whose grace and nobility make all those who hear her plea unable to deny her their assistance.[22] The basic imagery by which Greece was thus represented – not just in Choiseul-Gouffier's work, but in countless others during this heyday of the Romantic era as well – thus converted philhellenism into a romantic (as opposed to merely romanticist), and above all masculine, ideology, by which, in juxtaposition to the allegorical female, distressed Greece, the West becomes a knight in shining armor, riding off to the succor of this helpless lady. Through the assumptions of the Hellenic Ideal, which saw Greece as the supposed fount of Western civilization itself, the act of rescue would not be a mere gesture of a disinterested good Samaritan, but rather would constitute an act that would benefit the West as well. To rescue the enslaved woman that was Greece would be an act of cultural philanthropy toward the West itself. The fundamentally colonial impulses undergirding travel to Greece were thus cloaked beneath a mythic narrative of salvation and redemption, not just of the Greeks, but of the West's own cultural origins.

Byron is but the most well known of the countless philhellenes who regarded Greece in this idealized, feminized fashion. In his "Maid of Athens, Ere We Part," a poem that initially seems to be directed toward a specific woman, we find by the final stanza that it seems that the woman of Byron's affections is as much the city of Athens itself as it is any particular person:

> Maid of Athens! I am gone:
> Think of me, sweet! When alone.
> Though I fly to Istambol,
> Athens holds my heart and soul:
> Can I cease to love thee? No![23]

Athens, indeed, was very much a female entity; indeed, the city's very name, Athena, is that of a regal female divinity from classical antiquity. Byron's true love, then, while it may be a specific "maid," is also the maid that is Athens, Athena herself. And it is this maid that "holds [his] heart," as indeed it held the heart, and romantic imagination, of European philhellenism in general.

Byron also personally embodies the image of the Western knight attempting to rescue Greece from her Turkish bondage. His interest in the Greek struggle for independence led the London Greek Committee to elect him a member in 1823 and, at the Committee's request, he went to Greece to lend his prestige to the Greek cause. He died there the following year of a fever, but not before writing the poem, "On this Day I Complete my Thirty-Sixth Year," which contains the stanza:

> The sword, the banner, and the field,
> Glory and Greece, around me see!
> The Spartan, borne upon his shield,
> Was not more free.[24]

Thus, travel literature of the period is filled with a desire to find the classical world in visits to modern Greece. When reality failed to meet Western travelers' expectations, they sought explanations that would preserve their ideals and hopes that the ancient world could be discovered despite their disappointment. This, in turn, led to preoccupation with the supposedly degenerate and reduced state of Greece, which they attributed to Turkish rule and, more especially, to the degraded state of Greek women. This preoccupation fed the understanding of Greece itself as an imprisoned woman. And as a woman who represented Western Europe's nostalgic understanding of its own cultural origins, Greece, the damsel in distress, cried out for the rescue of the Western European male. Through such gendered themes, the colonialist impulses undergirding much philhellenic sentiment were romanticized, deepened, and justified.

4

Wild Irish Women: Gender, Politics, and Colonialism in the Nineteenth Century

Tamara L. Hunt

In an essay written in 1923 to mark the birth of the Irish Free State, author and poet Susan Mitchell declared:

> Men playing alone at their moss-grown games of politics have made a mess of human society. The entrance there, not of two or three, but of two or three hundred women partners, might take the game into wider fields and fresher airs, broadening the humanity of Government. Women would come into the game, not to herd together and fight in a feminine corner, to triumph over man and force a petticoat government on him; not to use their sex as a weapon to fight sex, or as a lure to snare it. As men and women working together, they need not attempt the impossible in trying to efface sex, nor the unnecessary in insisting on it. But they might find in it a clue to the wider understanding of each other's nature. Thus should woman move graciously to her place in Irish politics; for only when the petticoat goes out of politics can the Woman come in.[1]

Mitchell's concern that women were seen as gendered beings and not rational individuals was a reaction to the existing political ideology that depicted women as frivolous, weak, and helpless. This view, however, was not one that was native to Ireland; rather, it had its roots in the colonial era, as English, then Irish, leaders sought to forge images of women that would serve male leaders' political agenda.

Ireland bears the dubious distinction of being England's oldest colony. By 1700, military conquests, widespread property confiscations, and legalized religious oppression conferred the bulk of the land and all state offices to a hostile foreign minority of Presbyterian Scots and Anglican gentry, while about seventy-five percent of the population were Gaelic-speaking Catholic peasants.[2] The establishment of these foreign predatory settlers and the displacement of the native Irish fostered an ideology that helped to rationalize the conquest, one that depicted the Irish as "barbaric." One way to do this was to emphasize the difference between Irish and English women, as did the author of one of the earliest texts for midwives, *Speculum Matricis* (1671). He declared that the book was for treating English women only, not hardy Irish women who rarely needed a midwife's assistance. As proof, he described an Irish soldier's wife who, unaided, gave birth to twins under a bush and less than an hour later marched another twelve miles that day "without the least prejudice to her health or the lives of her children."[3]

Throughout the eighteenth century, English depictions of the Irish remained negative, especially on the stage. Men were portrayed as simpletons and common soldiers, or as the "stage Irishman," a caricatured figure who was excessively talkative (in a strong brogue), vulgar, boastful, hard-drinking, bellicose yet cowardly, unreliable, and perpetually insolvent.[4] Irish women usually appeared as camp-followers, servants, or upper-class hoydens. David Garrick reflected the public's low opinion of Irish women in his popular play *The Irish Widow* (1772). The "Dedication," addressed to Mrs. Barry, the actress who played the title role, read: "You were before rank'd in the first class of our Theatrical Geniuses, and now you have the additional merit of transforming the GRECIAN DAUGHTER into the IRISH WIDOW, that is, of sinking *to the lowest note, from the top of the compass!*" The plot features a hitherto modest young Irish widow who discourages an unwelcome elderly English suitor by feigning a heavy brogue and implying she will spend all his money, take lovers, make him go to frivolous entertainments, and, ultimately, drive him to an early grave. He breaks the engagement, declaring "That of all dreadful things I should think of a woman, and that woman should be a Widow, and that Widow should be an Irish one; *quem Deus vult perdere* [Whom the gods would destroy]–."[5]

Such stereotyped images of wild Irish women reinforced the belief that the Irish needed English guidance to become "civilized," for by this time, the English were coming to assume that a domestic structure that emphasized male control and female domesticity constituted an essential component of civilized life.[6] The unrest that arose in the wake of the American and French Revolutions, however, suggested that the Irish were still far short of this goal, for the United Irishman movement of the 1790s had widespread female participation. This group, which initially formed to agitate for parliamentary reform, was forced underground by English repression and became a revolutionary movement. It is difficult to pinpoint this secret organization's membership, but there is no question that women swore oaths to the society and participated in its activities.[7] To the English, however, this proved the danger of the situation: the Secret Committee of the House of Lords investigating the Irish disturbances listened to the alarming evidence that "every woman from Tinnahinch Bridge to Roundwood was 'an United Irishman.' "[8]

When open revolt broke out in 1798, women played a prominent role, acting as spies and couriers, bringing ammunition and supplies to men in battle, and even leading troops in some engagements.[9] Their sexuality could also serve the movement; in Derry, one loyalist commander complained that Irish girls were seducing his men from their duty.[10] This image of English soldiers and Irish girls was one that United Irish leaders could use to inspire their troops; young men were told that the Irish women were in danger from the lustful English soldiery, just as Ireland itself had been ravished by the English oppressor.[11]

Even though the United Irishmen used the image of defenseless females to inspire the rebels, they also used traditional images of strong women for propaganda purposes. Of particular interest are the poetry and ballads that featured the character of Grace O'Malley (known as Granuaile or Granuweal). The original Granuaile had lived in the sixteenth century and, after a long career as a pirate, went to sue for pardon before Elizabeth I. According to legend, the courtiers were scornful because she lacked manners, but she ultimately triumphed over them. Her freewheeling life, coupled with her refusal to submit to England except on her own terms, was enormously appealing, and she became the heroine of United Irishmen poetry and ballads. "Granuweal, An Old Song," published in 1794, is particularly revealing. In it Granuweal rejects an Elizabethan English suitor, saying: "I always still lov'd to be free; / No foe shall invade me in my liberty, / While I've Limerick, Derry, and the fort of Kinsale, / I'll love and not marry, says Granuweal." Thus, this song – and the legend itself – praises a woman whose life was not domestic, and in order to keep her liberty, she rejected marriage because it meant being under the control of a man.[12]

Such sentiments, coming in addition to open rebellion, seemed to prove to the English that the Protestant Anglo-Irish landlords were incapable of controlling the country, and after the United Irishmen were defeated, the English government incorporated Ireland into the national state, allowing direct rule from London. Yet even though Ireland legally became a full partner in the United Kingdom, in reality, it remained a colonial state. This fact was highlighted by a series of Coercion Acts intended to keep down unrest, but which had never been used elsewhere in the United Kingdom. The traditional images of the "wild Irish" thus did much to legitimize the self-serving idea that Britain's role was to tame, educate, and improve the country – in other words, to "civilize" it.

By the early nineteenth-century English literature about Ireland often reflected such concepts by portraying the colonial relationship in specifically gendered terms, such as the "wild Irish girl" being tamed by her English lover. One of the earliest and most popular of this genre was Lady Morgan's novel, *The Wild Irish Girl* (1806). The heroine, Glorvina, lived with her princely father in remote and medieval splendor, and personified Ireland through her love of singing, dancing, and nature. The hero, Mortimer, is a jaded young man who is banished to Ireland by his father, an absentee landlord. They meet at her father's castle, where Mortimer is asked to remain and "invest her with sufficient rudiments in the art [of design]" for which she has a natural but untrained talent.[13] This led to the perfect colonial ending in which both benefited from the union; the English man taught the Irish girl to control and develop her raw talents, while she awakened him to the beauties of nature.[14]

Maria Edgeworth's 1812 novel, *The Absentee*, presented a variation on this theme.[15] Lord and Lady Clonbrony are Irish absentees, and although Lord Clonbrony wants to return to his estates, he remains in London at his wife's insistence. Like Lady Morgan's novel, Edgeworth's portrayal of both Lord and Lady Clonbrony suggests that the "naturalness" of Ireland is preferable to the artificial nature of London society. Lady Clonbrony is so anxious to deny her Irish background that her speech and manners become a caricature of Englishness, making her a laughing-stock. Lord Clonbrony, who has left the management of his lands to his agents, one of whom is utterly unscrupulous, has no natural occupation, turns to gambling, and becomes heavily indebted. To resolve this situation, their son and heir, Lord Colambre, undertakes a voyage to Ireland incognito, where he concludes that his family – and his father's tenants – would be much happier if the family lived in Ireland. Young Colambre returns to London and, after resolving questions about the parentage of his Irish cousin, Grace Nugent, declares his long-standing love for her. With her assistance, he persuades his parents to return to Ireland and their natural setting.

Domestic ideology is central to this resolution. Edgeworth plainly states that the "domestic peace of families" is the cornerstone on which "public as well as private virtue and happiness depend."[16] If Lord Clonbrony overrules his wife and brings his family back to Ireland, their happiness and that of their tenants will dramatically improve and he will rule over all as a benevolent patriarch. Edgeworth stresses that women such as Lady Clonbrony need to be controlled by their husbands or disorder will result.[17] This was also the colonial allegory – the feminine Irish needed to be controlled by the masculine English, and this happy arrangement would at last achieve domestic harmony within the United Kingdom.[18]

Even legislative proposals for Ireland utilized the language of familial relations. In his discussion of the Poor Laws, Rev. Thaddeus O'Malley argued that through "wise parental legislation . . . the most barbarous and degraded portion of [the Irish] lower classes . . . [could be raised] in a few years to a high pitch of civilization."[19] Others noted that some English and Anglo-Irish elites were fulfilling their patriarchal roles by living on their estates and encouraging their tenants to adopt English ways. In 1828, an Englishman visiting Ireland said of the village of Piltown on Lord Duncannon's estate: "I defy anything in the most civilised district of England to surpass it in neatness, comfort and really ornament." He added, however, that this "rapidly spreading civilization" was "begun, of course, and mainly promoted by Lord and Lady Duncannon during the three years they have lived in Ireland."[20] Similarly, when Lord Palmerston wrote to his sister about improvements he had ordered on his Irish estates in 1826, he noted with satisfaction: "The people too are beginning to understand how to labour & that is the first step in civilization."[21]

Palmerston probably meant men's wage labor only, for Victorian ideology was predicated on a patriarchal family whose sole breadwinner was the husband. In the eyes of many Victorian moralists such as Sarah Stickney Ellis, the author of several social guides for middle-class women, a wife had to be protected from the public world in order to be "a companion who will raise the tone of [her husband's] mind from . . . low anxieties, and vulgar cares" which arise from business, whose "purely material" aims tend to "lower and degrade the mind."[22] In other words, women were the repository of civilization, but only if they could maintain their spiritual purity by being separated from the venal concerns of money-making.

However, in most Irish peasant families, income-earning wives were both independent and self-sufficient, generating essential funds for the household's survival. In the mid-1830s, Irish wives earned between sixteen and thirty-seven percent of the total family income, not counting the unpaid family labor they performed.[23] Moreover, government investigators discovered that even if Irish women did not work for wages, poverty still kept them from the "proper" woman's role. Commissioners examining the state of the Irish poor in 1835 noted that when the supply of potatoes ran out, poor husbands and wives temporarily went their separate ways: "the wives and children of those [men] who left home in search of work, used invariably to leave their own part of the country and beg."[24] During a tour of Ireland in 1852, Harriet Martineau worried about the consequences of this situation, "whether the men are to turn nurses and cooks, and to abide beside the hearth, while the women are earning the family bread . . . such a distribution of labour is an adopted symptom of barbarism."[25]

Hardworking women who supported their families while lazy men lounged at home were a stereotype that intensified during the Great Famine (1845–49). The London *Times* actually claimed that Irish men welcomed the famine as an excuse not to work, citing the shiftlessness and improvidence of the Irish character as barriers to improvement of the people.[26] *Punch*, London's leading satirical weekly paper, agreed that Irish men needed to learn to work and published a cartoon entitled *Union is Strength* in 1846, showing hearty John Bull holding out a basket of bread and a shovel to a despairing Irish laborer: "Here are a few things to go on with Brother, and I'll soon put you in a way to earn your own living."[27]

The Famine even led some to speculate that the racial character and temperament of Catholic Celts made them unsuitable for civilization, compared to other subject peoples of the Empire.[28] In 1848, the London *Times* declared that the Irish were "listless, improvident, and wretched . . . [and] have not participated in the great progress of mankind. We do pity them, because they have yet to be civilized. In Canada we have Indians in our borders, many of whom we yearly subsidize and maintain. In Ireland we have Celts equally helpless and equally the objects of national compassion."[29] *Punch* went even further, suggesting satirically that the Irish "Yahoo" was a "creature manifestly between the Gorilla and the Negro. . . . The somewhat superior ability of the Irish Yahoo to utter articulate sounds, may suffice to prove that it is a development, and not, as some imagine, a degeneration of the Gorilla."[30]

Yet, for many Victorians, such comments were not just vicious satire – they appeared to be supported by science. As L. Perry Curtis has shown, "the newer forms of evolutionary thought associated with Darwin, Wallace, Huxley, and their disciples, tended to polarize Englishmen and Irishmen by providing a scientific basis for assuming that such characteristics as violence, poverty, improvidence, political volatility, and drunkenness were inherently Irish and only Irish."[31] Further, some believed that physiognomy – the theory that facial features reflected one's character – provided additional evidence of Irish inferiority. In the 1830s, Gottfried Schadow's extensive study of national physiognomies concluded that the lesser races of Europe such as the Celts had prominent jaws, ill-formed noses, and dark hair or skin.[32] In their *Crania Britannica* (1856) Joseph Barnard Davis and John Thurnam argued that the Celtic facial type and coloring revealed a character that was "wild, superstitious, vengeful . . . [and] timidly susceptible to every impression . . . [tending to] fall into confusion and a state of degeneracy." In 1885, John Beddoe's *The Races of England* included an "Index of Nigrescence," which placed the "Africanoid" Celt with a jutting jaw at the lowest end of the scale.[33] Several physiognomists specifically used women's images to illustrate this Celtic degradation; S.R. Wells' *New System of Physiognomy* (1866) contrasted the image of Florence Nightengale – who at that time epitomized womanly self-sacrifice – with Bridget McBruiser, whose tangled hair, snub nose, and prominent jaw give her a vaguely ape-like appearance.[34]

Some used these views on racial inferiority to explain unrest in Ireland. In a letter to *The Times* in 1868, Benjamin Disraeli declared: "[The Irish] hate our free and fertile isle. They hate our order, our civilization, our enterprising industry, our sustained courage, our decorous liberty, our pure religion. This wild, reckless, indolent, uncertain, and superstitious race have no sympathy with the English character."[35] A decade later in an essay entitled *The Incompatibles*, Matthew Arnold acknowledged that many believed Ireland's "lower" civilization rebelled against England's "higher" civilization, pointing out that English "exactness and neatness, for instance (to say no more than what everybody must admit) – are disagreeable to Irish laxity and slovenliness, and are resisted by them."[36]

Such views on Irish racial inferiority were reinforced by suggestions that national characteristics were gendered. Powerful and dominant countries were "masculine," while poorer, weaker, or conquered countries were "feminine." Indeed, "feminization" of the "Other" – in this case the colonized country – was one means of defining English national identity.[37] This ideology was summed up in a conversation recorded by the Irish playwright Lady Gregory, in her diary in 1882; an Anglo-Irish supporter of English rule told her that the Celtic countries were "female" countries which had the "soft, pleasing quality and charm of a woman, but no capacity for self-government." He added that it was necessary for male countries like England to "take the female countries in hand."[38]

Political cartoonists also drew on this ideology, and Erin/Hibernia was used most frequently to represent Ireland in the 1870s and 1880s, often depicted as a girlish figure who needed English assistance or protection. For example, *Punch* published *Two Forces* in October 1881 which shows Hibernia, a girlish, weeping figure, being comforted by a powerful and strapping Britainnia, who fends off a stone-throwing, degraded-looking Irishman (whose hat is inscribed "Anarchy") with her sword, inscribed "The Law."[39] Another cartoon, entitled *Bravo, William!* (1881), also shows Ireland as a beautiful young woman cradling in her arms the Irish Land Bill that was intended to bring relief to tenant farmers, and she is defended from unseen enemies by Prime Minister William Gladstone, dressed as a British sailor.[40]

This image of Ireland as a weak, helpless woman incapable of coping with political problems did not reflect reality for Irish women, who had long been involved in politics and public affairs. Women had provided support to the United Irish soldiers in 1798, and in some instances actually led troops. During the agitation for Catholic Emancipation in the 1820s,[41] women attended political meetings, and in the 1830s and 1840s, penal transportation records indicate they were active in the agrarian unrest.[42] During and after the famine, women joined the Fenians, a physical force nationalist movement, and women from the gentry joined Young Ireland, an intellectual, liberal, Protestant group which promoted Irish independence in the immediate post-Famine years. Still others participated in politics more informally on a local level; for instance, some women apparently negotiated the sale of their husbands' votes in an electoral system rife with corruption. They could also be used to sway voters: Lord Eglington, wrote to J.H. Walpole in 1852: "The non-electors, women and children have been invited in the chapels to attend every polling place and mark the men who voted against their religion."[43]

By the 1870s, however, female activism had come to be viewed as a problem by male Irish political leaders, probably because it seemed to suggest that Ireland was still "uncivilized" or "feminized" and thus incapable of reasoned independent political decisions. The English had portrayed the Irish as sub-human creatures who had national characteristics that made them "weak," "feminine," and unfit to rule their own country. In English eyes, this unfortunate situation could be rectified only when stable bourgeois homes – like those in England – had been established throughout Ireland. Thus, because Irish leaders wanted to be seen as capable politicians and earn the respect of their peers in Europe and America, they had to prove that the Irish had become manly and civilized, and to do that, they adopted the language and paternalistic attitudes of the colonial power which barred women from formal participation in public life.[44]

These beliefs were central to the controversies that developed over the Land League agitation, 1879–81.[45] By 1879, questions involving the rights of Irish tenants to the land they farmed had become the most pressing issue in Irish politics, and Michael Davitt, Charles Stewart Parnell, and others founded the Land League with the intention of forcing the issue on Parliament through (relatively) peaceful agitation to resist excessive rent and boycotting landlords and tenants who opposed the League's principles. Women participated in both these activities, and while widows who were tenants of family farms could be League members, the organization's paternalistic principles forbade them from having leadership positions or from speaking at rallies or political meetings.[46] However, when the League's leaders faced arrest in late 1880, Michael Davitt proposed the formation of a Ladies' Land League (hereafter LLL) to carry on their work. Although Parnell and others considered this a "most dangerous experiment," the motion passed and Parnell's sister, Anna, was asked to organize the group.[47] According to Davitt, the LLL was "vehemently opposed" by Charles Stewart Parnell and others solely because they were afraid "we would *invite public ridicule* in appearing to put women forward in places of danger [emphasis added]." Yet Davitt's support for the LLL was also based, to some extent, on a concern for appearances.[48] Although he acknowledged that women were "in certain emergencies, more dangerous to despotism than men," he saw their participation in the Land war as an extension of women's domestic role in a fight to "save the homes of Ireland – the sacred, domestic domain of woman's moral supremacy in civilized society." He further believed that the idea of endangered womanhood could be valuable to the cause: "what of the effect this would have on the public opinion of the United States and the world if fifty or a hundred respectable young women were sent to jail as 'criminals,' without trial or conviction, by England's rulers in Ireland?"[49]

This view of the LLL clearly saw its members as symbols, not as vigorous political activists, a fact Anna Parnell and her supporters quickly learned when the Land League refused to help them identify and assist tenant farmers who followed the Land League's instructions and refused to pay excessive rents.[50] Consequently, the LLL began the first comprehensive survey of tenant holdings for all of Ireland, sending out women to the most remote parts of the country to inquire into the rents and types of landholdings. Ultimately, the LLL adopted its own course and, instead of following the Land League policy of paying the rent of those who withheld it on the League's instructions, the LLL constructed hundreds of houses throughout the country for those who were evicted.[51] With impressive organization, the LLL encouraged the founding of local chapters, including children's branches; as one member later recalled: "the Ladies' Land League was established in every town."[52] Members of the LLL were publicly active, organizing rent strikes and addressing and attending political meetings; women were also prominent in the crowds that defied the police or prevented process servers from evicting tenants.[53]

This activism led some to question whether these women – and in particular, Anna Parnell – could be proper "ladies" at all. For example, one of Charles Stewart Parnell's early biographers declared that when Irish women "take to politics, [they] have a capacity for fanaticism which is almost inhuman," and went on to refer to the LLL as "Miss Parnell's band of harridans," ultimately suggesting that Anna Parnell was insane.[54] In contrast, Katharine Tynan, one of the original members of the LLL, asserted that "there were no furies in the Ladies' Land League . . . we were a harmless pack of very harmless girls and women."[55] Yet ironically, Tynan also illustrated the contradiction the LLL presented when she said of Anna Parnell's organizing abilities: "One would have said she was masculine if she had not been so feminine."[56]

Yet the English government seemed to agree that the LLL's members were women of questionable repute, for when it began arresting the women in December 1881 in an effort to stop agrarian unrest, it did not use the political legislation drawn up to muzzle the men of the Land League; rather, it began enforcing a medieval statute against prostitutes ("take and arrest all those that . . . be *not* of good fame, where they shall be found"), interpreting this to mean any woman who attended or spoke at LLL meetings and demonstrations or who encouraged tenant farmers to defy the law.[57]

Even before this point though, male Irish leaders had begun to denounce the LLL as "improper." According to Anna Parnell, the LLL faced opposition from their male allies from the start: "the first thing that happened to the women who complied with the request [to form the LLL] was to find themselves condemned wholesale for having done so by members of the Land League executive." Nor did things improve; Land League leaders found "fault with everything we did. . . . As time went on the hostility manifested towards the Ladies by the authors of their being, increased instead of diminishing."[58]

The LLL faced condemnation from other quarters as well; the *Belfast News-Letter* declared that "sensible people in the north of Ireland dislike to see woman out of the place she is gifted to occupy, and at no time is woman further from her natural position than when she appears upon a political platform."[59] The same journal also condemned as "distasteful" the "spectacle of women making a harangue from a public platform," expressing the hope that other young girls would not become "such as Miss Parnell."[60] Archbishop McCabe of Dublin, who opposed the land agitation itself, also issued a ringing condemnation of the LLL in March 1881, telling his diocescan clergy: "Do not tolerate . . . the woman who so far disavows her birthright of modesty as to parade herself before the public gaze in a character so unworthy of a child of Mary."[61]

Some blamed the Land League for this gender inversion. Archbishop McCabe was certain that "this attempt at degrading the women of Ireland comes very appropriately from men who had drawn the country into her present terribly deplorable condition."[62] The *Connaught Telegraph* was even more forthright, denouncing the Land League's leaders for betraying both Ireland and their manhood:

> God or nature never intended . . . that the manhood of any nation could be so cowardly and demoralized as to intrench [*sic*] themselves behind the fair sex. . . . We do not see how any man or body of men having Celtic blood coursing in their veins can be found to descend to or condescend to female leadership. . . . [We] enter our solemn protest against having the responsibility of Irish affairs vested in women.[63]

In October 1881, the London *Times* showed contempt for Ireland's "feminized" political movement by declaring that "when treason is reduced to fighting behind petticoats and pinafores it is not likely to do much mischief." Nevertheless, a few months later, it expressed admiration of the LLL's dauntlessness, calling them the "irrepressible ladies of the Land League" who defied police threats to arrest their members by vowing to "meet next Sunday at the same hour" and to continue "as long as any of them were left."[64] With some mortification, the Land League's own newspaper noted in February 1882 that the women had shown more courage than the men when threatened with arrest.[65]

These reports confirmed Charles Stewart Parnell's fear that the Land League would look ridiculous if they were thought to be hiding behind the women.[66] What was worse, the LLL was not obeying the orders issued by the imprisoned Land League leaders.[67] This independence, coupled with the LLL's success in organizing the people and defying the authorities – which had surpassed the achievements of the Land League in 1879–80 – only deepened the condemnation made by male leaders. Years later, Timothy Harrington, the secretary of the Land League, baldly told Maud Gonne that the LLL was disbanded because "They did too good work, and some of us found they could not be controlled."[68] Charles Stewart Parnell was particularly displeased and, reportedly, believed "that the organization was being used 'not for the purposes he approved of, but for a real revolutionary end and aim.' "[69]

This was the crux of the matter; after negotiation with Prime Minister William Gladstone, Parnell and his supporters proposed abandoning the resistance tactics of the Land League and planned instead a constitutional campaign to secure Home Rule once they were released from prison. In consequence, they feared any actions that might jeopardize their plans. They wanted to prove to England and the world that the Irish were a civilized, rational people, capable of making their own political decisions. The openly political activities of the LLL, however, directly challenged Victorian ideology which equated women's domesticity with civilized behavior. By the time of his release from prison, Parnell was convinced that the women – his sister included – were uncontrollable and insubordinate.[70] He reportedly complained that the LLL "told me in Dublin, after my release, that I ought to have remained in Kilmainham [gaol]. I fear they have done much harm along with some good."[71] However, the Land League leaders did not immediately disband the LLL. According to Anna Parnell, the women were told to continue assisting evicted tenants, and they sent their bills to the Land League's banker, as they had done for the past year. However, unbeknownst to the LLL, the Land League refused to pay the bills, and when their overdraft reached about £5,000 the men acted. According to Anna Parnell, their motives were contemptible:

> At the beginning of August [1882] we were officially informed that the Land League would not discharge the debt to the bank unless we agreed to their terms. . . . the Ladies' Land League should dissolve, and *afterwards*, were to consider all applications for grants made to the Land League and make recommendations on them for that body. . . . For us it was the most laborious and sickening of all we had to do. . . . there was every reason against [this agreement], and not one for it. Except that the other side, understanding perfectly well the unpleasant nature of the tasks they had so intelligently planned to put, once and forever, on other shoulders, wanted us for a buffer between them and the country – *a perpetual petticoat screen behind which they could shelter*, not from the government, but from the people. [emphasis added][72]

Without the funds or support of the Land League, the Ladies' Land League disbanded. Anna Parnell would later remark bitterly: "If the men of that country have made up their minds it shall not be done, the women cannot bring it about."[73]

Charles Stewart Parnell and his supporters not only dismissed the women, they also began to dismantle the Land League itself, for they were in the process of adopting British parliamentary rhetoric and tactics, which would further restrict Irish women's political role. The Land League was replaced by the Irish National League, a political organization dedicated to securing Home Rule from Parliament, a change that reflected the virtual abandonment of land issues and public resistance in favor of parliamentary maneuvering. Given the fact that women across Europe were excluded from political participation, it is hardly surprising that the National League was described as "an open organisation in which the ladies will not take part."[74] When Maud Gonne met with the leaders of the National League to volunteer to work for Irish independence, she was told flatly: "A woman's place is in the home."[75] While nationalist leaders apparently did not mean this literally, Gonne and other female patriots were restricted to fundraising, supporting men's organizations, or organizing women's groups to promote Gaelic culture – direct political action was the province of men only.

In consequence, when the non-political Gaelic League was formed in the 1890s to promote the Irish language and culture, women were encouraged to participate at all levels of the organization. Indeed, some believed that women were central to the revival of Gaelic culture, either through forming groups celebrating Irish culture such as *Inghinighe na h'Eireann* (Daughters of Erin) or promoting Irish language and culture in the home. As the Gaelic League pamphlet *Irishwomen and the Home Language* (1901) declared, in "the life and death crisis" Ireland faced, patriotic women should "shake themselves free from the dead hand of denationalisation which has weighed down on them in the past . . . [and] make their homes centres of Irish life. They will have the proud consciousness of knowing that in making the homes of Ireland Irish, they will be doing the best day's work that has ever been done to make Ireland a nation in fullest, truest sense of the word."[76]

Thus, in some respects, Ireland's fight for independence seems to fit Edward Said's model for liberationist colonial struggles, when he declares that "one of the first tasks of the culture of resistance was to reclaim, rename, and reinhabit the land . . . [which makes possible] the search for authenticity, for a more congenial national origin than that provided by colonial history, for a new pantheon of heroes and (occasionally) heroines, myths and religions . . . [and] an almost magically inspired, quasi-alchemical redevelopment of the native language."[77] In the process, however, women tend to be marginalized, regardless of past traditions, as nationalist political leaders adopted ideologies and political structures from their oppressors.[78] Yet Ireland's traditions included numerous examples of strong and independent women, which did not appeal to the leaders of a late Victorian nationalist movement. Thus, the women in nationalist literature and drama could be ambiguous figures. The best-known example is the play *Cathleen Ni Houlihan* (1902) by Lady Gregory and W.B. Yeats. Maud Gonne electrified Dublin audiences in the title role, in which she played the personification of Ireland, but this figure had a slightly more sinister side. By the end of the play, she has enticed a young man on the eve of his wedding to give his life in a futile rebellion, leaving his heartbroken bride and family to mourn his loss. A similar tension exists in works that utilize Ireland's ancient historical sagas, especially the *Táin Bó Cuailnge*, one of the oldest surviving vernacular tales in Europe. The female figure used most often by late nineteenth-century authors was not the powerful and independent Maeve, Queen of Connachta, who dominates the *Táin*; instead, they more frequently used Deirdre, a princess whose uncontrolled passion led to the death of her lover and his followers, as well as her own suicide.[79] In both these examples, a woman's unchecked power can lead men to disaster.[80]

Certainly, many male politicians feared women's activism, and Irish women soon discovered that their concerns would be ignored or downplayed if they seemed to conflict with the male leaders' nationalist agenda.[81] When Dublin suffragettes began a campaign of civil disobedience, they were accused of being anti-Home Rule, anti-Irish, and unwomanly.[82] Although many Irish Members of Parliament claimed to support women's suffrage, when anti-suffragist

H.H. Asquith became Prime Minister they dropped their support for fear of blocking a Home Rule Bill.[83]

Women's exclusion from politics became increasingly important among nationalists, as gender became a focus of the growing movement to "recover" Celtic manhood. Leaders such as Parnell and Patrick Pearse publicly expressed fears about their supporters "becoming women" or "old women" and being politically impotent; according to Mary Condren, this fear "reached almost pathological proportions" by the time of the 1916 Rising, and she points out that "These taunts were used consistently as political weapons, as though political potency depended upon a rigid reassertion of gender boundaries."[84]

Women also took up this gendered ideology, even those who were long-time activists. For example, Mary O'Donovan Rossa was opposed to independent women's political groups, even though she had been politically and publicly active for decades:[85]

> I believe in votes for women, of course. . . . But I am old-fashioned enough still to cling to the notion that men are the lords of creation and women at their best when kindly cooperating in all that reason and conscience approve, and under guidance, with modesty, not self-asserting. Maybe you don't want to hear my ideas about women's societies – I approve of them for as much good as they do for women and particularly for as much help as they can give men in patriotic matters. But they must be absolutely under obedience to the authorised [*sic*] men and take willing guidance from them if they profess to be patriotic societies. If they are social or church or charity societies, they are sufficiently competent to manage their own concerns independently of men. But patriotic -! I would give the men a despotism over them and ban whoever murmured. . . . Don't be asking them [the women] to oblige you by doing this or that, but take the reins in your hand and lay down the law for them. Do that to-morrow evening and if they are mutinous, believe me you may be glad if they disband.[86]

The contradiction presented by O'Donovan Rossa – a female political activist who nevertheless believed that women should be kept out of politics – in some ways reflects the conflicted ideologies that existed when the Irish Free State finally was born in 1922. As Mary Condren has suggested: "colonized societies often develop political identities by rigidly asserting their moral purity over against the foreign 'invader' . . . [and Irish women's] 'purity' became the indicator of national identity over against 'pagan' England."[87] Yet the virtues that nationalists claimed were also those of the colonial power. As Maryann Gialanella Valiulis argues, when the new Irish Free State government came to power in 1922, it

> wanted to achieve a state based on those virtues that the British had proclaimed in the nineteenth century as the basis of all civilized society – the Victorian virtues of respectability, sobriety, hard work, self-help, thrift, and

> sexual puritanism. . . . Finally, by defining women's primary role as that of mother and guardian of the hearth to the exclusion of a political and economic identity, the government emphasized women's role as transmitters of culture. In so doing, the government assigned to women the responsibility for insuring the 'Irishness' of the new state, that is, of preserving and transmitting traditional Irish culture.[88]

In some ways, the view of Irish women had come full circle from that of Lady Morgan's *Wild Irish Girl*. Again, they were assigned a role to convey culture, but only under the direction of Irish men who remained the true leaders of society. Thus, despite the contributions Irish women made to nineteenth-century politics, society, and culture, the end result was that they were doubly colonized – first because they were Irish, and again because they were women.

Part II
Colonialism in the Americas

5

French Views of Native American Women in the Early Modern Era: The Tupinamba of Brazil[1]

Laura Fishman

European travelers to the New World in the sixteenth and seventeenth centuries provided their contemporaries with numerous, richly detailed accounts of Native American societies. Both the writers and the readers of this literature regarded its contents as factual, eyewitness reportage of newly discovered peoples. Present-day analyses of these travel accounts, however, continue to unravel a web of European prejudices, stereotypes, myths, legends, and even literary genres, which meshed with the travelers' observations.[2] Attempts to separate fact from fiction will always leave some room for doubt, since Europeans provided the only written sources. In addition to the problem of cultural bias, one must also consider the role of gender bias as a factor that influenced European conceptions of New World societies, since virtually all the explorers, missionaries, and early colonizers who provided written accounts of their experiences with the native inhabitants were male. To what degree did gender influence the perception of early modern Europeans in the New World? And especially, how did gender affect the portrayal of Native American women, and the evaluation of their roles in native society? This study will examine the attitudes of Frenchmen who went to Brazil in the sixteenth and seventeenth centuries; there they met the Tupinamba.

Anthropologists have begun to recognize the problems inherent in the studies of primitive societies in those cases where men provided the observation and evaluations. Male anthropologists have tended to project the dominant patterns of gender relationships in their own culture onto the societies that they observed. Their underlying assumptions regarding gender relationship have led them to undervalue the role and contribution of women in primitive societies, and to assume that women were accorded status inferior to that of men. Anthropologists of the Victorian era maintained that women in non-Western societies were mistreated and subjugated by men. This stereotype of the oppressed and exploited native female served as an indication of the supposed savage nature of primitive societies and the concomitant need for the alleged uplifting benefits of Western civilization.[3]

Twentieth-century anthropologists continue to minimize the significance of women in primitive cultures by focusing on male activities such as hunting, dismissing any work performed by women as secondary and assuming that childbirth automatically relegated women to an inferior and dependent role. This purported evidence serves to confirm the pre-existing beliefs of the observers in the universality of male superiority and dominance.[4] Furthermore, the assumption that women played a secondary and inferior role in primitive cultures is not so much an accurate observation of aboriginal gender relationships as it is a reflection of charges brought about by centuries of contact with Western colonizers and missionaries. Native social systems that may have originally maintained more harmonious and egalitarian relations between men and women succumbed to Western patterns of male dominance and control. Latter-day anthropologists then assumed these adoptive practices to be natural to native culture.[5]

Western observations of primitive societies often contain an additional dynamic that expresses gender stereotypes on a metaphorical level. The female body, especially in a virgin state, has typically served as a symbol of the land, and of unexplored territory in particular. Thus, the activities of exploration, colonization, and hence domination appeal to male members of society on a variety of levels. Specifically, the newly discovered continent of America was artistically personified as a naked female, often decorated with feathers. Such allegorical depictions were common in paintings and prints; they decorated plates and tankards. Maps and books portraying the New World often contained such artistic representations of America as well. Thus, Europeans were introduced to America as a female. The equation of the primitive with the feminine served as both a further indication of the inferiority of native societies and a justification for Western control. These images also intensified erotic visions of "savage" women.[6]

European observers in the early modern era assessed the societies of the New World natives according to the dominant values and norms of contemporary Old World culture. A strong anti-female bias was one key element of their worldview. Misogynist sentiments had intensified since the late Middle Ages, as evidenced in numerous philosophical and literary works. This trend was, in part, a reflection of the deterioration in women's status that accompanied the process of state formation in this era. Local and familial units of power, in which some women had been accorded a measure of influence, were under attack. The increase in the authority of the central state also affected women's domestic position. The emergence of the patriarchal, nuclear family further subjected women to male authority, and the state enforced regulations that helped to solidify this development. Subjugation of wives to husbands was regarded as important in promoting social order by establishing patterns of obedience.[7]

In light of this dominant misogynist cultural milieu, it strikes the modern reader as surprising to note the degree of attention that Frenchmen paid to Native American women in the travel literature. These accounts contain much detailed observation regarding physical appearance, sexual activity, childrearing, marriage patterns, and the routine work performed by women. Written at the time of initial contact between people of diverse cultures, this travel literature provides the closest look at Native American societies prior to the impact of a sustained European presence. The details recorded may be deemed factual to a large degree, especially when more than one traveler to the same region reports similar findings. A twentieth-century anthropological study has confirmed the ethnographic reliability of many of these sources.[8] The evaluative conclusions drawn by contemporary Frenchmen concerning the nature of Native American women and their status in society, however, reveal many of the biases of their European culture. Still, surprisingly, these travel accounts contain a curious mix of both positive and negative appraisals of the female population native to the New World.

Jean de Léry has provided a lengthy account of his journey to Brazil, first published in 1578, which includes substantial information about the Tupinamba Indians who inhabited that region. Léry was part of a French Huguenot colonial venture headed by Nicholas Durand de Villegagnon and operating under the initiative of Admiral Coligny. Villegagnon reached Rio de Janeiro in November of 1555; five years later, his settlement was destroyed by a Portuguese attack. Léry was sent by Calvin in 1557 to minister to the religious needs of the approximately three hundred colonists, but had a heated quarrel with Villegagnon regarding the religious regulation of the colony. Léry was forced to abandon his compatriots and live amongst the Tupinamba for about one year, until a ship arrived to take him back to France in 1558. Jean de Léry's personal experience of finding more hospitality amongst the Native Americans than the French undoubtedly influenced his assessment of Tupinamba life and society. The subsequent religious warfare that he encountered upon his return to Europe, and his ensuing disillusionment, also led him to portray Native American culture in a more positive light.[9]

Léry's depictions of Tupinamba women are generally quite favorable. Like most European travelers to the tropical regions of the New World, Léry is initially struck by the natives' nudity, "men and women go about entirely naked, as when they were born." The writer, however, displays no horror or disgust, and proceeds to describe matter of factly other aspects of the Tupinambas' physical appearance. The women have long hair, which they wash and comb carefully; pierce their ears, but not their lips; and use feathers to ornament their heads. Léry also describes large bracelets made of bones and the manner in which the women paint their faces.[10]

Jean de Léry reports that the natives have "well formed and proportioned bodies," and the women possess a "natural beauty." He feels compelled, however, "to respond to those that say frequentation among completely naked women incites promiscuity . . . it is otherwise than appearance may lead one to believe." Léry does state that he is not approving of nudity and it is shameful to view naked women, but within the context of native society nudity appears ordinary, "as opposed to what appears striking in an individual case." This Frenchman defends the reasoning of Tupi women who refuse to adopt European clothing when they argue that it is too much trouble for them to constantly dress and undress, since they dive into the river several times a day in order to wash themselves.[11]

What first impresses the reader as a rather surprising expression of tolerance of non-European cultural practices, accompanied by an even more striking respect for Native American women, turns out to be a means for Jean de Léry to convey his anti-female bias toward contemporary European women. Léry points out that the "artifical things, wigs, dresses, infinite trappings which women never have enough of, without comparison are the cause of more evil than the ordinary nudity of Brazilian women." He then emphasizes his role as an eyewitness to both societies, and invites those who disagree with him to travel to Brazil and make the comparison for themselves.[12]

A similar pattern is evident in the report of a Capuchin missionary to Brazil, Claude d'Abbeville. The Capuchins accompanied another French colonial venture, this one launched in 1612 to the Marañhao region, south of the Amazon River.[13] Abbeville admires the physical appearance of both men and women Tupinamba. He reports that their bodies are "well proportioned" and that there are "as handsome boys and beautiful girls as seen elsewhere." Women wear their hair long, wash it every morning, and rub it with oil; they also pierce their ears, and then insert long pieces of wood.[14]

Claude d'Abbeville devotes a whole chapter to the topic of nudity. He conveys his initial shock: "One hardly can find a nation, although barbarous, that did not at one time have the usage of clothes."[15] Here, as well as at other points throughout his account, Father Claude is ambivalent in his assessment of Tupinamba society and culture. He is a Catholic missionary and thus condemns many of the practices of a "pagan" people. Yet since his goal is to convert the Tupinamba to Christianity and convince his European readership that this is both a worthwhile and feasible goal, he often highlights positive actions and character traits of the New World natives. On the one hand, this missionary states that the practice of nudity is "abnormal," "shameful," and a sign of "brutality," and that "many believe it is a monstrous thing to see these people all nude, and that it is dangerous to go among the girls, the attraction will lead to sin." On the other, like Jean de Léry, Claude d'Abbeville immediately counters this assumption with a strong defense of the behavior of Tupinamba women. He reports that they are "modest and restrained in their nudity, offering no movement, word, or action to offend, very careful of their integrity." But once again, as in Léry's account, this positive depiction ultimately emerges as a critique of the behavior of European women, whose "artificial devices, unrestrained simperings and new inventions . . . cause more mortal sin and ruin more souls than do the Indian women with this brutal and odious nudity."[16] Abbeville thus substantially qualifies his admiration of nudity among the female Tupinamba. However, it is the contemporary European woman who bears the brunt of the missionary's disdain.[17]

Claude d'Abbeville also shows admiration for Tupinamba women by idealizing their role as mothers. Here again, his motive is to critique the practices of European women. Abbeville praises native women for the deep love and constant attention that they give to their children. He also praises the absence of swaddling; native children are permitted to grow freely, without pain and difficulty, and thus develop well-proportioned bodies – physical deformities are rare. Abbeville admires Tupi women for nursing their own children and sees this as an indication of maternal love and devotion. But once again, this praise of native women turns out to be a means for the author to express criticism of European mothers who do not have patience and give babies out to be nursed.[18]

A similar pattern is found in the writing of Jean de Léry, who lauds the absence of swaddling and praises Tupinamba mothers for breastfeeding their babies. According to Léry, European women are "inhuman" to send their infants to a wet-nurse, and he declares that mothers should nurse their own children.[19] Thus, the idealization of Tupinamba women serves as a vehicle to reprimand their European counterparts.

Yet, other observers who were contemporaries of Abbeville and Léry found nothing admirable about the Tupinamba society, and viewed Tupi women with distinctly misogynistic sentiments. André Thevet was part of the expedition led by Villegagnon, and he describes the natives as "lecherous, carnal, more than brutish, especially the women, who use all means to move men to lust." Thevet warns Christians to avoid sexual relations with Tupi women, since they are the source of the "pocks."[20] Yves d'Evreux, a Capuchin missionary and colleague of Claude d'Abbeville, also portrayed the Tupinamba women as promiscuous in his lengthy and detailed account based on his two years at Marañhao. Evreux analytically divides Tupinamba life into six chronological states, and discusses the activities and customs of both males and females during each phase of their lives. He expresses some sympathy for the "poor young barbarian girls," ages seven to fifteen, but concludes that they are not to be esteemed because they "need not preserve their purity." Regarding the next stage of life, ages fifteen to twenty-five, Evreux declares that he chooses to "be silent about abuses committed in these years," concluding it is the custom of these people to live in "error." During the ages of twenty-five to forty he reports that Tupi women grow ugly and dirty, and their breasts hang long; in the final phase of life, after age forty, they are said to be dirty, rough, and wrinkled. Evreux here goes against the consensus of his contemporaries, who emphasize the attractive physical appearance of native women. He asserts that sexual license is the cause of the deterioration of female Tupinamba, and comments that the "rewards of this world go to the pure and incorrupt."[21]

Evreux abhors the sexual freedom enjoyed by young Tupi women prior to marriage and depicts them as extremely promiscuous. Evreux links this "lubricity" to the nudity of the Brazilian natives. He also asserts that venereal disease is the result of the sexual "excesses" of Tupi women and a "just punishment" for those Frenchmen who engage in "illicit" relations. Evreux's account gives evidence of sexual activity between Tupi women and French men. The natives offered their daughters as "concubines" to the French as a sign of hospitality and friendship when they concluded an alliance. Evreux reports that the natives considered it an honor if a child was born of this union, and he goes on to describe the physical characteristics of these children. But the author urges his countrymen to live chastely and have sexual relations within marriage only, provided that their native partner has been converted to Christianity. According to Evreux, veneral disease would not be contracted if these precautions were taken.[22]

Yves d'Evreux, like his colleague Claude d'Abbeville, had as his highest goal the conversion of the Tupinamba to Christianity. He regarded their nudity and sexual promiscuity as two of the greatest obstacles he faced. However, Evreux could not view the native as inherently evil or barbarous, since that would negate the plausibility of his mission. He asserts that "nature has given to all men of this world, without exception, the foundations and seeds of virtue." Evreux sees the Devil as responsible for the offensive conduct of Tupi women. They are promiscuous because they are "infidels." Their sexual conduct illustrates the "blindness of souls in captivity of a foul spirit, which does not desist from precipitating filth upon filth on the souls that serve him."[23] In Evreux's account, however, it is Native American women, more than men, who appear to be engaging in this diabolically motivated frenzy of sexual activity.[24]

The remedy, according to this missionary, is not merely religious conversion, but the introduction of French customs, language, and literacy. Yves d'Evreux emphasizes the importance of building schools, and also stresses that "respectable" French women should be sent to the Marañhao colony. It would be their job to "instruct in Christian doctrine, as well as other things well suited and requisite for that sex . . . respectability, modesty, hand work or crafts."[25] Evreux is optimistic that, within a few years, the Tupinamba can be rendered more orderly and "civilized." He cites the example of a young native girl who was raised among the Portuguese and "now one cannot distinguish if by birth she is Portuguese or savage." Evreux was impressed by the degree to which she had acquired the "modesty and decency that a woman must have to carefully cover the imperfection of her sex."[26]

That women of both the Old World and the New ultimately have a common nature appears to be Yves d'Evreux's conclusion. The virtues that he esteems for all females, modesty, respectability, and purity, are all acquired traits that both French and Native American women must practice in order to overcome an "imperfect" nature. Evreux and his contemporaries agree that one of the key flaws in women's characters is their tendency toward excessive sexuality. André Thevet and Yves d'Evreux portray Tupinamba women as promiscuous; Claude d'Abbeville and Jean de Léry idealize the perceived modesty, restraint, and simplicity of female natives in order to condemn the sexually forward and flirtatious manner of European women.

Early modern European travelers were products of a society in which the basic family structure was patriarchal.[27] Accustomed to the dominance of male authority, they were astonished by the degree of sexual freedom accorded to young Tupinamba women. The family structure of Native American societies was sharply distinct from that of contemporary Europe. The most striking native custom was polygyny, but it was also the case that women enjoyed a large degree of influence and independence in native societies, and divorce was easily obtainable.[28] In Tupinamba culture, marriage initially followed a matrilocal pattern. Daughters were highly valued by their fathers and regarded as an asset, since a girl's suitor, and then her husband, was obliged to serve his father-in-law and increased the latter's authority and prestige. Ultimately, young men did attain independence from their fathers-in-law, but only after providing them with substantial favors and presents. Men were then able to take other wives, but the first wife was considered the principal one. Either spouse could renounce the marriage should they become dissatisfied; adulterous wives were usually not severely punished.[29]

French observers of Tupinamba society in the sixteenth and seventeenth centuries recorded many comments pertaining to native marriage patterns. Female members of native society thus occupy a substantial place in the travel literature. However, these accounts do not clearly portray a culture characterized by more egalitarian gender relationships. Instead, the travelers' depictions of Native American women tend to mirror their own European experiences and expectations.

For Yves d'Evreux, a male-dominated family unit was the ideal, and he depicted Tupinamba society as adhering to this "natural" pattern. Here, as elsewhere throughout his account, this missionary continually searches for elements that reveal the workings of "nature" in the New World. Believing the Tupinamba to be devoid of any civilization or culture, Evreux seems to have regarded their society as a laboratory in which he could examine the operation of nature in a pristine state. But those aspects of Tupi life and society which Evreux upholds as "natural" mirror the missionary's own beliefs regarding ideal patterns of human conduct.

Yves d'Evreux's account does provide evidence of matrilocality, noting that the wife's family provides lodging and other necessities. But Evreux asserts that native parents love their sons more than their daughters. He comments that this practice is "similar to our custom," and clearly implies that it is a proper and universal sentiment, stating that the natives "follow nature" in this matter.[30] Evreux emphasizes the respect and obedience that he reports is accorded to Tupi men. In describing the organization of native villages, he notes that the family is the basic unit and the father is its head – wives, children, and slaves recognize his authority. Evreux also praises the most honored phrase in the life of a male Tupinamba, after age forty, when he is respected as a "captain." When he speaks at a council he is listened to in silence, and the youths are especially attentive; his wives care for him and serve him, and mourn him when he dies. According to Evreux, this respect for male elders is taught to the "savages" by "nature alone." By contrast, the author sees no such respect for older Tupi women, whom he portrays as dirty and disgusting.[31]

Jean de Léry is interested in the structure of marriage and family life among the Tupinamba and devotes a chapter of his account to "marriage, polygamy, and the degree of consanguinity observed by the savages and the treatment of their little children." He notes that marriage is concluded with less formality than in Europe, and that there are only three blood relationships that restrict marriage – a man cannot marry his mother, sister, or daughter – but may marry his niece. Léry, however, does not report that Tupi women experience any greater freedom or equality within marriage, but instead portrays a family structure that is male-dominated. He comments that a young man must ask permission of a girl's father before marriage, adultery of wives is "regarded as a horror," and that a husband can kill his wife for adultery. Léry's discussion of polygyny also emphasizes his perception of the Tupi male as dominant. A native man can have as many wives as he chooses; multiple wives are a sign of prestige and valor. Léry does not condemn Tupi men for having multiple sexual partners. In fact, he praises their "modesty" when he reports that men "never have relations with their wives in public, as some might imagine they do." Léry's only surprise is that the wives live together in "unparalleled harmony." One wife is regarded as pre-eminent by her husband and is "loved best," but the other wives are not jealous of her.[32] Thus, while Léry reports the Tupinamba family structure as being decidedly different from that of contemporary Europe, he nevertheless portrays the relationship between husband and wife within the family as being similar to that of Old World society, that is, the man is the source of authority and prestige, and women are obedient and docile.

A less favorable view of Tupinamba marriage practices is provided by André Thevet, who reports that the "Americans are no more discreet in their marriages than in other things." He appears shocked that natives marry their cousins, and uncles marry their nieces. Thevet often compares native practices that he regards as strange and bizarre to those of other cultures, past or contemporaneous, about which Europeans already had some knowledge. Thus, what was the novel and unknown was understood by establishing relationships with what was already familiar.[33] He does report that Tupi women may easily dissolve their marriage ties, but the implication is that he does not find this fitting behavior, since he notes that it was also common among the "ancient Egyptians . . . before they had any laws." Thevet notes the practice of polygyny, and comments that this is also the custom of the Turks and Arabians. However, he adds that "this though does not make it honest or allowable," and he urges Christians to avoid such things.[34]

Claude d'Abbeville also condemned polygyny among the Tupinamba, since he viewed the custom as one of the biggest obstacles to his goal of converting the natives to Christianity. Since Christian marriage is regarded as a sacrament, religious conversion entailed more than altering native belief systems – the essential structure of the family had to be redesigned as well. Abbeville asserts that the Tupinamba are "not all capable of receiving baptism, especially those married in the native fashion, with many wives." Adding that "God wishes man to be content with one wife," Abbeville advises that young children and unmarried men be baptized first, but only on the condition that they renounce the native practice of multiple wives. Abbeville also notes that both marriage and divorce in Tupi society are concluded easily, with little formality, but he tends to portray the male in a more dominant position – a wife cannot end her marriage without her husband's permission, and all wives live together peacefully and obey their husbands.[35]

Claude d'Abbeville, however, expresses ambivalence in his discussion of polygyny among the Tupinamba. His ultimate conclusion is that this practice should be eradicated, but he nevertheless exhibits a fuller understanding of the function of polygyny in native society. He explains that men do not have multiple wives to satisfy their lust, and even comments that many Christians ignore God's commandments and "lose themselves with women. . . . Are they not more brutal and savage than the savage Indians . . . who had no prior knowledge of God and His commandments?" Abbeville notes that multiple wives are a sign of status and prestige among Tupi men, but also points out that this form of marriage had benefits for Tupi women. Since warfare was frequent among the Tupinamba, there were not enough men for each woman to enjoy monogamous marriage. As with other observers, Abbeville notes that multiple wives cooperate and share the heavy load of household and garden work, and he expresses astonished admiration for Tupi wives within each household who "live in peace, without envy, jealousy, or riots." He adds that this should serve as "a good lesson for many Catholic families" who continually experience domestic discord, even though they "received the light of faith and the sacrament of marriage."[36] As noted above, praise of certain aspects of Native American behavior and culture often served as a vehicle to highlight moral shortcomings of contemporary European society. Claude d'Abbeville's admiration of the harmonious nature of Tupi households emphasizes what he interprets as the obedient and docile characteristics of native women. The implication is that the tumultuous nature of many European households is due to unruliness on the part of the female.

In their discussions on marriage and family structure among the Tupinamba, Claude d'Abbeville and other French travelers provide details about patterns of social organization which are distinct from their own societies. Yet the personal characteristics that they attribute to the Tupinamba reflect the ideals of contemporary European culture. Female natives are depicted as passive and obedient; men are portrayed as dominant. Yves d'Evreux's discussion of polygyny reveals his view that Tupi men occupy a superior position, while women assume a subservient role. He also notes that Tupinamba men have numerous wives as an indication of their esteem in society. Native men are compared to the *grands seigneurs* of Europe, who flaunt their possessions as a sign of status, but Tupi wives are compared to the mules that follow the great lords, carrying their baggage.[37] Thus, Yves d'Evreux's discussion of native polygyny ultimately reveals his contempt for Tupinamba women.

Here, Evreux's account points to a key aspect of the European assessment of Native American women: the division of labor by gender. Virtually all travelers appear keenly interested in the routine work performed distinctly by men and by women in Native American society. The details reported in the travel accounts portray a culture in which women play a crucial economic role – their work is necessary for the survival of their society. Among the Tupinamba, and primitive societies in general, both men and women cooperated in performing essential tasks. Division of labor by gender was practiced, but work done by women was not necessarily accorded a lower status. Instead, female members of society generally enjoyed respect and esteem due to their key economic role. Tupinamba women provided the major portion of food for their society – they did all the planting and harvesting, as well as collecting wild fruits and nuts.[38]

In spite of the data recorded by French observers which attest to the extent of the work performed by Tupinamba women, these travelers do not reflect upon the details they recorded, nor do they fully recognize the essential nature of women's economic contributions to native society. Instead, European standards of productive labor are applied. From the late medieval period, women's economic status had begun to deteriorate as the work that they performed became relegated more and more to the domestic sphere. In addition to infant and childcare, European women continued to engage in productive occupations, notably textile manufacture. These activities, however, were accorded less esteem, as women were increasingly excluded from more prestigious, higher paying occupations, which were reserved for men.[39]

French observers of Tupinamba society in the sixteenth and seventeenth centuries reported that native women performed numerous and varied occupations. They portrayed native women as hard-working and industrious, but failed to acknowledge the full extent of women's economic contribution to New World society. The travel writers appear genuinely surprised at the amount of work performed by female Tupinamba, but they do not conclude that this society is egalitarian or that women occupy a position of greater respect and esteem than was the case in contemporary Europe.[40]

Jean de Léry describes diverse tasks performed by Tupinamba women linked to their responsibilities for tending crops and providing basic foodstuffs. They cut wood, planted gardens, harvested and dried roots, and prepared cereals. Léry testified that this food was tasty and easy to digest. He also described the manner in which "caou-in," the Tupi beverage, was made by women from roots they gathered. Léry emphasized that the preparation of food and drink is done exclusively by women and that they are in "complete charge of the household." They make earthern vessels and pots, fashion drinking cups out of gourds and other large fruits, spin thread of different textures, make hammocks, and produce garments made of feathers. But in addition to these important functions, Tupi women also assisted the men on their war expeditions, an activity one might expect to fall exclusively within the male domain. Women accompany the men to war, carry the cotton hanging beds, and bring all necessary provisions. Léry also reports that Tupi women make weapons. Overall, Léry concluded, Tupinamba women "without comparison work more than the men."[41]

Léry's sentiments were echoed by other French observers of Tupinamba culture. André Thevet noted that women accompanied men on war expeditions, and if they traveled by water, women were responsible for bailing out the boat should that necessity arise. As was the case with other travelers, Thevet lists the myriad other tasks of Tupi women related to the preparation of food and drink, and ultimately concluded that "[Tupinamba] women work more than men."[42] Claude d'Abbeville made similar observations, noting that even in old age, women "never cease to work at what they are accustomed to do," but he does add that older men also continue to work at difficult tasks. However, it is Tupinamba women who are described as being "usually more occupied than the men," since it is their sole responsibility to take care of the household, plant gardens, and "prepare everything necessary for food."[43]

Yves d'Evreux's account differs somewhat from his contemporaries as he depicts a society in which both men and women cooperate in essential tasks. This missionary praises the well-ordered households of the Tupinamba. Although the natives are taught by "pure nature," nevertheless, according to Evreux, they follow the dictates of St. Thomas regarding good domestic conduct, since they have "enough of the necessary things to live and . . . each one knows what he is required to do." Father Yves emphasizes that the Tupi have nothing that is superfluous. He discusses the work performed specifically by men and women – the former hunt, fish, cut wood, build boats, make bows and arrows, and work in gardens, while the latter dig, plant, prepare food, and make cord and thread. Women do all the household work, and are "in charge of what is necessary for the life of the family." Men and women each have baskets that contain various utensils and ornaments "peculiar to their own sex." Young children, from about age eight, learn the tasks appropriate to their gender by following and imitating the parent of the same sex. Evreux distinguishes men's work by noting that it is performed outside of the house, but he does indicate that both men and women cooperate in the important task of gardening. In addition, preparations for war involve both male and female – the men construct canoes, the women prepare victuals.[44]

Yves d'Evreux expresses ambivalence in his assessment of work in Tupinamba society. As a Capuchin missionary, trained to uphold the ideals of St. Francis, he admires what he regards as the simplicity of the native society of the New World. The Tupinamba do only what is necessary to sustain life and nothing that is superfluous. However, elsewhere in his account he describes the natives as "unbelievably lazy," since they "prefer to do nothing and live meagerly, than to work and live better."[45]

The other French observers concur with Evreux's assessment that the Tupinamba are not a productive society. Although their remarks are not as derogatory as Evreux's, the travel writers ultimately ignore the hard work and resulting economic contributions of Tupi women in their final negative assessment of the productivity of native society. André Thevet notes that when the natives are not at war, they have "little occupation but to make gardens"; they work out of necessity and "do not labor too hard."[46] Jean de Léry asserts that the land occupied by the Tupinamba is "capable of supporting ten times as many people as are there now."[47]

Léry, though, idealizes this purported absence of hard work. He attributes the good health and long life enjoyed by the Tupinamba to their lack of concern for worldly goods. Europeans, by contrast, "die before our time, consumed by avarice, envy, and ambition."[48] Claude d'Abbeville likewise depicts a society characterized by the absence of hard work and idealizes this supposed leisure. Abbeville maintains that the Tupinamba are content and lead a joyous life, "without care to work very much." The cause of their happiness is their lack of concern for temporal goods or riches. If the Tupi are not engaged in war, they spend a portion of their time at leisure, otherwise they dance, hunt, and fish. Abbeville acknowledges that the latter activities do procure food, but says they are also a source of recreation.[49] Thevet also minimizes the efforts of Tupi men when he reports that they "only" hunt and fish.[50]

French travelers to the New World applied their own concepts of productive labor in their ultimate evaluations of Native American culture. The efforts of the Tupi women were dismissed, and Tupinamba men were perceived as contributing little to the maintenance of their society. European observers minimized the economic aspects of hunting and fishing, and instead viewed these activities primarily as recreation. In European society, hunting was regarded as one of the prime sports or exercises practiced by the upper classes.[51]

One of the earliest images of the New World in European culture was of a land that resembled Paradise – man did not toil and the earth freely yielded its fruits. On his third voyage to America, Christopher Columbus believed that he had indeed arrived at the Garden of Eden. Deep-seated myths of terrestrial paradise had long permeated European culture, and many travelers utilized these images in their interpretations and portrayals of New World societies.[52] Thus, they minimized the level of productive activity so that Native American men might more closely resemble Adam before the Fall.

There is a blatant contradiction, however, between the details recorded in the travel accounts and the Europeans' ultimate evaluation of New World culture and society. The natives are said to enjoy leisure and be free of hard work. For this, they are either condemned as lazy, or idealized as content and carefree. Yet the travel writers attested to the myriad tasks performed by Tupinamba women, noted that they worked hard and were continually occupied, and commented that native women performed work necessary to sustain life. Once again, it is contemporary European standards regarding productive labor which are applied. Work performed by women is undervalued or even denied. The crucial and necessary work performed by Tupinamba women is seen not as an indication of the significant role of women in native society, but rather serves to enhance the image of native men as idle.[53] French travelers ultimately evaluated New World society in terms of what native *men* did or did not do.

In view of the misogynist attitudes that permeated early modern European culture, it is surprising to note the amount of detailed attention devoted to Native American women in the accounts of the contemporary French travelers to the New World. These men were fascinated by the new cultures that they observed and prided themselves upon the information that they recorded. America was indeed a New World for Europeans, and those who made the journey emphasized that they were contributing to knowledge that surpassed that of the ancients. Jean de Léry asserts that he can no longer uphold the opinion of Pliny and other authors, as he has seen things himself which others thought were non-existent.[54] André Thevet likewise maintains that his writing is contrary to that of ancient cosmographers, but they had not traveled to the lands that he did.[55]

However, these travel writers do not take the evidence they recorded to its full conclusion. Their ultimate assessment of New World peoples and culture appears to be derived not from their own observations, but rather is determined by the values and standards of Old World society. Data about Tupinamba women, and New World societies in general, were used to confirm rather than challenge contemporary social norms and practices.[56] Students and scholars today can read the sixteenth- and seventeenth-century accounts of the Tupinamba and find a society where women performed work vital to the maintenance of their society, enjoyed substantial control over their own sexual activity, and cooperated on equal terms with men in many key aspects of life. Contemporary European observers and their readers instead saw a culture where women were obedient, overworked, and oversexed. Those accounts that emphasized the modesty and docility of Tupinamba women did so only in order to chide European females for their alleged lack of these supposedly desirable traits. Upon reading this travel literature with a more critical eye, feminists today can take heart that male domination and control is neither a natural nor a universal aspect of human life. Or does this conclusion merely reveal that present-day readers can be as biased as early modern Frenchmen, continuing to evaluate other cultures in terms of their own standards, values and beliefs?

6
Women as Symbols of Disorder in Early Rhode Island[1]

Ruth Wallis Herndon

King Philip's War is generally acknowledged to have precipitated the decline of Indians in southeastern New England. With the massacre of defenseless Narragansett non-combatants at the Great Swamp in 1675 and the subsequent selling into slavery of captured Narragansett warriors, European conquest of the region seemed complete. Over the following century, many native people migrated to western land less settled by whites, and those who stayed "behind the frontier" found their options severely limited. Some tried to eke out an existence on the ever-shrinking reserved lands set aside for the Narragansett in 1709 in the heart of their ancestral territory. Others abandoned both the reservation and traditional ways, conforming to Anglo-American expectations by living as bound servants in white households (often victims of debt peonage) or as free neighbors who conducted their own native households along patriarchal lines. Still others moved back and forth between Indian and white worlds, periodically living among whites but not living like them. Most of these were women, whose daily, weekly, or seasonal labor in Anglo-American households brought them into official view long enough to be scrutinized, discussed, and subjected to harassment by town authorities. These women are the focus of this study.

Officials complained that such Indian women followed traditional native ways instead of adopting white ways, thus undermining the race and gender order of Anglo-American communities. Indeed, these women can be understood as rejecting the quiet coexistence or submissive accommodation that whites expected from women of color. Deliberate allegiance to native tradition, and not necessity only, prompted these women to behave in ways that officials found so irritating. They did not group themselves in patriarchal households, but lived separately from their mates and communally with other kin. They did not follow Anglo-American conventions of marriage and so produced children whose fathers could not be identified with ease by white officials. They migrated on lengthy sojourns, not bound by law or convention to remain in any one place or with any one employment. Their private lives frequently were hidden from official gaze and their productive and reproductive labor often eluded official management.

As they struggled to bring these women under "proper authority," town leaders left a paper trail of official actions, showing that the poor law (warning out, indenture, poor relief) was used to control the presence and absence of Indian women in the white community and that literacy and record-keeping (naming and designating) were used to control the presence and absence of these women in the historical record. For this study, I followed the paper trail through the records of community organization and maintenance in half of Rhode Island's eighteenth-century towns.[2] Especially helpful are the minutes of the town council, which detail the "trouble" caused by free Indian women as well as the attempts of authorities to bring order out of disorder in Indian–white gender relations.

Most Indian women existed on the margins of Rhode Island town life then and on the margins of the remaining records now. They did not vote in town meetings, appear on tax lists, or register the birth of their children. Even their fleeting and shadowy presence in the council records is complicated by the sensibilities of the record-keepers. After King Philip's War, town clerks made little effort to identify Narragansett and other native people by tribal membership. Further, by the late 1700s, clerks routinely blurred racial distinctions to the point of redesignating Indians as black, thereby virtually erasing "Indians" from most official town records by 1800.[3] Since the records reflect not Indians' self-identification but only white designations, it is impossible to separate women of Native American descent from those of African descent. Further, sexual liaisons between the two groups resulted in children of dual Indian and black ancestry. Accordingly, to reconstruct the experience of women of Indian heritage, I have cast a wider net and have gathered data pertaining to all women designated as non-white: "black," "Negro," "mulatto," and "mustee," as well as "Indian." While I privilege the particular information about women specifically identified as "Indian" or "mustee,"[4] I consider in the aggregate all information that pertains to women of color.

In eighteenth-century Anglo-America, the ideology of household and communitarian patriarchy placed all women under the authority of men in both private and public life. Every woman, it was assumed, was a member (wife, daughter, mother, servant, slave) of an individual household headed by a white male. Every household was in turn part of a public family, headed by elected officials who styled themselves "fathers of the town." Every inhabitant of the town came under their oversight and had claim to the care of these authorities. If individual households fell into disarray through the death, departure, or disability of the male head, then town leaders stepped in to manage the lives and direct the future of each household member.[5] In this social organization, free Indian women seemed out of place, floating loose from the moorings of white male oversight and authority. Since they did not live as servants or slaves within white households, they fell under the "government" of no individual white male. Instead, they were seen as the responsibility of town leaders, who struggled to prod and push them into household arrangements that conformed more closely to the patriarchal ideal.

The six town councilmen, elected by the white, land-owning, Protestant men in each town, were more prosperous, educated, and socially connected than most, and were trusted to uphold and perpetuate the traditions and values of the community.[6] Tasked with "maintaining order" in their towns, they scrutinized and harassed those who threatened that order. In their regular meetings to solve problems in the community, they frequently discussed what to do with the Indian women who lived among them yet did not live like them.

English poor law, adapted and implemented by all Anglo-American colonies, equipped these local officials with three principal instruments of control. *Warning out* rid the community of people who "belonged" legally to another town – a home town – where they were entitled to poor relief. *Indenture* put poor children into labor contracts with local residents, who agreed to provide the necessities of life in exchange for work. And *poor relief* put needy people into the care of "respectable" inhabitants, who would receive payment in money or goods from the town treasury for their support of the poor.[7] Despite these apparently gender-neutral and color-neutral poor laws, Indian women (and other women of color) were the *least* likely to benefit from such laws and *most* likely to suffer from their application. In fact, as shaped by colonial leaders, the poor laws privileged those who owned real estate, lived in one fixed place, and were part of English-style households, and simultaneously punished Native Americans and others who owned no real estate, moved around frequently, and lived in non-patriarchal households.

Settlement law, the heart of the eighteenth-century poor law, was critically important in reinforcing English concepts of community in North America.[8] A newcomer could gain a "legal settlement" in a town by being born there, serving out an indenture or apprenticeship to a master there, purchasing a significant amount of real estate there, (for a woman) marrying a man who belonged there, or living there for a year without being sent away by officials. All who had not gained a settlement were legally "transient," no matter how long their residence or how strong their connections to their jobs, churches, or neighborhoods. Transients were subject to being warned out at any time by officials in response to a "complaint" lodged by "respectable" people – sometimes a matter of transients appearing to be needy and likely to require poor relief, other times a matter of transients irritating their neighbors. This "warning out" was the favorite instrument of white authorities dealing with native people. Nearly one-quarter of those persons warned out of Rhode Island towns in the eighteenth century were designated "Indian," "mustee," "mulatto," "Negro," or "black," at a time when all persons of color constituted less than ten percent of the population.[9]

Indian and black women account for two-thirds of the warnouts of people of color in the late eighteenth century.[10] Certainly, Indian women were more visible as they labored within the white community, while Indian men often pursued a livelihood by fishing, hunting, sailoring, and soldiering out of view of local officials. Still, the disparity suggests that women attracted official attention as people of color without masters and as women unrepresented by men. This double violation of racial and gender order spurred town "fathers" into doing their duty of "governing" these households without male heads to prevent them falling into poverty and trouble.

Mary Pisquish, for example, defied conventions of place in Jamestown, Rhode Island by not keeping a permanent residence there; she "was some times in this town and at other times elsewhere." When this Indian woman became "lame and incapable of supporting herself" while living in Jamestown in 1759, the town councilmen warned her out, not wanting to shoulder the financial burden of her poor relief.[11] Sarah Greene, on the other hand, defied conventions of gender relations by producing nine children over twenty-four years in Providence, although "she was never married to any person"; in 1786, she became involved in some unsavory activity (prostitution, perhaps) that prompted the councilmen to judge her "not of good fame and reputation" and have her removed.[12] Elisabeth Heary, "an Indian or Mustee woman," offended authority by trying to live an independent life, unregulated by a master, after having grown up in indentured servitude in Sandwich, Massachusetts; as soon as she moved to Providence, the town council ordered her back to her home town.[13]

Sometimes community officials tried to apply poor law *en masse* to people of color. In 1779 the East Greenwich councilmen, galvanized by a "complaint" that "a number of Indians, Molatos & Negro women" had moved to the town to work for the Continental Army stationed there, warned out all these people and threatened that they would be "severely whipped" if they came into the town again for more than twenty-four hours at a time. They could collect and deliver laundry and food, then, but they could not live in the town. A few months later, the council unconditionally warned out all "Indians Molatoes & Negroes that does not belong to this Town."[14]

Even those Indians who legally "belonged" to a community and could not be sent away found themselves affected by similar group round-ups of "the poor." In 1757, the voters of Middletown, Rhode Island, decided that "all Indians & Molattos that are free born," regardless of their economic situation, would be placed under the management of the overseers of the poor, just as impoverished "white people" were.[15] Similarly, in 1800, the Providence town council ordered that a list be made of "all transient white people in poor circumstances, as also of the blacks of all descriptions whatever dwelling in this Town."[16] Such measures, which associated race with poverty, trouble, and disorder, revealed official assumptions that Indians and other people of color needed watching and that the poor law was the best *means* of controlling them.

Indentured servitude, another key component of the poor laws, was the most frequently employed method of dealing with Indians who were legally settled in a town. In this system, town "fathers," acting *in loco parentis*, took children from "disordered" households and placed them in "ordered" ones, where these youngsters would come under the official "government" of a white man and under the daily care and management of a white woman.[17] Overall, at least twenty-three percent of such forced indentures of children in eighteenth-century Rhode Island towns involved Indian and black youngsters, highly out of proportion to their numbers in the general population.[18]

Officials rationalized indenture in several ways: the children had been orphaned; the children were "bastards" without the economic support of a father; the parents were seriously ill; or, most significantly for this study, the children required management because of their race. In one-fifth of the cases, indenture was enacted simply because the child was "Indian," "mustee," "mulatto," "Negro," or "black"; no other explanation was offered or, apparently, needed. For these children of color, servitude brought few rewards and long service. An analysis of the contracts reveals that black and Indian children were far less likely than white children to be taught to read and write. Further, their terms of indenture were usually longer: while white girls' indentures ended at eighteen and white boys' at twenty-one, children of color could expect to labor at least one year longer and often several years longer. Public indenture was a highly useful means of control: white masters had free access to many years of Indian labor while they discouraged traditional ways by raising Native American children in patriarchal, English-style households.

"Poor Indeon Child" John Seton, for example, was bound out to prosperous farmer Caleb Gardner by the South Kingstown council because "the Father being Dead, and the mother Neglecting to take any Care of it." By the indenture, Gardner acquired rights to the boy's labor for over thirteen years.[19] The two children of "Indian squaw" Betty Jack were bound to Jamestown inhabitant Dan Weeden, the man who had been "maintaining" them for six months, when he complained that the children had caused him "Extraordinary Trouble." Without waiting to consult Betty Jack, the council bound out her fifteen-year-old daughter for three years and her four-year-old son for eighteen years.[20] Luranor Strum, adolescent daughter of Indian parents, was bound out by the New Shoreham town council when they judged her to be "an Idle, luce [loose], Runagate hussey" who needed the discipline of servitude to bring order to her life.[21]

Indenture had a distinct gender bias: Indian and black boys were twice as likely as girls to be bound out.[22] Male labor was more prized, perhaps, and authorities more anxious to secure that labor for white households. Thus Indian girls less often received even the dubious protections of indenture – a minimal level of physical care, a rudimentary education, and training in some skill. Indian girls certainly labored for whites, but not in contracts regulated by town authority. Instead, any recompense for their labor depended upon the good conscience of their white masters. As a result, when they reached the age of freedom, they faced severely limited economic futures.

Indenture was a system designed to rescue impoverished but healthy children; it did not serve the case with ill, aged, and helpless people. Public poor relief, drawn from the town treasury, sustained those who could not labor for their own support. It was meager charity, involving only the barest "necessities of life," but it applied to all legally settled members of the community. Some inhabitants petitioned for relief for themselves and their families; more often, neighbors and employers reported desperate circumstances to town authorities.[23] This often thin maintenance was seldom granted to people of color, who rarely received disbursements from the town treasury. Many Indian people doubtless took refuge in Indian enclaves during times of distress, weathering illness or disability out of sight of town officials; indeed, some repaired to the Narragansett reservation in southern Rhode Island, where the tribal council managed care of the poor within their borders.[24] But those Indians who were legally settled members of Rhode Island towns supposedly had full rights to town welfare.

Unfortunately, few Indians received that care. No town supported an Indian or black person for more than a few weeks and then usually only at the end of life. Those few who were virtually pensioned by the town, spending years on poor relief, were white. Several white people who were mentally handicapped spent decades on public support; no Indian or black person ever did. This inequality of support is unlikely to reflect inequality of need, since free persons of color were widely acknowledged to be poor and comprised a measurable percentage of the population. Instead, this inequality indicates an official bias against aiding Indian and black persons. Only in times of gravest and most obvious necessity were officials willing to spend public money on frail, ill, injured, or aged people of color.

In the few instances when Indians received poor relief, it usually went to women rather than men.[25] This is not surprising, since Indian women were more vulnerable economically and more likely to come to official notice than Indian men. But this trickle of relief usually was too little too late, most often coming only when a "final illness" visited aged and ailing native women like Sarah Fitten, for whom the Jamestown treasury covered the costs of a coffin and burial in 1755, and Martha Sawnos, who died of smallpox in Exeter in 1760.[26] For Fitten, Sawnos, and others, such "last rights" were the only time the women ever cost the town a cent.

In sum, free Indian women were more often punished than rescued by Anglo-American poor laws. Their visibility to officials made them likely targets for warning out and for having their children forcibly indentured. But their visibility did not prompt officials to open the town treasury on their behalf; instead, they were granted support, if at all, only when their cases were most desperate and then for only brief periods of time.

When town authorities looked behind Indian women, they saw numerous "Indian," "mulatto," and "mustee" children. The frequent appearance of these children in the town records indicates the extent to which they gave rise to official anxieties – and official action to remove the mothers, so that the children also would disappear. Numerous "Indian" youngsters suggested a flourishing population of supposedly diminished native people; even worse, "mulatto" and "mustee" youngsters represented sexual activity across the color line and were the best and most obvious evidence for a world of disorder within officials' jurisdictions.

"Mulatto" and "mustee" are terms with complicated meanings, but clearly denote miscegenation among European, Indian, and African.[27] In eighteenth-century Rhode Island, white officials most often used "mustee" to refer to people of part-Indian ancestry and "mulatto" to refer to people of part-African ancestry. For example, the children of "Indian" women Elizabeth Broadfoot, Moll Pero, and Deborah Anthony are all described as "mustee."[28] Children described as "mulatto" included those born to "Negro" woman Sarah Tony, "mulatto" woman Betty Church, and "Capt Rowland Barton's Negro man" (this last by "mulatto" woman Catherine Talbury).[29]

The frequent use of terms such as "mulatto" and "mustee" underscores a general upheaval in race relations in New England in the latter part of the eighteenth century, occasioned by a steady rise in the number of free people of color. In the late 1700s, revolutionary fervor and rhetoric resulted in numerous voluntary manumissions, and growing numbers of free people of color migrated towards Providence and its satellite communities in search of work on the ships and docks and in the warehouses and upper-class households of this booming seaport. Rhode Island's 1784 gradual emancipation law, which declared that children born to slaves after March 1, 1784 would be free when they reached the age of majority (eighteen for girls, twenty-one for boys), promised to introduce a steady wave of free young people of color into the general population beginning in 1802. And in the 1790s, an influx of mixed-race refugees from slave uprisings in Saint Domingue (later Haiti) placed before the eyes of Rhode Island's whites additional evidence of interracial mating.

In response to these new demographic realities, white authorities labored to categorize people of color. While Rhode Island officials had once clearly designated people as "Indian" or "Negro," in the mid-1700s they relied increasingly on the terms "mustee" and "mulatto." But "mustee" survived only as an interim designation; by 1800, officials had pretty much abandoned it and had resorted to describing all people of color as "Negro," "black," or "mulatto." Rather than sorting out "Indian" from "Negro" or "part-Indian" from "part-Negro," local officials erased Indianness and turned to a bipolar color system that separated "white" from "Other."[30] The capstone to this sorting came in 1798, when the Rhode Island legislature passed a law that no minister or justice of the peace "shall join in marriage any white person with any Negro, Indian or mulatto, on penalty of two hundred dollars."[31]

The 1798 anti-miscegenation law not only prevented Indian and black women from legitimating their relationships with white men, it also categorized the offspring of such relationships as bastards. In so doing, it provided a further rationale for the existing practice of removing children of color from their birth families and placing them in indentured servitude. It also illuminated the long-standing practice of describing children of color in other than legal terms when they were taken under official management. The terms "bastard" and "orphan" were used almost exclusively for white children in the Rhode Island records. Of the 720 child indentures examined for this study, twenty-five percent (179) were identified as non-white and another nineteen percent (134) were identified as "bastards." The categories are nearly mutually exclusive, with only six children being identified both as both "bastard" and non-white. "Orphan" even more emphatically excluded non-white children. Of the 720 indentures, another fifteen percent (110) were identified as "orphans," but not one of these was also described as non-white, and clerks seem to have made an effort to avoid using the term "orphan." For example, when ten-year-old "mulatto" child Betsey Richmond was bound out as an indentured servant, the clerk described her as a child "who has no Parents living," but did not use the term "orphan" in her contract.[32]

The terms "bastard" and "orphan" point to a particular relationship between a child and its father. "Bastard" indicated that a child's mother was unmarried and that the child had no legal rights to the father's name or property; the father would not regularize either present support or future inheritance for the child. "Orphan" indicated that a child's father had died, for in English law a man's death orphaned his children legally, whether or not the mother still lived. When town leaders learned of "bastard" and "orphan" children in their community, they stepped in to regularize the children's situations. In many cases, Indian and black children taken under management by town officials were in fact born of unmarried mothers or left fatherless by a man's death. But officials avoided using the terms "bastard" and "orphan," suggesting their thin knowledge of the non-white world over which they had legal jurisdiction.

Simply stated, officials did not always know the marital status of a non-white child's parents. Free Indians in particular lived on the margins of Rhode Island towns in the late eighteenth century, laboring for a time on the farms and in the households of whites, but never fully "belonging" to the town. Men and women joined together in ways that were not formalized by Anglo-American ceremony, and women bore children out of sight of the "respectable" white community, their names never appearing on official lists. In a particularly revealing interview, Indian woman Mary Fowler told the South Kingstown councilmen that she had lived with James Fowler "for about thirty years & had ten children by him" but she had not married him "in the manner white people are married in these parts." Her daughter Mary Champlin testified that she had lived with John Champlin eleven years and had six children by him, "but never was married to him according to the form used by the white people in these parts."[33] This carefully chosen language suggests that these women considered their relationships to be conventional in Native American or some other terms, but they had not participated (as some people of color did) in the civil or religious marriage ceremony of "white people" that would have validated their relationship before local officials and entitled them to an entry in the town books.

Here and there in the record, town officials silently acknowledged the existence, and perhaps the equivalence, of such alternative conventions. The East Greenwich councilmen tacitly endorsed the bond between "Indian man" Winsor Fry and "Indian woman" Lucy Davis when they issued the pair a single settlement certificate, as if they were a married couple, even though they recorded the two separate surnames on the certificate, indicating that Fry and Davis were not married according to Anglo-American law.[34] Similarly, officials routinely avoided declaring children of color "bastards" unless they knew their particular family history.

Further, avoiding the terms "bastard" and "orphan" allowed town officials to skip the usual steps of tracking down the father and securing a maintenance (for bastards) or locating the estate and administering it (for orphans). Such tasks were difficult, if not impossible, when Indian mothers had died, abandoned their children, or refused to give information about the fathers. Without a working knowledge of the Indian and part-Indian community that existed on the periphery of official vision, town leaders preferred to assume there was neither father nor estate. They moved directly to indenture the child in an appropriate household where its material needs would be met and where another man would shoulder the financial responsibility of childrearing.

Finally, officials presumed a right to indenture children of color without an explanation. Town "fathers" meddled freely in the lives of people of color and in the lives of women unrepresented by men. Children of color, born of free women of color, were thus "natural" targets of official regulation. The treatment of Indian and black children reinforces what other historians have discovered for non-white adults: people of color were presumed to need oversight, no less so as free people than as bound.[35]

Many free Indian women resisted official efforts to control and manage their lives and the lives of their children. Some openly defied authorities by refusing to provide information during warning out interrogations or by refusing to mark an 'X' on legal documents, as did Judah Wanton who said "she never did sign any writing."[36] But most simply avoided confrontation. Some melted out of sight before officials could lay hands on them or left town only to reappear later. Almy Cooper, for example, was one of many Indian women who returned after being warned out, but one of the few who got caught and had to endure the punishment of "nine stripes well laid on upon her naked back."[37] Some spirited away their children from white households, as did the mother of young Jem, thus galvanizing Joseph Clarke to appeal to the Jamestown council to enact an official indenture of the Indian boy, to counteract the mother's intent "to take him away."[38] Many Indian women complied with official regulation only as a last resort. Martha Bristol, for example, dodged the Jamestown town council for five years, but after receiving her fourth warning out, she finally obtained a departure certificate from her home town to avoid further harassment.[39] Such maneuvering around authorities was facilitated by the presence of a functioning community of native people who provided advice, support, and refuge. Even white officials recognized that Indians cared for Indians, as when the Jamestown council decided that the best way to support Mary Mew, an elderly and lame Indian woman, was "to put her into some Indian family."[40]

Sarah Gardner's interactions with town councilmen in two communities illustrate official frustrations over "disorder" and Indian women's resistance to official dictates. Sarah Gardner was born in 1730 in the town of Warwick to Indian parents. Her father, Thomas Gardner, owned a house and land in the town, probably his legacy of belonging to the Narragansett tribe.[41] Although her father was a property owner, Sarah was put into an indentured labor contract as a child and grew up as a servant to David Greene, one of the wealthiest colonial landlords.[42]

After her indenture, Sarah Gardner attempted to build an independent life for herself, but she had to struggle against her children replicating her own experience of servitude. There is no mention of a husband in the official records, but she bore twelve children and managed to raise them with only the barest one-time assistance from the town, suggesting an Indian mate who pursued a livelihood "off-stage."[43] In 1762, Warwick officials, worried about the ability of this "Indian Squaw" to raise her growing family without more substantial and visible means of support, ordered that her two oldest sons be bound out as indentured servants.[44] Later that year, as winter approached, the council rented a house for Gardner and her three youngest children, tacit evidence that she did not live in an English-style house during the warmer weather.[45] One month later, the Warwick councilmen tried to complete their management of the family by ordering that Gardner bind out four more of her children in indentures to "suitable" masters, preferably to the four men with whom the children were already living and working.[46] With six of her children in servitude contracts and the youngest ones with her, Gardner managed to stay out of the view of town officials for the next five years. In 1767 she moved to Providence, where she set up a household with six of her children back in the fold, some of them newly sprung from their indentures.[47]

For the next twenty years, Gardner alternately avoided and accommodated Providence authorities in her efforts to maintain a household there. She came before the town council, was questioned by them, and was ordered out of town five times: in 1770, 1772, 1780, 1782, and 1787.[48] Each time she reported a different household composition, but one always bursting at the seams as her adult children moved in and out with *their* children in tow. Four times she returned quickly and unobtrusively, even though the council ordered her whipped if she came back. The council wanted her elsewhere, for she and her adult daughters were considered people "of bad character and reputation" who stirred up complaints by respectable neighbors.[49] The 1782 warnout was occasioned by a scandalous incident in which a mob rioted and "pulled down" the "wicked nest" of a house where Gardner lived with a number of other women, and where "drinking, tippling, whoring" and other offensive behaviors had occurred.[50] Gardner was clearly *persona non grata*.

Nevertheless, Gardner persisted in returning and consorting with other women who were of concern to authorities. In two instances, she was questioned in the company of other women of color, and the implication in the record is that these women had formed a community of support.[51] More importantly, Gardner had the support of her adult daughters, who accompanied their mother on her removals and her returns. On the last removal, when Gardner was delivered personally by the Providence town sergeant to the Warwick overseer of the poor, she was accompanied by two of her daughters and one grandson.[52] Sarah Gardner was not alone.

When she was removed to Warwick in 1787, Gardner, then nearing sixty years old, apparently ended her career as irritant to the Providence council. She did not appear before Providence authorities again. Officials may have had the last word, but Gardner had managed to live as an unwanted person in their jurisdiction for two decades.

Sarah Gardner came under official scrutiny because she was Indian and because she was female.[53] She lived in ways that offended magistrates' sense of order: she had many children, yet appeared to be without the support of a husband; her father had owned land in one place, yet she moved about from town to town; she associated with people of bad repute; and she refused to obey council orders when they conflicted with her own interests. From an official perspective, Sarah Gardner embodied disorder, she needed to be controlled, and her attempts to resist this control were simply further evidence of the disorder she threatened.

Sarah Gardner's story is nowhere stated plainly in the official records, which focus on the activities of worthy white officials, not on the actions of a troublesome Indian woman. Reconstructing her story required the careful sifting of thousands of pages of council minutes in different towns, and then piecing together the scattered references. This labor highlights the power of record-keepers to marginalize and obscure the lives of those they considered unimportant. Eighteenth-century town clerks crafted community records to highlight men of power and influence and to leave women like Sarah Gardner in the shadows. We find the lives of Indian women between and behind the lines of the written record.

The power of the record-keepers was three layers thick in the case of Indian women. First, such women were eliminated from or obscured in the written record by clerical decisions based on what properly "belonged" there.[54] Second, where such women entered the record it was usually under an inaccurate racial designation. By the early 1700s, Narragansett women and men had lost their cultural distinctiveness in the written records of Rhode Island towns; they had become "Indian." Before the century was out they would become "mustee" or "black." And in the 1800s, they would become "colored." Third, native women were frequently labeled pejoratively by white male record-keepers, and these labels were often substituted for real names, as when an unnamed "Indian or Mullato Wench" was sent out of Jamestown in 1785.[55] Young Luranor Strum and others were labelled "hussy." But eclipsing all terms by far was "squaw," a term used widely and almost always with negative connotations in the written record.

In the official view, "squaw" meant trouble and disorder. An unnamed "squaw" drowned in Tiverton in the winter of 1760; another met misfortune in Tiverton in the deep winter a few years later, a householder reporting that the nameless "scaw" had "hapned into his hous & Died there"; yet another unnamed "squaw" "left" her child with a white farmer in South Kingstown in the summer of 1770.[56] A disgruntled Warwick inhabitant applied to the town council for repayment because of "an Indian Squaw named Sarah and her Child who Lately died at his house and Created a Considerable Charge."[57] Another Indian woman with only a first name – "Experience, a Mustee Squaw" – was chased out of Warwick, along with her child, as soon as she tried to settle there.[58] Betty Low, "an Indian Squaw," needed help from Jamestown when she was "old," "very poor," and "helpless."[59] These few representative quotations drawn from the many "squaw" entries show the persistent theme of desperation, grief, and trouble associated with the term.

From town officials' point of view, "squaws" symbolized disorder: they bore children outside the conventions of marriage, abandoned their children to the care of others, disappeared and reappeared according to no pattern that officials could discern, and burdened the community with their care when they were past useful labor. But by reading between and behind the lines of the official record, we can also see that it was Indian "squaws" who maintained their heritage by pursuing native tradition on their own ancestral lands in the face of open hostility. It was Indian "squaws" whose persistence forced white authorities to acknowledge the presence of a surprisingly strong remnant of a once vigorous people. And it was Indian "squaws" who reminded officials most often that not everyone cherished Anglo-American concepts of "order."

7

Native Women and State Legislation in Mexico and Canada: The Agrarian Law and the Indian Act

Verónica Vázquez García

The impact of colonialism on women's work and status in traditional subsistence economies has been well documented. However, there is considerable debate on the exact nature of the effects of colonial processes on women's lives. Leacock, Brown, and Bell[1] have suggested that men and women in precolonial societies are autonomous individuals with positions of equal power and prestige. Women make a substantial contribution to the domestic economy and control the access to resources and the conditions of their work. By contrast, other scholars point to accounts of male violence against women, and patrilineal patterns of resource allocation where women have access to land and other critical resources only through male kin.[2] Thus, these and other authors believe that women's degree of autonomy and independence in pre-colonial societies should not be overestimated.[3]

This debate has mostly centered on the impact of market economies on subsistence economies.[4] Studies have examined the changes in women's lives resulting from the introduction of new technology, the commercialization of agriculture, migrant labour, paid labour, and other forms of income-generating activities.[5] However, less attention has been paid to the role of the colonial and post-colonial states in constructing gendered civil rights through legislation. This chapter studies the impact of two particular legal instruments on native women in Mexico and Canada: the Agrarian Reform of Mexico and the Indian Act of Canada, whose purpose in both cases, was to regulate land use in native communities. The chapter shows that both pieces of legislation were influenced by a European-based liberal tradition, which defines civil rights as individual property rights, where individuals are male. The chapter argues that by using the European model of the nuclear, monogamous, and male-headed family to legislate, the Mexican and the Canadian states have limited native women's access to land in their own communities and have placed them in a vulnerable position vis-à-vis their male counterparts.

Before the arrival of the Spaniards, what is now Mexico was inhabited by various ethnic groups, most of whom lived under the military rule of the Aztec Empire. The Spaniards had to defeat Tenochtitlan militarily in order to found New Spain in 1521. Most of the information on pre-hispanic land tenure systems focuses on Tenochtitlan, the core of the Aztec Empire and what later became Mexico City. The unit of the land tenure system in Tenochtitlan was the *calpulli*, which was associated with kinship groups and professions that were passed on from parents to children. Members of households within each *calpulli* cultivated collectively a common area and had rights to specific tillable plots, which were cultivated individually. At the time of the Spanish invasion, however, the equivalence between kinship groups and *calpullis* was no longer clear,[6] and there were clear signs of inequality in the distribution of land. Landed states of the Aztec nobility had to be worked by tenants, who also cultivated their own subsistence plots.[7]

We know very little about women's involvement in agricultural work in *calpullis*. Hellbom, Cline, and Rodríguez[8] agree that only women belonging to the professional group of agricultural workers or female slaves performed all agricultural tasks. Other women participated mostly in planting and harvesting. However, we do know from early colonial evidence that residence groups in late Tenochtitlan were formed by units larger than the nuclear family. They were based on a parent–child or, more often, a sibling tie. Usually more than one person, typically siblings, received rights to residential sites, as well as other parental property. Brothers and sisters inherited equivalent rights in parental estates. However, men were more likely than women to receive landed estates.[9]

With the Spanish invasion, it was established that the ownership and management of land was vested in the Spanish Crown, which could in turn grant land rights to private persons. Two forms of land ownership were created: *corregimientos* and *encomiendas*. The first were territories and tribute obligations on the aboriginal population controlled by the Spanish Crown, while *encomiendas* were designations to Spanish soldiers who had aided in the invasion. However, hardship inflicted by excessive tributes and epidemic diseases soon devastated the aboriginal population. The Spanish crown sought to "protect" its new subjects from abuse and replaced the *encomiendas* with *mercedes*, or permanent land grants to Spanish soldiers that did not involve tribute from the resident population. The crown also called for the concentration of aboriginals into *pueblos*. The *pueblo* was composed of a town site and an *ejido* comprised of individual agricultural plots and a common untilled area of forest and pastures.

In Culhuacan (central Mexico) the decline of native populations coupled with a temporary abundance of resources increased native women's ability to inherit and bequeath property. In her analysis of wills, Cline shows that women could receive all types of property, land, houses, and movable goods from male and female donors and likewise pass them on to heirs of their choice.[10] In early colonial Mexico City (1540–1600) native women left land, houses, and movable property primarily to their daughters and granddaughters, while men left land, houses, and movable property to wives, siblings, and children in a more balanced manner. When it came to residential sites, the sibling group continued to be a major unit of inheritance. Kellogg points out that these sites "were rarely inherited by only one person; instead, siblings, cousins, and sometimes other relatives were given such rights to share."[11]

However, the nuclear family was gradually enforced among the aboriginal population by Spanish officials through religious indoctrination and legal sanctions. Tribute had to be paid by each (nuclear) family and Spanish officials started to identify and name one male as head per household, despite the fact that often more than one couple shared a household. Spanish inheritance stressed lineal ties from parents to children rather than lateral ones to brothers and sisters. Spanish inheritance rules also showed a far greater tendency to choose one person, or a very small group, particularly the nuclear family, to inherit. A weakening of ties between siblings gradually came about, making it harder for native women to inherit as someone's sister. Increasingly, native women began to inherit land only as custodial heirs, that is, only if they had children to support. Thus, women's access to land became limited to their roles as mothers and grandmothers taking care of young children. Native women learned that they could maximize their chances to receive land by emphasizing in colonial courts their roles as guardians of young children.[12]

In the seventeenth and eighteenth centuries population pressures reasserted themselves and the *hacienda-latifundio*[13] became the most predominant productive unit in rural Mexico. In this context, it became more difficult for women to assert land rights. In Calimaya and Tepemaxalco (central Mexico) the number of houses and the amount and extension of land bequeathed in wills declined between 1672 and 1821. According to Kanter, native men held a much greater share of land than native women.[14] Although women (both married and widowed) tended to choose female descendants as heirs (daughters, sisters, nieces, and granddaughters), they had to fend off usurpations by male relatives, the village or (if widows) in-laws. Widows inherited land in their capacity as custodial heirs and were not considered owners in their own right, but property mediators between a man and his children.[15]

Mexican Independence in 1810 and the liberal governments that followed throughout the nineteenth century which were shaped and influenced by European ideas and traditions brought about a further commoditization and privatization of land. Legislation against collective land ownership was introduced by liberals inspired by laissez-faire and private property ideals. They believed that private property and the integration of aboriginal populations into the wider society would result in economic development and "elevate the Indians into useful citizens."[16]

With these changes, land became even more attached to individuals rather than communities. Once personal allotments were legally owned, land acquired a commercial value and could be sold without regard to kin groups or the community. This resulted in the erosion of traditional patterns of property acquisition and residence, and contributed to strengthen men's position of dominance within the family by making their right to inherit and bequeath land almost unquestionable.[17] Moreover, the colonial judicial system through which women's land rights as guardians of young children were somehow protected in courts expired with Independence from Spain. As a result, female landholding among native women in central Mexico declined.[18] During the Porfiriato regime, widows in one district of this region continued to be entitled to land, but they had to arm themselves and keep watch over it.[19]

Just as independence from Spain in the early nineteenth century had a significant impact on native land ownership, so too would the Mexican Revolution of the early twentieth century, which joined the discontent of a rising class of professionals and capitalists with the misery of the rural and urban poor. Francisco I. Madero's call for elections in 1910 forced dictator Porfirio Díaz to flee the country and initiated ten years of social upheaval. Changes in the definition of land ownership was one result, and the Revolution gave way to three forms of land property, the *ejido*, the agrarian community, and private property. The first two are collective forms of land ownership and they represent close to fifty percent of the national territory. About ninety-two percent of the 28,958 collective landholdings of Mexico (totalling 95,108,066 hectares) are *ejidos*; most native communities in rural areas live under this land regime. Politically, *ejidos* are associations of independent producers with exclusive rights to specific parcels and to common untilled lands (usually forests).[20]

Official pronouncements affected women's land rights within *ejidos* in the years following the revolution and have continued throughout the twentieth century. While the first Agrarian Law (1915) and the land right clauses of the 1917 Constitution made no reference to gender, the *Ejido* Law (1920) and the By-Laws (1922) established that "wherever land is granted to *ejidos*, the heads of households or individuals over the age of eighteen shall receive from three to five hectares of irrigated or rainfed lands." Article 97 of the 1927 agrarian law establishes that "*ejido* members shall be Mexican nationals, males over the age of eighteen, or *single women or widows supporting a family*" (emphasis added).[21] On the death of a male *ejidatario*, his wife has legal priority to keep the parcel, which must be transferred to one of his children. As in colonial times, women in post-revolutionary Mexico became eligible for land rights only in their role as guardians of young children.

Women's organizations asked for amendments to the law during the 1920s and 1930s. In the first Congress of Women Workers and Peasants held in 1931, activist Cuca García argued that young *campesinas* were condemned "to live at the poor economic level of their father, their husband or brother" because the law denied them access to land. The issue was raised again at the Second Congress held in 1933. Juana Gutiérrez de Mendoza spoke of the need for women peasants to have the same opportunities as men to receive land under the Agrarian Reform program.[22] Women's organizations asked for amendments to the Agrarian Code in 1935 and 1937,[23] but they had to wait until 1971 to see some changes take place. By that time, Mexico City was getting ready to host the first International Women's Conference, held in 1975. President Echeverría took an active stand in defending women's rights in order to promote his image as a Third World leader and re-establish his credibility after his followers massacred protesting students in 1968.

The code was modified to give women equal rights to receive land. The new law states that Mexicans by birth, "male or female over sixteen years of age, or of any age if with dependants" are eligible for land rights, and women can keep their land right even after they marry. On the death of an *ejidatario*(*a*), his or her spouse has legal priority to keep the parcel.[24]

Although changes to the Agrarian Law were necessary and welcomed, the number of female landholders in rural Mexico did not increase significantly after the amendments: in 1984 they accounted for only fifteen percent of the total *ejido* members.[25] The changes had arrived a bit late, when most *ejido* land had already been distributed in all rural Mexico. Where land distribution did occur, the changes were simply not enforced by federal government officials and male-dominated, well-established *ejido* organizations, which continued to determine women's land rights on the basis of their marital status – only widows with young children, preferably male, had some chance of receiving land. Although the law had changed, male-dominated *ejido* authorities went on operating in the old way, with passive government support.[26]

The amendments to Article 27 of the Constitution made in 1992, which establish that *ejido* land can be sold and private investment can be made in *ejidos* (in "association" with *ejidatarios*) is having a negative impact on women. It means, among other things, that *ejidatarios* (mostly male) can sell or bequeath their land to anyone of their choice.[27] In other words, the *ejidatario*'s spouse and children have lost the legal priority that they used to have to inherit the land on the death of the landholder. In the new laws of the market, all women in rural Mexico have lost all legal access to land, unless they can afford to buy, or their husbands choose to bequeath, their land rights to them. As surprising as it may seem, the pre-revolutionary liberal ideals based on the notion of individual, private and male property are back in place, thereby continuing the male-dominated social system originally envisioned for Mexican natives by Spanish officials in the sixteenth and seventeenth centuries.

The economic marginalization of native women was not simply the result of one method of imperialism, that is, rapid conquest followed by large-scale redistribution of land mainly to the conquerors. As the actions of nineteenth- and twentieth-century Mexican government show, colonization carried with it a patriarchal ethos whose impact was both extensive and long-lasting. Thus, it is useful to compare the Mexican case with that of Canada; not only was colonization carried out by a different European power, but the establishment of colonial dominion was strikingly different from the Mexican case. Nevertheless, the end result was the economic and social marginalization of women as a result of land legislation that linked citizenship and private property to males only.

Two major linguistic groups occupied what later became Eastern Canada: the Iroquois and the Algonkian. Iroquois society was matrifocal, matrilineal, and matrilocal. This means that "descent was traced through women and after marriage the husband went to live with his wife's family. Each dwelling was owned by a senior woman."[28] A household among the Iroquois "consisted of a woman, her female relations, their spouses and dependants."[29] The economy of the Iroquois relied on corn and fish. They stayed in one place for ten to twelve years, until soil exhaustion forced them to move on. Women were responsible for agricultural operations (except for clearing the fields, which was men's responsibility) and had a prominent social and political role. Senior matrons had the power to elect and depose the elders of the highest ruling political body, and hereditary eligibility to this council was through the female line.[30]

The other major linguistic group in Canada, the Algonkians, were migratory peoples who relied on hunting and gathering for subsistence. An Algonkian band was a group of male kin who hunted together, their spouses and their dependent families. Among the Montagnais-Naskapi, an Algonkian-speaking group, men and women had complementary functions. Men hunted and women brought home the game slain by their husbands, prepared the food, tanned the skins, and made them into clothing. Women controlled the apportionment and distribution of meat as well as the assignment of living space and the selection of campsites.[31]

Given their migratory condition, there was no such thing as European-style private property among the native peoples of Canada. The Kaianerakowa, the ancient constitution of the Haudenosaunee Nations Iroquois Confederacy, states that land was and is invested in the power of the women: "The lineal descent of the people of the Five Nations shall run in the female line. Women shall be considered the progenitors of the Nation. They shall own the land and the soil. Men and Women shall follow the status of their mother."[32] Thus, ideas about property and social roles among the Algonkian and Iroquois were dramatically different from the patriarchal, property-owning French and British explorers who first made contact with them. However, as opposed to Mexico where the Aztecs were militarily defeated by the Spaniards, the first centuries of European colonization in Canada were distinguished by cooperation in expeditions, trade and war between French and British powers and aboriginal people. Natives were interested in European technology and exchanged fur for iron items. During the seventeenth century the Europeans were few and New France remained a commercial colony rather than an agricultural settlement. As such, it did not represent a serious threat to aboriginal people. However, the status of native women was gradually undermined by patriarchal French religious missions and commercial contact with merchants who were interested only in the furs obtained by native men. Thus, "the orientation of many female tasks began to shift from the creation of an useful end product, such as clothing or tools, to assistance in the preparation of furs."[33]

The eighteenth century was distinguished by military alliances between native people and European powers, and native support became vital to the British government as it attempted to maintain peace on its vast American frontier. In 1763, British victory in the French and Indian wars forced France to cede its Canadian holdings to Britain. As a result of this sudden and dramatic extension of its North American colonial holdings, the British Crown tried to maintain peace and "protect" aboriginal peoples through the Royal Proclamation of 1763, which established that native people were subject to the "paternal care" of the British Crown. Native land was under royal "sovereignty, protection and dominion, for the use of the said Indians," and could not be granted to new settlers. Like the Spanish crown in Mexico, the British crown gave itself the power to regulate land grants and to "protect" its native subjects from European settlers.

However, aboriginal land was gradually colonized through the signing of treaties in most parts of Canada. In these treaties, land was surrendered to the crown in exchange of lump-sum payments or annuities, where native peoples retained hunting and fishing privileges. While in western Canada fur trade continued to be an important activity well into the nineteenth century, in eastern Canada it was gradually replaced by agriculture. Once native peoples were not needed as economic or military allies, the government attempted to concentrate them in settled areas and to subject them to European-style agriculture and Christian education. Reserves were first established during the 1830s and residential schools during the 1840s. Newly arrived British women became models for morality and wifely virtues.[34]

These efforts to assimilate native peoples into white society were furthered by more comprehensive legislation in 1857, when the Gradual Civilization Act was made applicable to both Upper and Lower Canada. "Enfranchisement" was introduced as a mechanism to facilitate the acquisition of property and the rights accompanying it, and it reflected existing European social and gender ideology. The law offered fifty acres on reserve land and a sum of money to native men who could speak, read, and write English or French, had "good moral character," and were free from debt. Their "dependants" were enfranchised with him automatically whether they wanted to be enfranchised or not.[35] As in the case of Mexico, "progress" was seen as losing all Indian traits, and civil rights were equated with male, individual rights to property.

Yet even enfranchisement did not necessarily release Indians from state interference and control. In 1867, the year of Canadian Confederation, the British North America Act (Section 91.24) gave the new federal government exclusive legislative authority for "Indians and lands reserved for the Indians."[36] In this sense, Confederation did not mean the birth of a new nation for aboriginal peoples, but the continuation of the paternalistic policy of the British crown. The federal government of the new nation granted itself the right over native peoples and lands, the authority to set up borders and to define people's identities, and the new government lost little time in exerting its powers. Less than a decade later, it passed the first "Indian Act" (1876) which defined as Indian "any male person of Indian blood reputed to belong to a particular band." According to the Act, any native woman who married a non-native man would lose all her rights as an Indian, except for collecting annuities. Moreover, the Superintendent-General could decide to stop paying these annuities if she deserted her husband and started living "immorally with another man."[37] In effect, a woman's identity was predicated on her relationship with men, similar to those women in Mexico who had identities as landowners only as caretakers for their male relatives. Further, in the Canadian legislation, women were subject to a foreign moral code that embodied a sexual double standard imposed by the white government.

As in the case of Mexico, this legislation did not take into consideration the great diversity of social and political organization of native peoples. The legislation enforced private property on aboriginal peoples and made the nuclear, monogamous, and male-headed family the model after which private property was acquired and civil rights were granted. In doing so, the legislation deprived native women of all autonomy before their husbands and the law.[38] Native women became dependent on their native husbands; marrying a non-native man would mean losing Indian status; and deserting her husband (native or non-native) to live with another man would end a woman's right to annuities. Needless to say, this legislation drastically undermined women's economic and political autonomy. Native women in Canada, like native women in Mexico, became subject to patriarchal controls over resources, marriage and reproduction.

Native peoples who chafed under the patriarchal and foreign institutions thus imposed on them by the Canadian government began undertaking organized political action early in the twentieth century. Aboriginal organizations asserted land claims and demanded respect for treaties, a better school system and agricultural assistance as well as the right to perform traditional rituals. However, it was not until 1946 that a joint committee of the Senate and the House of Commons was appointed to re-examine the Indian Act. Some native representatives called for the abolition of the Act, while others stated that women who had lost their status through marriage and were deserted or widowed should be allowed to rejoin their communities. However, the committee ignored aboriginal people's recommendations, and the Indian Act did not change substantially. While the most obnoxious features, such as compulsory enfranchisement, bans on the potlatch and the Sun Dance, and prohibitions on consumption of alcohol, were deleted, the general outlines of the policy remained unchanged.[39] In fact, the revised law now contained new clauses that further affected the identities of native women who married non-natives. As of 1951, these women could not continue collecting annuities after marriage and were deleted from the band list. Any property that they held on the reserve had to be sold or otherwise disposed of in thirty days. In exchange, they would be given twenty years of treaty money (if the band took treaty) plus one per capita share of the capital and revenue moneys held by Her Majesty on behalf of the band. In short, these women were subject to involuntary enfranchisement, and these compensations have proved inadequate in most cases. For example, between 1966 and 1977 payments averaged $261.80 per each person enfranchised.[40]

Native women began to struggle against this situation during the 1970s. In 1970, Jeanette Lavell, an Ojibwa woman who had married a non-native, contested the deletion of her name from the band list by arguing that such deletion constituted discrimination on the basis of race and sex, and was contrary to the Canadian Bill of Rights. Lavell was joined by Yvonne Bedard, a native woman who had married out and then separated from her husband. She was fighting the Six Nations band council's attempts to evict her from the house which had been willed to her by her mother. The Supreme Court of Canada ruled against Lavell and Bedard by a controversial five-to-four decision, by arguing that the Bill of Rights could not take precedence over the Indian Act.[41]

It would take world pressure to force Canada to rethink its stand on native women's rights. In 1981, the United Nations Human Rights Committee argued that Canadian law had violated the human rights of Sandra Lovelace, a Maliseet woman from the Tobique Reserve in New Brunswick who had been denied the right to live in her natal reserve. As a result, the Canadian government agreed to make a commitment to the UN to introduce legislative changes. A special parliamentary committee recommended in 1982 that discriminatory sections be eliminated from the Act, and that women who had lost status, and their first-generation children, be reinstated. The implementation of the 1985 Charter of Rights and Freedoms (which prohibited discrimination on the basis of sex) a few years later made it absolutely essential to undertake the necessary changes to the Indian Act. In 1985, the Conservative government introduced Bill C-31, which was passed four months later. Under the amended Act, no one loses status through marriage. Women who lost their Indian status before these changes are eligible for reinstatement to band membership, and for re-registration as Indians under the Act. Their first-generation children and all people enfranchised for any reason, and their children, can also apply to be registered Indians, but are not entitled to band membership. Second-generation children of restored persons are not granted legal status or band membership. In the future, Indian status will be granted to those with at least one parent having status.[42]

This bill separated formally and legally Indian status from band membership. While the federal government kept for itself the right to determine Indian status, band membership and reserve residency is determined by bands. The bill was considered a compromise between women's rights to equality and the interest of male-dominated native organizations in self-government. However, the bill created further divisions between people of native origin: those who had both Indian status and band membership, and those who regained only Indian status but not band membership. The latter do not have the right to live on an Indian reserve, share in resources, or take part in band politics. Moreover, the bill failed to ensure a role for reinstated women in developing band membership codes.[43]

According to the Department of Indian Affairs, about 16,000 women and 20,000 other individuals would be entitled to have membership in Canada's almost 600 bands after the changes. The Department calculated that the total number of those eligible to regain status, though not necessarily band membership, ranged from 76,000 to 86,000. But these figures were underestimated. Since the amendment, 95,153 of 153,903 natives who applied for status have been reinstated. By December 1991, the population with Indian status had increased by nearly sixteen percent. Unprepared for such an influx of applicants, the Department was ineffective in the implementation of the new policy.[44] Although the federal government assured at the time of the changes that "no band would be worse off" because of the revised Indian Act, the funds committed to cover the needs of reinstated people have proven insufficient, and bands have had to cope with these problems on their own. Thus, attitudes towards returning women and their children vary regionally, from liberal postures in British Columbia and southern Ontario to the more intolerant Prairies. In Alberta, where 10,026 of 21,137 applicants have won back status, male native leaders have challenged the amendment, claiming that bands and not the federal government have the right to determine their own membership. Some bands have claimed that they have insufficient funds to accommodate new members and have passed strict membership codes excluding Bill C-31, while others have taken the women and their children back with restrictions, such as being placed on probation, paying a fee or not being allowed to open businesses. The National Aboriginal Inquiry on Bill C-31 reported in 1990 several charges of blatant discrimination against women by bands. According to the report, a new category of persons with diminished social status, the returning "C-31," had been created. They had become scapegoats for the wider ills of some communities.[45]

This chapter has examined the ways in which the colonial and postcolonial states of Mexico and Canada have contributed to the construction of gendered civil rights through legislation. Two legal instruments were examined for this purpose: the Agrarian Law of Mexico and the Indian Act of Canada. In Mexico, the colonial state was responsible for the introduction of a new legal system that granted civil and property rights to native peoples using the model of the nuclear, monogamous, and male-headed family. In doing so, the system undermined the preference of siblings over children as heirs, and the equivalence of male and female siblings of the pre-hispanic period. The new laws also limited native women's ability to own land, by restricting their rights to land to their roles as guardians of young children or grandchildren. Thus, Spanish law focused on women's family roles as wives and mothers and assumed that they were dependent on their husbands. Women had no legal or political rights of their own, and were perceived as property mediators between men, namely a man and his sons.

Native women's rights to land did not increase significantly in spite of radical changes in the country – a war of Independence, liberal programs in the nineteenth century, a social revolution in the first half of the twentieth. Patriarchal family structures simply served the post-colonial system too well. For example, in order to make tax collection more effective, liberal programs attached land to families rather than to communities, thereby contributing to strengthen men's position of dominance within the family. After the Revolution of 1910, the Agrarian Law acknowledged various forms of communal ownership of land (e.g. agrarian communities and *ejidos*), but following the colonial legal system, it limited women's land rights within *ejidos* to their roles as guardians of young children. That is, only women "supporting a family" became eligible for land rights.

After the changes of 1971, which aimed at ensuring gender equality under the Agrarian Law, female landholders still were a minority within *ejidos*. Most land had already been distributed and where land distribution actually did occur, male-dominated *ejido* authorities continued to give land to women only if they were widows and had young children, with the silent support of federal government officials. Moreover, the amendments to Article 27 of the Constitution made in 1992 have deprived women of their rights even further, by making it legal for *ejidatarios* (mostly male) to sell or bequeath their land to anyone of their choice, not necessarily their wives or children. Unless they can afford to buy, or their husbands choose to bequeath the land to them, native women have no legal access to land in Mexico.

In Canada something similar has occurred. Prior to the arrival of the Europeans, aboriginals had no sense of European-style private property. Women in pre-contact societies played a major economic role and retained control over the product of their labour, which in turn translated into social and political influence. In the first centuries of European colonization, native women continued to participate in expeditions and fur trade activities, although their political influence was undermined by the gradual deterioration of subsistence economies. Aboriginal people were increasingly confined within a particular territory and subject to segregational practices.

The Indian Act of 1876 triggered a process of legal differentiation within native communities and placed women in a disadvantaged position vis-à-vis their male counterparts. In the Indian Act, native women found themselves "marginalized in their own country and in their own community."[46] A woman who married a non-native man would lose her status as an Indian; if she married a native man, she was subject to her husband's desire to become "enfranchised," and could also lose her Indian status at his will. In both cases, the woman was legally dependent on her husband. As was the case in Mexico, property and civil rights were designed after the model of the male-headed, nuclear and monogamous family, where women and children were considered the male's property. Women were perceived as wives and mothers dependent on men, and had no political or legal rights of their own.

The 1985 amendments to the Indian Act, aimed at re-establishing women's rights, left many unsolved problems. While some wealthy reserves did not want to share their riches with the reinstated women, others simply lacked the resources to accommodate them. Even though women are allowed back, their living conditions are often inadequate.

Both pieces of legislation were influenced by a European-based liberal tradition that defines civil rights as individual and property rights. Within this tradition, the individual is male and has as his dependants his wife and children. In both countries, women were seen as incapable of exercising any legal or political rights: in the words of Jamieson, they were considered citizen minus.[47] This view conflicted with the diversity in forms of social organization in both pre-hispanic Mexico and pre-contact Canada. While in pre-hispanic Mexico siblings were an important grouping for inheritance purposes and women could inherit in their own right, women in pre-contact societies in Canada controlled their access to resources and enjoyed social status and political power. Even today, native people living in extended families do not fit the model of the male-headed, nuclear, and monogamous family after which land rights have been designed and civil rights granted.

Both pieces of legislation were developed in the period of nation-state building of each country. The Spanish and British Crowns started a policy of paternalism which was continued by independent nation-states. In both cases, the governments asserted their right to "protect" natives, but then proceeded to define native identity, as well as social and civil rights, in terms of European views of what these should be in a "civilized" country. Even when these colonial states were replaced by independent nation-states, the new governments adopted a similar ideology, thereby fostering a patriarchal system that marginalized native women by gendering concepts of land ownership and citizenship. In both countries, these nation-states granted themselves the right to rule over aboriginal territory, set up borders and define people's identities. Although they were justified as a way to "protect" native peoples and land, these legal instruments are state mechanisms aimed at controlling native land and resources and policing aboriginal populations. Both the Mexican and the Canadian states viewed native women as wives and mothers dependent on men, and made them incapable of exercising any legal or political rights. In doing so, they both placed women at a disadvantageous situation when forms of land tenure in Mexico and membership codes in Canada were established. By reproducing the model of the male-headed, monogamous, and nuclear family to regulate access to land, state legislation limited women's access to land and other critical resources in their own communities.

Thus from the time of first contact between Europeans and the native peoples of Mexico and Canada, colonial governments effectively imposed a dependent role on women as part of what colonial rulers saw as a process of "civilizing" the aboriginal peoples by transforming them into model European-style nuclear families. The land laws discussed here thus not only undermined native women's pre-colonial status and power, they fundamentally changed native social structures, laws, and lifestyles – so foreign to European society – into something more familiar and less threatening, while at the same time allowing the dominant power to exert maximum control by allowing it to determine the very identity of native peoples.

8

The "Male City" of Havana: The Coexisting Logics of Colonialism, Slavery, and Patriarchy in Nineteenth-Century Cuba*

Luis Martínez-Fernández

Throughout most of the nineteenth century, Cuba, and its capital of Havana in particular, remained simultaneously trapped between the two worlds of colonialism and neocolonialism. Within this arrangement, the island remained a Spanish colony while enduring a neocolonial relationship with the United States. But this reality also placed Cuba between two worlds in another sense: a Hispanic one tied to tradition and hierarchy and an Anglo-American one heralding modernity. The island was also trapped between the contradictory structures of a slave-based system and the demands of agro-industrial capitalism. Nineteenth-century Cuba, thus, was neither Spanish nor North American; it was neither fully capitalist nor fully slave-based; it was neither black nor white.

The complex political, economic, and social realities of nineteenth-century Cuba produced a cultural web with a peculiar, and often contradictory, set of internal logics that regulated relations between the colonizers and the colonized, rich and poor, black and white, and women and men. Often these coexisting hierarchies reinforced each other, but on occasion they were contradictory, and the foreign observers who visited Cuba in large numbers during the nineteenth century often failed to understand the social logics of the island. This chapter, which rests heavily on travelers' accounts written during the nineteenth century, seeks to explain the social logics behind the practices and rituals of gender relations so carefully described yet misunderstood by those foreigners who visited the island. It focuses on the social restrictions imposed on women residing in Havana and on how women from different racial, social, and ethnic backgrounds responded to them.

Havana, with the phallic Morro Castle as its gatekeeper, was characterized by nineteenth-century travelers as a "male city," likened to the mythical "Rome of Romulus."[1] "Where are the women and where are they to be found in Havana?" inquired one concerned visitor.[2] According to another traveler "the absence of the female form" constituted one of Havana's "most striking features."[3]

Indeed, there were considerably fewer women than men in Havana as well as on the island as a whole. According to the 1861 census there were 149 men for every 100 women in Havana and its environs, while the ratio for the entire island was a less sharp 134.[4] Although the overall sex imbalances were in great measure the result of slave-trading practices favoring males over females at a ratio of between 4:1 and 5:1,[5] similarly striking sexual imbalances were found among the white population, and particularly among whites residing in Havana. In the island as a whole, the white male: white female ratio grew steadily throughout the nineteenth century from 114 (1827) to 127 (1846) to 150 (1862) per 100.[6] The sexual imbalance among whites was even sharper in Havana, the island's administrative-military-mercantile center to which the exclusively male population involved in such activities gravitated. Havana was also a city of immigrants and transients, most of whom were men. In 1861, according to census figures, there were 1.8 men for every woman among Havana's residents of European descent.[7]

Women in nineteenth-century Havana were not only a demographic minority, they were also subjected to seclusion, discrimination, limited options, and gross double standards of acceptable social behavior. The seemingly obsessive desire on the part of society to protect and seclude women of the upper classes appeared – was, in fact – stronger in Havana than in any other Western society, colonial or metropolitan. In other societies, the United States among them, women faced similar forms of restriction, segregation, and exclusion but to a much lesser degree. What, then, accounted for Havana's more restrictive codes of female behavior? The answer to this question lies in the particular structure of its society: its slave base, the imbalance of its male: female ratios, its population of color constituting a majority, the strong correlation between color and class, its highly hierarchical social structure, and the very limited opportunities for social mobility.[8]

Sexual codes were thus intimately linked to issues pertaining to demographic patterns, class, color, and restrictions on social mobility. Paradoxically, it was the women of the native, white upper and middle class who became the primary targets of seclusion and discrimination. Otherwise disempowered white *Habaneras* were, for example, forced to carry the burden of controlling access to society's white elite. As Verena Martínez-Alier concluded in her now classic *Marriage, Class, and Colour in Nineteenth-Century Cuba*: "the device through which the purity of the group was achieved was virginity, that is female purity. By controlling the access to female sexuality, control was exercised over the acquisition of undesirable members of the group." Through seclusion, high regard for female virginity and chastity, and legislation obstructing interracial marriages, society "protected" white women and their race – and by extension their class – from what was perceived as "racial pollution."[9]

Interestingly, the same central tenet that shaped the Cuban elite's political postures during the middle decades of the nineteenth century – the fear of the black man – also shaped, to a great extent social rules regulating female behavior as they pertained to virginity, courtship, and marriage. Some of the island's key political figures of the mid-century justified Cuba's annexation to the United States on racial and sexual terms. The annexationist editors of *La Verdad*, for example, referring to events in neighboring Venezuela, denounced "the most lamentable spectacle, the most repugnant liaisons to our instincts, the most shocking to our present state of civilization and public opinion, the most degrading and shameful to our race, marriages between white women and blacks, mulattoes, *zambos*, and *mestizos*."[10] Note that the editors' concern was not with miscegenation per se – a long-accepted way of dealing with Cuba's "racial problem" – but specifically with men of color having sexual access to white women. Another contemporary observer hiding behind the title of "Yankee" but suspiciously familiar with Cuban ways referred to the seclusion of Havana's "ladies" (meaning white women) as a "necessity" to spare them the "risk of meeting blasphemous, odorous, and drunken negroes."[11] At one of the moments of highest racial tension, stemming from a temporary suspension of laws interdicting interracial marriages in 1854, a critic of the suspension pointed out that this and other reforms had encouraged blacks to salute Havana's ladies and to pay them "compliments in impudent and audible commendations of their beauty." He added that such "insolence . . . carried alarm into the bosom of every family."[12] Prison terms and other penalties were applied against men of color who dared approach white women in obscene or intolerably familiar ways.[13]

Clearly established social rules designed to both "protect" and subdue women contributed to keeping white *Habaneras* under seclusion. The prevailing etiquette did not allow "ladies" to walk on the streets, "not even two blocks."[14] According to Mercedes de Santa Cruz y Montalvo, the countess of Merlín, even when crossing a narrow street to visit a neighbor, Havana's ladies dashed as "fearful doves that flee from the sound of the lumberjack's axe."[15] Arriving in Cuba in 1848, the wife of Captain-General Federico Roncali sought to put an end to female seclusion by herself walking the streets of Havana. It was to no avail; her bold steps were not followed by other women of the local elite.[16]

Women of color and others not pretending to the title of lady, however, walked about as they pleased, sold fruits and other goods out in the open, and frequented places like cockpits which were completely barred to white women.[17] These privileges granted to Havana's women of color reflect a paradoxical situation resulting from the overlapping and somewhat conflicting logics of a slave-based and male-dominated society. The most evident distortion of these conflicting yet mutually reinforced power structures was that women of color, slave or free, appeared to enjoy greater liberties than the women of the master class. Needless to say, Havana was still first and foremost a slave-based class society and not a few black or mulatto women would have gladly given up the right to walk up and down Obispo or O'Reilly streets in exchange for the standard of living and privileges of the women of the elite.

Nonetheless, the highly visible "freedoms" enjoyed by black and mulatto Habaneras appear to have been a point of friction between women of different classes. The countess of Merlín, in her famous epistolary travelogue, scorned the almost snobbish pride with which *Habaneras* of color walked the streets, "cigar in mouth, almost naked with their round shining bare shoulders." The tone of the countess's comments reflects a degree of jealousy directed toward black women, who by virtue of their physical mobility and more revealing attires were made more visible, and therefore more accessible, to men of all races, including whites.[18] Other contemporaries also noted a degree of rivalry between the secluded white *Habaneras* and their sable sisters and commented on the proud and "jaunty" air that the latter displayed while walking in Havana's streets. One observer described black women walking nonchalantly, allowing their low-cut garments to "slip with picturesque negligence from their dusky shoulders."[19] A mid-century moralist criticized Havana's women of color for seeking the status of white women by using bleaching devises and by luring "men of all classes."[20]

Foreign visitors often expressed their dismay at the sight of home-bound white *Habaneras* clinging to the iron bars of their glassless windows from which they gazed at the forbidden world of the outside "like captives in durance."[21] One obviously amused visitor recorded in his travelogue that he had seen "[m]any a bright lustrous eye, and fairy-like foot . . . through the wires of her cheerful cage."[22] Another traveler likened Havana to a "zoological garden, in which the insiders and the outsiders have changed places."[23] Julia Ward Howe, a Bostonian feminist, found less to joke about and scorned the practice as a form of "Oriental imprisonment."[24] Havana folklore had it that one North American visitor on passing threw a few coins through an iron-barred window thinking that the sad- looking woman behind it was a convict, her home the city jail.[25]

While behind bars, *Habaneras* struggled to remain visible to those outside; custom could keep them from stepping outside but not from keeping their windows wide open. The compromise, thus, was to remain out of reach but not out of sight. A variety of contemporary sources attest that most windows were kept open and that the women came "freely . . . to the windows to chat with passers-by."[26] According to one visitor accustomed to Yankee privacy, wide open windows made it "nearly impossible to avoid glancing in upon domestic scenes that frequently exhibit the female portion of the family in déshabillé."[27] According to another observer, "one has the inspection of the interior arrangement of all the front parlors of Havana, and can see what every lady wears, and who is visiting her."[28] Passers-by complimented the women with witty *piropos*. Every night, after sundown, an army of bachelor *Habaneros* – one visitor called them *lechuzos* (night owls) – proceeded to call on the single, captive *Habaneras*, whom they courted "like monkeys" through the iron-barred windows that extended from the floor to the ceiling of their homes.[29] According to the description by one keen observer of Cuban social life, gentlemen callers positioned themselves at an angle outside the windows to avoid being seen by their lover's family.[30] William Henry Hurlbert hinted that iron bars failed to keep lovers from engaging in the most intimate expressions of tenderness.[31]

Female travelers and long-term foreign residents of Havana faced the dilemma of either complying with the roles and behavior expected of white women or challenging them and facing the consequences. They were for the most part shocked by the prevailing odious restrictions but also faced considerable pressures to conform with the norms, particularly if they were planning a long-term stay. According to one contemporary observer, foreign female travelers who challenged the social codes by walking the streets of Havana faced passing remarks, "annoyance and even insult," which in the end forced most to comply.[32] Another recorded incident described an episode in which several men and boys chased a group of North American women while shouting insults at them.[33] Quite significantly, license to harass women appeared to cut across class and color lines, as attested by an incident in which "a couple of half-naked, horrible looking negroes" harassed the Swedish visitor Fredrika Bremer.[34]

As one United States consul put it, his female compatriots would try walking once or twice but would eventually conform to the restrictions and "be quite miserable."[35] Julia Ward Howe reported that even "the hardiest American or English woman will scarcely venture out a second time without the severe escort of husband or brother."[36] In a humorous tone she added that the North American woman, usually very jealous of her own space and time alone in the United States, "suddenly becomes very fond of her husband" on whom, while in Cuba, she comes to depend as saving escort and bodyguard. As to the general rule of seclusion of Cuban women, she ended up rationalizing it by saying that in a place like Cuba where "the animal vigor of men is so large in proportion to their moral power . . . women must be glad to forgo their liberties" for their own protection.[37] Not all foreign women complied with Havana's strict norms about not circulating in the streets. One woman, Rachel Wilson Moore, and her friends, while recognizing that walking was not considered safe, stuck to what she called their "republican habits" and tried to ignore the stares and remarks that were thrown at them.[38] Julia Louisa M. Woodruff, a visitor from New York, tired of being able to walk only up and down the halls of her hotel, decided to go shopping "after the American fashion." Her daring move attracted a storm of long and mean stares but she persisted.[39]

For the otherwise imprisoned white *Habaneras* – at least for those whose families could afford it – there was an "Angel of deliverance": the *volanta*.[40] "Ladies" could move about freely throughout the streets of Havana only when riding on *volantas*, *quitrines*, and other horse-drawn carriages, whether these belonged to their families or were rented at a fixed fare. They were not, however, allowed to ride by themselves or to be accompanied by men, but only with one or two female friends or relatives. Men rarely rode on *volantas*, preferring instead to walk or ride horses.[41] One North American traveler recounted an incident about a female compatriot of his who was momentarily left alone in her *volanta* by her male companion and was soon approached by a daring *Habanero* who "with the greatest familiarity [proceeded] to take a flower from her hand." The woman responded by smacking the man, who immediately left the scene shouting obscenities of all sorts.[42] Yet another instance of harassment included the gathering of a laughing and insulting mob provoked by the daring Woodruff going for a drive with a local male resident.[43]

Volantas were peculiar-looking carriages of Cuban invention which elicited obligatory comments – mostly criticisms – from almost everyone encountering one for the first time. This type of carriage consisted of a low-cut chaise-like body, sometimes ornamented with precious metal trimmings, resting on a pair of disproportionately large wheels measuring about six feet in diameter. *Volanta* cabins were set up for two passengers but a third seat – significantly called "el de la niña bonita" – could be added for a third passenger. From the body of the *volanta* emerged two long shafts, sixteen to twenty feet long, attached to the sides of one or two small horses with their tails tightly braided and tied to the saddle or harness. In all, from the end of the wheels to the tip of the horse's nose, *volantas* extended a distance of around twenty-two feet.[44] On the horse sat the driver or postilion, usually a black slave or freedman dressed up in a most colorful livery consisting of a buckled top hat, a swallow-tailed scarlet coat trimmed with a generous dose of silver or gold braid, and leather jack-boots with oversized spurs and silver buckles.[45] One contemporary ridiculed the entire costume, describing it as "three parts jack boots and one part silver laced jacket."[46] The liveries of postilions working for some of the wealthiest families could cost several thousand pesos.

Most foreigners visiting the island were quick to criticize the ubiquitous *volanta* as odd-looking and impractical. One contemporary referred to it as comical and another dubbed it a queer vehicle.[47] Yet another observer described the *volanta* as the "oddest vehicle conceivable."[48] They failed, however, to understand that this peculiar Cuban invention reflected the needs and the structure of the society in which it was created. First and foremost, the *volanta* afforded mobility and visibility to the city's elite, particularly its women of marriageable age. At the same time, given the carriages' proportions and elevation from the road, *volantas* allowed a considerable distance between the passengers (mostly women) and pedestrians (mostly men). Like the barred house windows, these vehicles kept the city's upper-class women out of reach but not out of sight.

Volantas also served to mark class boundaries in a society obsessed with maintaining distinctions between its classes. Such carriages, along with grand pianos and a coterie of domestic slaves, became the trademarks of the elite.

The wealthiest families were said to own a *volanta* for each marriageable daughter. Middle-class families would go out of their way to purchase one such vehicle, setting aside for this purpose the household's very first savings.[49] One traveler remarked that middle-class Cubans "would sooner live on beans and cold water, dress in rags, and lie on straw . . . than go without a *volanta*."[50] Given the exorbitant cost of purchasing and maintaining a *volanta*, most middle-class families could simply not afford to own such vehicles. *Volantas* helped establish hierarchies within the elite as well. The richer the family the more carriages it owned and the greater the extent of their ornamentation, including fancy woodwork and gold leaf, with postilions and horses dressed to match.

Given the narrowness of most streets inside the walled city of Havana, the length of the *volantas'* shafts appears senseless and cumbersome; this detail, however, secured a considerable separation between the passengers and the postilion and horses. The nature of the postilions' attire, which matched the gaudy ornamentation of the carriages and the horses, further established them as objects far removed from the human and individual qualities of those they served. Significantly, *volantas* as modes of urban transportation peaked precisely during the peak decades of the slave trade and "Africanization" fear; they went out of style later during the process of gradual emancipation and lingered a bit longer in Matanzas, perhaps the island's most racially stratified town.[51]

The time of the *paseo* in the *volantas* was the daily high point for upper- and upper-middle class *Habaneras*. According to one observer, most women spent their mornings and afternoons "killing time" in rocking chairs, fanning themselves in their déshabillé in anticipation of *paseo* time.[52] "It is for their hour on the *paseo*," said Anthony Trollope, "that the ladies dress themselves."[53] According to other accounts, young women preferred to go without food rather than skip the *paseo*.[54] During the evening *paseos*, women of the upper classes displayed their charms and fancy clothing and elaborate coiffures from their *volantas* for the pleasure of the scores of gallant *Habaneros* who either walking or on horseback saluted the ladies whom they passed over and over again.[55] At *paseo* time the covers of the *volantas* were pushed back to allow maximum visibility. Over the cabin's side panels were spread the folds of the occupant's skirts. According to one observer: "The full, flowing skirts of these ladies were spread carefully out at each side of the *volanta*, hanging nearly to the ground, and giving the vehicle, when viewed from the rear, the appearance of being furnished with wings."[56] Another contemporary described a similar sight as "the most staring description that I ever witnessed."[57]

Volantas served another important function: they allowed white *Habaneras* to go shopping. So strict were the norms regarding not walking on the streets that upper- and middle-class women went out shopping on the basis of a curious predecessor to drive-by shopping or window service. As custom had it, "ladies" would order their carriages halted in front of a given shop, then the shop's clerk would jump over the counter and proceed to walk outside carrying a handful of goods for the inspection of his prospective costumers. Shoes and other items were tried by women on their carriages parked outside the stores.[58] This system allowed the mostly Peninsular, mostly male retailers to foist off on their female customers their slower-moving merchandize as well as their higher-priced, lower-quality items. The fact that the entire transaction was carried out in the street and in what had to be a hurried manner must have also put female customers at a disadvantage, given the bargaining fashion in which purchases were usually made.[59] Women also had their carriages driven to the portals of the city's famous cafés, La Dominica and El Louvre, where they were not expected to sit at the tables but could place orders of ices and other refreshments to go from *mozos* serving the drive-by customers. Another shopping custom was that merchants sent articles for inspection at the ladies' homes. Servants were used in these transactions, which could take an entire day of bargaining before a price was agreed upon.[60]

Another place allowing *Habaneras* some mobility and visibility was the interior of the city's churches. Church was, in fact, the best place for foreign visitors and Havana residents to catch an unobstructed glimpse of the proverbial beauty of the elusive *Habaneras*. Several sources attest that this was in fact the only place to see white women.[61] Given its conservative stance on many other matters it appears rather paradoxical that the church was the one Cuban institution where white women found freedom, comfort, and a space to call their own, and where there were no segregated spaces on the basis of gender or race. In some ways the church was in fact more progressive as an institution than the state, and more liberal than the attitude of the general population. Canonical law, for example, did not differentiate between male and female adultery as did Spanish legislation and social custom.[62] A quite revealing episode in mid-nineteenth-century Havana demonstrates these postures. In the summer of 1852 the members of the all-male Real Archicofradía del Santísimo Sacramento of the church of Nuestra Señora de Guadalupe wrote to Queen Isabella II, patron of the Catholic Church in Spain and its possessions, requesting permission to erect railings to segregate the sexes inside the church in order to "maintain the composure and decorum required in the Lord's House . . . and to avoid the distractions with which the common enemy would try to disturb devotion and concentration." Both the bishop of Havana and Captain-General Valentín Cañedo had prohibited the use of the railings, the latter scorning it as "a disagreeable distinction in the House of the Lord."[63]

Under the umbrella of the church, women of the elite were also able to take upon themselves the responsibilities of charitable work and raising funds for and taking care of the vestments of their church's female saints and virgins.[64] Since it was considered sacrilegious for any man to touch or even lay eyes on an undressed statue of a female saint or virgin, only women could fulfill the task of taking care of their vestments. This exclusively feminine activity allowed some women to come together and establish yet another area of activity they could call their own.

Church attendance was almost exclusively feminine; most accounts agree that less than ten percent of attendants to Havana's thirty-odd churches were male and that most of the men seemed to be more interested in the devout *Habaneras* than in either mass or the saints that lined the naves and side chapels.[65] Julia Woodruff commented in her travelogue that she "could count on the fingers of one hand, all the males that [she] had seen, during [her] whole stay in Cuba, engaged in any voluntary act of devotion."[66] Another observer remarked that men appeared to have "no religion at all."[67]

Male "worshippers" for the most part remained strategically positioned either behind the interior columns or preferably just outside the doors where they could catch "a glimpse of the pretty ankles ascending the steps of the volantes."[68] According to one account, their actions and smiles showed that they were "neither believers, nor ashamed of their unbelief."[69] Another chronicler recounted that many of the men "merely come within the door, drop one knee, with their faces turned toward the principal altar, and utter a short, but scarcely audible prayer."[70] Church authorities denounced the irreverent and disrespectful crowds of young men who habitually gathered outside the city's churches to see and talk to the young women before and after mass.[71]

Despite the fact that church ceremonies were led by male priests, the church was, indeed, a woman's domain. There they were not only the overwhelming majority, but by most accounts they ran the show and were able to create spaces for themselves, establish communication networks, and move about freely. The fact that Havana churches had no pews facilitated mobility, as *Habaneras* were able to set up camp almost anywhere within the church. Those who could afford it were usually accompanied by servants of color who carried pieces of carpet and folding chairs for their mistresses' comfort and convenience.[72] White women attended church dressed in black, their heads covered with black mantillas, while black and mulatto women wore white.[73]

Good Friday was the one day of the year when the church spilled over to the streets; interestingly, it was also the only day when Havana's "ladies" were allowed to go out and walk in the streets. As one traveler put it, it was the "only day of the year when dainty Havanese [*sic*] female feet press the pavements."[74] Referring to Holy Week in Matanzas, Woodruff wrote: "On this occasion alone, of the whole year, the entire population may be seen in the streets and on foot, without exception of class, color, sex, or age."[75] Women from the United States and England sojourning or residing in Havana, most of them Protestant, could find little comfort in the spaces that church ceremonies provided for Cuban women.

Several nineteenth-century travelers' accounts written by men include detailed, and somewhat lusty, descriptions of churchgoers of the opposite sex "whose graceful, voluptuous figures, bent down before their shrines."[76] One visitor referred to the sight of a church filled with "pretty women" as a "source of amusement"; another described it as "a beautiful sight": "their necks and arms bare, and often resplendent with jewels; their dark glossy hair ornamented with pearls or flowers, and their exquisitely wrought fans, inlaid with gold and precious stones, 'glittering in their hands like so many butterflies'."[77] Another traveler described female behavior inside the church as irreverent and somewhat disorderly:

> She kneels, but in the course of a few minutes sits. An ill-bred person would say, squats. Tired with the course of the ceremonial, she at length reclines. In the middle of the service the floor is strewn with a choice assortment of ladies' dress-goods with the ladies inside of them. At certain places in the ceremonial, it is necessary for everybody to place themselves again in a kneeling posture, and there is a general struggle to attain this end. To see two or three hundred women scrambling at once from a reclining to a kneeling position, has a tendency for the moment to destroy the solemn feeling one should have under the circumstances.[78]

Yet another observer described church as a rendezvous place of "gayety [*sic*], and flirtation" where women communicated using the "telegraphic fan."[79]

Yet another place where white *Habaneras* were able to become visible were the special upper boxes at the city's theaters which were designated for single women. There they sat "in full dress, décolletées, without hats."[80] Although highly visible, the box sections were separated by gates and zealously guarded by older women and armed guards. Along with the glances and fan signals, hand written notes passed back and forth between the balconies and the exclusively male pit section.[81] Here again, Havana's women settled for being out of reach but not out of sight.

Descriptions of *Habaneras*, of course, varied from observer to observer, but most agreed on their "exotic beauty," "endearing charm," and "dignified grace."[82] Most descriptions highlighted the *Habaneras'* lustrous dark eyes that "swim in melting lustre, and sparkle in expressive glances" and abundant jet black hair, "well formed," "full developed," "magnificent busts," which seem "to expand from year to year," and feet so tiny that "they do not afford a sufficient support to the body."[83] Of the much celebrated *Habaneras'* feet one visitor said that they were so small that it appeared they were "evidently never intended by nature to walk on."[84]

Foreign visitors and residents alike commented on the fleeting nature of female beauty in Havana. Women aged twelve to fourteen were considered marriageable, those in their late teens and early twenties in their prime, and those thirty or older ranked as "old."[85] The fleeting beauty of the *Habaneras* was referred to by contemporaries as the "beauty of the devil," lasting only as long as "the freshness of youth."[86] At least some women accepted these notions as exemplified by a fifteen-year-old's confession to a foreign visitor of "her sorrow at getting so old."[87]

A chart published in a newspaper in neighboring Puerto Rico with an obviously humorous intention, reveals the very real low estimation for maturing and aging women prevailing in the Hispanic Caribbean. While women between the ages of twenty and thirty were described as turtledoves and doves, those in their thirties, forties, and fifties were equated to parrots, owls, and frigid birds ("ave frías"), respectively. Those over sixty were simply dismissed as "neither birds, nor women, nor anything." The clear message in these associations is that after the age of thirty the qualities of tenderness, grace, and shapely bodies gave way to new characteristics marked by obnoxiousness, obesity, disfigurement, and frigidity. Beyond the age of sixty, for all practical purposes, women did not exist. Men, on the other hand, according to the chart, which was obviously produced by a man for a predominantly masculine readership, gained desirable qualities with age and began to develop negative traits such as those associated with turkeys and ostriches only after the age of sixty; that was, at twice the age at which women metamorphosed from doves to parrots.[88]

Most contemporary accounts presented rather unflattering portraits of the *Habaneras'* intellectual capacities and aspirations. One traveler observed that Cuban women were civilized only in appearance and that even the very rich were illiterate.[89] Another contemporary noted that they had "no intellectual resort."[90] A woman traveler quizzed several *Habaneras* and concluded that they were quite ignorant about matters that she deemed essential knowledge.[91] A well-traveled foreign visitor who had mostly good things to say about Cuba and its people, said that during his sojourn on the island he "rarely ever saw a lady sitting quietly reading a book."[92] It is significant to note that the two best-known Cuban women writers of the nineteenth century, Gertrudis Gómez de Avellaneda and the countess of Merlín, developed as authors not in Cuba but in Spain and France, respectively. One attempt by Gómez de Avellaneda to establish a women's magazine in Havana failed after the publication of only twelve biweekly issues of *Álbum Cubano de lo Bueno y lo Bello*.[93]

Nineteenth-century Habaneras were usually described as vain and overtly coquettish beings who wasted their time gossiping, sitting in rocking chairs, dancing, playing cards, and engaging in frivolous conversations and activities.[94] White Cuban women were also fond of wearing excessive amounts of whitening make-up (*cascarilla*), a paste made of pulverized egg shells mixed with egg whites which produced a clown-like effect meant to contrast sharply with dark eyes and hair. A credible source estimates that 40,000 pounds of *cascarilla* were produced annually in the island.[95] One female visitor said that in Matanzas – not coincidentally a highly racially stratified region of the island – women were particularly fond of *cascarilla*, which they abused "to a degree that is positively ghastly."[96]

The marked emphasis on make up, fine clothing, elaborate coiffures – some of which included live fireflies – and other attention-catching aspects of the Habaneras' female material culture and behavior, paralleled those of other slave-based societies.[97] The ideal of the southern belle in the American South emerged under demographic and social circumstances similar to those of nineteenth-century Cuba. In both Cuba and the American South white women of the upper classes struggled to look their best as they faced the competition of women of color for the attention of white men. Slavery as an institution ultimately based on force made women of color, as a caste, especially vulnerable to the sexual desires of those belonging, *de facto* or potentially, to the master class. In the other direction, as demonstrated by Martínez-Alier's research on Cuba, not a few black or mulatto women saw sexual liaisons with white men, even outside of marriage, as means of upward social mobility for themselves and their children.[98] Whatever the motivation, liaisons between white men and black and mulatto women were not uncommon in nineteenth-century Cuba. The opposite was of course socially unacceptable and quite rare.

Law and custom severely limited the educational options of *Habaneras* of all races.[99] According to statistics from the 1830s, the proportion of white males of school age receiving an education was twice that for white females. By midcentury there were 238 boys in school for every 100 girls. Access to education was also disproportionately higher for boys of color than for girls of color; within this group there were two and a half times as many boys in school as there were girls.[100] Educational opportunities for women were also of lesser quality, focused on domestic and manual crafts, such as sewing and embroidery, and included considerably less contact hours: while boys had five to six daily hours of instruction, girls received only one.[101] Like most aspects of Cuban life, education was also segregated. As one observer noted, it was a means to avoid mischief for the girls' own sake. "The Spanish mind is firmly fixed in the idea," he concluded, "that when the male and female of the human species are thrown together, there is sure to be mischief of some kind concocted."[102] Many families preferred to hire tutors to instruct their daughters in the safety of their homes rather than send them to school in Cuba or abroad. Colonial education was thus yet another area in which discrimination and segregation were justified in terms of protection for women, but ended up limiting their options and full integration into society.

Higher education for women was, to be sure, out of the question. Julia Ward Howe was scandalized by the fact that in Cuba women were not allowed to attend the university or most public places of entertainment, nor to engage in intellectual activities of any sort. When she and a group of friends inquired about visiting the University of Havana, the professor in charge, through an intermediary, responded that he "would be happy to show the establishment to the ladies on Sunday" when the all-male student body would be gone. When not satisfied with the answer they asked "Why?," the forthcoming response was: "For your own sake."[103] According to another contemporary North American observer, Cuban women knew nothing about "côöperative kitchens, or the Sorosis, or [their] inalienable right to serve on committees, edit newspapers, and lecture." "There never was a woman's rights' convention in this happy land," he continued, "or a Dorcas society, or even a crusade."[104]

In summation, of all the major cities in the West Havana placed the most strict social restrictions on the female portion of its population. A combination of several demographic, social, and cultural factors explain why white Habaneras faced seclusion, segregation, and other restrictions to a higher extent than women elsewhere in the hemisphere. The places in which Habaneras could move about freely, express themselves, and retain a semblance of visibility were few: behind the barred windows of their homes, in *volantas*, inside churches, at the opera boxes. In such settings they strove to establish communication with one another and with the opposite sex. Foreign observers, whether female or male, were struck by the social restrictions that women in Cuba endured and were amused by their creative responses to those restrictions. They failed, however, to understand both the restrictions and the responses in their broader contexts of slavery, patriarchy, colonialism, and neocolonialism. Still, that did not keep them from criticizing Cuba's social arrangements and from prescribing "better" ways of doing things. Yet these would not have worked in the racially stratified context of Havana, where the restrictions on women of the ruling class served as a constant a visual reminder of the separation between elite white society and the people of color they ruled.

9

Imperial Eyes, Gendered Views: Concepción Gimeno Re-writes the Aztecs at the End of the Nineteenth Century

Carmen Ramos-Escandon[1]

On the night of May 6, 1890, an upper-class Spanish woman, by the name of Concepción Gimeno de Flaquer, addressed the social and intellectual elite of the Madrid society at the Ateneo de Madrid: the topic of her speech – Mexican indigenous cultures. In some respects, this was an unusual occurrence: although Spain had a strong literary tradition focusing on Mexico, this had dealt with government administration or the conquest itself, but Gimeno spoke about the history of Aztec culture and society. Further, it was out of the ordinary for a woman to give such a lecture at the Ateneo, a stronghold of local tradition and thus patriarchal in character. Yet it was also fitting that Gimeno gave her lecture to this group, for it had a rich legacy as a venue for intellectual and artistic events, and had inspired the creation of similar societies by Spaniards residing in the former colonies.[2] Gimeno, like these clubs, served as a cultural interpreter, a contact zone where information and ideas about Spain and the Americas was exchanged.[3]

Gimeno's lecture before this gathering and her topic choice thus suggest the complex relationship between colonial discourse and feminism. Yet it would be a mistake to classify Concepción Gimeno as simply another imperialistic Spanish observer, for her feminist literary background and lengthy residence in Mexico would give her a unique view of native Americans and their history. The theme of her speech revealed both her rebelliousness against traditional travel literature and her fascination with the culture of the country in which she had resided for so long.[4] Hers is a case of conquered conqueror, a unique voice in which a fairly traditional woman uses feminism to partially overcome her colonial viewpoint.[5] By doing so she reveals that gender plays a definite role in the production of colonial discourse and the complex relationship between writer and "Other," for her fascination with Aztec society betrays her imperialist perspective.[6]

Gimeno's road to the Ateneo de Madrid began some forty years earlier, and from her first appearance as an author, she showed an intellectual interest in feminism. According to the scant information about her youth, she was born in Aragon, in the small city of Alcariz, Teruel in either 1850 or 1852, and attended grammar school in the town of Zaragoza.[7] At age nineteen she began her writing career with an article entitled "To the Detractors of the Fair Sex" ("A los impugnadores del bello sexo").[8] In it, Gimeno used sound arguments about the need for men to acknowledge the newly improved role of women, and encouraged readers to recognize women's intellectual achievements as well as their educational needs (an argument that recurred in many publications throughout her life). Subsequently she moved to Madrid and was able to complete her studies by educating herself through broadly-based reading and exposure to the most important writers and cultural circles of the day.

In Madrid during the late 1860s under the reign of Isabel II, upper-class women were often active in charitable and educational organizations such as the Junta de Damas de Honor y Merito de la Sociedad Económica Matritense de Amigos del País.[9] Although there is no evidence that Gimeno was a member of this society, she probably knew about these female-sponsored organizations which promoted culture for young girls. She was a frequent participant in a less likely feminine venture, the culture-oriented gatherings, or *tertulias*, where the intellectuals of the day discussed, read, and commented on each other's work, and the relevant cultural and political issues of the day.[10] In these "*tertulias* madrileñas," Gimeno was introduced to the most influential literary and intellectual Madrid circles, where most of the participants were older men of established reputation. By attending the *tertulias*, Gimeno did not conform to the expected intellectual pattern of femininity of her day, yet in all other aspects of her life, she carefully conformed to the expected values, conduct, attitudes, and physical appearance which were expected of a "proper lady." In an 1873 photograph included in her first book, she appears as a slim brunette with long, carefully braided hair with plenty of hair ornaments. Her young features show the expression of focus and concentration of an intellectually oriented woman.

Her beauty, probably as much as her brains and social connections, gained her access to the De la Torre *tertulia*, where writers such as Juan Valera and Carolina Coronado were regular participants. Coronado, well known for aiding and encouraging young women writers, invited her to poetry readings and recitals of her own work, along with such female writers as Patrocinio de Biedman, Faustina Saez de Melgar, Josefa Pujol de Collado, and Sofia Tartilán. Gimeno's association with female writers' circles lasted throughout her life. However, unlike her *tertulia* colleagues, Gimeno wrote poetry only occasionally, as she was far more interested in journalism, essay writing, and novel-length fiction.

Gimeno's first novel, *Victorina o el heroismo del corazón*, published serially in a Madrid newspaper, *La Epoca*,[11] is a typical romantic saga of a woman trapped between duty and her own feelings.[12] Victorina, the heroine, suspects that her husband is in love with a younger woman, and in turn, he accuses her of infidelity to mask his own guilty feelings. Against this background, Victorina's moral character is put to the test by her desire for a younger man, and in the end, she cannot make a choice that would allow her to be both happy and morally stronger. In consequence, she decides to put an end to her moral dilemma by entering a convent, thus allowing religious dictates and the established social order to prevail over her own feelings.

The narration builds the reader's interest by creating critical situations in which the heroine has to solve the moral problem of being caught between desire and duty. This means that Gimeno's main female character represents women who were responsible for maintaining social order and moral standards. While Gimeno draws on the love triangle theme which had appeared in some Golden Age Spanish literature authors such as Zayas Enriquez and Lope de Vega, Victorina's moral paradox reflects a common theme in Victorian morality: the inner struggle between duty and desire.[13] While some have read Victorina's character as a triumph of will over passion and ultimately as a woman's assertion of her own life, a more contemporary reading suggests that Gimeno is presenting a heroine much like herself who embodies the values of a prescribed femininity which characterized late nineteenth-century Hispanic society on both sides of the Atlantic. The contradictions between the social and moral prescriptions of her day and her own desires ultimately destroyed Victorina, who embodies the social restrictions on female conduct. The novel constructs women as the weaker sex who mistrust their own feelings. In this stereotype of a woman's character, females needed a strong supportive system of rigidly enforced values which would guarantee that they would not fall victim to their own emotions and desire.

By identifying her female characters with a rigid sense of duty and moral righteousness, as well as a strong respect for appearances and the need to follow social rules, Gimeno, as an author, also becomes a supporter and conveyer as well as the subject of some of the most traditional values of a colonized society: obedience, submission, and endurance. The contradiction in her writings between this ideology and her developing feminist consciousness became increasingly apparent in later articles, where she supports initiative, autonomy, and rebelliousness among indigenous women.[14]

On a personal basis, her own conduct often reflected a compliant attitude towards society's mores. Throughout her career she consistently embraced traditional values in her private life and in her writings. This might have been for expediency's sake, for she was able to win recognition as a lecturer, essayist, writer, and magazine publisher among both the Mexican and Spanish intellectual elites. Surprisingly, recognition came even from the male literary establishment and is well documented by the fact that she was one of the very few women who gained the right to address the conventional audience of male writers and intellectuals at the Ateneo de Madrid. The only woman previously to have gained such recognition was Emilia Pardo Bazan, whose role as creative author and critic is echoed by Gimeno's career, even if Pardo Bazan had both more talent and greater recognition in her day.[15]

However, Gimeno's role as a promoter of Hispanic culture and defender of patriarchal traditions in her society is overshadowed by the role she had as cultural entrepreneur. Not only did she found her own newspaper in 1869 in Spain, but as an active member of the literary circles of Madrid, she received literary support from the titled and most influential classes of Spain and Mexico. Founder and editor of her own magazine *La Ilustración de la Mujer*, she established contact with some of the most renowned male writers of her day and built a network of connections that included, among others, the well-known writer Juan Valera who, during Gimeno's later residence in Mexico, described her as a bridge between the close yet divergent cultures of Mexico and Spain.

Gimeno arrived in Mexico around 1880 as the wife of a Catalonian journalist and businessman, Francisco de Paula Flaquer. During her long residence there, she became editor and proprietor of one of the first and most widely read Mexican feminist newspapers in the nineteenth century, *El Album de la Mujer* (1880–93). For the decade following her arrival, Concepción Gimeno became deeply acquainted with Mexico and its people, far beyond the fleeting impressions of most travel writers, and mixed socially with the Mexican political and cultural elite. Yet her books and newspaper articles were perceived by Spaniards as only the observations of an experienced traveler whose work was no more than an exotic adventure. In the early 1890s she returned to Madrid as a visitor, and was ready to resume her role as a cultural emissary, but this time interpreting Mexican culture to the Spanish. This was reflected in her lecture at the Ateneo de Madrid on the eve of the fourth centennial commemoration in 1890 on Mexican indigenous cultures before the arrival of the Spanish.

By lecturing at the Ateneo de Madrid that night – and again in 1895 – Gimeno broke the traditional boundaries that confined women to the domestic sphere, and especially the taboo against women as public speakers.[16] Furthermore she was breeching the divide between the public and private in several ways. Her appearance as a public speaker was not only an intrusion into the traditional space of men, but the subject of her address transcended the traditional themes of women's travel writing (such as domesticity and everyday life).[17] Gimeno astonished her audience by taking a bold, original perspective, broadly different from the traditional unflattering viewpoint of Mexicans that was prevalent among Spanish intellectuals and travelers at the time, and this boldness attracted the notice of Madrid's most influential newspapers. In her description of old Mexican culture, Gimeno portrayed the Aztecs as a highly civilized society and explained their custom of human sacrifice as a religious ceremony that had more to do with devotion than with primitive savagery. While this perspective coincides with present-day anthropologists' views, it was much too innovative and advanced for Spanish public opinion a century ago.[18]

Gimeno also took a highly unusual feminist approach by focusing on the role of women in ancient civilizations, comparing Mexican mythical figures with those of ancient Greece. For instance, she compares the mythical figure of the Aztec goddess Coatlicue, with the Greek deity Hecate, as described in Hesiod's works. She stresses the motherly role of both figures, but emphasizes her belief in the superiority of the Aztec society by its acceptance of Coatlicue as a woman who participated in public life. In this myth, Coatlicue (the earth mother) while sweeping her house finds a bird feather. This pierces her chest and magically makes her pregnant. Being a widow, her pregnancy raises the suspicion of her elder daughter Cocyolchautli (the moon), who doubts that her mother is really pregnant. When the time of birth arrives, the new-born Huitchilopochlti (the sun) appears as an adult warrior who, defending her mother, kills his sister and throws her body to the sky.[19]

While this origins myth has been interpreted by modern scholars as a power struggle between an agriculture-based religious system and a war-oriented one, such as that which dominated in late fifteenth century Aztec society, Gimeno emphasizes the cross-gender alliance between Huitchilopochtli and his mother, Coatlicue, arguing that the two appear as equals. For the Aztec myth of the mother earth and the sun served her purpose of emphasizing the importance of women in that society by focusing on their mythic role.[20] Gimeno believed that the role of mothers in Aztec society was far more important than among the ancient Greeks. She also asserted that Aztec society gave women a far more important status and role than in Western civilization.

Gimeno's analysis of Malintzin, the guide and lover of Cortes, likewise underlines her point about the importance of women in the Aztec society.[21] However, Gimeno goes even further in her feminist interpretation, acknowledging Malintzin's superior intelligence and exceptional talent as an interpreter. Yet in keeping with colonial ideology, she also transforms Malintzin into an instrument of the Catholic mission by making her into an extraordinary figure whose remarkable traits embody the masculine conquistador ideal of converting the indigenous Aztecs to Catholicism. Gimeno reinterprets Malintzin's personality not just as a new convert, but a devoted, fervent Catholic believer who wants to spiritually conquer her fellow Indians to rescue them from religious error.[22]

Gimeno's Malintzin is not only colonized through her identification with the male conquistadors' goal of religious domination, but also in her physical description. Gimeno portrays her more like a Greek deity than an Aztec woman: "She was tall, with big bright eyes, white teeth and small feet. Slim, arrogantly handsome, and dressed in a white tunic embroidered with colors, her long, shiny hair adorned with pearls and corals made her like a poetic mermaid who abandons her emerald palace under the sea."[23] Gimeno had published an idealized portrait of Malintzin on the front page of the 11 September 1881 issue of *El Album de la Mujer*, showing her with handsome European features, and wearing a head piece in the shape of a vestal or an ancient Greek deity. Gimeno further occidentalizes Malintizin by usually referring to her by her Spanish name, Doña Marina; and in typical romantic fashion, explains Malintzin's role as translator and strategist for Cortes by her love for him. For Gimeno, Malintzin became a passionate heroine, not much different from the characters in her novels.

As a well-to-do Spanish woman married to a Catalonian businessman, Gimeno fits into the pattern of a metropolitan imperialist intellectual, who is also well connected and supported in Mexican political circles.[24] In her public address, however, she added distinctly different elements. By focusing on women and specifically on the Spanish conqueror's lover, Gimeno re-reads Aztec civilization, and its female representative, Malintzin, becomes a character in an fictitious tale of love and power. In interpreting the Spanish conquest as a love story, she introduces a new narrative, one in which adventure and the exotic nature of Mexico predominate. This perspective on the Spanish conquest ignores the brutality of imperialism, and fits well with the late nineteenth-century Spanish vision of Latin American societies as marginalized border cultures, a remote world existing beyond the boundaries of reason and civilization.[25] Gimeno's discourse thus echoes that of the colonizer, for she is looking at Aztec culture as an alien, peripheral reality that borders on the unattainable. However, her feminist ideology somewhat overcomes the imperialistic Spanish perspective, for she depicts Malintzin as an Aztec woman who embodies the initiative, self-assertiveness, and autonomy that Gimeno advocates for all women. Her views are thus colored by concern for her fellow women, and in spite of nationalistic views, she succeeds in forging a transatlantic dual perspective, in which each one observing the other also becomes a way for each to look into his or her own self, as in a two-way mirror.

Part III

Colonialism in Asia and Africa

10

The Indian Other: Reactions of Two Anglo-Indian Women Travel Writers, Eliza Fay and A.U.[1]

Nupur Chaudhuri

As European imperialism expanded in the eighteenth and nineteenth centuries, the domestic public's understanding of foreign and seemingly exotic colonies was shaped primarily by published descriptive accounts. Yet while travel purported to provide an accurate description of these distant lands and their peoples, it also reflected the ideas, prejudices, and beliefs of the traveler. As several essays in the present volume suggest,[2] travel writers thus served as interpreters of culture and points of contact between Europeans and the "Other," and scholars have suggested that the gender of the author can and does shape the way he or she views foreign cultures. Shirley Foster has maintained that the female genre of writing travel narratives is different from that of males.[3] Gender-based connotations have been drawn in several recent works, such as those of Susan Blake, Mary Louise Pratt, Sarah Mills, Susan Morgan, and Inderpal Grewal, among many others, who have analyzed colonial travel narratives primarily written by European women.[4] Pratt's *Imperial Eyes* has found that scientific knowledge about flora and fauna of colonized countries is a common theme in the travel literature by women. Mills has claimed that knowledge contained in a travel literature within an imperial context is definitely gendered and that women's travel narratives should be a part of colonial discourse. Morgan has analyzed the complex relationships between gender, imperialism, and geographical locations. Grewal established a linkage between the culture of travel on social divisions in Britain and India and the impact of imperialism on travel. In her discussion of Mary Hall's travel, Blake has incorporated an analysis of class differences.

My essay is part of these ongoing scholarly studies on gendered experiences and expressions of imperialism reflected in travel literature. It relates to travel narratives of two British women, Mrs. Eliza Fay and A.U., who disseminated their knowledge about India and its inhabitants to British readers in search of information about India. These two women visited India nearly a century apart under very different circumstances, and both explained the role and position of Indian women for their British readers. An analysis of their writings shows that each reflected the colonial *mentalité* of her era, and thus also represent different stages in British imperialism, where the colonial power defined and justified itself through its portrayal of the native "Other." Thus, although both Fay and A.U. represented and reconstructed Indians and Indian culture for their British readers from a perspective of superiority emerging from Britain's increasing political domination of India during the eighteenth and nineteenth centuries, their ultimate judgments about Indian women contain sufficient differences to be revealing about colonial attitudes. By emphasizing the "difference" and belittling the "Other," Fay and A.U. defined for themselves – and other British women – a role in the enterprise of empire-building. Finally, I examine these two authors' writings to see if Pratt's concept of "contact zones" where "the relations among colonizers and colonized, or travelers and 'travelees,' not in terms of separateness or apartheid, but in terms of copresence, interaction, interlocking understandings and practices, often within radically asymmetrical relations of power" can be applied to their writings.[5]

The experiences of Mrs. Eliza Fay and A.U. were separated by nearly a century of colonial rule. Nevertheless, their reflections on Indian women and India were very similar. This relatively unchanging portrayal of the subjects of the British empire is evident in their travel narratives, making the two accounts a valuable tool in further understanding the complex relationships between gender and imperialism. Both authors constructed the texts of their travel accounts on India by often combining their travel experiences and observations with derogatory remarks about Indian women. They put the socio-cultural values of the Indians in opposition to the values of the British reading public, which emphasized their own civility as British. Thus, although it is impossible to say how many people actually read the works of Fay and A.U., it is safe to say that their works reflect the tastes and inclinations of at least a portion of the British reading public.

Eliza Fay was born in mid-eighteenth-century England, and from her letters to her family members, we learn that at the age of twenty-three she married Antony Fay. Like Concepción Gimeno de Flaquer, the central figure of Carmen Ramos-Escandon's essay in this volume, Fay accompanied her husband abroad. He had been called to the Bar at Lincoln's Inn in 1779, and left England with Eliza to practice at the Supreme Court of Calcutta, where he was admitted as an advocate in June 1780. The Fays took up residence in Calcutta for economic reasons, but Antony Fay's career failed to prosper because of his constant opposition to local British authorities, his financial improvidence, and his disregard for social obligations. Although Eliza Fay stood by her husband throughout these difficulties, in July 1781, she learned of "a circumstance . . . [that] determined me no longer to bind my destiny with that of a man who could thus set at defiance all ties divine and human."[6] Although she is not more specific, E.M. Forster's introduction to her letters suggests that this circumstance was probably the fact that Antony Fay had fathered an illegitimate child.[7] Eliza Fay insisted upon a legal separation drawn up by local attorneys, which, in her words, rendered her "wholly independent of Mr. [Fay's] authority, with power, to make a will &c. in short conceived in the strongest terms our language could supply."[8] Since marital separation among people of the professional classes was relatively uncommon in late eighteenth-century Britain and carried with it the potential of social stigma, this step suggests that Eliza Fay was ready to challenge traditional values by her refusal to accept the dictum of a patriarchal society.[9] In this respect, she is quite different from Concepción Gimeno, who in her personal life remained obedient to Spanish societal rules, and in her novels depicted heroines whose obligations to their husbands superseded all other considerations, including personal happiness.[10] Although Eliza Fay returned to Britain in 1782, she traveled to and from Calcutta three more times between 1784 and 1815, and died there in 1816.[11]

When Fay first went to India in 1779, traveling there from Britain took anything from less than two months to more than six months; in this age of sailing ships, bad weather could substantially lengthen a journey that entailed sailing around Africa. As Rashna B. Singh points out in her study of British fiction on India, "The decision to go to India [in the late eighteenth century] was practically a self-imposed sentence of exile."[12] Because of this long and difficult journey until the mid-nineteenth century, only a handful of British women traveled to India, which made her perspective on India and Indian women relatively unique.[13]

When the Fays arrived in Calcutta, the government of the province of Bengal was technically part of the Mogul Empire but was actually under the control of the East India Company. In 1773, the British Parliament had passed a "Regulating Act" which created a Supreme Council at Calcutta, with a Governor General and four councilors and a Supreme Court of Judicature with a Chief Justice and three other judges. The Governor-General in Council could control the Presidencies of Bombay and Madras. This Act introduced British parliamentary supervision over the East India Company and gave the British a sense of imperial responsibility and self-consciousness.[14]

Eliza Fay hoped that Calcutta would provide an opportunity for economic advancement for her husband, and in this, she clearly reflected the ideas of many who saw a career in India as a guarantee of wealth.[15] She wrote from Calcutta to her friends at home on May 22, 1780: "I may now indeed call for your congratulations since after an eventful period of twelve months and eighteen days, I have at length reached the place for which I have so long sighed, to which I have looked with innumerable rational expectations of future prosperity and comfort."[16] Fay's letter is a typical acknowledgement of the ways India offered late eighteenth-century British subjects opportunities for jobs with security for life.

Yet her first views of India must have served to remind her that she was clearly in a foreign and alien environment. After being forcibly removed from their ship, they were marched several miles to the town square of Calicut in the pouring rain. According to Fay, they were "surrounded by all the mob of Calicut, who seemed to take pleasure in beholding the distress of white people, those constant objects of their envy and detestation."[17] They were imprisoned by local Indian authorities at Calicut during the first months after their arrival in extremely uncomfortable conditions. However, they eventually gained their freedom, journeyed to Madras and then to Calcutta.

Fay discovered that the English community was relatively small, and the city itself bore little resemblance to any European urban center, as Calcutta in 1780 consisted mainly of wharves, fishing boats, weaving villages, and Hindu holy places.[18] Not surprisingly, in view of the separateness she must have felt from her surroundings, she presented herself in her letters as objective and distant from her subject matters – the Indians – by making it clear that she collected much of her information from others. For many customs of which she was not a direct observer, her *banian* (secretary/overseer), Dattaram Chukerbutty, a Bengali Brahmin, seemed to be Eliza Fay's source of information regarding religious and social customs of the Bengalis, which she then extended to all Indians. She recorded that Hindu women, whom she referred to as "ladies," are "never seen abroad." In their infrequent outings, they traveled in carriages that were covered with curtains. Fay notes that on one rare occasion, she saw two of these women who were "apparently very beautiful," but she added that it was difficult to judge whether they really were attractive since "they use so much art . . . it is difficult to judge what claim they *really* have to that appellation." Fay concluded that these women spend all their time adorning their persons and making themselves "completely fascinating," due to prevailing Hindu marriage practices, particularly plural marriage which made it necessary to secure the affections of their husbands and to counteract plans of another wife.[19]

Fay described the rituals of marriage of an Bengali/Indian woman, having had the opportunity to observe a marriage procession. She was told by her informant that the bride and bridegroom sat in the same enclosed palanquin, which was splendidly ornamented. Dressed in the most superb manner, all the relations on both sides accompanied the bride and bridegroom. Some were on horseback, some in palanquins, and several on elephants with bands of dancing girls and musicians preceding them. Fay recorded that there were much feasting and fireworks at the house of the Hindu bride's father, although she took pains to report that no Europeans were present at this wedding. To her sister Fay wrote:

> This wedding was of a nature by no means uncommon here; a rich man had an only daughter, and he bargained to dispose of her, or rather to take for her a husband out of a poor man's family, but of his own *Caste*; for this is indispensable. In this case the bridegroom is brought home to his father-in-law's house and becomes a member of the family; so that although the law prohibits a man from giving a dowry with his daughter, yet you see he

> does it in effect, since he gives a house to a man who wants one . . . in a few years the old man may die, and the young one having fulfilled the wishes of his parents, and provided for his own wants, may employ some of his female relations to look round among the poorer families of his caste for a pretty girl, whom he will take as a second wife, tho' the first always retains the pre-eminence, and governs the house.[20]

Here, Eliza Fay is recording knowledge about Indian private sphere – an unknown landscape to her correspondents and the British reading public. Fay's descriptions of a foreign societal practice like polygamy and arranged marriages were intended for people at home who would look at these practices as alien to their own culture. Her description of Bengali women/Indian women's segregation also highlighted the difference between the two societies. By emphasizing the difference in cultural functions and social practices between the British and the Indian societies, Fay assigned an alien status or "otherness" to Indian women.

She also included a discussion of the custom of *sati*, whereby Hindu wives immolated themselves on their deceased husbands' funeral pyres.[21] She distances herself and other Europeans from the practice by noting that "I have never had an opportunity of witnessing the various incidental ceremonies, nor have I ever seen any European who had been present at them."[22] She speculates on the origin of this custom,[23] concluding that it has nothing to do with affection within marriage but is instead "a political scheme intended to insure the care and good offices of wives to their husbands, who have not failed in most countries to invent a sufficient number of rules to render the weaker sex totally subservient to their authority." She expanded upon this idea of a sisterhood of oppression shared by all women by humorously suggesting that women everywhere were such slaves to habit that if English custom demanded that a widow burn herself at her husband's death, many women would do so even if they felt no affection for their spouses and had done their utmost to contribute to their discomfort and outright ruin while they were alive.[24]

Yet even while she draws these parallels between women in England and India, she also emphasizes their separateness:

> She who wages war with a naturally petulant temper, who practices a rigid self-denial, endures without complaining the unkindness, infidelity, extravagance, meanness or scorn, of the man to whom she has given a tender and confiding heart, and for whose happiness and well being in life all the powers of her mind are engaged; – is ten times more of a heroine than the slave of bigotry and superstition, who affects to scorn the life demanded of her by the laws of her country or at least the country's custom; and many such we have in England, and I doubt not in India likewise: *so indeed we ought, have we not a religion infinitely more pure than that of India?* [emphasis added][25]

Felicity A. Nussbaum has argued that though Fay degraded *sati* "as an irrational solution to practical oppression and as less heroic than Englishwoman's self-abnegation in the face of loveless or unsatisfying marriage," yet Fay's depiction of it as a protest by Indian women against patriarchy made them similar to the British women.[26] However, I believe that Fay's depiction of *sati* in her narrative presented India as a land of strange and alien practices and Indian women as backward and primitive. This seems to be borne out by her suggestion that Western religion was more "pure" than Hinduism. As she further describes Hindu religious beliefs, she notes that only believers can enter Hindu temples, yet even though she has not seen their interiors, she goes on to state that "the Idols worshipped there are of the very ugliest forms that imagination can conceive; and to whom Pope's description of the heathen deities may, in other respects be strictly applied. 'Gods changeful, partial, passionate unjust. / Whose attributes *are* rage, revenge, or lust'."[27]

The conditions Eliza Fay experienced and described changed dramatically over the following century, as A.U., author of *Overland, Inland and Upland: A Lady's Notes of Personal Observation and Adventure* (1873), discovered when she arrived in Calcutta in about 1870. Part of this change was due to the Indian Rebellion of 1857, which resulted in a dramatic turn in Anglo-British relations. British men, women, and children were massacred during the uprising, and once the rebels were crushed, the administration of India was transferred from the hands of the East India Company to the crown. The British nation felt jubilant over the acquisition of the "jewel in the crown" of the Empire, and in 1876, Queen Victoria was named its Empress. The change in control coincided with a change in the British perception of the indigenous population. Between the period of initial consciousness of the building of an empire and the age of imperial confidence, the Anglo-Indians believed ever more strongly in their own racial superiority and assumed that it was their responsibility to improve the physical fabric and moral fiber of the indigenous society.[28] This belief in racial superiority and imperial responsibility influenced the relationship between the British and Indian women throughout the nineteenth century. British women now openly expressed their disdain for India and the Indians with an intensity that was not apparent in the previous century.[29]

With the opening of the Suez Canal in 1869, traveling from Britain to Calcutta became easier and the number of women going to India increased substantially. Communications between the two countries became frequent. Channels of information increased, dispelling apprehension about daily life in India and encouraging more British women and men to avail themselves of the opportunities in the subcontinent. From her published work we learn that A.U. stayed in Calcutta for some time before she traveled into the interior. Otherwise little can be discovered about her personal life. Perhaps her reluctance to write about herself, or even to provide her full name, can be interpreted as an unwillingness to be exposed to the public as a writer – to claim for herself an identity as a writer. Literary scholars have pointed out that many women writers refused to take center-stage as authors and for this reason used either initials or pseudonyms, or simply wrote anonymously.[30] A.U. could have traveled to India alone and had contact with some missionary families. But her work indicates that she was single.

By A.U.'s time, earlier imperialistic goals had emerged with a perception that it was the duty of British men and women to bring civilization – their term for Western culture – to the Indian subcontinent. This is in noted contrast to the approach of Eliza Fay, who described Indian culture and found fault with it, but never expressed a belief that it was the duty of Europeans to change it. One of the ways empire-builders justified their views was to argue that the Indians were different or strange, which to them was the same as saying that Indians were inferior to the British. Although when A.U. arrived in Calcutta in the early 1870s she came to a well-known place, her writings about Calcutta and the indigenous people emphasize the otherness and the inferiority of the country and the people, and reflected an aura of superiority that was common to the British community.

In direct contrast to Fay, who characterized upper-class and upper-caste Indian/Bengali women as ladies, A.U. wrote: "it seems only a sad mockery to call any of these poor creatures by our noble English name of lady."[31] She argued that in England ladies had some degree of rank, wealth, and education, and that rank implied either personal achievement or generations of refinement and intercourse with civilized society. But in India, according to A.U., only very poor women moved around freely while the movements of women from higher classes were restricted. A.U. further claimed that wealth provided an opportunity for British women to gain an education, to travel in foreign countries, and to cultivate tastes for everything beautiful and refined in nature and art. Thus, although she agreed with Eliza Fay that many of the wealthy Indian women spent their money and time on personal adornment, A.U. drew very different conclusions: "in India, [wealth] can clothe a woman with transparent frippery and load her with jewels, furnish her with the finest tobacco for her hookah, and with abundant attar to sprinkle her garments; but it is powerless to elevate her mind, or to bridge over the immeasurable gulf that separates the mere female from the lady."[32] She claimed that Indian women lacked education and skills in fine arts, and wrote that Indian women were not exposed to books, needlework, or pictures, "except the vilest daubed prints from their most vile mythology, [and had] no accomplishments except cookery, no employment, except smoking and playing with their jewels and their children, no knowledge of the grand past, or the busy present, or the eternal future!"[33]

This emphasis on colonial women's education – or lack of it – was very common throughout the colonized world. Westerners often concluded that indigenous education was insufficient or flawed, and this situation could only be rectified by introducing Western-style education, complete with European notions of "proper" feminine behavior.[34] A.U. acknowledged that she had heard of Hindu ladies who were well versed in Sanskrit literature or mathematics, but she believed that "they are few in number. . . . The vast masses, in every rank, are condemned from childhood to old age, to the purely animal existence described above."[35] Thus, A.U. could project a superior status for British women by painting a negative image about the status of Indian women in their own society.[36]

A.U.'s opinion of Indian women was drawn from her observations of poor Bengali women, with partly clad bodies. A.U.'s disgust with their appearance was apparently not an isolated response, as Bernard S. Cohn made a general observation that during the nineteenth century British travelers to India were shocked to see the nakedness of most of the Indians whom they encountered upon their arrival.[37] A.U. described the Bengali women in bazaars as being "bare armed and bare legged, their heads and bodies loosely wrapped in coarse white calico or muslin, or in the dark blue and crimson stuffs of the country, with rows of bracelets on their dusky arms, and heavy metal ornaments upon their ankles, and generally carrying astride upon their hips black-eyed children, absolutely naked but for the rows of coloured rings circling their sleek brown legs and arms."[38] This nakedness perhaps was an element of A.U.'s depiction of the backwardness and barbarism of the Indian race. The blackness of the skin of Indian women emphasized the "otherness," i.e. the racial inferiority of indigenous women. To the Victorians, any one with a dark complexion, regardless of geographic identity, was classed as black. Binary color division identified the dominant "white" group as superior in legitimizing its rule over the subordinate "black" group in a colonial framework.[39] In the realities of race relations, color contrast matters the most, as we see in Luis Martínez-Fernández's account of nineteenth-century Cuba, where white women used excessive amounts of whitening make-up to contrast sharply with people of color.[40]

A.U. also contrasted English and Indian marriage customs, maintaining that in England many women remained single because marriage would have required resources to set up a separate establishment. But in India, she wrote, owing to the family system, bringing home a wife did not necessarily involve any appreciable expense. She painted a bleak picture for newly married couples, claiming that parents did not have to spend money on children because the children "require no clothes, no nurses, and no furniture, and merely share family provisions of curry, rice and sweetmeats." A.U. clearly thought that people with such backward customs would benefit from British rule, and as evidence, she pointed out that due "to the fearless humanity of Lord William Bentinck the widow-burning [*sati*] was abolished."[41]

For Eliza Fay and A.U. the city of Calcutta and its surrounding areas served as a "contact zone" between two disparate cultures with their positions as colonizer and the colonized. Both narrators described the clothing and complexion of Indian women. They described in minute detail various social and religious practices which presented Indian women and their culture in stark contrast to British women and their culture. Both authors conveyed to their readers their own perceptions of Indian women as a group of uneducated and unskilled individuals. Although Fay more clearly sees India as a land of opportunity for Europeans rather than a savage place in need of rescue, both her account and that of A.U. can be seen as reinforcing the commonly held nineteenth-century notion that British imperialism in India could be justified on the ground of liberating the indigenous women from strange social customs. To Fay and A.U., these faceless, nameless women blended into a landscape that simultaneously helped to create British women's own identity in the imperial scene. Thus they made Indian women a "supporting cast" for the British Empire.[42] Fay's and A.U.'s narratives also lend support to Stephen Greenblat and Deirdre David's assertion that by recording indigenous practices authors have brought particular cultures "into the light for study, discipline, correction, transformation" which expresses "one culture's desire to control and thereby transform another."[43]

However, there are some differences between the writings of Fay and A.U. In the century that elapsed between their visits, the historical reality of India changed. When Fay came to India in the 1780s, the British Parliament was gradually taking over the administration of the country, the number of British women in India at that time was quite low, and the British reading public was not familiar with the city of Calcutta or Indian societal customs and manners. Against this backdrop, Fay wrote her letters about Calcutta/India and Bengalis/Indians to her relatives. Her informant was her Bengali overseer, which suggests that she had at least some contact with Indians. Although in her discussion about the status of Indian women, marriage customs, and widow-burning, Fay emphasized the otherness of the Indians, her tone was milder and less arrogant than that of her compatriot A.U. Although Fay sees her own customs as superior to those of the Indians, she presents herself as an observer only, and one who is willing to see some similarities between European and Indian women.

By the 1870s when A.U. arrived in Calcutta, India was totally under British rule, the number of British women in India had increased and many of the British reading public had heard of Calcutta, which at the time was the capital of India. Against this backdrop, A.U. wrote about Indian society and its culture and traditions by gathering impressions apparently from her own observations and contacts with other *British* inhabitants in India. After reading her narrative, one is left with the impression that she had little contact with the indigenous population. Like Fay, she presented Indians as the "Other," but she was much more presumptuous. For example, Fay did not hesitate to describe upper-class and upper-caste Hindu women as "ladies," while A.U. felt it would be a "mockery" to describe Indian women as such. A.U.'s response to India was summed up on her description of a Bengali bazaar with women, birds, and animals "more like some strange phantasmorgia, the imagery of a hideous magic lantern or a bewildered dream, than like a sober, waking reality."[44] Her writing reinforces the British imperial ideal that non-European colonies had to be "civilized" by their conquerors by being forced to adopt Western customs, traditions, and ideals.

The writings of Fay and A.U. are expressions of various stages of imperial relationships that existed in the colonial environment and reflect the bounds of religious, cultural, and national identities. Fay's narratives provide partial support for Pratt's assertion of "copresence, interaction, interlocking understanding and practices," a claim that is not consonant with A.U.'s writings, which provided a vision "only in terms of their difference to objects and people in Britain."[45] Emphasizing the value differentiation between two cultural groups, A.U.'s narratives on India presented Indians as culturally inferior or different, as "Other," in order to "signify British culture as central, stable, and coherent."[46]

11

Image and Reality: Indian Diaspora Women, Colonial and Post-colonial Discourse on Empowerment and Victimology[1]

Karen A. Ray

During the colonial era in India, the image emerged of the "native woman" as a weak and powerless being who needed male colonial protection to save her from hopeless exploitation. While the development of this view certainly owes much to imperialist aims and agendas, a closer examination suggests that a similar ideology which emphasized women's helplessness was inherent in "native" paternalist ideas. This made the image more invidious because it arose at the beginning of the demand for independence from the British Raj, and was enshrined in the propaganda of the abolitionist movement in early twentieth-century India, which sought to end the system of bonded Indian immigration to other colonies within the tropical British Empire.[2] Abolition was the first great campaign in India to involve all nationalist factions, Hindu and Muslim, moderate and extremist, and, in addition, introduced a new player to the Indian political scene: M.K. Gandhi. Its ideology emphasized the figure of vulnerable, exploited Indian village women, an image so pervasive it still haunts the current campaign to empower Indian women in village *panchayats* (local councils).[3] This representation of abused immigrant women was a powerful one, embodying absolute purity defiled and absolute innocence ravished; at the same time, these women were portrayed as frail creatures seeking protection from emancipated men, rather than wanting to achieve their own political empowerment.

To what extent were these images a reflection of reality? The stories of the women themselves[4] are here juxtaposed with evidence that can inform our post-colonial discourse:

> *Minnu was eighteen years old, married by her family to a boy of nine. She had come with no dowry, her marriage a favor owed by the groom's family to her own. In her new place she was less than a servant, and no one in her own home village wanted her anymore. She looked after her husband, and his younger sisters,*

> *played with him, fed him, tidied for him, was beaten by him, and by her mother-in-law, cried herself to sleep and dreamed of love. . . . A handsome young man appeared in the bazaar. He found her hiding place on the river. He spoke soft words, touched fires, offered escape. How could her life be worse? He knew a place where they could be together, could work honestly, raise a family, together forever.*[5]

But the beautiful young man was a deceiver,[6] a recruiter paid Rs 100 for every woman he could entice away and broker to the British Colonial Civil Servant recruiting for Trinidad. After she makes her mark on paper, which says she is willing to emigrate, he abandons her:

> *Minnu is thrown in a sealed boxcar and shipped to the coolie depot in Calcutta. She is held there, incommunicado – but who would she dare tell? At every stage she is raped, passed from overseer to male recruits. She must clean the chamber pots. She must live on tinned beef, an element so foreign she suffers from chronic illness.*[7]

In an archetypical ending to a sad morality tale, Minnu should have found herself on a coolie plantation in the West Indies, Fiji, or Mauritius. There she would have lived a life of degradation and shame, illustrating the iniquities of the "coolie system" perpetrated by the British Raj, but also of the innocence and naïveté of the unprotected and unguarded female. What in fact happened was that Minnu was rescued from the Coolie Depot at Calcutta by abolitionist Indian men, who had heard of unwilling women being held captive there. She was brought before a justice of the peace to swear out her testimony, but that witness was discounted by both the colonial magistrate and the abolitionists: she had been unfaithful to her in-laws, so it was not totally unexpected that she had met such a fate.

Indentured labor in the nineteenth century was a "new system of slavery," as the first wave of post-colonial historians has demonstrated.[8] When the British reformers, full of justifiable self-congratulation, came to the end of their long struggle to abolish slavery in the British Empire in 1833 they acquiesced in the establishment of a new system of Indian indentured emigration[9] to replace the recently liberated African laborers. Planters and colonial governments looked to the presumably teeming millions of the Indian subcontinent, where the British had only recently become the paramount power, and decided that they had there the perfect solution to the problem of the Empire's labor shortage. Just as English and Irish peasants were given the chance to make new lives in America by working out their passage in bondage to colonists and plantation owners in need of labor,[10] so too could the peasants of India be given a chance to improve their lot by emigrating to Mauritius, the Caribbean colonies, and other places where tropical labor was "unsuited" to the surplus European population.[11]

But, according to the labor recruiters, the problem was that most Indian peasants were more reluctant to emigrate than impoverished Europeans, especially "native" women and "jungley villagers."[12] Seasonal migration was already common in the newly absorbed parts of the British Indian Empire: it was the difference between survival and extinction for both peasant and planter,[13] and when labor migration expanded overseas to the Crown Colonies and Protectorates of the British Empire, it was done without any official notice. In 1830, anticipating the abolition of slavery, planters from Mauritius began sending their recruiters to India for laborers. The British Government of India only came to realize that this emigration was occurring when it was confronted with deciding whether "coolies" were passengers or freight in the reform of shipping regulations.[14] While deciding that each coolie[15] should have accommodation not greatly inferior to that formerly provided for slaves, it also considered which other conditions should be placed on the coolie traffic. By 1837, British Guiana, too, had indented for this handy supply of labor, the cost "not half that of a slave,"[16] but while Mauritius was a two-month voyage by sea from India, the Caribbean colonies were five months away: how could the British Government of India be expected to protect its subjects so far from home? The question of the role of women in the system did not arise immediately because, when recruitment for the Caribbean began in earnest, the planters wanted male labor only and very few women were taken on each coolie ship.

Women might not have been encouraged to emigrate had it not been for Victorian morality, which was offended by two unnatural circumstances inherent in all-male coolie lines on the plantations. Miscegenation was rampant, particularly in British Guiana. And there were even greater "moral dangers" lurking. With only other men for company, as a Parliamentary committee was told, North Indian males (unlike their Tamil counterparts) would almost certainly engage in homosexual practices. Thus, in the new overseas migration pattern, there was not only now more time away from home,[17] and more distance traveled, but the inconvenient factor of sex as well: Indian women seemed an unavoidable adjunct to Indian male labor.[18] Thus the indenture system was structured to ensure that the sexual needs of hard-working young or middle-aged adult males were served with as little trouble and expense as possible. Women were not highly valued as workers, but, of course, had to work for their keep, even as they met those inconvenient male sexual needs and bore the consequent children. Some did housework as maids and nursemaids, but the majority worked as field laborers, many even giving birth in the fields. The system could not work with them, the planters said, but it certainly could not work without them. It was the failure of those who ran the system of indentured emigration to adapt the system to female emigration that ultimately brought the system to its end.[19]

Forced by the morality of the reformed parliament to import working women for working men, the colonies wanted as few women as possible: but how few women could keep how many men from "unnatural acts" and miscegenation? The colonial agents claimed women were difficult to recruit in India. Eventually the British government intervened to preserve moral order: ships could not sail unless they had forty to sixty[20] women for every 100 men on board. This was not adequate for normal family life, of course, and the situation was exacerbated by the tendency of the sirdars and overseers to claim the most desirable women, married or not, for themselves. The women themselves were blamed for this and accused of "barter[ing] their virtue."[21] Even after Indian marriages were recognised by law, both marriage and divorce could be procured for a five-shilling fee in some colonies: a woman could always be sold to the highest bidder.[22] Suicide of either the woman or her abandoned husband often followed,[23] and the suicide rate among Indian emigrants was many times that in India. Some women had been prostitutes before they left India, of course, and many of these continued their occupation in the coolie lines where there was, not surprisingly, a brisk trade. The British Cabinet's representatives were horrified, but they had a solution to all this immorality: compulsory, all-day field work for all women to keep them from the temptations of the coolie lines.[24] Women were exempt for two weeks after giving birth, after which they were expected to take their children to the fields with them. But there were other Minnus, whose testimony tells a different tale. This other

> *Minnu emigrated to Trinidad, with her young man. They both worked under conditions not much better than slavery on a sugar plantation. The first five years paid for the passage to Trinidad, and the next five for passage home or a grant of land. This Minnu and her husband remained in Trinidad and took a grant of land in lieu of passage home. They farmed, became prosperous, opened a shop. Business grew. Their children owned chains of businesses, and if you go to Trinidad today, Minnu's great grand-daughters, are working as lawyers, or drinking tea in the Trinidad Hilton, looking over the Botanical Gardens and chatting about their daughters at McGill or Dartmouth.*[25]

These women clearly were no longer "natives." But what if the young man were a recruiter, a deceiver, and Minnu had not escaped from the coolie depot in Calcutta, how dire would her fate have been? Exploited, assaulted, she might have died in childbirth, or from the overwork required even of mothers as young as fifteen or sixteen. She could have lost her baby, as well as her own life. The absentee plantation owners were certainly not exercised at the prospect. They had, after all, filled their female quota merely by importing her. However, to the men she lived and worked with, the other "natives" of her India, she was a desirable and valuable commodity, if nothing more. Women were in short supply and few were unmarried by choice:

> *If she chose, this Minnu could marry, produce children, work out her contract – or have a husband pay it off. In this version, too, of her tale, she could have descendants on the terrace of the Hilton or studying feminist theory at Mt. Holyoke.*[26]

But any happy resolution of the fate of these women was offensive too, both to most in the imperial hierarchy and to the Indian nationalists. While the emigration system was still in operation, it was already evident that women who emigrated to places like Trinidad were able in many cases to transcend caste and class; they were a vital part of an emerging petty bourgeoisie.[27] However, the abolitionists represented a vaster, more powerful economic and political interest in India.

Opposition to the indentured emigration system did not begin with any concern for the fate of emigrants, male or female. It began as a result of Gandhi's activities in South Africa, when the Indian middle class had become convinced that the reason for the "color bar" was the "coolie stigma" which attached to all Indians in the colonies because most Indian emigrants were indentured workers. Their chief concern was to differentiate themselves from the "coolies" and claim for themselves middle-class status as imperial citizens. However, when Gandhi became convinced that he needed the sheer numerical strength of the indentured emigrants to make his techniques of mass nonviolent resistance work,[28] he studied their concerns, and campaigned to address some of the most egregious problems in the coolie "lines."[29] Although he used women in the mass movement he created and credited the women's march with mobilizing mass worker support, he too regarded the image of the woman as more important than the fate of the women themselves.

The "honor" of Indian women therefore became a convenient symbol of colonial oppression, and thus the image of the exploited native woman was a powerful argument against the system. Although the indenture system gave options to women, they were too ignorant to be trusted with such choices, as Gandhi's lieutenant from South Africa reported to Indian and British audiences in 1909. On the large and well-run estates especially, "the indentured laborers' material welfare [was] far better than it would have been had they remained in India,"[30] he said. Indian women were often induced to go to Natal by "the best recruiting agents . . . famine and want,"[31] but whatever women's material condition, the temptations of coolie lines could prove disastrous to their morals:

> *Viliamma was the very attractive wife of Sornachellan Padiachy. She began a flirtation with the powerful plantation sirdar/overseer, Muthialu. In fact, an affair – which could never have happened in just such a way in India – began. Sornachellan complained to the estate owner. But the owner had a much greater interest in keeping his sirdar happy than returning Viliamma to her rightful owner. Not only did he not get his wife back, but the indignant husband was whipped for complaining and transferred to another estate. This left the sirdar with a clear field, and he quickly*

> *registered his marriage to Viliamma with the Protector of Immigrants.*[32] *Several children later Muthialu and Viliamma's indenture expired, and they left the protection of the first owner for another plantation. At this point their records came before the Protector again and he chose to institute proceedings against Viliamma for bigamy. She was convicted and fined £5, which was paid for her by the still faithful sirdar, with whom she continued to live happily.*

It was "a modern case of David and Bathsheba."[33] This story of a faithless wife provoked newspaper columns of protest in the India of 1910: how could the government collaborate in such immorality?[34] It was an example of the kind of wife-stealing which would have been severely dealt with in India, and the image of the bigamous Viliamma made clear the message that women removed from the structures and strictures of traditional Indian village life were likely to become untrustworthy wantons. This conclusion ignored the fact that Viliamma seems to have ended up as happily as Bathsheba, but perhaps without the subsequent family problems.

While these stories still occupied editorial columns, even more horrific images of degraded Indian women came from Fiji, another colony at the other end of the Empire. Originally, Indian indentured emigration to Fiji began for the most noble of reasons: to save the indigenous population of the islands, people who had voluntarily joined the British Empire to put themselves under the protection of *pax Britannica*. Fiji was not a colony of sturdy pioneers but was one of the earliest instances of almost total control of land by agribusiness: the Colonial Sugar Refining Company. The Company's profits depended largely on cheap Indian labor. The system of absentee ownership from Canada and Australia, and unsupervised overseers, produced the most corrupt imposition of the system of indentured emigration. The exploitation of Indian women by the capitalist structures of the white Commonwealth was so blatant that it was responsible, in a very great measure, for the refusal of Indian leaders to willingly join the imperial structures intended to keep the Empire together after World War I. It was the beginning of the end of the British Empire itself.

Using the colonial civil service structures already in place for the West Indies, the Colonial Sugar Refining Company obtained in India the cheap labor it needed. But as the century turned, the needs of these "colonial" capitalists came up against those of the newly emerging capitalist community in India and this group became the backbone of the abolitionist movement in India.[35] Chief among the abolitionists were the Marwaris, a caste grouping prominent in the ports of Bombay and Calcutta as agents and bankers.[36] Introduced to Gandhi over the abolition issue, they were later to give the Mahatma the financial backing he needed to live in poverty for life. Marwari fortunes had been made in opium and jute, for which cheap labor was important. The colonial recruiters were taking labor for overseas colonial capitalists from the very areas where jute and opium were grown, and where there had been recently a decrease in population.[37] Thus emigration clearly violated both the commercial interests of the Marwaris and their orthodox beliefs against travel over the black water of the ocean, a step which they felt was bound to result in personal pollution. After several years of fruitless opposition to indentured emigration, the Marwaris effectively used the violence done to the image of Indian women to mobilize abolitionist support; they entered and came to control much of the abolitionist discourse. Further, by talking about women and their vital role in preserving India's honor, they succeeded in turning the discourse away from their self-interest in abolishing the emigration system and to the evils inherent in the system itself.

The Marwaris, whatever their motivation, created a hagiography of a Hindu heroine caught up in the indenture system, who, through her own ingenuity and courage, successfully escaped its clutches. The Marwari benevolent association (*Marwari Sahayak Samiti*) had long helped those who escaped from the coolie depots,[38] providing free legal aid and buying them tickets to their homes.[39] In 1913, however, they were thrust into a more active role because of the actions of a Marwari lady of substance, who in her escape exposed the powerlessness of the other, ignorant, village women:

> *A Marwari lady of substance, Lakshmi, left her home in Agra with her six-year-old daughter to inspect a shop she had inherited.[40] She had wired the manager of the shop to meet her at the station, but another man met her and, well informed about her business, claimed to be the manager's assistant.[41] Then Lakshmi was told that her manager had gone to a village called Jamaica where he had expanded the business. The assistant was to take her there, but he said that he was afraid of being arrested for enticing another man's wife, so that the best plan would be for Lakshmi to go before a magistrate and swear that she was going to Jamaica of her own free will. This she did.*
>
> *She was then told that to reach Jamaica she must go via Calcutta. This surprised her, but she was mollified by being installed in a railway carriage with several villagers – ostensibly labourers for the new business – who were told that she was to be their mistress. She entrusted her money and ornaments to the assistant for safekeeping. She then found herself in the coolie depot at Calcutta, where it turned out that the "assistant" was a recruiter and that she and her small daughter were bound for the cane fields of the West Indies. There, she said, "My grief then knew no bounds. After a few days I thought that if I could send word to the Marwaris of Calcutta, they would surely rescue me."*
>
> *Through the bars of the coolie depot, Lakshmi noticed a newsboy who agreed to take a message for her. She sent a message that the Marwaris should come and rescue a kidnaped kinswoman and her daughter.[42]*

The newsboy rushed into the offices of a major Marwari company and gave the message that a lady was imprisoned in the coolie depot. He managed to spread this exciting news throughout the shops and stands of the big bazaar, which buzzed with the news. The local Marwari leaders decided that if a Marwari lady were indeed imprisoned in the coolie depot, active intervention was necessary to free her.[43]

The next day a delegation of businessmen, community leaders, and lawyers went to the coolie depots and found Lakshmi, her daughter, and another woman whom she identified as her servant. The men were horrified at their first glimpse inside a coolie depot, packed with more than a thousand recruits who "began to cry and to entreat us to arrange for their release":

> *One woman said that she had been separated from her child, only six months old. . . . Still another said she was a Brahmin woman and there she was falling from her religion by having to take her meals with low caste men. . . . While all this was going on, some depot officers reprimanded the poor helpless women and forbade them to speak to us and threatened to turn us out of the depots if we spoke to the coolies.*[44]

"An opportunity having presented itself, we then began to take down in pencil, unperceived by the depot officers, the names of those who were not willing to emigrate."[45] They got fourteen names in this way before leaving with Lakshmi, her daughter, and a "maid servant." "Lakshmi's" anonymity was protected, because what had happened to her was a shameful disgrace for her family:

> *I have fallen on evil times and hence these troubles and indignities; but I won't tarnish the names of my people by mentioning them. You have worked hard to secure my discharge; if you will now send me to Jagannath Puri, I will go home from there with our Panda who knows me and in that case the names of my relations will not be affected.*

And so she went.[46] But her courage and ingenuity made her a legend whose story was told again and again from Calcutta to Bombay, in broadsides, by Marwari benevolent association "missionaries" who journeyed up-country to the recruiting districts to tell the story as a warning against the wiles of recruiters, and even in the pages of the imperial journal, the *Round Table*. Even more horrific stories emerged, for the Marwari lady had been clever once again. The "servant" was in reality a Brahmin woman, also kidnapped, whom Lakshmi had rescued through her ruse. The Brahmin woman then told her story:

> *"I was going to Brindaban but finding that all my money had been spent in coming up to Mathura only, I was crying at the railway station, when a Munshi came and asked why I was crying."*[47] [Easy game. What was a Brahmin woman doing away from her family and menfolk?] *She was promised enormous*

> *wages (9 annas a day) if she would go to Jamaica. In Calcutta she learned that the "Munshi" was a recruiter; and that she would have to cross water and dig earth – both actions forbidden to Brahmins. She had to eat with "untouchables." She was told she was no longer a Brahmin but a coolie. Then "several coolies came to me and asked if I would be their mate." She told them her husband was still alive. They told me that my husband was lost to me forever and that I was to choose one from amongst them for a husband. My sorrow was simply boundless. May God bless you and Sethani Lakshmi through whose instrumentality I got my release and have been able to turn my back on the coolie depot."*[48]

Refused further access to the depot by the Colonial Agents, the delegation were able to get release orders only for the fourteen women whose names they had taken down.[49] As the delegation sped to the docks the first steamers were sailing for the West Indies: only five of the fourteen women emigrants were still in the depot. The furious Marwaris resolved to spare no resources to end this hideous system which preyed on the innocence of Indian women. Victorian prose and national outrage combined to make a powerful polemic. They already had a well-organized community charitable organization and they now turned this organization into an anti-indenture machine. They sent young men up-country to the villages to warn people about what the indenture system meant. They published broadsides and posters warning that Fiji and British Guiana were not colonies, but hell: "There you will be sold into the hands of the sahibs."[50]

The Indian abolitionists were particularly unhappy with the reports of the Royal Commissions on indentured emigration, which painted a rosy picture of opportunity for men and independence for women,[51] and in response, they financed an independent inquiry. They commissioned the irrepressible Charlie Andrews and his companion, Willie Pearson, to go to Fiji and file an independent report. The powers that be might dismiss the hysterical women's testimony as egregious exaggeration, but Andrews was a friend of the Viceroy and especially of the Vicereine of India, Lady Hardinge. He would be believed; and he was.[52] He gave additional fuel to the nationalist press in their campaign to save Indian womanhood. In the most "respectable" lines, the ones where the lucky women went, Andrews and Pearson reported, there was a fairly orderly system of organized polyandry, "on the ground that there are fewer fights, murders and suicides under this condition than under general promiscuity."[53] The debate changed in a qualitative way. In the beginning, the image of dishonored "Indian womanhood" had been a tool to spark nascent national pride in the nationalist press.[54] Now, the failure of nationalist Indian men, or even the British government, to protect the deceived and defiled native woman, the soul of "Mother India," became intolerable, an appalling example of the difference between the conquered and the conquering races. Native newspapers, as they were called, compared the way "native" and European women were treated: "Let members of the Government think how they would feel if white women were sent out with white men in proportion of one to three, to serve as indentured labourers under coloured planters. The very idea would cause in them a feeling of indignant revolt; yet why should it be less revolting when the colours are reversed?"[55] In the Calcutta abolitionist movement, emigrants returning from Fiji were questioned about conditions on the plantations and their testimony was publicized. After Lakshmi's rescue, the evidence that received the widest currency was that relating to sexual exploitation of women in the coolie lines. One emigrant told of attending a sale of women on a large estate, some being taken from their husbands. One women went blind from the trauma, another was a young girl who was sold to two men who were intending to share her.[56] The most moving stories were compiled in *My 21 Years in Fiji*,[57] a book allegedly written by a returned indentured emigrant who, according to the government readers, "describes in stirring language the brutal atrocities practiced on Indians in Fiji and the numerous ways in which violence is done to their feelings."[58] To spread the word in villages, a play, *Coolie System, Slavery in the Twentieth Century*,[59] was written, based on the book, and became so popular throughout northern India that the British government banned it.

Newspapers throughout India published excerpts from the book and the play and then rejoiced in the flood of letters they provoked.[60] Governments from the United Provinces to Madras warned that the revelations were bound to arouse intense feelings, "particularly the allegations *in re* the women,"[61] and queried, "What shall we do?"[62] What they did was abolish the coolie system. Although many in the Government of India hated to see the chance to emigrate denied to "their" coolies, the honor of India had to come first. Nationalists asked: "Is the chastity of our mothers and sisters so lightly regarded that it is considered of less significance than the profit of colonial traders [who] fill their coffers with such tainted money?"[63]

The British Government of India was left with little choice. The unanimity of Indian opinion, largely a result of the power of the image of the defenseless and exploited Indian woman, and the political imperatives of keeping domestic peace in India during World War I were potent incentives. When Gandhi threatened to call the first all-India civil disobedience campaign to ensure abolition, the British government capitulated and allowed the Government of India to use its war-time powers to suspend recruitment for indentured emigration without the consent of the colonial planters.[64] It was never resumed; abolition had come. Much misery was avoided, honor was satisfied, and Indian widows perforce were faithful to one man "in life and through death."

What was the result for the "native" women, for whom so much ink had been spilt and whose well-being was declared so important? Their image had been used to score important political points, but what alternative had they now to poverty, bonded labor in India, or perpetual widowhood? In "saving" Indian womanhood, whose honor was being assuaged? Nupur Chaudhuri[65] has emphasized the "creation" of Indian women as a background to the

British Raj, and this was especially important as the diaspora spread these "helpless" women throughout the Empire. If conflicts over the paternalistic nature of the imperial apparatus were egregious in the case of male emigrants, when women were involved the whole British Indian Empire seemed endangered. The conflicts depended on which scenario seemed the most likely representation of female emigration, and this same dilemma is reflected in the historiography of the Indian diaspora during the indenture period. The classic study of the system of indentured emigration was volume one of Hugh Tinker's work, written in the stormy days of 1970s protest when he was the beleaguered head of the Institute of Race Relations. Tinker cites case after case of kidnapping and deception in recruitment – decidedly the weak point of the system.[66] He accepts the nationalist arguments that indenture is a "badge of helotry"[67] and is converted by the arguments of Andrews and his account of his experiences in Fiji.[68] Other, more recent studies have questioned Tinker's stance. One writer defended his positive account of the system in Trinidad and British Guiana:

> Professor Tinker would no doubt say of me . . . that I have been reluctant to pursue the sordid far enough. It seems to me that he himself has sometimes allowed his vigorous pursuit of the sordid to lead him a little too far, and that his account is too much coloured by the attitudes of the later twentieth century to questions concerning conditions of labour.[69]

Many current analyses come to the same conclusion, impressed with the safeguards against impressment, and the

> relatively low percentage of runaways between the moment of first registration and embarkation indicate that indentured emigration was usually the result of a choice made by the intending emigrant himself, albeit not always based on rational grounds. In this respect, indentured emigration had more in common with the "free" emigration out of Europe during the 19th century than the slave trade during the preceding centuries.[70]

While, by the end, most British officials in India, including the Viceroy, were eager to abandon a system which gave them so much political grief,[71] some still worried about the lack of alternatives for women after abolition, since seasonal migration offered no avenue of escape for them. Overseas emigration had offered opportunity.[72] This is the current construction used by feminists, many from India, seeking to mobilize women in overseas Indian communities.[73] The independent Indian woman throwing off the shackles of superstition and male dominance and seeking her fortune abroad is an tempting image:

> Literature suggests that Indian women came to Trinidad as already independent women who made a conscious decision to move out of the difficult

> social situations which confronted them in India. These included deserted women, practising prostitutes and brahmin widows. But soon enough they were constrained to accept the androcentric ideal of Indianness which was coterminus with subordination.[74]

This was the crux of the problem. Were the women free, were they empowered either socially or economically, or were they exploited in both body and soul for the benefit of colonial planters and capitalists? Indian nationalists clearly believed the last.

Yet of these two principal kinds of discourse, the discourse of victimology and that of empowerment, who was served by each mode of discourse during the nationalist phase and whom does it serve now? First, the idea of Indian women as victims/saints was necessary to the Indian anti-indenture forces as a focus for making opposition to the system almost universal. To the "nationalists" and to Gandhi, this same image served as a unifying cause at a time when unity was essential and non-divisive images were at a premium. Second, to the Government of India the image of the exploited woman and the indignant native populace was essential in its struggle with the Colonial Office to persuade the British Cabinet to abolish a system so fraught with danger to British rule. Faced with an "Imperial Government which is naturally predisposed towards the Colonies,"[75] and a nationalist press which knew this only too well, the Government of India needed every weapon it could muster to achieve abolition and avoid political turmoil in India. Third, in the modern struggle for power among the ethnic "detritus"[76] of the British Empire, the image of the Indian population as unwilling victims of an exploitative system has given them a counterpoise to the post-slavery entitlement of African or indigenous groups.

The discourse of empowerment, too, serves several purposes. First, the feminist movements in post-colonial societies can use this image as a stimulus in current struggles. For them, the concept of strong female forbears is an attractive one.[77] Empowerment did come to many women who went from being defiled, despised prostitutes – or defiled, despised widows – to desirable attractive mates. Having a chance to "barter" one's virtue might have been an appealing alternative to a life of submission in a family or village. In the colonies Indian women were sought-after and important. On the other hand, it would have been almost impossible for female emigrants to remain single and completely independent of male ascendancy, but a few stalwart women managed even that.

Finally, most immigrant communities have a strong sense of the future: one generation's experiences may sow seeds reaped only in the second and third generations. For the women of Trinidad, Guyana, and Mauritius an image of empowerment may someday overcome the need to have "chaste" ancestors, as, in Australia, a convict forbear is now a matter of pride. Recently, I went in a matter of months from a road tour of the Bhojpuri region, from which most of the women emigrated, to a stay in Trinidad, and still could not answer the question: would those women who chattered as they drank their tea on the terraces of the Trinidad Hilton Hotel have made such a brave showing in a "backward class" – or Muslim – Bhojpuri village? Would their daughters be at university? Does the difference justify a sordid system? However sordid, did the system empower these women? If we cannot reach a definitive answer to these questions, we can at least make these women and their emigrant grandmothers part of the discourse.

12

Civilizing Women: French Colonial Perceptions of Vietnamese Womanhood and Motherhood*

Micheline R. Lessard

In July 1927, the *Collège des jeunes filles indigènes de Saigon* invited a local physician named Coulognier to give the prize-day speech marking the end of the school year. He had some experience at such public speaking engagements, since he had also been asked the previous year to speak to the young graduates of Saigon's *Ecole primaire supérieure des jeunes filles*. In his speech, Coulognier asked the graduating young women to cultivate qualities of generosity, charity, and self-sacrifice, qualities he claimed they had developed as a result of the education they had received at the *Collège*. Coulognier made no mention of the young Vietnamese women's academic achievements or potential. Instead, he focused primarily on his own field of expertise, medicine, and on how it related to these graduating students. He emphasized the importance of hygiene, breastfeeding, and child-rearing skills in the future of the young Vietnamese women's lives.

Coulognier's speech is the focal point of this essay for a number of reasons. First, it reflects French metropolitan concerns and fears which were transported to the colonial context and which affected educational policies there. Chief among these was the concept of degeneration, the notion that French society and culture were in decline. Second, Coulognier's speech reflects the idea that women, both in France and in the colonies, were considered partly responsible for this phenomenon and that they needed to be educated in order to be able to counter and reverse the process of degeneration. Third, the solutions proposed by the French authorities reflected definite perceptions of womanhood and motherhood. In Vietnam, the solutions prescribed to solve the problem of degeneration illustrate not only French perceptions of womanhood and motherhood, but also French perceptions of the Vietnamese character and Vietnamese customs. In their attempts to solve certain political and social problems in Vietnam, French colonial authorities resorted to facile stereotypes concerning Vietnamese culture. They also infantilized, through their colonial rhetoric, the entire Vietnamese population, and this infantilization served to justify and explain the French colonial educational mission. Driven by fears of degeneration in France, French colonial authorities developed educational policies towards women which, for the most part, were suited to the European rather than the Vietnamese context, but which also worked well to serve the colonial "mission."

The appearance of a physician in a school context was commonplace at the end of the nineteenth and the beginning of the twentieth centuries, and the close relationship between French physicians and education was not unique to the colonial setting in Vietnam. In turn-of-the-century France, as well as in other European nations, including England, Germany, and Russia, physicians played a key role in instituting social reforms.[1] During the nineteenth century France was a country in flux: it vacillated between empire and republic, between liberalism and conservatism. While industrialization and urbanization benefited certain elements of French society, those processes also resulted in serious social problems: congested cities, pollution, disease, crime, alienation, and confusion.[2] The infant mortality rate in the French *faubourgs* was high. In addition, statistics in late nineteenth-century France seemed to indicate a falling birth rate. Ultimately this decline proved less drastic than earlier perceived, but French officials' social policies nonetheless reflected such misperceptions. Within the context of competition between France, England, and Germany, dwindling birth rates were considered a national peril. Competition on this scale required a population large and healthy enough to support a strong military and a solid industrial base.

Equally troublesome to French political leaders of the late nineteenth century was the quality of life of those children who did survive. While urbanization and industrialization did not proceed in France at a rate comparable to that of England, by the eighteenth century, France's urban living conditions were abominable. France's laboring urban poor were for the most part relegated to the *faubourgs* located on the peripheries of metropolitan centers. By the nineteenth century, the popular masses represented a growing interest of the French political leadership, as the poor became a source of fear and concern. French *faubourgs* were mired in poverty and populated by people suffering from physical and psychological illnesses. There were slums and filth. In the minds of many, the laboring poor were a dangerous mass. It was in the *faubourgs*, after all, that prostitution, infanticide, suicide, sexual promiscuity, and other so-called deviant behaviors were most *obviously* widespread.[3]

The fears engendered by these conditions also resulted in the sexualization of the urban poor. Many contended that the members of this particular socio-economic group were more sexually precocious and promiscuous, that they had more immediate sexual needs.[4] As Michel Foucault has pointed out, this process of sexualization resulted in an emphasis, if not an obsession, in France on drawing and analyzing statistics on a number of phenomena. Birth rates, the number of births within or outside of marriage, the age at which sexual relations began, the frequency of sexual relations, the nature of sexual relations, and cases of fertility or sterility were recorded and tabulated. The assumption was that deviance in sexual behavior would necessarily bring negative social consequences.

Compounding these internal social problems was France's devastating defeat by Germany in 1871. Increasingly, French political leaders and legislators sought remedies for what they considered were France's two most serious ailments: depopulation and degeneration. During the Third Republic, this analysis of France's social and political problems resulted in an alliance between the medical and the political worlds. Physicians, perceived by French legislators as scientists with the expertise to solve these problems, gained significant political power. As historian Rachel Fuchs has noted, French physicians spearheaded social reform programs, served on parliamentary committees, sat on municipal and departmental councils, and, increasingly, themselves became legislators. In 1902, for example, there were thirty-three physicians in the French National Assembly.[5]

In addressing the problems of depopulation and degeneration, French physicians developed social reform policies that revealed particular attitudes toward women as mothers and toward women's bodies. In the wake of a unified and developing Germany, France's depopulation "crisis" led French political leaders to believe that mothering was no longer strictly a private matter. Because it was now considered a matter of national integrity, mothering required state intervention.[6] In 1896 the *Alliance nationale pour l'accroissement de la population française* was formed by a physician named Jacques Bertillon.[7] The purpose of the organization was to protect the welfare of infants, and one of its chief methods was to promote maternal breastfeeding and denounce and discourage wet-nursing. The beneficial, medicinal properties of mothers' milk were emphasized, since they were deemed crucial in reducing the rate of infant deaths. In the eighteenth century, Jean-Jacques Rousseau had elaborated on this in his *Emile*, but during the Third Republic French women who had used the services of wet-nurses for their infants were often blamed for the high infant mortality rate.[8] There developed a glorification of breastfeeding in France and elsewhere because it symbolized "selfless devotion" since a mother's milk "was her own blood, her own life-sustaining fluid."[9]

Jules Michelet, in particular, amplified what Rousseau had begun earlier by suggesting that mothers' duties entailed not only nurturing their children but also laying the groundwork for "the future generations and the future republic."[10] Because of this latter role, legislators decided that women required the support and protection of social reform legislation. In 1874 the National Assembly passed a law intended to regulate wet-nursing.[11] Prior to that, there had been an attempt, in 1872, to legislate maternal breastfeeding.[12] As historian Joshua Cole points out, the purpose was "to demonstrate that the roots of France's social welfare could be found in the feminine half of the population."[13] The conclusions drawn by a number of French policy-makers was that the high infant mortality rate was the result of "poor hygiene and maternal indifference,"[14] and that each of these phenomena bore moral connotations. On the one hand, the process of urbanization had made women turn away from their "natural" instincts as mothers.[15] On the other, the lack of proper hygiene in some families' homes necessarily signified also a lack of morality.[16] The widespread belief in the nineteenth century was that "anyone who transgressed 'the laws of hygiene' deserved to get sick, and anyone who got sick had probably broken those laws."[17] These conclusions were drawn despite the fact that the great majority of French mothers breastfed their own children and that those relying on wet-nurses were a minority unlikely to significantly alter infant mortality rates.[18] Nonetheless, after 1884, French schools incorporated these notions and developed courses on hygiene and child-rearing based on the expertise of a physician named Pinard who had himself coined the term *puériculture*.[19]

In France's colonies, particularly in Vietnam, policies reflected these metropolitan concerns. The problems of depopulation and degeneration did not exist in Vietnam. Birth rates were high, and there could be no degeneration in an area in which, French colonial authorities maintained, generation had not yet begun. The most immediate problem was that of French consolidation of political control in Vietnam. From its inception, the French colonial administration faced immediate, constant, and fierce resistance to its rule and authority. Rather than searching Vietnam's history for explanations to such resistance to foreign domination, French colonial authorities resorted to stereotyping Vietnamese culture, often referring in their memos and reports to the inherently traditionalist and conservative nature of Vietnamese culture. The burden of ridding Vietnam of such perceived traditionalist attitudes would eventually fall on the shoulders of French educators and on those of Vietnamese women.

Concerned about high infant mortality rates, colonial officials emphasized poor hygiene, climate, ignorance, and promiscuity as the perceived causes of these problems among the Vietnamese. There was little mention of the socioeconomic conditions that might have led to such problems. There were few reports concerning the abusive labor conditions existing on the rubber plantations or in the mines. There was also no mention of the fact that Vietnamese peasants for the most part were unable to survive due to French colonial taxation, monopoly, and *corvée* policies. French colonial officials never doubted that the transformation of the Vietnamese peasant economy from one of subsistence to one of surplus agriculture would benefit *colons* and Vietnamese alike. Unfortunately for Vietnamese peasants, the reality was far removed from the ideal. As French rule in Vietnam became more deeply entrenched and involved, fewer Vietnamese peasants were able to hold on to their small plots of land. They became tenant farmers or itinerant workers. The result was, in some cases, an exodus from the countryside to the cities in search of new means of livelihood. For Vietnamese women there were few options. In desperate attempts to hold on to their land, some Vietnamese families hired out their daughters as factory workers, domestics, or nannies. Some flocked to the cities to work as wet-nurses, often finding themselves in such precarious financial situations that they were forced to feed *colon* children at the expense of their own infants. The least fortunate women ended up as bar girls or prostitutes. The plight of Vietnamese migrating from the countryside to the cities is well documented in a number of sources, including Vu Trong Phung's *Household Servants*, written in 1936. But such reports are rare in French colonial sources, where all too often the problems engendered by this migration were attributed to Vietnamese women's ignorance or lack of morality.

Vietnamese workers found themselves in situations similar to but often much worse than those of their French counterparts in the *faubourgs*. In addition, the French colonial government continued to enforce the practice of separate pay scales for Vietnamese and European workers, a practice that meant that for similar positions, the highest paid Vietnamese could make no more than the lowest paid European.[20] This not only emphasized Vietnam's colonized status but also ensured that most Vietnamese would be unable to live beyond a subsistence level. Instead of focusing on such socio-economic problems, French colonial authorities attributed the growing pauperization of the Vietnamese to a lack of formal, modern education and to what they considered was Vietnamese conservatism. With respect to the high rate of mortality among young Vietnamese children, French colonial authorities pointed the finger at Vietnamese lack of knowledge concerning modern hygiene. The impetus was then to create an educational system that would eliminate such ignorance and loosen the Vietnamese people's attachment to its own culture and traditions. It was also determined that many of these problems were caused by Vietnamese women and that this new educational system should include them.

Just as French women had been held responsible for the creation of and the need for social welfare in France, Vietnamese women were considered an impediment to French colonial rule in Vietnam. In the eyes of many French colonial officials, only a western, modern education could solve this problem:

> It is therefore in our interest to give the young *annamite* girl a Western education, because it is the female element that ordinarily opposes our culture; it is the female element that is most attached to traditional customs.[21]

These sentiments were echoed in the reports of the *Commission Guernut*, a body created by French authorities to investigate and analyze political unrest in Vietnam. One of the authors of the report maintained that "for more than thirty years in Indochina, one of the greatest obstacles I have encountered . . . has been the lack of evolution among Vietnamese women, their conservative spirit . . . which has made them act instinctively and in a retrograde manner."[22] In addition, French colonial authorities complained that despite their educational efforts, young Vietnamese students, particularly boys, were not developing a fondness for French culture. This led some educators to maintain that the reason for this lay in the child's early, pre-school development. It was then determined that an understanding, and thereby also an embracing, of French culture would have to begin in the home prior to a child's formal education. As such, Vietnamese mothers were to become their children's first teachers of French culture. As in France, motherhood, within the context of a proper education, would provide a better quality of male "citizens." It became all the more imperative, therefore, to rid Vietnamese women of their perceived conservative tendencies and to teach them how to teach their own children.

Much of France's justification of its colonization of Vietnam employed the language of schooling, motherhood and adoption. In its colonies, the Republican mother's arms opened even wider. Jules Michelet had referred to France as the "glorious mother who is not only our own and who must mother every nation into freedom."[23] In the case of Vietnam, these opinions were shared and expressed by Edouard Marquis in 1935:

> French philosophy is a beacon towards which must sail, from the depth of their ignorance, their miseries, their needs, those peoples who have had faith in our nation. It must light the forward march of the large French family, spread throughout the world. It is not only for those we call *les attardés* or *les arrièrés*, but for all those who manifest a drive towards a superior culture.[24]

To French *colons* in Vietnam, the "children of the colonies" referred to all Vietnamese, regardless of age or educational level. Vietnamese boys and girls sitting on the wooden benches of French colonial schools were children in the literal sense, while Vietnam itself was perceived as a child in need of the political, philosophical, and economic guidance and nurturance only France was willing to provide. French colonial literature, its memos, letters, reports, and newspapers often referred to the Vietnamese as *non-evolués* (non-evolved). The language of French colonialism described Vietnamese politics, philosophy, and culture as immature and unsophisticated. With respect to philosophy in particular, French *colons* perceived the Vietnamese as children, even toddlers, whose ideas were still unformed. In an article published in the *Avenir du Tonkin* in 1926 such attitudes vis-à-vis the Vietnamese were quite clear:

> The expression "young man" has with us a definition which reconciles the notions of youth with virility; on Annamite soil, a young man reveals himself mostly a child, and in mature men there survives something puerile in most circumstances.[25]

Mother France would therefore teach some of its adoptive children, Vietnamese women, how to mother their own children.

In their conception of the role of Vietnamese motherhood, French colonial authorities were projecting their vision of the colonial mission. Faithful to the rhetoric of colonialism, Coulognier reminded the young Vietnamese women that France had "always been generous to her children of the colonies."[26] The notions of motherhood and patriotism, and later motherhood and imperialism, were irrevocably linked. It was also hoped that these patriotic sentiments, proffered by Mother France, would envelop the children of Vietnam. Furthermore, it was up to Vietnamese women to inculcate in their children these values and qualities. As such, Vietnamese women were enlisted to become France's chief propagandists. "You must," stated Coulognier, "give France infinite gratitude for all its kindness, and it is your duty to spread that kindness in order that others may know and love France better."[27] All of this would translate itself in the creation and opening of girls' schools and in the development of a curriculum deemed suitable for Vietnamese girls.

The creation of girls' schools in Vietnam was a slow process, however. French educators insisted that Vietnamese society, its family structure, and its Confucian values made it difficult for them to persuade Vietnamese families to send their daughters to school. A report dated 1910, addressed to the Governor General and written by French educators, stated that the Vietnamese had never been preoccupied with the education of their daughters: "Among them [the Vietnamese] a woman was devoted exclusively to the life of her family and to housekeeping." The report suggested that this was why, in part, French efforts at creating and opening girls' schools had been so minimal.[28] These perceptions were shared by French and some Vietnamese men alike. While their motives were significantly different from those of French colonial authorities, some Vietnamese nationalists also maintained that Vietnamese families were largely unwilling to educate their daughters. In 1927, an article in *l'Annam Scolaire* examined this problem and further suggested that Vietnamese girls should be educated, either in Vietnam or in France: "If it is a consolation to see Annamite boys travel abroad for their studies, it is, however, disappointing to realize that our sisters do not follow that same road."[29] Its author, Le Hoa, suggested that the reason for this was largely traditional, that the less educated Vietnamese continued to follow an old Vietnamese proverb: "for the boys, the lakes and the mountains of the four regions, for the girls the four walls of the home." Still, Vietnamese scholars Mai Thi Thu and Le Thi Nham Tuyet point out that the education of girls had long been a concern for the Vietnamese and that from at least the fifteenth century, there existed a tradition of didactic texts which illustrate the Vietnamese concern for the education of girls:

> Specialized works with such titles as "Education of Girls," "Duties of Women and Girls," educational songs and poems took pains to illustrate the rules of the Four Virtues and the Three Obediences, using the form and the content most suitable for each social stratum, from the common people to the aristocracy.[30]

Although these texts were Confucian in nature and were largely intended to maintain and justify Vietnamese women's place in society, they nonetheless demonstrate that the Vietnamese had for centuries been concerned about the education of their daughters. During the French colonial period, the resistance to educate Vietnamese girls in French-created schools was motivated not so much by an unwillingness to educate girls, but by a fundamental difference as to what constitutes a proper education for girls. In addition, by dismantling the village school system, French colonial authorities had placed Vietnamese peasant families in the position of having to send their daughters (and sons) away from their villages to attend school. Because of Confucian mores and because of the role played by Vietnamese girls in their families' economy, there was an understandable reluctance to have them removed from the villages in order to attend school. Furthermore, school fees made it impossible for most peasant families to afford an education for their daughters or for their sons.

The unwillingness to provide a French-style education for girls in Vietnam cannot be attributed solely to Vietnamese tradition, however. In the early stages of French colonization, the schooling of Vietnamese girls had been the purview of Catholic missionaries. The sisters of St-Paul de Chartres, for example, had opened numerous small schools for girls. This proved cost-efficient for the colonial government, yet the same report which placed responsibility for the slow development of Vietnamese girls' and women's education on the Vietnamese themselves also conceded that the colony's most immediate concern was the education of Vietnamese boys. It was Vietnamese boys, after all, who needed to be integrated first into the French colonial economy. French colonial officials may have been slow in opening girls' schools out of budgetary concerns, but there were also ideological considerations. French educators held specific notions of womanhood and motherhood. If these notions were to be properly imparted to young Vietnamese girls, French teacher training colleges (écoles normales) needed to properly train the teachers of these schools. The creation and the opening of girls' schools therefore needed to be accomplished more gradually.

While it would be wrong to suggest that Vietnamese society, prior to French colonization, advocated the formal education of girls, it must be stated that, specifically within the colonial context, attitudes changed. In fact, sources reveal that some Vietnamese officials were exerting considerable pressure on the French colonial government to create girls' schools. There were numerous and frequent requests on the part of Vietnamese to open private girls' schools, and many Vietnamese actually opened their own private institutions when colonial officials proved slow to provide funds for the building of such schools. But fearing that these schools were not advancing the cause of French rule, colonial authorities decreed in 1924 that no private school could be opened in Vietnam without the approval of the colonial government. The truth of the matter is that French authorities intended to exercise complete control over private schools since they were considered hotbeds of Vietnamese anti-colonial resistance. This perception had developed early on and was manifested in 1908, when the *Dong Kinh Nghia Thuc* was closed.[31] The need for Vietnamese villages to petition the French colonial government in order to open private schools greatly slowed the process of providing Vietnamese girls with a formal education.

By that time Vietnamese nationalists had come to the conclusion that in order to wrest power from French colonial authorities, Vietnam would have to enlist the help of Vietnamese women, as it had done so often throughout the course of its history. Within the context of French colonization in Vietnam that meant that women needed to extend their focus outside the home and onto the larger issue of Vietnamese political independence. A "modern" education would help Vietnamese women understand and justify this shift in focus.

By the early twentieth century both French and Vietnamese men had joined in defining the role of Vietnamese women and in advocating the education of Vietnamese girls. Anti-colonial Vietnamese patriots such as Phan Boi Chau urged young Vietnamese women to become "mothers of the nation." Both Phan Boi Chau and French colonial authorities, albeit for different motives, made the connection between motherhood and patriotism. According to David Marr, "If girls were teased with the question 'Do you have a husband yet?' They should reply, 'Yes, his surname is Viet and his given name is Nam'."[32] A 1930 Vietnamese political tract aimed at Vietnamese women suggested that "good women are those who are interested in the political life of the country."[33] In an article titled "Young Sisters, What Will Your Role Be?" one young Vietnamese nationalist congratulated those Vietnamese girls and women who had participated in a fundraiser for flood victims in Than Hoa and stated that women no longer needed to be engaged in their traditional "inactivity" which had been so detrimental to the nation's economic and social life.[34]

Even among the more radical Vietnamese nationalists, however, in the attempt to convince Vietnamese women of their role within the anti-colonialist movement, there remained powerful strains of conservatism and tradition. In the article from *l'Annam Scolaire*, cited above, Le Hoa called on her fellow Vietnamese women to leave Vietnam and to study other countries' "ingenious ways." She also asked them, however, to do this while "remaining good and virtuous in order not to betray the trust of your parents" and to "renounce your lives of leisure, to no longer have a servile spirit, to devote your precious bodies, like gold and jade, to the service of the country, and to imitate your famous predecessors, the Trung Sisters."[35]

A number of Vietnamese who favored French rule also called for the education of women. Conservatives such as Pham Quynh agreed with the French colonial mandate to educate Vietnamese girls. In his newspaper *Nam Phong*, Pham Quynh wrote numerous articles on the status of women in Vietnam.

Pham repeated that Vietnamese girls needed to be educated to become good wives and good mothers, but he added his own brand of conservatism to the equation. Pham Quynh agreed that Vietnamese girls ought to be educated in French schools, but was adamant in his belief that certain Vietnamese (Confucian) qualities should be preserved. In an article published in *Nam Phong* Pham highlighted the qualities of the "Asian" woman: she was gentle, kind, and docile. In another series of articles published in his newspaper, and titled "Oriental Women," Pham Quynh delineated these definitions of Vietnamese womanhood by providing short biographies of both virtuous and non-virtuous women. The didactic purpose of the articles was clear.[36] In 1931, an article in the *Trung Bac Tan Van* stated that "while working to achieve, among Vietnamese women and young girls, a measure of progress in modern studies, we must also ensure their moral education by making them respect the Four Virtues in order to keep them from committing reprehensible errors concerning the application of the principles of equality and liberty."[37] That same year, *Phu Nu Thoi Dam* also published a series of articles aimed at Vietnamese women. They varied in focus and scope. Some instructed women on what books were considered proper reading (novels and romances were to be avoided), and others bore titles such as "How to Prepare Oneself to Become a Virtuous Mother."[38]

In time a number of girls' schools opened in Vietnam and promoted French conceptions of womanhood and motherhood. The French ideal was that of a Vietnamese woman who would be adequately literate, that is literate enough to engage her husband in pleasant conversation. She would encourage the diligence and faithfulness of her husband through her own virtues, and would keep him from gambling and running around, providing an orderly, clean, stable, home. Reflecting the nineteenth-century French obsession with hygiene, French colonial educators pointed out that the ideal Vietnamese woman would keep the house swept and clean, would keep animals out of the house, would open wide the windows and allow in fresh air, would use tablecloths which she had sewn and embroidered herself, would place objects neatly on doilies which she had made herself, and would spend quiet evenings at home sewing and mending.[39] Furthermore, she would be the children's first educator and would teach them French morals and values. Finally, she would remind them of France's generosity and civilization, virtues from which she had so obviously benefited. Moreover, Vietnamese women were to stay away from activities not considered appropriate for them. In 1937, the *Commission Guernut* proposed that Vietnamese girls' schools needed to offer classes primarily in family hygiene, child care, motherly duties, housekeeping, laundry, and cooking, but its recommendations also made it clear that female education was to include nothing that would allow them to become interested in politics.[40] "What is necessary," stated the authors of these reports, "was a girl's education which will correspond with our goals." Those goals were, as written, "not to create politically emancipated women, but mothers educated just enough to be fond of their roles and their missions as wives and mothers."[41] The Commission's authors suggested careful planning to ensure that young Vietnamese women refrain from pursuing work outside the home. While a few places admitted Vietnamese women as teachers, nurses, or nannies, French colonial authorities stressed the importance of limiting such options for women lest they take away positions from young male Vietnamese graduates.[42] The idea that young Vietnamese women would ultimately compete with Vietnamese men for employment was problematic for French colonial authorities. Many French administrators attributed the political unrest in Vietnam to the *déclassés*, those Vietnamese men who were either unable to find employment or were unwilling to perform manual labor. In 1927, the *Résident Supérieur* of Tonkin stated in a memo that: "It is necessary to avoid that they [Vietnamese women] also become a class of 'unemployed intellectuals.' That is why we are striving to make them understand that their place is within the family and not outside of it."[43]

The *Commission Guernut*'s proposals were merely a reiteration of what had been suggested at the onset of colonial rule in Vietnam. As early as 1908, the *Ecole de la rue Jules Ferry* in Hanoi offered its pupils a curriculum more than half of which was based on hygiene, childcare, and home economics. The Hanoi school offered its female students the basics of *quoc ngu* (the romanized Vietnamese script), French, Chinese characters, and simple arithmetic. Female pupils spent approximately two-thirds of their school day learning the following: hygiene of the body, of clothing, of the home; the preparation and cooking of food; child care; children's first aid; the ability to recognize the symptoms of infectious disease; the care and keep of animals. One half of the school day was spent on what was considered practical work: sewing, mending, embroidery, knitting, cutting, laundering, bleaching, and ironing. Time was also spent teaching young girls how to keep house.[44]

With respect to the more immediate problems of degeneration and the high infant mortality rate in Vietnam, colonial authorities embarked on what Laurence Monnais-Rousselot refers to as a "colonial crusade" which would link "the doctor, the administrator and the teacher."[45] She points to the creation in 1897 of sanitation authorities. In 1902, a public health law was enacted and a school of medicine was opened in Hanoi. The promise of modern medicine made doctors, both French and Vietnamese, promoters of the benefits of French colonial rule.[46] This promotion of the benefits of French rule was to take place in the classrooms, in conferences, and in speeches throughout the colony.[47]

As an expert in such medical matters, almost half of Coulognier's speech, which was printed in the *Echo Annamite* of 15 July 1927, was concerned with promoting breastfeeding. Coulognier discussed at length the benefits of breastfeeding, regardless of the fact that Vietnamese women were, and had been for a long time, breastfeeding their children. In many ways, Coulognier was projecting France's fears onto its colonies. He was also choosing to ignore the fact that those Vietnamese women who were not breastfeeding their children were, in large part, unable to do so. In an article written for the *Bulletin de la société académique indochinoise* in 1882 Tran Nguyen Hanh had described Vietnamese customs pertaining to breastfeeding: "To raise a child, we use a wet-nurse only if a mother is unable to breastfeed as a result of illness or other such serious circumstances."[48] With few exceptions, Vietnamese women adhered to such prescriptions and practices. Still, French colonial authorities did much to develop a Western educational system aimed at helping Vietnamese girls develop skills in "modern" hygiene and child-rearing techniques and practices. Much like their counterparts in France, Vietnamese mothers were blamed for the high infant mortality rate. In the March 23, 1923 issue of the *Bulletin général de l'instruction publique*, French colonial educators denounced Vietnamese child-rearing practices as well as Vietnamese women's mothering skills:

> The habit, which some mothers have in Indochina, of ingurgitating mouth to mouth to their infants rice which they have chewed for a long time is not only dirty but it is very dangerous for the child. Many children are overcome with illnesses which have no other origin but this defective nutrition. It is a mistake to believe that from the moment the infant can eat, that what he will eat will not be dangerous to him. The large numbers of children who die in infancy die victims of a lack of care from their mothers.[49]

Vietnamese scholars have acknowledged the existence of high infant mortality rates in colonial and pre-colonial Vietnam. As Mai Thi Thu and Le Thi Nham Tuyet have noted: "children were born in conditions completely lacking hygiene, and grew up in a state of permanent under-nourishment."[50] Contrary to the contentions of French colonial authorities, however, such conditions were the result of poverty and not of Vietnamese women's ignorance or neglect. Still, the *colons* saw the majority of Vietnamese in the same light as France's urban poor: a degenerate mass. Furthermore, French colonial authorities believed this degeneration was an illness, and a contagious one at that. The pages of colonial newspapers were filled with advertisements for all sorts of products intended to prevent such contagion: elixirs, powders, balms, antiseptics, tonics, and infusions. It was believed that the longer a French citizen stayed in Vietnam, the more likely he or she was to become ill or listless. Certainly the climate played no small part in this, but as Ann Stoler has pointed out, it was also perceived that sexual contact between French men and Vietnamese women would result in "not only disease but debased sentiments, immoral proclivities and extreme susceptibility to decivilized states."[51] Again, according to Stoler, French physicians advised French women to have separate quarters built for their Vietnamese domestics and workers. This would in some measure protect French families from contamination.[52]

As their metropolitan contemporaries had done with respect to the French working poor, French colonial authorities sexualized the Vietnamese. Colonial educators in particular complained that Vietnamese students were not only sexually precocious and promiscuous, but also that they were threatening to influence more innocent French students in the colony. In 1922, a report on the *Lycée de Hanoi* stated that the quality of French education at the school was undermined by the presence of too large a Vietnamese student population, and by the social quality of these Vietnamese students. As was the case in France, French educators in Vietnam feared the degenerate nature of the Vietnamese working classes:

> Not only are there at the *lycée* much too many Annamites, but too many from the inferior classes of the indigenous population. And what is even more serious, of the inferior classes of the indigenous *urban* population, whose sense of morality is not the highest. Those children lack all education. The promiscuity within which the Annamite live, and the mores of the Annamite family have too soon informed these young *indigènes* about many points which westerners have the habit, and no doubt the wisdom, to keep from their children. The young Annamites take it upon themselves to educate the young French students in the most deplorable manner.[53]

This sexualization of the Vietnamese made it all the more urgent for French colonial authorities to educate Vietnamese women in a way that would counter such promiscuity. It was Vietnamese, after all, and not European women who worked as prostitutes and bar girls. Also, it was Vietnamese women who, in the early days of colonization, became the concubines of European men. In order to be rid of such dangerous habits, Vietnamese women were to be schooled in French morality and in French conceptions of ideal womanhood and motherhood.

In addition, French colonial officials were highly concerned about the emancipation of Vietnamese women. From its inception, the education of young Vietnamese girls led to unforeseen problems. Vietnamese women were sometimes emulating French women. French educators claimed that their efforts to educate young Vietnamese girls were being ruined because some Vietnamese girls were wearing Western clothes, drinking alcohol, smoking cigarettes, and dancing the tango. French school teachers and some French politicians in Vietnam maintained that the Vietnamese people's philosophical and political infancy prevented them from properly understanding French society and culture, and led them instead, to favor the less savory aspects of French society. In other words, Vietnamese students, both male and female, were adopting the values and habits of the French working classes. This, coupled with the perceived "natural" promiscuity of the Vietnamese, and their dubious morality, could spell disaster for the colony. Such women could not be counted on to properly educate young Vietnamese boys. Furthermore, this problem became more urgent given the phenomenon of concubinage in Vietnam. Few European women were emigrating to the colony. Ann Stoler notes that "as late as 1931" European men outnumbered European women 14,000 to 3,000.[54] While concubinage between European men and Vietnamese women was tolerated, if not actually encouraged, in some instances, the fact remained that Vietnamese women involved in such relationships were considered little more than prostitutes. Faith in the power of a proper education prevailed, however, with the *colon* belief that "if *métissage* girls were rescued in time, they could be effectively educated to become *bonnes ménagères* [good housekeepers]" of a settled Indochina, wives, or domestics in the service of France.[55]

In sum, French colonial authorities believed that the education of Vietnamese girls in French-created schools would serve the colonial mission in a number of ways. First, they maintained it would "raise" Vietnamese women and girls from their perceived debased state. Second, French-educated Vietnamese girls and women would necessarily abandon their traditionalist nature and embrace French culture. As the mothers and the earliest educators of Vietnamese children, these women would represent the living proof and would promote the benefits of French colonial rule in Vietnam. The education of these girls would rid them of their "ignorance" with respect to hygiene and the "science" of childcare, and would rid them also of their promiscuous tendencies, which were the result of such ignorance. In his speech, Coulognier linked education, medicine, and motherhood when he told his audience:

> *Mesdemoiselles*, you are the women of tomorrow and you will be therefore called upon to create a home. New responsibilities will be placed upon you, as wives and as mothers, and you are not unaware of the impact upon a child, for his entire life, of the memory of maternal love. More than anyone, I have been able to witness, as a physician, the power of that sentiment upon a man mortally wounded on a battle field or upon an ailing man, dying far away from his country or his loved ones. Always the name they call before they render their last breath is that of their mother.[56]

13

Social Construction of Idealized Images of Women in Colonial Korea: the "New Woman" versus "Motherhood"

Jiweon Shin

In contemporary Korea, motherhood is much respected and glorified. What Chizuko Ueno states about Japanese motherhood can also be applied to Korea;[1] according to Ueno, the word "mother" connotes "a cultural representation rather than a clearly defined female sub-group"; an idealized crystallized personification which is characterized by "devotion to children, parental affection, and self sacrifice."[2] However, motherhood is not the only virtue that has been expected of women historically, nor is the modern cultural construct of motherhood inherent in women. As Edward Shorter states, "[g]ood mothering is an invention of modernization."[3] Different sociopolitical conditions require different roles for women, and the image of an ideal woman is constructed and reconstructed as an ongoing process according to society's needs at any given era. Research in this field argues that a society requires and endorses certain types of women depending on its stage of modernization, industrialization, and/or international/political environment.[4] This is clearly reflected in late nineteenth- and early twentieth-century Korea.

Prior to the 1870s, the traditional image of Korean women can be described as primarily that of procreating: the foremost responsibility of married women was to bear sons to continue the family lineage. But this role changed during the Enlightenment Period (1876–1910), when the image of the "educated mother" emerged as a new ideal.[5] After annexation by Japan in 1910, the feminist image of *shin yosong* (new womanhood) emerged, and Korean society became infatuated with this new ideal. But by the late 1920s, it had become the target of severe criticism from conservative Korean intellectual circles and the Japanese colonial government. *Mosong* (motherhood) was asserted to be the proper role model for Korean women, and by the early to mid-1930s, "motherhood" was established in public sphere as a sort of officially correct ideal. This image differed from earlier images of motherhood in that it was linked to nationalistic ideology rather than the traditional Confucian roles of daughter-in-law or wife. Moreover, it was largely a response to Japanese imperialism. By the mid-1930s, the image of women as mothers raising an enlightened next generation for the sake of national well-being was firmly established in Korea.

This chapter argues that the image of motherhood in contemporary Korean society has its roots in the colonial period when the construction of this version of motherhood was conditioned by strong nationalism and a vigilant Japanese colonialism. This research is based on an analysis of women's journals that were published by leading intellectuals and were intended to shape and direct the nation toward modernization and independence. These journals basically come from two distinct time periods: published either before 1910 or after 1920.[6] Although modern publishing began in Korea in the 1890s, and the first women's journal appeared in 1906, Japanese annexation in 1910 was followed by a decade of severe censorship of all Korean media as a part of the colonial power's policy of ruthless repression. But after the March First Movement in 1919, the biggest nationalistic political event in colonial Korea,[7] Japanese policy shifted, and the publication of journals and newspapers resumed in the 1920s and henceforth flourished. Women's magazines reappeared, but their content continued to change as the political and social situation under colonialism developed.[8]

The beginning of the public discourse on women can be traced to the 1890s, when the image of "educating mothers" began to appear. Confucian ideology, which stressed the inferior position of women, dominated Korea until the late nineteenth century. Women were regarded as inferior to men, and obedience, subjugation, chastity, and endurance were considered the highest virtues that they could attain, while education was reserved exclusively for males. Women were regarded as merely ignorant and subordinate, and even the "seven bases for divorce" (unfilial behavior toward parents-in-law, failing to bear a son, gossiping, stealing, jealousy, improper conduct, and disease) which had formed the fundamental code of conduct for women during the Yi Dynasty (1392–1910), did not contain any reference to education.

In the arranged marriage system, women were primarily significant for producing sons and as cheap labor. In this patriarchal marriage system, any close link between a husband and wife was neither meaningful nor encouraged. The most important family relationship for a married woman was with her parents-in-law, not with her own children nor her husband, since the foremost responsibility of women was to serve them.[9] But as Korea came under increased military pressure from Japan in the last decade of the nineteenth century, some leaders questioned whether the country could afford to maintain this traditional female role in an increasingly hostile international environment.

As the military threat increased and aggressive Japanese colonialism expanded into Northeast and Southeast Asia, Korean intellectuals and political leaders opposed this aggression in many forms. These included the struggles within the Choson imperial dynasty to reinstate its fading power; memorials were made to the throne from Confucian literati which pleaded for a more effective defense policy. "Righteous armies" were formed by both Confucian literati and common people, with anti-Japanese guerrilla warfare reaching a peak in 1908. Political and social movements sought internal institutional and political change to preserve national independence, and publications (including newspapers) sought to raise the social and political consciousness of the people. Progressive elites also sought to foster a contemporary, nationalistic culture to instill modern education and nationalism within the people.

In this socio-historical context, Korean intellectuals began to realize the importance of women's education for this struggle, and in the 1890s initiated the *Kaehwa Undong* (Enlightenment Movement). Pak Yong-hyo, one of the progressive political leaders of the time, mentioned several women's issues for the first time in an official petition to the King in 1888: these included abolishing the legality of domestic violence against women, establishing equal opportunity education for boys and girls above the age of six, banning child marriage and concubinage, and permitting widows to remarry.[10]

These issues, however, were not circulated in public until the *Tongnip Shinmun* (*The Independent*), the most influential daily newspaper of the time, began to advocate women's rights for equal education in 1896. Through a series of editorials, *Tongnip Shinmun* argued that if women were not given a proper education, half of the Korean population would remain ignorant, thus jeopardizing the education of future generations. Hence the neglect of women's education would ultimately result in the deterioration of the national well-being.[11] The paper also encouraged women to fight for more education and rights: "So we are urging you, women of Korea, to strive for high education, conducting yourselves in an exemplary manner to become models for men. In this way not only will you gain rights properly due you, but guide ignorant men in the right direction."[12]

Tongnip Shinmun tried to foster social consensus on the necessity of educating women, and succeeded in gaining the attention of both the government and public. Their efforts bore fruit in several significant ways. In 1908, the first law on women's education, "the article on public higher schools for women," was proclaimed by the government, and in the same year, the first government girls' high school was founded.[13] Intellectuals' emphasis on the importance of women's education increased during the first decade of the new century, as various segments of the Korean intelligentsia attempted to educate the people and mobilize nationalist opinion, while Korean sovereignty eroded, since the government did not have the resources to reorganize and redirect an effective defense.

By this time, *Kajong Chapji* (*Home Journal*), published from 1906 to 1908, was circulating the novel idea that mothers should be responsible for the education of their children at home. This approach emphasized the importance of women's education for the sake of the next generation who would be responsible for the nation's fate in the hostile international political environment. *Kajong Chapji* also attempted to enlighten the people by first changing their attitudes regarding sons: "To those with sons, when you love and raise your sons, do not expect any payback from them; do not consider them as yours. Instead, consider them as social resources, and raise them as such. When your sons make great contributions to this society, the society will reward you properly."[14] This was a major break with past views of motherhood. Raising children, especially sons, was the only guarantee for support in retirement, and thus filial piety was considered a primary virtue. Encouraging the people to give up their privileges as parents, and to consider their sons more as social resources, was thus a significant departure from tradition. Yet, within this revolutionary view, women were still regarded as being important only for educating their sons at home.

In the realm of domestic education, however, it was asserted that women – rather than their husbands – should have indisputable authority in educating their children. In 1906, *Kajong Chapji* states:

> For children's education, women's role is far more important than men's. Since men are busy earning money outside home, they do not have enough time to spend with children. On the other hand, women give birth to children, breast-feed them and raise them with their own hands. Until children reach the age of 20 when they go out to the society as adults, they are under the direct influence of their mothers. . . . If mothers are intellectual, smart, sincere, and socially conscious, children will grow to be as such. . . . If women got married and raise such wonderful children, those children will again be wonderful parents. In this way, this nation will be full of good people and will prosper. Therefore, we can say that *women are the teachers of the whole nation.* [emphasis added][15]

This idea of giving enormous significance to women's education attained popularity among the intellectuals, and they founded over fifty women's schools during the Enlightenment period. Although many of these private schools suffered from lack of adequate financial support, they helped to generate widespread enthusiasm for learning by Korean women. By 1910, educating daughters had become an established custom for middle- and upper-class Koreans. Official records show 7,000 women students in Seoul in 1907; by 1910, 2,250 private schools were registered, and it was estimated that there were as many unregistered schools.[16] The notion that women were the teachers of the whole nation was a further step away from the idea that women were primarily responsible for children's education at home, and it is much beyond the Confucian view of women as mere procreators.

Following Japan's forced annexation of Korea in 1910, the role of women in Korean society changed once again.[17] The first decade of Japanese colonial rule "has been called the 'dark period' (*amhukki*) because of the repression of political and cultural life in the colony."[18] Political organizations were dismantled and the right of public assembly was abolished; publication of newspapers, magazines, and books were strictly controlled and censored. The slightest sign of political opposition was crushed by military force; intellectuals and nationalist leaders were put under police surveillance, and the Japanese colonial educational system provided Koreans with only minimal, basic learning with the goal of molding them into loyal and obedient subjects. Japanese was taught as the "national language," and Korean became the second language; colonial education likewise aimed to implant ambivalent attitudes toward Korea's culture, history, and heritage.

This repressive colonial policy and social atmosphere changed after 1918. Following World War I, US President Woodrow Wilson declared the principle of humanism and respect for the self-determination of peoples in the post-war settlement. Korean nationalists considered Wilson's principles as a basis to prepare a nation-wide nationalistic protest and to proclaim the independence of Korea. National leaders in exile, religious leaders, and moderate nationalists combined their resources to prepare the Declaration of Independence. On March 1, 1919, this was proclaimed in Seoul by so-called "national representatives," and a copy was dispatched to the Japanese Governor-General.

Non-violent demonstrations and nation-wide rallies were then staged over the following months in which more than a million people participated. The Japanese overlords reacted with their customary imperial brutality; Korean nationalists estimated that the subsequent repression resulted in over 7,500 deaths and approximately 15,000 injured, with some 45,000 arrests made between March and December of that year.[19]

The severity of this repression meant that the Japanese colonial administration's authority was severely damaged; by June, the government in Tokyo had begun to realize that a policy change was inevitable. Admiral Saito Makoto was appointed as a new Governor-General, and the colonial administration was reorganized. This new strategy brought out a new style of colonial rule in Korea: Saito's reform was known as the "Cultural Policy" or "Cultural Ruling." Various controls in cultural, political, and social aspects were altered, and the discriminatory educational system, publication restriction, and restrictions on organizations were either removed or greatly improved. The Cultural Policy provided an environment for Koreans to forge a cultural and political renaissance in the 1920s. Although publications were still supposed to be censored, hundreds of popular magazines and specialized journals appeared, and Korean national leaders were developing their own "cultural nationalism" in a more relaxed colonial atmosphere.[20] Thus, the 1920s blossomed into a radical and progressive age for every aspects of Korean society, including women's issues.

The new stage of the public discourse on women revolved around the concept of *shin yosong* (new woman), which had originally meant women who received education from newly established Western-style schools, called *shin kyoyook* (new education); these "new women" were those who attained the new education. Those who were opposed to them were the "traditional women," meaning all those – regardless of age – who stuck to the old ways. The "New Women" were easily distinguished from "traditional women" by their appearance: they wore Western- style clothing, with suits and shoes, or the modernized version of *hanbok* (traditional Korean dress), and either cut or permed their hair.

However, appearances alone were not enough to be a "New Woman," and they were expected to espouse both a new philosophy and a new way of life.[21] "New Womanhood" was defined in the first issue of *Shin Yosong* (New Woman) in 1923 as "characteristics of women who have found their real, inner individuality," which was central to this new identity of the 1920s; women were thus advised to discard their traditional collective identity, to discover their own individual personalities, and to reject the old, false, pathological identity and all hypocritical, face-saving customs that the old society had demanded which limited their freedom. To become a true "New Woman," they had to be reborn.[22]

Educated women were taught that without first discovering their inner selves through this intense revolution from within, they did not deserve to be called "New Women."[23] "Traditional women" depended solely on their husbands; "New Women" were supposed to guide their own fates.[24] A radical new code of conduct for women was clearly suggested. According to the July issue of *Shin Yosong* in 1926, the first thing that "New Women" should do was destroy all negative remnants of the past:

> Recently people hear a lot about women's education, women's liberation, equality, and freedom. But you [Korean women] should not be satisfied since nothing has been changed and you are not respected enough as whole selves. You should make fierce efforts to become complete human beings and to be treated as such. . . . You must burn everything from the past in your mind and create a new mind, new thought, and a new personality. Things from the past cannot be improved; they should be eradicated.[25]

For women who wished to remake themselves into "New Women," three suggestions were offered: first, women should develop self-respect. In the past, women did not have an opportunity to assert their identities as autonomous people; their identities were simply subordinated to those of men. To recover their individuality, they had to realize their value as a human beings. Second, women should liberate their thoughts; without free will, they could not cultivate an individuality separate from that of men. Third, women were strongly advised to cultivate both financial and mental independence. However, these recommendations were accompanied by an acknowledgment that Korean society at that time did not provide women with a favorable environment to achieve these goals. But they were advised not to give up, and to at least strive to the will to achieve both financial and spiritual independence.[26]

By 1925, *Shin Yosong* was advocating absolute equality for women,[27] and their education was thus perceived as a necessity.[28] However, this educational agenda aimed at creating "New Women" and was therefore different from the earlier ideal. The Enlightenment Period stressed only the necessity for women to educate the next generation. But by the 1920s, it was understood that women themselves should contribute to society, and their social participation was viewed much more favorably. This perspective became the basis of the concept of the "new morality."

In addition, the Western model of the nuclear family became idealized during the 1920s, and intellectuals criticized the traditional arranged marriage system as barbaric and inhumane. They wanted to liberate Korean women, stressing that the foremost condition for marriage should be love, and romantic love and marriage based upon love received eager endorsements. In 1924, *Shin Yosong* stated that: "For human beings, marriage is not just for procreation. Marriage makes life beautiful and sacred; it satisfies the spiritual desires of people. And the indispensable element for a great marriage is love. Then what is love?" The author then quotes Ellen Key: "Love cannot be defined solely by body or spirit. Love is the elegant unity of mind and body. Sensation should not oppress the spirit; the spirit should not expel the sensation. . . . True love exists only when body and spirit are combined."[29]

Feminists thus audaciously challenged the traditional conventions of marriage and morality, arguing that as long as there was love, any kind of relationship was moral. For them, even a legal marriage was considered as immoral of love did not exist between a husband and a wife. According to the new morality, marriage was defined as true love – the unity of mind and body – and that such a marriage was sacred regardless of its legal status.[30]

Challenges were also made against the traditional female virtues of virginity and absolute chastity, and feminists argued that the traditional virtue of chastity was merely a tool of a patriarchal social order to suppress and control women:

> Chastity was applied only for women, who were forced to follow this rule, even to the extreme of forfeiting their lives for violating it. Men, who are the beneficiaries of this system, can believe and easily claim that "chastity is the essence of a good women," yet it is truly both degrading and ironic that women would believe in this myth. It is only a coerced moral concept, and should not be considered to be an obligation. It is a sick ideology that was only established by men with power to monopolize women's minds and bodies.[31]

The feminists thus suggested a new concept of chastity as a relative concept that was renewed over and over with new lovers.[32]

Along with this radical view on gender equality, feminists also recommended a new, progressive type of marriage. They argued that both husband and wife should continue to work after marriage, property should be equally divided between the husband and wife, women should be financially independent, and have the right to divorce.[33] Henrik Ibsen's play, *A Doll's House*, and the works of Ellen Key were frequently quoted. Kim Maria's poem succinctly represents the spirit of feminism that prevailed in the 1920s:

> *Come out, Friends!*[34]
> The darkness is alive.
> Even for us, who are lost in the dark,
> The darkness is alive.
> Friends, get up, and come out!
> This is not the time to be in a dark room.
> Nor is this the time to agonize over traditions.
> Look, isn't the road visible?
> Do not hesitate and come out.
>
> Out of your beautiful silk dress,
> Out of the tide of your vanity,
> Out of your high, arrogant tower,
> Friends, come out.
>
> Can't you hear?
> The weak voices of hunger, echoing in the dark.
> Wake up from your idle dream,
> Throw away your vanity.
> Friends, come out fast,
> Hasn't the time already come?

In contrast to these feminists, there were also conservative groups of "New Women," though their influence was much weaker. They cherished the traditional domestic role of women and the charm of the old feminine role. What they wanted was equal status for women at home, and they continued to stress women's education as preparing them to be good "educating mothers."

In the late 1920s, strong reaction set in against the progressive "New Women" agenda among conservative Korean intellectual circles and the older generation who advocated the Confucian social order. In addition to the practical difficulties of getting education and finding employment, marriage was the biggest problem for the "New Woman." Those who graduated from the higher schools had nowhere to go; changes in the social structure and labor markets were not fast enough to include all these highly educated women. These "New Women" had to face the gap between their ideals and hard social realities, yet even achieving compromises could be difficult.

Due to the traditional custom of child marriage, most of the educated men whom "New Women" wished to marry already had wives and children. This lack of eligible men, combined with the radical perspective of "New Women" on chastity and morality, encouraged most of the "New Women" to became mistresses or "second wives." Combined with extraordinary growth in the divorce rate in a very short time, this trend elicited severe criticisms against the "New Women" and the leaders in feminist opinion. Even the term "New Woman" began to acquire the connotation of promiscuity, or of being a high-class call girl. The term "modern girl" replaced "New Woman," and intellectual women no longer wanted to be categorized as "New Women." Instead they began to designate themselves as *intelli yosong* (intelligent women or intellectual women). By the late 1920s, the term "New Woman" was regarded as disgraceful. Thus, during the decade of Japanese reform, the Korean view of culturally progressive women underwent a dramatic change.

The emphasis on the self promoted for women during the decade of Japanese reform did not sit well with nationalists who called upon all Koreans – and especially women – to devote themselves to maintaining Korean culture and identity in the face of Japanese oppression. For women, this meant a return to an emphasis on selfless motherhood, this time in the service of the nation, and it was directly related to actions by the Japanese colonial authorities. By the early 1930s, Japan's military had expanded its influence, both at home and abroad. Japan renewed its imperial interests in Manchuria, setting up the puppet state of Manchukuo in 1931. Korea was its strategic stepping stone and was integrated into Japan's plan for dominating northeast Asian, with a greater mobilization of Koreans to support its political and military goals. This change brought about the end of Cultural Policy in Korea. In 1931, the new Governor-General Ugaki Kazushige devised a more stringent policy to wipe out Korean cultural autonomy and to carry out a more rapid cultural, historical, and political assimilation of the Korean people into the Japanese Empire. A new education policy in 1934 enforced intensified teaching of the Japanese language, history, and ethics, as well as an enforced pledge of allegiance for all imperial subjects; the Korean language was prohibited. After 1937, all Korean organizations were disbanded and Japanese colonial policy henceforth specifically focused on tightening control over the social and cultural aspects of Korean society. The Japanese attempted to force Koreans to become loyal, obedient imperial subjects, with an intensive mobilization of both people and economic resources to serve Japanese colonial interests.

These developments provided the basis for a dramatic change in Korea's domestic atmosphere, which in turn strongly affected the ideals of the image of Korean women. The changes in colonial policy, especially those aimed at erasing Korean culture and national identity and assimilating Koreans under Japanese subordination, created an enormous sense of national crisis among Korea's nationalist leaders and people. They were now confronted with an historic juncture in the face of the imminent obliteration of their unique national identity and cultural heritage. This crisis superseded all other issues, including the feminist discussions and leftist activities that had prevailed in the 1920s. Thus to show concern for women's status or feminist issues was regarded as extremely selfish, unpatriotic, and anti- nationalistic.[35]

This social reaction created an alternative image of the ideal woman; instead of the 1920s progressive image of the "New Woman," from the early 1930s, a new conservative idealization of women as mothers began to emerge. By the mid-1930s, this new ideal of "glorified motherhood" had become firmly established. The very same authors who had promoted the ideal of female individuality in the 1920s were now praising the virtues of motherhood. Now the highest, most beautiful, goal for women was to become good mothers so that they could give their love and soul to the next generation:

> The most wonderful goal for a woman lies in becoming a good mother. By becoming a mother, she transmits the long cherished love and the beauty of her deepest heart, of her soul, to a new generation. Let's devote all of our lives and beings to our children. After all, the highest goal and ideal for a woman is to give her love and soul to the next generation. For a woman, the very reason to live in this world is to become a good mother.[36]

Practically every issue of *Shin Yosong* (*New Women*) and *Shin Kajong* (*New Home*) was flooded with poems, essays, novels, and articles that praised "motherly love," which was typically characterized by selfless sacrifice and the endless devotion of women to their children. "My mother," "A letter to my mother," "Thinking about my mother," "At my mother's grave," "A song for my mother," "Missing my mother," are typical examples of these contributions. Good mothers were those who dream of their children's beautiful future, weave the clothes of hope for their children,[37] and endure the endless pains of sacrificing everything they have for their children.[38]

This "sacred motherhood" was justified and supported by nationalism, since the urgent political crisis of the nation called for sacrifice. Many Koreans considered it to be inappropriate to waste time arguing for the rights and status of women, when the fate of the whole nation was at stake. In her article, "Choson [Korea] needs mothers like this,"[39] Whang Shin-tuk asserted that Korea needed mothers who could raise tomorrow's nation-builders and transform today's misery into a prosperous future.

What, then, were the virtues such mothers should have? Whang Shin-tuk specifically set out the following four qualities. First, mothers should be determined to carry out what they believe in; they need to have a critical understanding of rapidly changing social issues, and have strong willpower to carry their thoughts into practice. Second, mothers should be progressive and keep up with social changes so that they can raise informed, strong children to become tomorrow's heroes. Korean mothers should be able to discard corrupt customs and conventions and construct new ones to build a better Korea.

Third, mothers should keenly understand Korea's current situation, since this was the environment in which their children would grow up. Mothers should thus know in what direction Korea needed to go and accordingly influence their children so that they could also help to change the environment as they matured. Finally, mothers should sacrifice themselves, discard self-centered vanity, and educate themselves to contribute to the well-being of the country. After all, the future of Korea rested upon on the mothers' shoulders, since each and every baby would become one of tomorrow's nation-builders.

Mothers were said to be the flowers and the stars of the nation; the ones who should give their children the true soul of Korea; and they should thus bear the burden of serving their country.[40] Raising children at home was thus considered the supreme nationalist virtue for women:

> The most important thing for a nation is to have the next generation / To bear and raise sons and daughters / Nothing can be compared to mothers' pains, endurance, and love / . . . / Mother's love is endless love / Do you have appreciation? / Dedicate it all to your mother / Do you have words of praise? / Present it all to your mother / Those who gave us our flesh and blood / Love, sacrifice, endurance, diligence / Mothers gave all these to us / They are our mothers / Our sacred mothers! / They are also mothers of our nation[41]

In addition to these neo-conservative ideals of motherhood, women were expected to be good wives. The image of equal companionship in marriage in the 1920s was replaced by that of a housewife who likes to clean and decorate her home, and who always smiles at and perfectly understands her husband. Having a job or being financially independent was no longer encouraged for married women. A wife was supposed to be the source of strength for her husband, her family, and the nation, and was even described as "an angel with an apron."[42]

The material analyzed in this study shows that the ideal images of women in Korea went though radical changes between the 1890s and the 1930s. The image of "educating mothers" in the Enlightenment Period before 1910 was an enormous break from the traditional image of the "procreating mother." Yet the image of the "educating mother" was superseded by the "New Woman" of the 1920s, whose foremost goal was to find her inner individuality. Nationalistic reaction to the changed colonial environment in the 1930s, however, brushed away all such feminist issues, and instead constructed a new ideal of women in the 1930s as strong mothers who are keenly aware of the political situation of the nation and who could raise the next generation accordingly. By the mid-1930s, this new image of motherhood was firmly established for Korean women; the mothers who were supposed to sacrifice themselves for their children and for the nation. They would raise the enlightened next generation, which was the only hope for Korean society to reclaim its national autonomy.

The colonial threat to the national identity thus superseded the possibility of Korean women to define and develop a feminist agenda, since the national interest always came first. As Bonnie Oh (1982) indicates, feminism and the women's movement in Korea "did not arise from a crisis of *conscience* which sought to rectify a basic inequity within a society, but from a response to the external threat and sought to ensure national survival."[43]

These two opposing ideologies, colonialism and nationalism, thus shaped social, political, and cultural conditions that constructed and imposed ideal images of women that shifted according to society's changing needs. The "educating mothers" ideal in the Enlightenment period was superseded by the "New Woman" of the 1920s, which finally gave way to the "selfless motherhood" ideal of the 1930s. Ironically, both the colonialist and nationalist ideologies, though for different reasons, seemed to direct the image of women toward the 1930s' "selfless motherhood" ideal. By the mid-1930s, this latter image of motherhood was firmly established and strongly promoted to Korean women by nationalistic leaders as well as by the Japanese colonial government. The motherhood image was also approved by the conservative circles in Korean society. However, if colonialism regulated and affected societal factors that limited the possible path of women's self-image, the subtle content of the image was more strongly influenced by nationalism. The 1930s' motherhood ideal was on the surface agreeable to the colonial government who attempted to make docile and submissive subjects out of Koreans; yet, in reality, this constructed image of motherhood embraced a strong, yet covertly patriotic, spirit.

The image of "selfless motherhood" became the basis of today's ideals of Korean motherhood. We can confirm Ueno Chizuko's conclusion, through these transitions of the idealized image of Korean women, that: "Motherhood is neither nature nor culture. It is a historical product, subject to historical change."[44]

14
Education for Liberation or Domestication? Female Education in Colonial Swaziland

Margaret Zoller Booth

The issue of female education under colonial powers and the impact that it had on the cultures of the colonized is gaining in importance among colonial historians, feminist scholars, and education specialists. While academic research addressing the British and French use of formal educational systems as a means to gain power, produce a semiskilled labor class, and spread European culture has flourished, only recent research has examined different colonial philosophies regarding the education of females as distinct from males.[1] Colonial educational policy, curriculum design, and targeted enrollments worked together to provide a different educational experience for boys and girls in many parts of Africa, including Swaziland. Furthermore, the interaction of these formal educational policies, together with Swazi traditional, patriarchal practices, may have worked cooperatively to weaken what power and status Swazi women had previously enjoyed in society.

Swazi society has traditionally been patriarchal, patrilineal, and patrilocal.[2] With political and economic power in the hands of men and the tracing of lineage through the male's family, Swazi women have historically been subservient to men in almost all aspects of society.[3] Gender role differentiation and gender-specific division of labor have influenced Swazi concepts of traditional education. Historically, before the coming of the Europeans, Swazi education was both age-related and gender-specific. Kuper discovered that the training of boys was designed to make them physically tough and mentally disciplined. Young boys spent most of their time in the veld with other males, learning all that was deemed necessary about cattle and manhood. Girls were allowed less freedom of movement. Their training was confined primarily to the homestead, developing domestic skills and learning the proper manners of Swazi women. Their daily routines remained largely unvaried from childhood through adulthood.[4]

One's level of education was also largely influenced by the age peers with whom one was raised. In the case of men, the age class system prepares them for leadership in the community. However, age classes play a relatively smaller part in a woman's life. Kuper points out that "the nature of the women's *emabutfo* [regiments] reflects the subordinate role of women, and the extent to which they are bound by domestic tasks and local interests."[5] For women, their only chance of advancement in society was through the age class system because "with increasing age the inferiority of women is lessened."[6]

Women's access to education was shaped by the colonial government's mission: but did it intend to produce a labor force or "civilize" the country? Since African independence, the vast majority of academic research concerning the purpose and goals of colonial education has embraced the presumption of a colonial policy which was designed to educate Africans just enough to produce a semi-skilled labor force to support the colonial economy. However, the truth of that policy argument was a partial truth. For in fact the colonial educational goal was aimed at only half of the population – men – while the other aim, of "civilizing" and Christianizing the colonized, was designed primarily for women.

It has been well documented in African historical literature (including Swaziland) that the colonial administrations and missionaries worked together designing educational systems that were separate and not equal according to race.[7] Furthermore, colonial administrations permitted the missionaries strong power in educational policy and curriculum decisions, thus freeing themselves from the duty.[8] While creating a semi-skilled labor force was important, missionaries stressed the importance of education as a socializing and Christianizing tool.[9]

The Phelps-Stokes Report, produced in the 1920s by American missionaries concerned with education in Africa, became a guiding document for colonial administrations throughout the colonies. The Report produced the following aims for the future development of colonial education: character, health, agricultural/industrial training, family life, and healthy recreation.[10] Those aims, the Report argued, were designed to meet the needs of both labor development and the Christian "civilizing" mission. The 1944 colonial office document, Mass Education in African Society, also emphasized the need for "technical training" for African "semi-educated juveniles."[11]

While policy documents influenced educational decisions in Swaziland, so too did neighboring countries like South Africa which developed an inferior education for Africans for the sole purpose of creating a "civilized" servitude class for white South Africans. This educational policy strongly influenced Swaziland whose colonial administration believed the protectorate would be incorporated into South Africa in the near future.[12] Elizabeth Schmidt found the same attitude in Zimbabwe as missionaries argued whether the larger purpose in education to be either developing semi-skilled labor or "civilization."[13]

In Swaziland, the debate was no different. Top policy analysts argued for teaching the "Native . . . some form of work" so he can then act in a "civilized manner."[14] Reflections of these sentiments can be found in the 1934 African Primary School Syllabus, which revealed a distinct bias toward the development of manual skills. Approximately one-third of the syllabus was dedicated to detailing the goals and objectives of "industrial work."[15] However, skills outlined in the syllabus were for positions primarily open only to men, while women received domestic training which was not professionally oriented. Therefore, it can be argued that this overall educational goal of industrial training was in fact designed strictly for the male Swazi population. Consequently, Western education in Swaziland never strayed too far from the Swazi traditional social goal of female domestication and in many ways reinforced it. For while the Western curriculum and methods specified for the proper training of a future wife and mother may have differed from the Swazi traditional view, the ultimate goal was the same – domesticity. While education for formal employment may not have been part of the grand scheme for Swazi girls, they were viewed by missionaries and colonial officials as vital participants in the move toward the "modernization" of the Swazi nation.

The majority of research focusing on the education of African girls during the colonial period concentrates much attention on the lack of girls enrolled in school in comparison to the number of boys and the rationale behind it. Most authors blame the biased attitudes of African parents who would not receive "monetary benefits" as they might from an educated male who would later secure employment as a result of his education.[16] However, from the beginning of Western education in Swaziland, enrollment figures at the primary level always were imbalanced in favor of girls. As indicated in Table 14.1, in all years girls consistently (and often substantially) outnumber boys at the primary level but fall behind by the time they reach the upper grades. Thus, while girls enrolled at higher rates, they dropped out at higher rates than boys.

It is important to note that the gender imbalance in these Swazi educational statistics reveal a trend rarely seen in the rest of Africa during the colonial or even post-colonial times.[17] Yet, as previously emphasized, the rationale given in other African territories for the enrollment of boys over girls was the economic gains in later employment to be anticipated for educated males. Consequently Swazi parents, unlike most other African parents on the African continent, were not convinced of the economic benefits for their sons of going to school. Boys were often kept from school because of duties related to the herding and tending of cattle which have been traditionally thought of as the main store of wealth among the Swazi.[18] Therefore, unless formal education was viewed as a means to increase one's most important economic asset, cattle, parents saw little rationale for sending their sons to school.

Yet Swazi parents surely must have desired some benefit from sending their daughters to school. For even if daughters dropped out faster than boys, they were enrolled in the school system at a much higher rate. Yet girls were not sent to school because parents envisioned economic benefits. In Swaziland's patriarchal society, women were not traditionally associated with the primary

Table 14.1 African student enrollments for various years

Year	*1932*	*1941*	*1944*	*1945*	*1948*	*1952*	*1954*	*1956*	*1959*	*1962*
Primary boys	1,100	3,571	3,955	4,578	4,958	7,668	8,441	11,823	13,690	19,625
Primary girls	1,870	5,341	5,560	6,221	5,935	8,793	9,393	12,593	14,721	19,638
Total primary	2,970	8,912	9,515	10,799	10,893	15,487	17,834	24,416	28,411	39,263
Secondary boys		33	57	105	108	288	276	267	373	1,181
Secondary girls		8	52	104	95	236	206	213	282	818
Total secondary		41	109	209	203	524	482	485	655	1,999
Total boys		3,604	4,012	4,683	5,066	7,956	8,717	12,090	14,063	20,806
Total girls		5,349	5,612	6,325	6,030	9,029	9,599	12,806	15,003	20,456
Total Students	2,970	8,953	9,624	11,008	11,096	16,985	18,316	24,896	29,066	41,262

*All statistics except 1932 taken from *Reports on Education in Swaziland*, Mbabane, Swaziland for various years. **1932 statistics taken from Pim Report.

means of economic support for the homestead – cattle. Until recent times, women have been banned from working with cattle.[19] Consequently, if daughters were not sent to school in order to increase their likelihood for economic gains, what were the potential benefits?

Ten Swazi women who went to school during the colonial period were interviewed by this author in 1998 to recount their thoughts and memories of the education they received. The average number of years they had attended school was 5.7. Nine of the ten interviewed believed the education they received was designed to better prepare them to be good mothers rather than to make them marketable professionally. They also agreed that education *could* have helped them get jobs *if* they had been able to continue through secondary school. All interviewees spoke with fond memories of the "home economics" classes they received, where they learned how to "behave as girls."[20] So the question becomes whether parents purposefully sent their daughters to school in order to receive European "domestic training" or whether they hoped their daughter might be one of the fortunate ones able to stay in the school system long enough to reap economic benefits.

As a part of the British "civilizing mission," the school curriculum for girls emphasized female socialization rather than academic subjects. But how were they "to behave as girls"? When analyzing the education of females in other parts of Africa, scholars have argued that the attitudes of the colonizers and missionaries toward the education of African females was influenced by their own European societies' opinions of women.[21] "According to their Victorian Christian ideals," Schmidt contends:

> good mothers stayed at home raising their children according to Christian values, while fathers went out to work in order to feed the family. This ideal corresponded neatly to the needs of the colonial state and the European-dominated economy. While African men were expected to work for Europeans and pay the taxes, African women were to reproduce the labor force and bear the social costs of production.[22]

Both Schmidt and Musisi stress the influence of missionary zeal in *proselytizing* and thus place most of the blame for the continuance of African patriarchy on missionary educational policy. Yet colonial administrations were just as influential, as they openly left African education in the hands of the missionaries and often expressed approval of the job they did. While disputes often arose between missionaries and colonial administrators, in the end missionary policy was usually approved and upheld by the authorities.[23]

While missionaries were constantly concerned about civilizing and making good Christians of their Swazi pupils, so too were colonial officials. Government documents throughout the twentieth century stressed the socialization of the "native," especially with regard to female education. The Phelps-Stokes Commission of 1925 dedicated an entire chapter to the education of women and girls. The Commission agreed that of the five primary aims presented in their Report, four of them (character, health, family life, and recreation) were dependent on the proper teaching of females. Agriculture and industrial training were omitted from their list.

In sum, the Report's chapter on women blames essentially all of the social evils of African society on the "ignorance of the women."[24] It supports this accusation by pointing out that three vital aspects of domestic care within African homesteads (cooking, clothing, and keeping house) are dependent on women. Therefore, when women are ignorant of the proper ways to perform them, the development of civilization is retarded. According to the Report, African women seem to hold the key to completely "make or unmake the individual and the social group."[25] In particular, the Report refers to the influence women have over the "recreational" practices within "native" societies. It blames demns the "rougher recreations of primitive society" on women and contends that the "elimination of the excesses of these will probably depend more largely upon the education of the woman than upon the training of the man."[26] It further warns that the "influence of ignorant and uncivilized wives and mothers upon semi-educated men and boys can do nothing but hamper and delay the development of civilization." Therefore, "tragic results will follow if the education of the African woman does not develop on parallel lines and simultaneously with that of her husband."[27]

In relation to Swaziland, in particular, the Phelps-Stokes Report does mention concern for the low attendance of Swazi pupils in general in comparison to other African nations. However, it also notes the "unusually large proportion of Native girls" in school in relation to the gender figures elsewhere in Africa. The authors of the Report stress the significance which this could make in the "civilizing" mission of the Europeans, and state that "There is therefore a real opportunity for the improvement of the home life of the people."[28] In essence, Swaziland, because of its high female enrollments, held the potential for reaching the Europeans' goals of Christianizing and civilizing.

As for the curriculum, what women needed to know was also listed in the Report. It stressed the need for "health and hygiene related to the life of womanhood and especially to the care of children; agriculture and gardening for food; the home and its responsibilities for the preparation of food, for restful sleep, for clothing, and for the full round of family life; recreation for childhood, youth and adults; [and] character development."[29] While the Report did recognize the need for some "rudimentary professional training," it limited this training to teaching and nursing, which were the only two professions "likely to open before the African woman in the near future."[30]

The Swazi school curriculum of the same era reflected similar concerns. In 1924, there was not yet established a set curriculum for all Swazi schools in the territory because they had been run primarily by individual missionary societies, each with its own curriculum. However, it was clear in a letter attached to the *Native Schools Report* for that year that in addition to religious instruction, particular attention was given by most missions to "the teaching of gardening, sewing and other manual work."[31] Furthermore, the 1931 *Report on Education in Swaziland* laments: "the most pressing requirements [among the Swazi] are more makers of good and satisfactory homes, and for men who can deal more satisfactorily with the land."[32] By 1932, a "code" had been adopted (in the absence of a real syllabus) for the native schools which was "specially prepared for use in Swaziland." The code paid special attention to "the teaching of the vernacular, arts and crafts, hygiene, agriculture, needlework, and the ordinary school subjects."[33]

Girls were limited in their access to knowledge in other ways. At this time, the only secondary school in the country was the Swazi National School at Matsapha which was created to "give to the sons of chiefs and headmen a training that will stand them in good stead when they leave school."[34] Consequently, at this time, girls did not even have access to secondary school. By 1938 girls were enrolled at Matsapha High School in small numbers. Furthermore, because the use of the Swazi vernacular (siSwati) was required in all native primary schools (at least for the first five years), girls rarely had access to English, which was an essential prerequisite for most occupations.

In addition to the medium of instruction, other aspects of the new 1934 African Primary School Syllabus limited female access to the substantive academic curriculum. Of the thirty-three pages describing syllabus requirements for each subject, eleven were dedicated to a detailed description of "Industrial Work." The other twenty-two were divided among all the other subjects. The section on "Industrial Work" for girls included very specific directions for the teaching of: laundry work, needlework, cookery, grasswork, clay modeling, and the "housewife's course." As an example, "cookery work" received one and a half pages of intricate detail, while by contrast the entire history syllabus was accorded one paragraph.

Furthermore, the content of each course syllabus included materials and practices which were suitable for European homes but not traditional Swazi homesteads. For instance, the "laundry work" syllabus contained almost an entire page dedicated to listing the care and cleaning of laundry utensils. Those utensils were ones which were far too expensive for most Swazi to purchase and therefore were rarely found in homesteads. The needlework syllabus included the making of a duster, or handkerchief, in addition to the making of button holes. Again, at that time most Swazi could never have afforded the types of materials needed to create such European objects, including buttons for the button holes.[35]

Some Swazi leaders feared that teaching women European-style domesticity would destroy Swazi culture. The Paramount Chief, *iNgwenyama* Sobhuza II, expressed his concern in a memorandum in which he complained that the methods used in school "treat Africans as Europeans, without first trying to discover what it was that produced good qualities in their own system of education." He further complained that the curriculum instilled certain "social leanings" which would have left the Swazi "with a feeling of intense frustration."[36] Finally, Sobhuza condemned the types of food and clothing styles which were being taught in domestic science classes.

By 1941 concern was being expressed in education reports regarding the quality of education for Swazi females. The colonial administration believed that "female education would also receive greater attention through the appointment of a woman to the inspectoral staff with special training and experience on the side of female education."[37] Thus government concern for the quality of female education was primarily limited to domestic courses. This concern continued through 1944 when, for the first time, the *Annual Report on Education* included an entire section dedicated to "Female Education." However, the bulk of this section concentrated on the domestic science syllabus and the special needs for those courses. One of the basic problems of teaching domestic science was described as the "extra expenses of the needed materials," for sewing and cooking. The two solutions which schools used were either to "charge the girls extra fees for the materials" (most likely increasing the female drop-out rate even more) or "permitting" the girls to "practice" their skills in the houses of the head teachers. Schmidt found the same treatment in Zimbabwe, and concluded that the missionaries harbored a "hidden agenda" in the teaching of domestic science. Many of the girls practiced in the homes of their teachers and missionaries what they had learned at school, and consequently these Europeans received free labor in the form of cooking, ironing, sewing, and cleaning.[38]

According to the *1955 Swaziland Annual Report*, the strong emphasis on domestic science courses in the girls' curriculum was partially to blame for the high drop-out rate of females through the primary grades. The report finally makes the connection between high female drop-outs and lack of economic opportunity after school. In other words, schools were not training girls to become anything other than housewives. "Many leave school after Standard VI and this is attributed to . . . economic reasons, and that few careers apart from teaching and nursing are open to girls even after secondary school education."[39] And yet, throughout the 1950s and even until independence (1968) female enrollments in the very first years of school continued to outnumber the males. Colonial administrators attributed this to the willingness on the part of parents, especially women, to send their daughters to school. The fact that "Swazi women show more concern about the education of their children than do the men makes for progress in the field of female education."[40] However, the question remains whether women *were* making progress, a question that would be put to the test in the post-World War II period.

After 1945, the Colonial Office began to reveal some concern for the general development throughout their African colonies and dependencies. London envisioned the institution of Western education as a means to rectify the poor place women held in society. It indicated in a 1948 report a clear desire to elevate African women from their lower place in patriarchal African society. The report gave the impression that the Colonial Office was ready to "liberate" and empower African women:

> the grim fact has to be faced . . . . that women and girls have so far taken little part in educational advance . . . . In the full balanced development of African society, woman must take an increasingly active share. To achieve this, her material lot must be improved, her knowledge extended, and there must be a general recognition of her place and her influence in all spheres of life and labour.[41]

Yet while colonial administrators agonized over the status of women in African society, they also produced an educational system that not only reinforced female domestic roles but at times even strengthened them. Gaitskell discovered the same contradiction in South Africa. While some academics have argued that Western education for women in South Africa helped them gain employment as domestic servants in European homes, Gaitskell did not. By contrast, she found that while a small percentage gained domestic positions, the majority were being trained to return home.[42] Furthermore, in Swaziland, the prospects for domestic employment were always low. In 1921, for instance, only 1.7 percent of all women were employed in domestic service, whereas almost 92 percent were peasant farmers. By 1950, less than 500 women were employed in domestic service in all of Swaziland.[43]

The same contradictions have been found in Uganda and Zimbabwe. While colonial powers viewed the education of women as an important part of "development," the role that women were to be allowed to play in development was no more extensive than what traditional African societies had already permitted. However, as Schmidt points out, in this case girls learned in a formal setting that it was their duty to stay at home and cook, clean, raise healthy Christian children, and respect and obey their husbands. "While African men were to work for wages in the European economy," she argued, "their wives were to stay at home, reproducing the labor force and bearing the social costs of production."[44]

The previously analyzed *Swaziland Education Reports* throughout the twentieth century referred to an education system which enrolled a larger number of girls than boys in the first year. However, this system discarded them before they could reach a standard of education which could provide high-level training, English instruction, and matriculation results to permit entrance into higher institutions of learning. With this as the case, the argument is compelling that the colonial administration was in no way even attempting to fulfill its stated goal in the 1948 conference, to "extend [a woman's] knowledge" and to recognize "her place and her influence in all spheres of life and labour."

Furthermore, the administration's stated desire to improve her "material lot" was also contradicted by colonial administrative practices. Not only was the curriculum for job training restricted to boys, but so too was agricultural training for cash crop production. For instance, the Phelps-Stokes Commission predicted in the 1920s that African society would be required to undergo some social changes. The writers of the report realized that traditionally in much of Africa (including Swaziland) agricultural production for the family's food supply had been designated as women's work. However in order not "to burden" the women with any more work, the Report suggested that "even if women still till the food crops the newly introduced money crops might be regarded as in the sphere of the men."[45] Thus women would once again be excluded from the formal sector economy where the real monetary power was located.

The curriculum available to girls and women in Swaziland ensured that they would increase their domestic skills and also allow for some extra cash to be made through the informal sector of the economy; basket weaving, pottery making, and other handcrafts were viewed as acceptable activities outside of the homestead. These skills provided women with a little extra cash to better run their homes without challenging the economic power of their husbands. In 1931, for instance, females attending the Mbuluzi Girls' School not only learned mat weaving and other crafts, but also learned how to sell them in informal markets. Missionaries, wanting to stress the practical significance of this, wrote to the *Times of Swaziland*: "Quite apart from the purely religious training, industrial training was everywhere in evidence. Articles made by students in their leisure were sold for their personal profit . . . . The school has a wide market for its mats and other products."[46] This emphasis is still clearly seen in the curriculum of the 1950s, when educational planners expressed delight with the high female enrollments in Swazi schools. As reported in 1953: "Every effort is made to capitalise on the large female enrolment. Needlework and Domestic Science . . . are given every encouragement . . . . a Housecraft Center has been established . . . . The two year course includes training in dressmaking, mothercraft, cookery, simple dietetics and general housewifery."[47]

Consequently, the smattering of education that girls received in school was generally enough to have a small effect on their lifestyles at home, supplementing their Swazi traditions with European customs (including of course religion) and adding a little pocket money to supplement the diet with store-bought goods or to save up in order to send another family member to school. To be sure, it was not enough to provide women with some education. They also had to have the opportunity to enter the professional sector in order to be motivated to finish school. Ironically, boys, who would have better job opportunities after school, failed to enter school at high rates. School administrators lamented this fact.[48] Consequently, schools provided a limited education for the majority of its pupils (girls), who were then not qualified to enter the job market. Yet, public and private sector positions went unfilled.

It is arguable that traditional Swazi male society did not want women academically and technically trained any more than Europeans did. The heavy emphasis on domestic science courses in schools for girls fit the pattern of what Swazi men wanted for their women. While it may not have been the same type of domestic science which girls would have received in informal traditional education, the emphasis was similar. To equip women with the ability to become economically independent would have gone completely against this patriarchal/ patrilineal society. Miles argues that the strict gender division of labor within the Swazi household was strengthened during the colonial era due to land alienation, environmental pressures and increasing levels of male migrant labor. This put further pressure on women to be even more dependent on men for economic support.[49]

While women were generally in favor of sending their girls to school, there was growing suspicion among the male Swazi population regarding the impact of formal education on acculturation and its influence on traditional family structure and the hierarchy of status within society. In particular, *iNgwenyama* Sobhuza expressed his deep concern regarding the impact that Western schools were having on Swazi social structure and culture in general. In a memorandum read to the Native Education Advisory Board, he complained that Western schools caused students to "despise Swazi institutions" and "indigenous culture." He also worried that these students would no longer fit in with their present "environment." But most importantly, Sobhuza worried that students in Western schools were "released" from "the wholesome restraints which the Swazi indigenous method of education inculcated."[50]

This last worry was particularly aimed at girls who traditionally had more "restraints" placed on them in Swazi society. For this reason, fear of too much schooling for daughters was voiced by many elders. The Rev. Mr. Robinson stated in a meeting of the Advisory Board on Native Education that parents were complaining that "in these days we are teaching girls that they need not bow to the control of their parents."[51] Fathers, in particular, were afraid that their educated daughters would leave home, find employment in town, and disregard their intentions to commit them to arranged marriages. For runaway daughters caused fathers to forfeit cherished *lobola* (bridewealth) which constituted an important underpinning of the homestead's economic wealth. This fear was made clear in a debate over the marriageable age for girls in letters to the editor of the *Times of Swaziland* during 1933. The letters pointed out that while traditionally girls were not married until 16 years of age, modern fathers were being tempted to marry their educated daughters off earlier "in order to keep them away from town mischief."[52]

The greatest resistance to schooling consistently came from Swazi elders, who stood to lose the most in economic and political power because of it. Kuper identified the principal elder concern that "formal education weakens the claim of the uneducated that the possession of the greatest knowledge is obtainable only through age."[53] It can be argued that this fear was especially true in the case of female education, for until recently girls had enjoyed very limited legal, political, or economic power.

The concern of Kuper's elderly Swazi over the education of women was well founded. The ten women who were interviewed by this author in 1998 felt that men traditionally have enjoyed much more power in society than women. They all agonized over the hard work which women performed in the homestead, yet were not rewarded for it. Furthermore, while women essentially ran the homestead, their men retained decision-making power over them. One woman reflected on the relationship between education and power: "Since women are not as educated, they can't do as much. Education gives you power – your salary will be higher." Yet another spoke about education or knowledge as powerful in and of itself. "Education has helped me a little because I am able to *see* when my rights are gone. Those without education can not even see that their rights are taken."[54]

"Changed men will require changed mates,"[55] is how the Phelps-Stokes Report summed up the rationale for educating girls. But what if the "changed mates" change too much? In many African colonies, small percentages of women took advantage of their missionary education in ways not always foreseen by Europeans or by their parents at home. Schmidt found in Zimbabwe that "African women and girls perceived mission education as a means of upward mobility." Education often permitted them to marry wealthier, educated men, or it opened up professional opportunities. She concluded that "despite missionary intentions" some women were able to build their own economic independence. While the only professions normally available to them were teaching and nursing, still some were able to climb the ladder in those fields and thereby enter the "emerging African female middle class."[56]

This was also the case in Swaziland, yet the fact remained that the most educated Swazi women recognized that the best professional opportunities to be across the border in South Africa. Before 1960, Swazi women needed no legal documentation from Swaziland to cross the border and women flocked to Johannesberg seeking better paid jobs than they could get in Swaziland. However, Swazi men have historically tried to prevent women from crossing the border, in order to keep them from gaining economic independence. Men objected to the bus service and the introduction of the railway systems because it enabled women to travel to town on their own and to cross into South Africa. It was not until after the 1948 political changes bringing official apartheid that travel to and staying in South Africa became difficult for any Swazi – male or female.[57]

However, because the best jobs for everyone, female and male, lay across the border, the numbers of Swazi men who migrated to South Africa as laborers escalated from 1914 throughout most of the twentieth century. When men departed, they often left behind women with children who had little means of support and therefore were forced to search for wage employment themselves armed with what little education they had.[58] Consequently, the institution of migrant labor created a working class of women who were not just earning wages out of a need for professional self-fulfillment, but also out of stark economic necessity. This circumstance created even further gender role disruptions. Those conflicts were expressed by one migrant laborer when he told Kuper that the "men have become the women of the Europeans. When we return home our wives are independent and disrespectful." He was also concerned that when they beat their wives, the latter would "run to the court of the European and complain that we maltreat them."[59]

This example of women running "to the court of the European" represents a growing trend in the twentieth century. One editorial in the local newspaper expressed concern that young, educated people would appeal "to whichever of the two Governments is the more likely to favour his cause and facilitate the object he has in view."[60] This was especially true of young, educated women who came to recognize that European courts would often rule in their favor. Alan Booth found that Swazi women sought protection from colonial courts especially in matters of forced marriage and male physical violence.[61] As Musisi found in Uganda, so too in Swaziland: "education beyond domesticity had begun to challenge men in a very sensitive area: their right as husbands to control their wives."[62]

To what extend did education serve to provide more opportunities for women in the colonial or post-colonial eras? "Her subservience is obvious, her ignorance is not questioned, her capacity is decried."[63] This is how the missionaries and colonial administrations viewed African women. Yet at the same time, they also recognized that historically African women have often exercised great power, especially in Swaziland. The Phelps-Stokes Report particularly recognized the Queen Mother of Swaziland whom it described as "a ruler as potent as Khama himself."[64] With such paradoxical opinions regarding African women, it is no wonder that educational policy in Swaziland regarding girls was historically unclear and often confused. Yet it is obvious that the policy of education for the training of skilled labor was for many years denied to the female gender.

This chapter finds it arguable that the primary purpose of colonial education for *all* Africans was to develop a semiskilled working class capable of filling positions needed in the civil service and private industry. While this may have been a primary motive behind male education, formal education for females was less specific. While it is clear that women were viewed as the key to "civilizing" the household, how that translated into female education was often incoherent and inconsistent. Europeans designed an education for girls that would primarily create good Christian housewives in the European model. Yet, their policy regarding curriculum content (academic vs. practical) and enrollment goals was, in retrospect, seemingly designed to fail. While girls enrolled in higher numbers than boys in Swaziland, their attendance was still not great enough to bring about a "cultural revolution" in the country. Furthermore, little was done to try to retain girls in the system sufficiently long to afford them enough education to truly affect their livelihood and empowerment as future female leaders.

Fundamentally, colonial administrations never developed a clear picture as to how education would truly affect women. While they envisioned it as a means to civilize the nation, in order to do so, they would have had to take the further step of helping women gain access to political and economic power as well. It is hardly likely that the Europeans, coming as they did from a patriarchal culture themselves would have done so. Furthermore, providing a high level of education for the Swazi female population would have been political suicide for the colonial administration who wished to befriend the Swazi monarchy in accordance with British indirect rule policy after 1922.[65] According to this approach, colonial administrators did what they could to rule through the present African traditional power structure. Accordingly, the creation of an educated female population which could gain access to economic and political power would have angered the monarchy, making it impossible for the colonial administration to rule indirectly.

While a small minority of Swazi women were able to take advantage of European education in order to qualify themselves for employment and therefore upward mobility, this was not what the missionaries and colonial administrators had intended. On the contrary, as we have seen, formal education was largely designed to domesticate African women according to British cultural values. In so doing, the official idea was to reproduce European and Christian values in Swazi children, thus reproducing the domestication of future generations of housewives, and thereby perpetuating the patriarchy.

15
Women, Gender History, and Imperial Ethiopia

Timothy Fernyhough and Anna Fernyhough

Ethiopia has long been a source of interest to Westerners. Christianized during the Roman Empire but cut off from the Mediterranean in the seventh century of the common era by the rise and expansion of Islam, Ethiopia remained at least partially Christian throughout its long separation from European contact. This, along with the country's rugged terrain, political organization, and ability to defend themselves from outside intrusion, kept the peoples of Ethiopia from being colonized by Europeans, even during the late nineteenth-century "Scramble for Africa." However, an abortive effort by Italy to establish a colony at that time was followed by a more determined effort under Mussolini in the 1930s, which temporarily deposed the Ethiopian emperor. Nevertheless, Ethiopia cannot be said to have been a colonial country, which raises a significant question: to what extent can a country that has never been fully or successfully colonized be the subject of the "colonial gaze"? As K.E. Fleming suggests elsewhere in the present volume, eighteenth- and nineteenth-century Europeans travelers treated Greek history as a "colonial" possession, molding it to fit their notions of what ancient Greece was and what contemporary Greece "should" have been.[1] The present chapter will use historiographical analysis to argue that a similar "colonization" has occurred in Ethiopian women's history, as mid-twentieth-century African scholars attempted to fit Ethiopian history into existing anthropological, sociological, or theoretical models that minimized or misread women's roles. It will further point the way for new, less patriarchal approaches to Ethiopian women's history in the wake of more recent studies of African, colonial and women's history.

Social history has since the 1960s been at the heart of the new historiography of Ethiopia. A now impressive volume of scholarly output has focused on such issues as the relations between state, society, and the economy, on modes of social protest, on revolution and its aftermath, and on agrarian history. Moreover, the recent work of social historians and anthropologists has started to fill several of the topical and thematic "gaps" identified by Donald Crummey in 1990 in an important "taking stock" article.[2] Thus the 1990s have seen the publication of three general histories of Ethiopia, new departures in the study of Islam, a new historical dictionary, and renewed opportunities for archaeologists and students of Ethiopian antiquity.[3] In recent years the historical origins and politics of identity, including the "restoration" of women's identity, have drawn particular attention, as social scientists have tried to understand how groups within Ethiopia have exploited opportunities to preserve their own cultures and history.[4] Given the current Ethiopian government's commitment to a devolved administrative structure based on ethnic autonomy and at least nominally to the equal rights of men and women, such works in ethnographic and women's history are particularly pertinent and reflect the longstanding contribution of social anthropology to the study of Ethiopian history.[5]

Amidst what is now a rich body of work on Ethiopian society, a most significant lacuna highlighted by Crummey in 1990 was women's studies. Not only was extant scholarship in the social sciences "all male," but worse it showed "no sensitivity to the issues raised by feminism."[6] Such pessimistic conclusions were by no means new. Writing in 1982 one of the authors of this chapter had commented that, very regrettably, research on Ethiopian women "has been written largely from a male perspective." She observed also that women tended almost invariably to be viewed in terms of their relations to men.[7] It was clear that during fieldwork, researchers had most often drawn their data from male informants.

As recently as 1992 Helen Pankhurst, who has written extensively on women in development in Ethiopia, could still bemoan a situation where there was "still no single book devoted to the position of women in Ethiopia as a whole" and that "most of the general works have been written by, and focused on, men."[8] If this was strictly accurate, times were changing. In the mid-1960s Comhaire Sylvain was almost alone as she studied the opportunities made available to Ethiopian women through their improved access to higher education and professional training.[9] But by the early 1980s the work of Daniel Haile, Salome Gebre Egziabher, Judith Olmstead, and Laketch Dirasse had introduced new diversity, though given the paucity of previous output they could scarcely fail in this. Their topics encompassed the legal, educational, and health conditions of women, women in rural communities in southern Ethiopia, the changing role and position of women in society, and prostitution.[10]

A decade later, Helen Pankhurst's lament for more scholarship on Ethiopian women still held, particularly for a general work, but several scholars had already picked up the baton, looking initially at social and economic status, life histories, and at women and rural development. Among these were Hirut Tefere and Lakew Woldetekle, Anne Cassiers, Hanna Kebede, and, more recently, Addis Tiruneh.[11] Their efforts were soon matched by other important contributions. Several derived from a pathbreaking seminar on gender issues convened at Addis Ababa University in December 1989. Published two years later by Tsehai Berhane-Selassie, the proceedings included substantive papers on women, their role in and access to education and training, on women and gender issues in health care, in the media and in rural development.[12] The collection also addressed the changing roles, economic occupations, and status of women in relation to specific rural communities in southern Ethiopia.[13]

Pankhurst has herself pioneered whole new areas for research and analysis. Her study of Amhara women in Menz, to the north of the Ethiopian capital Addis Ababa, in the late 1980s and early 1990s, explored peasant–state relations, and the failure of nationally inspired agrarian reform programmes. However, it entered a new domain in its analysis of how local custom and household dynamics, tradition, folklore, religious and spirit beliefs, reflected, shaped, and upheld feminine identities in rural Ethiopian society. Particularly exciting was her analysis of *conjonctures* in rural gender history, especially the intersection of social and economic contexts with issues of culture, human biology and the life-cycle: birth, reproduction, death.[14] Thus Pankhurst's work, with that of Almaz Eshete, has moved our focus well beyond the role of women in economic production.[15] Conversely, Zerihun Asfaw has argued that in Ethiopian literature women "are primarily portrayed in their biological roles as mothers, wives, girlfriends," mostly in urban contexts, and usually in their relation to men, at times simply as "sexual objects."[16] In her view, Ethiopian literature will come of age only when it embraces "women's roles in economic, social and political activities." Clearly a fruitful point of convergence with social scientists lies in rural women, and in the social and spiritual issues which govern their lives. In pursuing these, Ethiopian authors may have to follow a lead already set by visual artists, especially women painters, who have not shirked portraying social conditions and the "burden" of both urban and rural women.[17]

Given the previous neglect of Ethiopian women as a subject of serious research, these are promising developments. Yet for historians, and especially social historians, there is still very little to go on. The few notable treatments of women in Ethiopia's past have merely highlighted how impoverished the field is generally, and how urgently Ethiopian Studies needs intellectual commitment by historians of women and gender. Thus Richard Pankhurst has taken a selective look at the role of women in Ethiopia between the medieval period and the eighteenth century, and at the history of prostitution.[18] Most recently he has turned his attention to a topic first considered by Bairu Tafla: dynastic marriage and alliance between royal and noble houses.[19] Chris Prouty's meticulous scholarship has shed new light on leading women of Ethiopia's *Zamana Masafent* (Ethiopia's "time of troubles", 1769–1855, lit. "era of the princes"), and on Taytu Betul, wife of the Emperor Menilek who repelled the Italian invasion in 1896 and constructed the twentieth-century imperial state.[20] Her subsequent monograph on Taytu discerned the hand of the empress in shaping policy through the major events of her husband's reign and thereafter, and discloses her consummate skills in diplomacy, administration, and intrigue.[21] Finally, Crummey has moved discussion decisively into the arena of social history by analyzing how far noble women in the heartland of historic Abyssinia enjoyed formal rights to land and the extent of their actual control over it.[22] Historians keenly await publication of his new book on land and society in pre-revolutionary Ethiopia, which promises further insights into the relations between family and property.

However, as members of imperial Ethiopia's ruling families and high nobility, the subjects of most of these studies were numerically a privileged minority, hardly representative historically of their sex. Thus a significant problem of the limited historiography of Ethiopian women is that it remains sharply skewed toward those of royal or noble descent. One imperative is to redress the balance from the elite to the plebeian, and thereby historically enfranchise the majority of women who belonged to the cultivating classes, the peasant women of rural Ethiopia. As in many countries, and as Almaz has reiterated, women constitute over half the Ethiopian population, and have "always figured prominently in the development of society." If we are minded to pause at her assertion that the historical data are not difficult to come by, nonetheless we fully agree with her that the lack of studies of Ethiopian women, particularly in their historical and cultural context, reflects an "absence of previous concern" both with women and especially gender issues.[23]

Clearly Ethiopian social history will be far the richer when "the majority find its past."[24] However, as Almaz, Hirut, and others recognize, the task is not simply to recover women in Ethiopian history, to merely reconstruct their past in isolation from the other half of the population. The art will be to depict gender within historic Ethiopian societies in the light of other variables, initially relations between and within the sexes, but also in terms of class, society and economy, politics, culture, religion, and family without imposing models which have often been developed as an aspect of colonial inquiry.[25] Nor should historians of Ethiopia be insensitive to the vigorous debates which have informed the relatively brief career of gender history, as discourse has moved from a point of conjunction with social and material history to a "postmodernist" preoccupation with gender and linguistic and critical theory.[26]

To date the historical literature has barely scraped the surface in applying concepts of gender to empirical studies of Ethiopian women. Indeed, we remain unclear even about the place of women in past Ethiopian societies, still less about how gender articulates with other social relations such as class, ethnicity, wealth, or status. Hence, the remainder of this essay addresses three critical themes: first, the place of Ethiopian women in the theoretical literature; second, images of Ethiopian women as viewed by their contemporaries and historians, where we look especially at the extent to which women exercised independence and control; and third, and briefly, avenues of future research. Chronologically, discussion of these covers a lengthy period, from the "restoration" of the Solomonic dynasty in the late thirteenth century, through the *Zamana Masafent*, to the reconstruction of the imperial state by successive rulers between 1855 and the 1974 revolution. However, for our purposes the period may be considered analytically as one because, apart from the brief interlude of the Italian occupation (1935–41), Ethiopia was neither colonized nor incorporated into the world economy to any significant degree. Geographically, the analytical focus lies in the largely Amharic- and Tegrenya-speaking heartland of Christian Abyssinia – the historic provinces of Bagemder, Shawa, Gojjam, Lasta and Tegre (including the Eritrean districts of Hamasen and Akala-Guzay), but does not exclude the vast, largely Oromo and Omotic, southern territories incorporated by Emperor Menilek after 1870, which extended Ethiopia to its twentieth-century frontiers. Necessarily, the reflections which follow are no more than prolegomena to substantive research and further discourse, to the books which have yet to be written.

Rather refreshingly, Ethiopian women have proved extremely difficult to fit within scholarly models and typologies. Long before heightened feminist awareness in the 1960s stimulated new interest in African women, and moved research away from considering women primarily in relation to marriage and the family, anthropologists had embraced theoretical constructs which analytically diminished their significance.[27] In some ways, this imposition of an outside model of social structure by observers is comparable to the colonial view of officials in Canada and Mexico as described by Vázquez-García in Chapter 7 above, who disregarded and undermined existing sibling and matrilineal descent groups by applying European patriarchal familial structures to concepts of land ownership.[28] In the case of Ethiopia, by relying heavily on unilineal models of social relations first proposed by Evans-Pritchard and Radcliffe-Brown, and used for instance by Meyer Fortes in his studies of the Tallensi and Asante, African ethnography underplayed the importance of women as political and juridical agents, and assumed that women only rarely controlled property and exercised legal rights.[29] Drawing inspiration in part from Firth's research in the Pacific, by the mid-1960s Schneider, Scheffler, and others had begun to question Fortes' assertion that only unilineal societies produced corporate, "closed," descent groups with legal, political, and property-holding functions.[30] Where ambilineal descent operated, as they did among the Amhara of Ethiopia, it was clear that men and women could manipulate political and legal claims as members of a "cognatic descent group."[31] Thus, the Ethiopian setting very early demonstrated the limitations of the "unilineal model," especially in its polarity of respective male and female roles in the conduct of politico-juridical and domestic matters.[32]

Nor have Ethiopian women fitted other than awkwardly into typologies of their position based on their role as agrarian producers and their modes of cultivation.[33] Baumann's broad historical correlation for Africa between hoe cultivation, vegetable crops, and female labour on the one hand, and more intensive agricultural techniques, cereal production, increasing male labor, and social stratification on the other, is a generalization now over sixty years old.[34] However, it underpinned Boserup's oft-cited conclusions that different modes of agrarian production, and different farming techniques, governed changes in the division of labor and delineated the role and position of women in diverse societies.[35] In most of Africa, she asserted, where female labourers worked root crops using hoes, women retained a large measure of economic power and social standing. In Asia, where plow and other more intensive forms of cultivation occurred, there developed more rigid gender roles in agriculture and society, in which men predominated, and in which women were marginalized, held subordinate, and constrained in terms of their social interaction, movement and clothing.

Guyer has rightly challenged the basic premise of Baumann's model, arguing on the basis of a number of case studies that the fundamental flaw of the root and cereal crop distinction in Africa is that "labour organisation differs at least as much within those two categories as it does between them."[36] Specifically for Ethiopia, Helen Pankhurst has made the manifest point that the strikingly hierarchical plow-based society of historic Ethiopia matches the Asian model more closely than the African one. She concludes that at the very least this could be used to highlight the dangers of geographical determinism. Moreover, she reminds us also that in Ethiopia the gendered division of labor was by no means as pervasive as in many parts of Asia. Women enjoyed considerable social and economic autonomy, and there was, and still is, "little segregation and veiling."[37] Nor, she asserts, should we be too ready to embrace the complementary arguments advanced by Jack Goody.

Goody has posited that across much of sub-Saharan Africa plentiful land, extensive agriculture, and low levels of technology, notably reliance on the hoe rather than the plow, modified political structures and worked against the emergence of distinct social classes and the division of labor by sex. Moreover, in political terms land surplus and low levels of productivity meant that chieftainship tended to be over people rather than land; women were controlled for their labor and reproductive labor.[38] Conversely, in Eurasian regions where plow agriculture raised productivity, and land was relatively scarce and competed for, elites appropriated surpluses and restricted commoners' control of their holdings. In creating a class society, they also marginalized women, controlled their property rights and reproductive capacities, and in so doing reinforced male authority in such areas as marriage and inheritance. Ethiopia appeared to fit the latter bill in several respects, though Goody clearly perceived the Abyssinian case as lying between his sub-Saharan and Eurasian norms.[39] Historically, state and ruling classes controlled fiefs (*gult*); there were degrees of subinfeudation and fragmentation of political authority. Rulers and nobles exacted peasant tribute in a plow-based milieu which more closely resembled a feudal society than any other. In this stratified and highly deferential context women were denied access to land and the means of production.[40] Nevertheless, women were never subordinated so decisively as in parts of Asia, and retained significant marriage and inheritance rights. In part this may have derived from relatively low levels of agricultural surplus produced in historic Abyssinia.[41] Perhaps more significant was the reality that the "overwhelming bulk of the land was under peasant control, as were the associated means of production, mainly oxen."[42] In Ethiopia ruling elites had only limited direct access to land, relying primarily on tribute and *corvée* labour as their primary mode of surplus extraction. Peasant control of land across much of the Christian heartland derived from inalienable rights called *rest*. These were vested in the cognatic descent group whose living members, the *balerest*, (owners of *rest* and descendants of the legendary first holder, the *wanna abbat* – usually a noble, soldier, or priest) claimed and exercised them in their lifetimes.

Thus application of current theoretical approaches to the position and role of women in Ethiopia has proved less than rewarding, even "puzzling."[43] This is not least because the empirical data are themselves often equivocal or contradictory. If these occasionally reflect the very diverse cultural contexts which scholars encounter in a far from homogeneous Ethiopia, their interpretations often say more about their preconceptions, preoccupations, and even prejudices than about the women themselves, and about attitudes towards them. Hence, scholarly images of Ethiopian women, whether historical or contemporary, are potentially very misleading, especially, as Crummey has warned, when they take male views as representative of those of society. In Crummey's view Donald Levine, the pre-eminent sociologist of Ethiopia, was an early offender.[44] Writing in 1965, Levine contended that such Amharic proverbs as "women and donkeys need the stick" and derisory expressions like "women's work" and "women's talk" accurately conveyed the low status in which women were held in Ethiopian society.[45] Reiterating this view almost ten years later, and extending a sweeping analysis across the whole country, he was even more forthright. Thus most Ethiopians, he believed, considered women inferior, had little respect for their femininity, and were derogatory of "alleged female attributes." By the same token, the "general Ethiopian pattern" was "to associate the highest values exclusively with masculinity."[46]

Such pejorative views of the opposite sex were familiar and frequently expressed. They underscore the depiction by many scholars of Ethiopian society historically dominated by men. Thus Hanna Kebede and Almaz Eshete, among many others, have described Ethiopian society as patriarchal and the position of women as clearly subordinate and inferior.[47] Nor are further Ethiopian examples hard to find. Meshesha affirms the male conviction that women should be submissive and behave modestly. Men expected that women neither ate nor drank to excess. Their male children were more highly valued, and girls were traditionally christened forty days after boys because this was the time a girl had to wait "to become the equal of a boy!"[48] Hence, our evidence indicates that Ethiopian men from diverse ethnic groups maintained negative opinions of women.

Where Levine and others enter dangerous waters is in assuming that these views were held "generically" by the majority of the different peoples of Ethiopia, and within each ethnic group equally between the sexes.[49] Levine is himself aware of exceptions to his "general Ethiopian pattern," acknowledging, for example, that non-Muslim Oromo societies have a "relatively benign view of women."[50] However, Hirut's recent survey demonstrates wide variation between ethnic groups, with Oromo respondents at one end of the spectrum according women high social status within their communities, Afar and Anuak low status at the other, with major groups like the Amhara lying somewhere between.[51] Moreover, it may be very wrong to assume that women from diverse Ethiopian cultures also shared pejorative views of their own sex, status, and role in society. Thus Hirut's survey also highlights how men and women differed markedly in their assessment of their roles as the family's breadwinners.[52] Further evidence, discussed below, demonstrates that even where a pervasive male hegemony prevailed, women were by no means always passive, deferential, and conformist. In their daily lives and consciousness they often questioned and rejected the ideological domination and hegemonic authority of men.

If ambivalence surrounds the social place of women, both recent and contemporary, and their perceptions of their own standing, there is no consensus as yet about their historical importance. Nevertheless, there is scope for preliminary observations. Hence, in the rest of this chapter we consider in turn, and as far scant data permit, the historical place and status of women politically, legally, and in rural society and economy. Analysis of these topics helps delineate the research opportunities which lie ahead, and in closing we offer a few cautionary remarks.

Women of the ruling elite and nobility clearly played significant political roles in pre-revolutionary Ethiopia, most often as advisors and mediators, and occasionally in their own right. As depicted by Prouty, Empress Taytu did both.[53] Well before her husband Menilek, she divined the true extent of Italian ambitions in Ethiopia and determined to frustrate them. Her resolution as the Ethiopians defeated the Italians at the battle of Adwa in March 1896, even perhaps as her husband Menilek's nerve wavered, is well attested. Between 1908 and 1910, as Menilek's health failed, she was *de facto* ruler of Ethiopia. Nor should we forget that Ethiopia's penultimate monarch was also female. Menilek's eldest daughter, Empress Zawditu (r. 1916–30) may have owed her elevation to the Shawan nobility and her own "political innocuousness."[54] However, she was no political cipher. Thus Marcus argues that in her relations with the regent and heir, *Ras* Tafari Makonnen (later Emperor Haile Selassie I, 1930–74), she always "had the last word."[55]

Empress Taytu was by no means the only female ruler to achieve real political pre-eminence and to demonstrate a sound grasp of government. Almost two centuries before, between 1722 and 1769, the ambitious and talented dowager Empress Mentewab had exercised power with her husband Bakaffa, and had ruled as she outlived him through her son and grandson.[56] Reaching further back, Richard Pankhurst's "collation of data" from the Middle Ages to the *Zamana Masafent* discloses how Emperor Zara Yaqob (r. 1434–68), for example, relied heavily on his two daughters to conduct state business, and appointed a number of noble "princesses" in his provincial administration.[57] His wife Elleni, originally a Hadya princess whom he married as early as 1445, disclosed impressive political talents over more than half a century. Her shrewd judgment in government and sound grasp of diplomacy served not only Zara Yaqob's son, Ba'eda Maryam (r. 1468–78), who allowed her to retain the title of queen, but his grandson, Emperor Na'od (r. 1494–1508), and his great-grandson, Lebna-Dengel (r. 1508–40), in whose minority she acted as regent.[58]

Remarkable as these figures were, they were too few to break the political mold. Imperial Ethiopia rested on gendered conceptions of political authority, occupational boundaries and social status.[59] Elite women occasionally enjoyed real political power, but the framework in which they operated was masculine. It barely mattered that women could on rare occasions participate actively in imperial political life, because the political process was geared, or gendered, to ensure that men were visible and empowered, the bestowers and the beneficiaries of the state's patronage and power. Both the prevailing discourse and the structure of power relations ensured that women were, save for the brief exceptions noted above, excluded from politics. Noble women might, as Salome Gebre Egziabher has argued, enjoy rank and privilege, and be apparently treated as equal to male members of their class, but there is little evidence that this translated into political clout.[60] Still less did it ever change where authority and legitimacy were located within the state. Men were never seriously threatened as masters of the political house. Women might rule, and occasionally reign, but the "Solomonic" heritage of the Ethiopian emperors was an almost exclusively male domain.

Legally women were more highly favored. Men monopolized the apparatus of the law as judges, officials, and elders. However, a number of scholars agree that women enjoyed substantial property rights.[61] According to Dan Bauer the prerequisite for claimants to land in Enderta in Tegre was actual residence in the district and descent from the founding ancestor of the village from whom all inheritance rights derived.[62] In pre-revolutionary Gojjam Allan Hoben observed that "with regard to the ownership of land and moveable property and the right to institute divorce the wife is very much the equal of her husband."[63] At Ankober in Shawa, site of a former nineteenth-century royal, later imperial, capital, land could come from claims activated by men or women.[64]

The reason for this is that in the ambilineal society of the Christian heartland, women could make such claims on an equal basis with men, for all children held equal hereditary land rights.[65] Like men, women could claim land bilaterally through up to twelve generations of both male and female ancestors. They were restricted only by the claims of other members of the cognatic descent group, tax and service obligations, and the viability of the *rest* plot in question. If overlapping claims reinforced the potential for conflict, women nonetheless enjoyed the same rights in litigation over property as men. In practice, maintaining active membership and claims in more distant descent groups was usually extremely difficult. Thus the widespread diffusion of property rights was restricted by geographical and social considerations. In this respect noble women perhaps fared better, for their political position and economic power may have enabled them to activate rights across different locales in ways not necessarily open to women of peasant origin. Nobles and peasants, and noble and peasant women, shared the same hereditary claims to *rest* so there was legally no distinction between claimants to land from different classes. As Salome has suggested, there may have been a substantial divergence in the extent to which noble and peasant women were able to exercise their rights in practice.[66]

It is in the exercise of these rights and in the degrees to which women actually controlled land that one can start to judge whether formal legal equality had meaning. Drawing on historical records of land sales and accounts of litigation over land, Crummey has posited that Abyssinian women may have historically enjoyed ambilineal rights, and manipulated these as men did, but that in practice they exercised them less frequently than men, probably in only twenty percent of cases, and often to their disadvantage.[67] Though he relies on material a hundred or more years old, Crummey believes that women's access to land changed little in the twentieth century. Only the revolution and the 1975 land reform changed inheritance rights, but the bias against women persisted as Yared Amare's recent fieldwork in northern Shawa has disclosed.[68] In short, Crummey's conclusion is that the possession of rights is very different from their execution. Thus he endorses Salome's view that women of the nobility and gentry exercised legal rights over land and property equal to men, but refutes the notion that they exercised these as frequently as men or that they ever enjoyed parity in control over land with men. The essence of his argument is captured in the pithy assertion: "Men dominated and controlled land, and where women had it men tended to get it."[69]

Reconstruction of the historical lives and aspirations of rural women lies at the heart of any future scholarship. In staking out new areas for study James McCann's pioneering agricultural history of Ethiopia has focused, albeit briefly, on gender issues, while Helen Pankhurst's work in Menz, the product of fieldwork in the late 1980s and early 1990s, offers a range of contemporary insights which shed light on peasant women in the past.[70] Both depict a world in which men exercised authority within their households and without. They organized household activities and production, allocating tasks and resources; they negotiated with local officials over tax or tribute obligations, and pursued litigation to press land claims. Male household heads enjoyed higher status than their spouses, expected and received their deference, and deprecated women's work as inferior, even degrading.[71]

Yet this was also a world in which men had to recognize the crucial role played by women in supporting the household, both through their labor and trade at local markets. Women had the primary responsibility for processing crops, preparing food, carrying water, and gathering fuel. Hence, for most peasant women the daily round was long, hard, and tedious. It was marked by drying, cleaning, pounding and milling grain, by baking *enjara* (fermented, thin, pancake-like bread), processing and cooking other foods and beverages (including *taj, talla*, and *araki* – mead, beer and barley spirit), by fetching water, firewood and dung (for fuel, fertilizer and building), and by washing clothes, and spinning wool.[72]

Beyond these domestic tasks, women played critical roles in petty trade and in agriculture. Thus women contributed directly to the household economy, earning small, but often critical, amounts of cash in local markets (by selling spun wool, dung cakes, small amounts of grain, vegetables, and alcoholic drinks).[73] They shared with their menfolk the task of tending cattle and livestock, though the "dirty work" often fell to the women. Depending on the financial well-being of the household and the labour at its disposal, the nature of the crop in question, and subject to regional variation, they participated with men in most aspects of cultivation, from land preparation to harvesting.[74] The result was "blurred gender roles in all parts of agriculture" and, as Guyer has observed of much of West Africa, a "complex interdigitation of male and female, group and individual tasks."[75]

The significant enduring exception across highland Ethiopia was that plowing was invariably men's work. In response to McCann's enquiry whether women had ever plowed, both male and female farmers "consistently laughed or showed derision."[76] In practice, despite women's apparently equal legal access to land, their need for men to plow it had three distinct effects: first, parents tended to favor their sons in making initial grants of land, particularly when they married, fearing the alienation to in-laws of land passed to or inherited by daughters; second, women were far less likely to press legitimate claims to land with success if they lacked male labor; third, and concomitantly, women who did hold land sufficient for subsistence or more were often unable to acquire or even retain essential oxen and agricultural implements, because of their persistent need to divert resources to pay men to plow and help harvest.[77] Hence, many of the 15–25 percent female-headed households were transitory, led by divorcees and widows between marriages. "Historically ubiquitous," they achieved economic independence only precariously, if at all.[78]

If women did not plow, and achieved economic security most satisfactorily through a husband or an adult son, all our contemporary evidence nevertheless suggests that in the past, as now, men and women discussed and committed themselves jointly to weighty decisions involving their households. As Yared has commented of Wogda in northern Shawa, women have always expected to express their view of all important domestic transactions, and to agree jointly any major sales or purchases with spouses. By the same logic, wives negotiated with their husbands about the crops to be cultivated in the light of specific household needs, and it was they who were responsible for reserving sufficient seed grain for the next year's planting.[79] In Wallo, as elsewhere in the northern highlands, the final say might ultimately rest with the male heads of households, but they had to take into account commitments made in "marriage contracts, obligations to children, inheritance and property law, and cycles of household growth and decline."[80]

For women, the most important of these were the marriage contracts.[81] The extent of the parental endowment at first marriage (land, livestock, equipment, and other capital resources), and potential claims to further *rest* land, often determined their future prospects. This was true not merely for a woman's first marriage, but following the divorce or death of the husband, perhaps through two or more further marriages. In theory there was equity of provision and control of resources at marriage, matched at divorce by an equal division based on each partner's original stake in the union, and their subsequent contribution to it. Yet just as parents failed to make equal parental endowments for daughters, preferring to reserve resources to their sons, so women were often less favoured at divorce. Though a newly divorced woman might gain a half-share of livestock and equipment, a sole oxen would always go to the husband who plowed. On marrying, most women had moved initially to the house of their in-laws, before constructing their own jointly with the spouse near his parental home. At divorce this pattern of virilocal residence usually required a wife to leave the marital homestead of her husband and return to her own parents and natal district, receiving cash or other payment in compensation.[82]

Yet divorce, and the disintegration of the original household created by the marriage, was extremely common. Indeed, even well-endowed first marriages were rarely expected to last.[83] Remarriages and serial marriages were a historical feature of rural Ethiopian society. Hence, approximately half the marital unions in Menz, for example, lasted less than five years. A similar pattern in Wallo ensured that "most mature households" may have still embodied the resources and land claims of the parental endowment, but the "accumulated holdings of either partner from previous marriages" were more important.[84] By no means so deliberately driven by economic considerations as the first arranged marriage, divorce occurred for a mixture of personal, emotional, social, *and* material reasons.[85]

Significantly, the "prime initiators" of divorce tended to be women, a phenomenon which Helen Pankhurst has explored in some depth. She rejects the narrow view that women's rights to divorce indicated their power within rural household and society, and also the notion that the frequency of divorce derived from "the instability of an egalitarian institution of marriage" in an otherwise hierarchical and deferential milieu. Drawing on the experience of other impoverished rural societies with high rates of divorce and serial marriage, she argues that high divorce rates in Ethiopia embrace a paradox, which is also reflected in the scholarly literature: women were empowered to escape an unsatisfactory marriage, but did so with striking regularity to maximise options in the face of extreme economic adversity and distress.[86] Perhaps the true yardstick against which to measure women's power to divorce lay in the very daunting prospects faced by any women who chose to remain single. Remarriage offered by far the best opportunity for renewed economic and emotional security, and real potential to construct a new household.[87]

"Careering through marriage" reflected women's power, but was an economic strategy often forced on them by remorseless economic hardship.[88] Equally ambiguous, and equally deserving of further scholarship, were two domains fundamental to women's experience, where they enjoyed degrees of control and were acknowledged as authorities: first the life cycle, where in procreation, childbirth and caring for offspring, women were biologically and socially key players; second, the world of religious and spirit beliefs. Thus women gained status and were defined by bearing children, a point of celebration, and by caring for them; a number of women were recognized for their specific expertise as midwives, healers, and practitioners of female circumcision. Women also exercised measures of autonomy over their own fertility, to an extent where a fear of further pregnancies often caused them to initiate divorce. Conversely, the commonly held view of women's blood as "polluting," which was upheld by the church, reinforced a degrading perception of female sexuality, menstruation, and childbirth as unclean.[89]

Equally contradictory, women played little official role in Ethiopian religious life, save as church "servers" [of food] and elderly, celibate "nuns." Excluded from the priesthood and the inner sanctuaries of the church, they nevertheless outnumbered men in religious observance. They participated in the important religious rituals of the life cycle, took vows, made pilgrimages, adhered to fasts and diverse religious proscriptions, and were often active members of women's *mehaber* – local religious associations to honor a chosen saint, or most commonly in women's case, the Virgin Mary. Moreover, women often played a pre-eminent role in spirit beliefs (*zar, wukabi*, and *chele*), interpreting personal fortune and misfortune, and major events, in terms of spirit intervention. Discouraged by the church, such beliefs represented a cultural arena in which women were not merely devotees, but acted as intermediaries for one or more spirits. For many women this presented an "opportunity for expression"; they represented their only public "sphere of power." Yet in their very peripherality and lack of challenge to male hegemony, Helen Pankhurst argues, spirit beliefs upheld women's subordination.[90]

Influenced by the international spate of scholarship on women's history since the 1970s, the reflex response of historians of Ethiopia was to infer that women were important in the Ethiopian past. According to Richard Pankhurst, they played "a major role in the country's economic, social and cultural life"; they were "not only wives, mothers and housewives, but also rulers and landowners, servants and slaves . . . "[91] The need for brevity here has dictated giving short shrift to many of the women Pankhurst depicts: the women of the high nobility, including those involved in government, the market sellers, the camp-followers (of both armies and the shifting imperial capitals), the singers and dancers, itinerant minstrels and poets, the prostitutes who plied a common trade with little opprobrium, or the thousands of domestic servants and slaves. Yet Almaz is surely right to argue that the visibility of dowager queens and ambitious noblewomen belies the fact that they constituted only a "minor segment" of the history of women in Ethiopia. She is equally sound in her judgment that viewing the camp-followers, hand-millers, water-bearers, and noble courtesans as evidence of "women's power," and of "endowment of strong identity and inclusion in the political process" is tenuous to say the least.[92] Noble women clearly could rise very high; peasant women were an integral part of the agrarian economy. Still, there is little evidence that women ever effectively opposed or changed the hegemonic masculinity of imperial politics or society.

Our view is that the challenges ahead are twofold and bear on the nature of further research and issues of interpretation. First, we believe that in writing women into Ethiopian history, it is the history of the majority of peasant women that should take priority. At the least we need to determine the accuracy of Almaz's suggestion that the historic "profile" of most Ethiopian women was framed by "arduous and exacting chores," suffering privation, poverty, and pestilence, and by lack of access to the resources enjoyed by men. Hence, the need for further research, in history as to date in anthropology and development studies, which focuses on rural communities and peasant women from diverse perspectives, including those suggested in the latter part of this essay (women in agriculture and the household, women's inheritance rights, marriages, life-cycle events, religious beliefs). Second, historians need to sharpen their analytical tools. The task is not simply to add women to Ethiopian history, but to add Ethiopian women's history.[93] To achieve this requires us to recognize that the history of Ethiopian women is distinct from that of men, but not to separate the two. Thus future research needs to elucidate women's experiences in terms of gender relations both between men and women, and as they articulate with such other factors as class, culture, ethnicity, and religiosity. It needs to explore how men gained and exercised power and advantage over women in Ethiopia, using the concept of gender to understand patriarchy, not the concept of patriarchy to explain the subordinate role of women.[94] And finally, and without embracing a postmodernist separation of language from historical agency and context, historians can take inspiration from Helen Pankhurst's preliminary analysis of gender differences in language, and their meaning.[95]

Notes

Introduction

1 See Edward W. Said, *Orientalism* (New York: Vintage Books, 1979), and *Culture and Imperialism* (London: Chatto & Windus, 1993). It has inspired a tremendous amount of historical debate and discussion, and scholars have either applied his theories to a wide variety of contexts, or shown how the paradigms he proposes fail to apply to specific instances. For a sampling of such works, see Nadia Malinovich, "Orientalism and the Construction of Jewish Identity in France, 1900–1932," *Jewish Culture and History* [Great Britain] 2 (1999), pp. 1–25; Neil McInnes, "'Orientalism': The Evolution of a Concept," *National Interest* 54 (1998–99), pp. 73–81; Michael Soldatenko, "The Quincentenary of an Erasure: From Caliban to Hispanic," *Mexican Studies/Estudios Mexicanos* 13 (1997), pp. 385–421; Arif Dirlik, "Chinese History and the Question of Orientalism," *History and Theory* 35 (1996), pp. 96–118. Geoffrey A. Oddie, " 'Orientalism' and British Protestant Missionary Constructions of India in the Nineteenth Century," *South Asia* [Australia] 17 (1994), pp. 27–42; Stephen Greenblatt, *Marvelous Possessions: The Wonder of the New World* (Chicago: University of Chicago Press, 1991); Rana Kabbani, *Europe's Myths of Orient* (Bloomington: Indiana University Press, 1986); Ernest J. Wilson III, "Orientalism: A Black Perspective," *Journal of Palestine Studies* [Lebanon] 10 (1981), pp. 59–69; Richard H. Minear, "Orientalism and the Study of Japan," *Journal of Asian Studies* 39 (1980), pp. 507–17.

2 "[Woman] is defined and differentiated with reference to man and not he with reference to her; she is the incidental, the inessential as opposed to the essential. He is the Subject, he is the Absolute – she is the Other." Simone de Beauvoir, *The Second Sex*, trans H. M. Parshley (New York: Alfred A. Knopf, 1980), p. 34.

3 Ronald Inden, *Imagining India* (Cambridge, MA: Basil Blackwell, 1990).

4 Mrinalini Sinha, *Colonial Masculinity: The "Manly Englishman" and the "Effeminate Bengali" in the Late Nineteenth Century* (Manchester and New York: Manchester University Press, 1995), p. 172.

5 Dominic David Alessio, "Domesticating 'The Heart of the Wild': Female Personifications of the Colonies, 1886–1940," *Women's History Review* 6 (1997), pp. 239–69.

6 Reina Lewis, *Gendering Orientalism: Race, Femininity and Representation* (New York: Routledge, 1996); Anne McClintock, *Imperial Leather: Race, Gender and Sexuality in the Colonial Context* (New York: Routledge, 1995).

7 Mary Louise Pratt, *Imperial Eyes: Travel Writing and Transculturation* (New York: Routledge, 1992), pp. 4–5.

8 Susan Morgan, *Place Matters: Gendered Geography in Victorian Women's Travel Books about Southeast Asia* (New Brunswick: Rutgers University Press, 1996), pp. 12, 17.

9 Susan L. Blake, "A Woman's Trek: What Difference Does Gender Make?," *Women's Studies International Forum* 13 (1990), pp. 347–55; Cheryl McEwan, "Paradise or Pandemonium? West African Landscapes in the Travel Accounts of Victorian Women," *Journal of Historical Geography* [Great Britain] 22 (1996), pp. 68–83. Other important works on women and travel writing include Sara Mills, *Discourses of Difference: Women's Travel Writing and Colonialism* (London: Routledge, 1991) and

Deirdre David, *Rule Britannia: Women, Empire, and Victorian Writing* (Ithaca, N.Y.: Cornell University Press, 1995).

10 *Journal of Women's History* 2 (Spring 1990), ed. Cheryl Johnson-Odim and Margaret Strobel.

11 See Ruth Roach Pierson and Nupur Chaudhuri, eds, *Nation, Empire and Colony* (Bloomington: Indiana University Press, 1998).

12 Clare Midgley, ed., *Gender and Imperialism* (Manchester: Manchester University Press, 1998).

13 For example, see *Gender and History, Special Issue: Gendered Colonialism in African History*. vol. 8, no. 3 (November 1996).

14 Ida Blom, Karen Hagemann and Catherine Hall, eds. *Gendered Nations* (New York: New York University Press, 2000).

15 The essays by Laura Fishman, "French Views of Native American Women in the Early Modern Era: The Tupinamba of Brazil," Chapter 5, and Luis Martínez-Fernández, "The 'Male City' of Havanna: The Coexisting Logics of Colonialism, Slavery, and Patriarchy in Nineteenth-Century Cuba," Chapter 8 are reprinted from *Terra Incognita* and *Cuban Studies*, respectively; all other essays are original to this volume.

16 "French Views of Native American Women in the Early Modern Era: The Tupinamba of Brazil," Chapter 5.

17 "Greece in Chains: Philhellenism to the Rescue of a Damsel in Distress," Chapter 3.

18 "Imperial Eyes, Gendered Views: Concepción Gimeno Re-writes the Aztecs at the End of the Nineteenth Century," Chapter 9.

19 "Cartimandua, Boudicca, and Rebellion: British Queens and Roman Colonial Views," Chapter 1.

20 "The Indian Other: Reactions of Two Anglo-Indian Women Travel Writers," Chapter 10.

21 "Wild Irish Women: Gender, Politics, and Colonialism in the Nineteenth Century," Chapter 4.

22 "Between Whipping and Slavery: Double Jeopardy against Mudejar Women in Medieval Spain," Chapter 2.

23 "The 'Male City' of Havanna: The Coexisting Logics of Colonialism, Slavery, and Patriarchy in Nineteenth-Century Cuba," Chapter 8.

24 "Women as Symbols of Disorder in Early Rhode Island," Chapter 6.

25 "Native Women and State Legislation in Mexico and Canada: The Agrarian Law and the Indian Act," Chapter 7.

26 "Education for Liberation or Domestication? Female Education in Colonial Swaziland," Chapter 14.

27 "Civilizing Women: French Colonial Perceptions of Vietnamese Motherhood," Chapter 12.

28 "Social Construction of Ideal Images of Women in Colonial Korea: 'New Woman' versus 'Motherhood'," Chapter 13.

29 "Image and Reality: Indian Diaspora Women, Colonial and Post-Colonial Discourse on Empowerment and Victimology," Chapter 11.

30 "Women, Gender History, and Imperial Ethiopia," Chapter 15.

Chapter 1 Cartimandua, Boudicca, and Rebellion

1 Stephen. L. Dyson, "Native Revolts in the Roman Empire," *Historia* 20 (1971), pp. 239–74. In this article, Dyson discusses five rebellions which "best illustrate the characteristics" of this phenomenon; the revolts of Vercingetorix (Gaul); Arminius

(Germany); Boudicca (Britain); and those in Panonia-Dalmatia and Batavia. Not only are these major examples, but they are also relatively well documented, in some cases by contemporary writers and even eye-witnesses and participants. Dyson is also concerned to make comparisions with modern native revolts, such as in Rhodesia in 1896–97 and in East Africa in 1917. Although this approach does not concern us here, his analysis is striking and provocative.

2 Dyson, "Native Revolts," p. 240.

3 For the date, which is controversial, see K. Carroll, "The Date of Boudicca's Revolt," *Britannia* 10 (1979), pp. 197–202. Tacitus, in giving the consular dating, *Caesennio Paeto et Petronio Turpiliano consulibus* (*Ann.* 14.24.1), places the revolt in AD 61, but others, including R. Syme, *Tacitus* (Oxford: Clarendon Press, 1958), 1:391; 2:756–66 and D.R. Dudley and G. Webster, *The Rebellion of Boudicca* (London: Routledge & Kegan Paul, 1962), pp. 144–5, opt for AD 60 Carroll believes it began in 61, but adds that "our evidence will not permit a definite chronology" (p. 202).

4 For a description of the territories of the Brigantes, see I.A. Richmond, "Queen Cartimandua," *JRS* 44 (1954), pp. 44–6.

5 G. Webster, *The Invasion of Roman Britain* (London: Batsford, 1980), p. 113.

6 Webster, *Invasion*, p. 113.

7 G. Webster, *Rome against Caratacus: The Roman Campaigns in Britain A.D. 48–58* (London, Batsford, 1981), p. 14.

8 For a very full discussion of Caratacus and his career, see Webster, *Rome against Caratacus*.

9 Richmond, "Queen Cartimandua," p. 49.

10 For the date, see D. Braund, *Ruling Roman Britain: Kings, Queens, Governors and Emperors from Julius Caesar to Agricola* (London; Routledge, 1996), p. 129.

11 See the notes on this passage in *Cornelii Taciti de Vita Agricolae*, ed. R.M. Ogilvie and I.A. Richmond (Oxford: Clarendon Press, 1967), p. 260.

12 The strongest proponent of this argument is S. Mitchell, writing in *Liverpool Classical Monthly* 3 (1978), pp. 215–19; Webster, *Rome Against Caratacus* concurs.

13 Braund, "Observations on Cartimantua," p. 4.

14 Braund, *Ruling Roman Britain*, p. 124. This idea is echoed by P.C.N. Stewart, who states that there is "a broadly accepted image of Britain in the minds of Roman writers (and readers) . . . which could be appropriated and exploited in different ways. We can suggest what Britain meant as a cultural icon. The emphasis placed upon difference serves to establish a foil to Roman civilization and culture. To assert the existence of somewhere that is *not* Roman is to reinforce the existence of Roman culture as a construct." P.C.N. Stewart, "Inventing Britain: the Roman Creation and Adaptation of an Image," *Britannia* 26 (1995), p. 6.

15 Braund, *Ruling Roman Britain*, p. 124.

16 Although one might regard Cartimandua's involvement with Vellocatus as a love affair, since Tacitus notes the *libido reginae* in his account in the *Histories*, I agree with Richmond that it was much more likely an affair "dictated by expediency rather than passion." Moreover, as it was the sort of thing well known to the ruling class in Rome, Tacitus' irony here, in describing the house as immediately convulsed by a scandal (*concussa statim falgitio domus*) is all the more appreciated. He treats the episode "as if he were introducing a solemn ode on morality." Richmond, "Queen Cartimandua," p. 52.

17 Braund, *Ruling Roman Britain*, pp. 123–4.

18 Braund, "Observations on Cartimandua," pp. 5–6, citing P. Galway, *Roman Britain* (1981), p. 133, n. 3.

19 Webster, *Rome Against Caratacus*, p. 38.
20 Dyson, "Native Revolts," p. 258.
21 Dio lived *c*. AD 150–235; his *Roman History* was written during his prime.
22 On the Romanization of Britain, and the organization of its peoples into governmental entities, see C. Haselgrove, "'Romanization' before the Conquest: Gaulish Precedents and British Consequences," in *Military and Civilian in Roman Britain: Cultural Relationships in a Frontier Province*, ed. T.F.C. Blagg and A.C. King (Oxford: BAR British Series, 1984), pp. 30–8.
23 Webster, *Invasion*, pp. 74–5.
24 Dudley and Webster, *Rebellion*, p. 53.
25 Dyson, "Native Revolts," p. 260.
26 Webster, *Invasion*, p. 74.
27 On the construction and dedication of the temple, see D. Fishwick, "The Temple of Divus Claudius at Camulodunum," *Britannia* 26 (1995), pp. 11–27, and the sources cited there, especially P.J. Drury *et al.*, "The Temple of Claudius at Colchester Reconsidered," *Britannia* 15 (1984), pp. 7–50.
28 On the variant reading *ara* for *arx* at 14.32.6, see *The Annals of Tacitus*, H. Furneaux, ed., 2 vols., 2nd edn (Oxford: The Clarendon Press, 1896–1897), 2:275.
29 C.M. Bulst, "The Revolt of Queen Boudicca in A.D. 60," *Historia* 10 (1961), p. 509.
30 Bulst, "Revolt of Queen Boudicca," p. 498, speculates that Prasutagus did not name Boudicca and her relatives as heirs "because he suspected or knew about their anti-Roman attitude." But Bulst does not explain her attitude satisfactorily; there is no evidence that it existed at all before the outrages against her and her daughters after Prasutagus' death. Bulst's other suggestions for the shape of the will are more convincing: that the daughters would be married off to other client kings chosen by the Romans, and that the deposition of Pratsutagus' kingdom was influenced by Roman advice, "since his own position as king was far from one of independence."
31 Prasutagus' bequeathing half of his goods to the emperor as "protection" "constitutes an indirect assault in the Tacitean narrative upon Nero and perhaps upon Roman imperialism in general" (Braund, *Ruling Roman Britain*, p. 134). Here we see Tacitus' hidden agenda at work again.
32 Dyson, "Native Revolts," p. 259.
33 Dio, *Roman History*, trans. E. Cary, 9 vols. (Cambridge, MA: Harvard University Press, 1954–1961), 8:83, 85.
34 See *Agricolae*, ed. Ogilvie and Richmond, p. 198. They believe this to be an exaggeration.
35 Dyson, "Native Revolts," pp. 261–2. Dyson further suggests that "the fact that Boudicca was one of the few surviving members of the tribal royalty in Britain made her a natural rallying point," but he does not give any evidence to support this claim.
36 Braund, *Ruling Roman Britain*, p. 123.
37 Braund, *Ruling Roman Britain*, p. 132.
38 Braund, *Ruling Roman Britain*, p. 132.
39 See, for example, K. Bradley, *Slavery and Society at Rome* (Cambridge: Cambridge University Press, 1994), pp. 110–15.
40 Braund, *Ruling Roman Britain*, p. 135.
41 More gruesome details are found in Dio, 62.7f., including instances of torture and what may have been taken for human sacrifice by the readers. See also A. Nice, "Superstition and Religion in Tacitus' and Dio's Accounts of the Boudican Revolt," *Pegasus* 36 (1993), pp. 15–18.

42 Braund, *Ruling Roman Britain*, p. 135.
43 Braund, *Ruling Roman Britain*, p. 137.
44 Braund, *Ruling Roman Britain*, p. 138.
45 Dio, *Roman History*, 8:83 and 85.
46 Braund, *Ruling Roman Britain*, p. 145.

Chapter 2 Between Whipping and Slavery: Double Jeopardy against *Mudejar* Women in Medieval Spain

1 I will refer to conquered Muslims as *Mudejars* despite the fact that the term *Mudejar* appeared only in Christian documents in Castile in the fifteenth century, and never in *Mudejar* documents.
2 Arxiu de la Corona d'Aragó, Reg. 74, fol. 5v. subsequently cites as A.C.A.
3 Ambrosio Huici Miranda and María Desamparados Cabanes Pecourt, *Documentos de Jaime I de Aragón*, vol. 3 (Zaragoza: Facsímil, 1975), doc. 587.
4 Bonnie S. Anderson and Judith P. Zinsser, *A History of Their Own. Women in Europe from Prehistory to the Present*, 2 vols. (New York: Harper & Row Publishers, 1988), 1:341.
5 A.C.A., Reg. 171, fols. 176r-v: "unum post alium."
6 A.C.A., Reg. 171, fols. 176r-v.
7 Elena Lourie, "Anatomy of Ambivalence. Muslims under the Crown of Aragon in the Late Thirteenth Century," in *Crusade and Colonization* (Norfolk: Variorum Press, 1990), p. 69.
8 Carmen Barceló Torres, ed., *Un tratado catalán de derecho medieval islámico: El llibre de la çuna e xara dels moros* (Córdoba: Universidad de Córdoba, 1989), IV.
9 Maria Teresa Ferrer i Mallol, *Els sarraïns de la corona catalano-aragonesa en el segle XIV. Segregació i discriminació* (Barcelona: Consejo Superior de Investigaciones Científicas, 1987), p. 24.
10 A.C.A., Reg. 285, fols. 179r-v.
11 David Nirenberg, *Communities of Violence: Persecution of Minorities in the Middle Ages* (Princeton: Princeton University Press, 1996), p. 132.
12 Ferrer i Mallol, *Els sarraïns*, p. 17.
13 A.C.A., Reg. 251, fol. 37v.
14 A.C.A., Reg. 209, fol. 244r.
15 A.C.A., Reg. 215, fol. 228v.
16 Nirenberg, *Communities of Violence*, p. 132.
17 A.C.A., Reg. 209, fol. 147r.
18 Louise Mirrer, *Women, Jews, and Muslims in the Texts of Reconquest Castile* (Ann Arbor: The University of Michigan Press, 1996), p. 2.
19 Mirrer, *Women, Jews, and Muslims*, p. 22.
20 Nirenberg, *Communities of Violence*, p. 138.
21 Ferrer i Mallol, *Els sarraïns*, p. 19.
22 A.C.A., Reg. 261, fol. 108v.
23 A.C.A., Reg. 282, fol. 127r.
24 A.C.A., Reg. 159, fols. 169v–170r.
25 A.C.A., Reg. 159, fols. 171v–172r.
26 A.C.A., Reg. 159, fols. 220v–221r.
27 Maria Teresa Ferrer i Mallol, *La frontera amb l'Islam en el segle XIV. Cristians i sarraïns al Pais Valencià* (Barcelona: Consejo Superior de Investigaciones Científicas, 1988), doc. 46.

28 A.C.A., Reg. 164, fol. 221r.
29 In January 1318, the king granted Berenguer 110 regalian pounds as compensation for the loss of Nuça and to cover the trial expenses that Berenguer had incurred A.C.A., Reg. 259, fol. 50r.
30 A.C.A., Reg. 259, fols. 27r–v.
31 A.C.A., Reg. 259, fols. 50v.
32 A.C.A., Reg. 285, fol. 171r.
33 Ferrer i Mallol, *Els sarraïns*, doc. 10.
34 Ferrer i Mallol, *Els sarraïns*, doc. 10.
35 According to the privileges the crown granted the *Mudejars* of Xàtiva in 1252, converts to Christianity were allowed to keep their movable property, while the real estate reverted to the crown. Huici Miranda, doc. 587.
36 Mary Elizabeth Perry, *Gender and Disorder in Early Modern Seville* (Princeton: Princeton University Press, 1990), p. 137.
37 Mark Meyerson, "Prostitution of Muslim Women in the Kingdom of Valencia: Religious and Sexual Discrimination in a Medieval Plural Society," in *The Medieval Mediterranean. Cross-Cultural Contacts*, ed. Marilyn J. Chiat and Kathryn L. Reyerson (St. Cloud, Minnesota: North Star Press of St. Cloud, Inc., 1988), p. 88.
38 Joan J. Ponsoda Sanmartin, *El català i l'aragonés en els inicis del Regne de València segons el Llibre de cort de justícia de Cocentaina (1269–1295)* (Alcoi: Editorial Marfil, 1996), any 1269, F10 R11.
39 Sanmartin, *El català i l'aragonés*, any 1295, F2v R628.
40 Mark Meyerson, *The Muslims of Valencia in the Age of Fernando and Isabel. Between Crusade and Coexistence* (Berkeley–Los Angeles: University of California Press, 1991), p. 250.
41 A.C.A., Reg. 110, fol. 115v.
42 *Ibid.*: "unde cum supradicte persone aliene sint a lege nostra." Christians in medieval Spain often referred to Muslims and Jews as peoples who had different laws.
43 Cases of sexual contact between Jews and *Mudejars* posed a great risk to the minority groups themselves. Even more than Christians, Jews and *Mudejars* wanted to protect their members from contact with outsiders in order to preserve their own religious and cultural identity.
44 John Boswell, *The Royal Treasure: Muslim Communities under the Crown of Aragon in the Fourteenth Century* (New Haven: Yale University Press, 1977), pp. 352–3.

Chapter 3 Greece in Chains: Philhellenism to the Rescue of a Damsel in Distress

1 Edward W. Said, *Orientalism* (New York: Vintage Books, 1979), pp. 2–3.
2 For an example of critiques of Said's thesis, see Bernard Lewis, "The Question of Orientalism", *The New York Review of Books* 11 (29 June 1982), pp. 49–56.
3 See, for example, Laura Fishman, "French Views of Native American Women in the Early Modern Era: The Tupinamba of Brazil" Chapter 5; or Micheline R. Lessard, "Civilizing Women: French Colonial Perceptions of Vietnamese Womanhood and Motherhood," Chapter 12.
4 Carmen Ramos-Escandon, "Imperial Eyes, Gendered Views: Concepción Gimeno Rewrites the Aztecs at the End of the Century," Chapter 9; and Nupur Chaudhuri, "The Indian Other: Reactions of Two Anglo-Indian Women Travel Writers, Eliza Fay and A.U." Chapter 10.

5 Sara Mills, *Discourses of Difference: Women's Travel Writing and Colonialism* (London: Routledge, 1991); Susan Morgan, *Place Matters: Gendered Geography in Victorian Women's Travel Books about Southeast Asia* (New Brunswick: Rutgers University Press, 1996).
6 Ronald B. Inden, *Imagining India* (Oxford, and Cambridge, Mass.: Basil Blackwell, 1990), p. 86.
7 According to Said, "The Oriental [was] irrational, depraved (fallen), childlike, 'different', thus the European [was] rational, virtuous, mature, 'normal'." *Orientalism*, p. 40. For other studies of the gendered nature of imperialism, see Edward Said, *Culture and Imperialism* (London, Chatto & Windus, 1993); Anne K. Mellor, "Romanticism, Gender, and the Anxieties of Empire: An Introduction," *European Romantic Review* 8 (1997), pp. 148–54. Reina Lewis, *Gendering Orientalism: Race, Femininity and Representation* (New York: Routledge, 1996) and Anne McClintock, *Imperial Leather: Race, Gender and Sexuality in the Colonial Contest* (New York: Routledge, 1995).
8 Artemis Leontis, *Topographies of Hellenism, Mapping the Homeland* (Ithaca: Cornell University Press, 1995), p. 46.
9 John Pentland Mahaffy, *Rambles and Studies in Greece* (Philadelphia: International Press, J. C. Winston, 1892), p. 247.
10 Mahaffy, *Rambles*, p. 342.
11 Edward Giffard, *A Short Visit to the Ionian Islands, Athens, and the Morea* (London: J. Murray, 1837), p. 266.
12 For the Grand Tour's place in aristocratic British society, see Jeremy Black, *The British Abroad: The Grand Tour in the Eighteenth Century* (New York: St. Martin's Press, 1992).
13 Percy B. Shelley, "Preface to *Hellas*," in *Selected Poetry and Prose of Shelley*, ed. Carlos Baker (New York: The Modern Library, 1951), p. 452.
14 Shelley, "Preface to *Hellas*," p. 452.
15 William Martin Leake, *Travels in Northern Greece*, 4 vols., (London: J. Rodwell, 1835), IV:150.
16 This conflict between Greek and Western European interests continued after the successful war for independence (1821–29), and it had significant implications for women. See Eleni Varikas, "Trop Archaïques ou Trop Modernes? Les Citadines Grècques Face à l'Occidentalisation (1833–1875) [Too archaic or too modern? Greek women and the encounter with Westernization during the years just after independence]. *Peuples Méditerranéens* [France] 44–5 (1988), pp. 269–92.
17 Thomas Watkins, *Travels through Switzerland, Italy, Sicily, the Greek islands to Constantinople; through part of Greece, Regusa, and the Dalmatian isles; in a series of letters to Pennoyre Watkins, esp., from Thomas Watkins . . . in the years 1787–1788, 1789*, 2 vols. (London: printed by J. Owen, 1794), II:166–7.
18 Choiseul-Gouffier, cited in Terence Spencer, *Fair Greece! Sad Relic; Literary Philhellenism from Shakespeare to Byron* (London: Weidenfeld & Nicolson, 1954), pp. 219–20.
19 Leake, *Travels in Northern Greece*, pp. 225–6.
20 Robert Pashley, *Travels in Crete*, 2 vols. (London: J. Murray, 1889), 1:197.
21 Spencer, *Fair Greece!*, p. 218.
22 Authors who attempted to show Greek women – or even Greek goddesses – as strong and heroic could face substantial criticism, as Kevin Eubanks has recently shown in his study of British Romantic author Felicia Hemans. Typical of Heman's early work was *Modern Greece* (1817), which focused on a strong and unconventional woman, the goddess Minerva; critics roundly denounced such depictions, which they saw as a challenge to women's domestic role. By 1830, however,

Hemans had come to praise domesticity in her poems, which, Eubanks argues, was part of her effort to be commercially and critically successful. "Minerva's Veil: Hemans, Critics, and the Construction of Gender," *European Romantic Review* 8 (1997), pp. 341–59.

23 George Gordon Byron, Sixth Baron Byron. *Selected Poems and Letters*, ed. with an intro. and notes by William H. Marshall (Boston: Houghton Mifflin, 1968), p. 164.

24 "On This Day I Complete my Thirty-Sixty Year," in *English Romantic Poetry and Prose*, ed. Russell Noyes (New York: Oxford University Press, 1956), p. 926.

Chapter 4 Wild Irish Women: Gender, Politics, and Colonialism in the Nineteenth Century

1 Susan Mitchell, "The Petticoat in Politics," in *The Voice of Ireland*, ed. William G. Fitzgerald (Dublin and London: Virtue and Co. Ltd. [*c*. 1923]), p. 166.

2 R.F. Foster, *Modern Ireland, 1600–1972* (London: Penguin Books, 1989), p. 130.

3 Jo Murphy-Lawless, "Images of 'Poor' Women in the Writings of Irish Midwives," in *Women in Early Modern Ireland*, ed. Margaret MacCurtain and Mary O'Dowd (Edinburgh: Edinburgh University Press, 1991), pp. 291–2.

4 Several plays feature a stage-Irishman as a hero, including George Farquhar's *Love and a Bottle* (1698), Thomas Sheridan's *Captain O'Blunder, or the Brave Irishman* (1743), and Charles Macklin's *Love à la Mode* (1759), but it was much more common to find him as a supporting, comic character, such as in Hugh Kelly's *A School for Wives* (1773), or Richard Brinsley Sheridan's early plays such as *The Rivals* (1775) and *St. Patrick's Day* (1775). Interestingly enough, in Macklin's play, the stage-Irish character of Sir Callaghan O'Brallaghan wins the hand of an heiress after he is the only one of her suitors – the others are gentry from England, Scotland, and France – to remain faithful to her during a time of crisis. Although the play was successful in London and Dublin, English reviewers complained about the Irishman's victory over men of other nationalities. Robert Welch, ed., *The Oxford Companion to Irish Literature* (Oxford: The Clarendon Press, 1996), pp. 533–4, 318.

5 [David Garrick], *The Irish Widow. In Two Acts. As it is Performed at the Theatre Royal in Drury Lane*, 3rd edn. (London: T. Becket, 1772), pp. v–vi, 37.

6 David Milobar has pointed out that contemporary British accounts of North American Indians that described women beating their husbands or plowing the fields assumed that such gender roles were "abnormal" and accounted for "character flaws" in Indian society. David Milobar, "Aboriginal Peoples and the British Press, 1720–1763," in *Hanoverian Britain and Empire*, ed. Stephen Taylor, Richard Connors, and Clyve Jones (Woodbridge, Suffolk: The Boydell Press, 1998), p. 76. In a similar vein, Edmund Burke, the famous Anglo-Irish statesman, argued that English inheritance laws and patriarchal family structure had to be adopted by Catholic Irish to attain a stable domestic and political structure for the country. Mary Jean Corbett, "Public Affections and Familial Politics: Burke, Edgeworth, and the 'Common Naturalization' of Great Britain," *ELH* 61 (1994), p. 888. Also see Laura Fishman's article in this volume "French Views of Native American Women in the Early Modern Era: The Tupinamba of Brazil" Chapter 5; some French observers thought that native American men were lazy because women seemed to do so much of the essential heavy work.

7 Thomas Bartlett, "Bearing Witness: Female Evidences in Courts Martial Convened to Suppress the 1798 Rebellion," in *The Women of 1798*, ed. Dáire Keogh and Nicholas Furlong (Dublin: Four Courts Press, 1998), p. 66.

8 Quoted in Anna Kinsella, "Nineteenth-Century Perspectives: The Women of 1798 in Folk Memory and Ballads," in Keogh and Furlong, *Women of 1798*, p. 188.
9 Kinsella, "Women of 1798 in Folk Memory and Ballads," pp. 191–2, 195–6.
10 Nancy J. Curtin, "Women and Eighteenth-Century Irish Republicanism," in *Women in Early Modern Ireland*, ed. Margaret MacCurtain and Mary O'Dowd (Edinburgh: Edinburgh University Press, 1991), pp. 134–5.
11 Curtin, "Women and Eighteenth-Century Irish Republicanism," pp. 135–6.
12 Mary Helen Thuente, "Liberty, Hibernia and Mary Le More: United Irish Images of Women," in Keogh and Furlong, *Women of 1798*, pp. 16–17.
13 Lady Morgan [Sydney Owenson], *The Wild Irish Girl*, intro. Brigid Brophy (London: 1806; new edn London and New York: Pandora, 1986), p. 69.
14 Similarly, Laura Fishman notes that some French observers of the Tupinamba of Brazil also tended to idealize the connection between the Tupi and nature. See "French Views of Native American Women," Chapter 5.
15 Both Sydney Owenson (Lady Morgan) and Maria Edgeworth were members of the Anglo-Irish gentry and lived much of their lives in Ireland. However, the viewpoint that they represent is a combination of Anglo-Irish and English, and the enormous popularity of their books in England suggests that they presented a view of Ireland that their English audiences wanted to see.
16 Maria Edgeworth, *The Absentee*, ed. W.J. McCormack and Kim Walker (Oxford and New York: Oxford University Press, 1988), p. 248.
17 In addition to the example of the Clonbronys, the Berryl family is ruined through "Lady Berryl's passion for living in London and at watering places." A widow, Lady Dashfort, is condemned as "one worthless woman," who "does incalculable mischief" by introducing expensive and frivolous fashions into Ireland, encouraging local women to follow suit. Edgeworth, *Absentee*, pp. 54, 92.
18 Corbett, "Public Affections and Familial Politics," p. 877.
19 Rev. Thaddeus O'Malley, *An Idea of a Poor Law for Ireland*, 2nd edn (London: Henry Hooper, 1837), p. 3.
20 Thomas Creevey, *The Creevey Papers*, ed. Sir Herbert Maxwell, 2 vols. (New York: E. P. Dutton & Company, 1903), 2:173.
21 Henry John Temple, Viscount Palmerston, *The Letters of the Third Viscount Palmerston to Laurence and Elizabeth Sulivan, 1804–1863*, ed. Kenneth Bourne, Camden Fourth Series, vol. 23 (London: Royal Historical Society, 1979), p. 185.
22 Sarah Stickney Ellis, *The Wives of England. Their Relative Duties, Domestic Influence, and Social Obligations* (London, 1843), pp. 99–100.
23 Mary Cullen, "Breadwinners and Providers: Women in the Household Economy of Labouring Families, 1835–6," in *Women Surviving*, ed. Maria Luddy and Cliona Murphy (Dublin: Poolbeg, 1990), pp. 105–6.
24 Commissioners for Inquiring into the Condition of the Poorer Classes in Ireland, *Selection of Parochial Examinations Relative to the Destitute Classes in Ireland, from the Evidence Received by His Majesty's Comissioners*. (Dublin: Milliken and Son, 1835), p. 279. Edgeworth describes such a scene: Colambre sees a peasant family lock its house and leave; the man walks away in one direction, while the woman took her three toddlers in another, a fourth infant strapped to her back. He asks about them, and is told that the man is going to England to work the harvest, while the woman is "going up the country to beg." *Absentee*, pp. 146–7.
25 Harriet Martineau, "Women in Ireland," from *Letters from Ireland* (London: John Chapman, 1852), pp. 65–72, in *Harriet Martineau on Women*, ed. Gayle Graham Yates (New Brunswick, NJ: Rutgers University Press, 1985), p. 188.

26 The *Times* (London), 22 September, 1846.

27 *Punch* 11 (17 October 1846), p. 160. Significantly, John Bull does not include the laborer's wife and children in this statement.

28 L. Perry Curtis, *Apes and Angels: The Irishman in Victorian Caricature*, rev. ed. (Washington and London: Smithsonian Institution Press, 1997), pp. 94–5.

29 The *Times* (London), October 4 1848. Travelers in Ireland made similar comparisons; Lord William Pitt Lennox recounted a humorous story in his memoirs about an accident involving the local mail cart, stating that after the Irish driver collected himself and his horse, "off started Paddy, shouting like an Ojibbeway Indian." Lord William Pitt Lennox, *My Recollections from 1806 to 1873*, 2 vols. (London: Hurst and Blackett, 1874), 2:235–6. Years later, during the agitation for Irish Home Rule in the 1880s, one nationalist leader reported that Lord Salisbury, the Prime Minister, "had declared the most loyal of Catholic peoples to be on a par with African Hottentots in their unfitness for self-government." Michael Davitt, *The Fall of Feudalism in Ireland or the Story of the Land League Revolution* (London: Harper & Brothers Publishers, 1904), p. 405.

30 *Punch* 43 (October 18 1862), p. 165.

31 Curtis, *Apes and Angels*, pp. 21–2.

32 *Physionomies Nationales, ou observations sur la différence des traits du visage et sur la conformation de la tête de l'homme*, 2 vols. (Berlin: J. G. Schadow, 1835), text volume, 63, pp. 91; *Crania Britannica*, 2 vols. (London, 1856, 1865), 1:200, both quoted in Mary Cowling, *The Artist as Anthropologist: The Representation of Type and Character in Victorian Art* (Cambridge: Cambridge University Press, 1989), pp. 125, 127.

33 Cowling, *Artist as Anthropologist*, p. 125.

34 Cowling, *Artist as Anthropologist*, p. 123. Cartoonists readily adopted these ideas, producing works such as *Mr. Pongo on 'The Situation'* (*Fun*, 1877), which shows a pensive gorilla giving more careful thought to Irish troubles than do two ape-like supporters of Home Rule. Reproduced in Curtis, *Apes and Angels*, xiv. The image was even picked up by cartoonists in other countries; for example, in America, *Puck's* "Gallery of Celebrities," included *The King of A-Shantee* published in 1882, which showed an ape-like Irishman, with huge jaw, snub nose, and receding forehead, wearing a chamberpot as a hat, and sitting on an overturned washtub outside his ramshackle house. His wife, also vaguely simian, looks out the door of the cabin. *Puck* 10 (February 15 1882), p. 378. Only one week earlier, *Puck* published *Social Types*, which linked highly caricatured American blacks (very black skin with large white eyes and lips) with Irish immigrants, one of whom bears a striking resemblance to a chimpanzee. *Puck* 10 (February 8 1882), p. 367.

35 Quoted in C.L. Innes, *Woman and Nation in Irish Literature and Society, 1880–1935* (Athens, GA: University of Georgia Press, 1993), p. 14.

36 Matthew Arnold, *The Incompatibles*, in *The Complete Prose Works of Matthew Arnold*, ed. R.H. Super, vol. 9, *English Literature and Irish Politics* (Ann Arbor: University of Michigan Press, 1973), pp. 270–1. Arnold also uses terminology that could have been applied to any other people colonized by Britain: "a great part of the Irish people is in a chronic state of misery, discontent, and smouldering insurrection. To reconquer [*sic*] and chastise them is easy; but after you have chastised them, your eternal difficulty with them recommences. I pass by the suggestion that the Irish people should be entirely extirpated; no one can make it seriously. They must be brought to order when they are disorderly; but they must be brought, also, to acquiescence in the English connection by good and just treatment." Arnold, *Incompatibles*, p. 253.

37 Mary Condren, "Sacrifice and Political Legitimation: The Production of a Gendered Social Order," *Journal of Women's History* 6/7 (Winter/Spring 1995), p. 173.

38 Quoted in Innes, *Woman and Nation*, p. 9.

39 *Punch* 81 (October 29 1881), p. 199.

40 *Fun* (May 25 1881), reproduced in Curtis, *Apes and Angels*, p. 163.

41 Catholic Emancipation refers to the effort in the decades after the union to secure Catholic rights to vote and hold government offices (if otherwise qualified) the same as Protestants. Since voting was based on property holding, this would actually enfranchise a relatively small number of Catholics, but opposition to it was fierce in England because of ongoing distrust of both Catholicism and the Irish. Ironically, emancipation passed during the premiership of the arch-conservative Duke of Wellington, who supported the measure only because he thought that to do otherwise would be to invite an Irish rebellion, which he believed was pending.

42 On October 23 1828, Thomas Creevey accompanied Lady Duncannon to a Catholic emancipation meeting held at Kilkenny in a Catholic Church, where her husband was to be voted into the chair. She was given a place on the speaker's platform, and Creevey noted that "There were women without end in the galleries" to hear the speakers. Creevey, *Creevey Papers*, 2:182. For women transported for agrarian crimes, see Maria Luddy, "Women & Politics in Nineteenth-Century Ireland," in *Women & Irish History: Essays in Honour of Margaret MacCurtain*, ed. Maryann Gialanella Valiulis and Mary O 'Dowd (Dublin: Wolfhound Press, 1997), p. 91.

43 Quoted in Luddy, "Women & Politics in Nineteenth-Century Ireland," p. 92.

44 Among the first groups to adopt English bourgeois ideology was Young Ireland. In *The Spirit of the Nation, Part 2*, (1843) an unnamed Young Ireland poet made it clear that the Irish masses' character was too feminine to achieve their goals: "Serf! With thy fetters o'erladen [*sic*]/Why crouch you in dastardly woe?/Why weep o'er thy chains like a maiden,/Nor strike for thy manhood a blow?" Quoted in Marjorie Howes, "Tears and Blood: Lady Wilde and the Emergence of Irish Cultural Nationalism," in *Ideology and Ireland in the Nineteenth Century*, ed. Tadhg Foley and Seán Ryder (Dublin: Four Courts Press, 1998), p. 157. Young Ireland's adoption of English values – as well as some of its perceptions about the Irish peasant – was influential, since Young Ireland's literature remained popular throughout the century, and some of its members joined other nationalist groups in the following decades. Howes, "Tears and Blood," p. 151.

45 The Land League grew out of agitation of the late 1870s that attempted to redress the inequitable property distribution in Ireland. While a disproportionate number of Irish peasants had been landless laborers in the eighteenth and nineteenth centuries, the Famine actually made this situation even worse, due to large-scale turnovers in landholding in which peasant proprietors were displaced by cattle-raising. Tenant farmers had no legal protection from sudden, unannounced evictions and dramatic increases in rent intended to drive them from their land, nor did they have a right to receive compensation for improvements they made on the property.

46 Janet TeBrake, "Irish Peasant Women in Revolt: the Land League Years," *Irish Historical Studies* 28 (May 1992), p. 67.

47 Margaret Ward, "The Ladies' Land League," *Irish History Workshop: Saotharlann Staire âeirann* 1 (1981), p. 29. Helen Bradford's "The Ladies' Land League and the Irish Land War 1881/1882: Defining the Relationship between Women and Nation," Chapter 9 in *Gendered Nations: Nationalisms and Gender Order in the Long*

Nineteenth Century, ed. Ida Blom, Karen Hagemann, and Catherine Hall (New York: Berg, 2000), appeared too recently to be included in this study.

48 Katharine Tynan recalled an interesting point about the title of the organization: "I do not know who was responsible for the alliterative title. . . . At one of the first meetings I said 'Why not Women's Land League?' and was told that I was too democratic." Katharine Tynan, *Twenty-five Years: Reminiscences* (London: Smith, Elder & Co., 1913), p. 75. Tynan suggests that either Anna Parnell or Michael Davitt was responsible, and if it was the latter, it would be in keeping with his concern for the "imagery" of the movement that he chose the term "ladies" which conveyed an aura of propriety, decorum, and womanliness to the movement.

49 Davitt, *Fall of Feudalism*, p. 299. English observers also viewed the LLL with a certain degree of paternalism, assuming that it would behave like genteel English women's groups: when the London *Times* first mentioned the LLL, it envisioned the "delicate, but very nimble, hands," of the ladies engaged in "writing letters, sending telegrams, composing addresses, freely interchanging their ideas, and telling their mind about the Ministry and the landlords." Moreover, when it came to the real management of the Land League's affairs, *The Times* used domestic ideology to explain the LLL's expected troubles: "But it is hard to expect them to prove their economic and administrative skill in managing an empty house, and they have reason to complain that they have not been left the key of the cash-box, but only an empty cupboard." *The Times* (London), 14 February 1881.

50 "We were supposed to be instructed in our work by the Land League, but their assistance confined itself to showing us the minute book in which they kept an account of their meetings, and allowing us access to their branch book, where the names and addresses of the principal local officials were written and – lastly but not leastly – finding fault with everything we did." Anna Parnell, *The Tale of a Great Sham*, ed. Dana Hearne (Dublin: Arlen House, 1986), p. 90.

51 For example, the London *Times* reported on 3 January 1882, that "Miss Marion Hawkes, an English lady, is at Kiltyclogher, county Leitrim, on behalf of the Ladies' Land League, providing for 40 families evicted by Mr. Tottenham, M.P. Over 30 wooden houses have been supplied by the Ladies' Land League." This was a country-wide policy, which the government tried to discourage, and Katharine Tynan was present in the LLL offices the day that Anna Parnell reported the following incident: " 'I met Lord Spencer [Lord Lieutenant of Ireland] in Westmoreland Street,' she said. 'He was riding with his escort. I went out into the roadway and stopped his horse. "What do you mean, Lord Spencer," I said, "by interfering with the houses I am building for evicted tenants?" He only stared at me and muttered something, lifting his hat. I held his horse by the head-piece till he heard me. Then I went back to the pavement.' " Tynan, *Reminiscences*, p. 83.

52 Senator Mrs. J. Wyse-Power, "The Political Influence of Women in Modern Ireland," in *The Voice of Ireland*, ed. William G. Fitzgerald (Dublin and London: Virtue and Co. Ltd., [c. 1923]), p. 158. On October 22 1881, the London *Times* reported that fifteen children's branches had been formed. According to Ward, there were ultimately 500 branches of the LLL. Ward, "The Ladies' Land League," p. 31.

53 The London *Times* of January 6 1882 reported that: "Three young women were arrested yesterday at Ballyfarnon for holding a Land League meeting in a Roman Catholic Chapel. The magistrate remanded them until next petty sessions, and liberated them without bail. On reaching the streets, they addressed a large assembly, urging the people to pay no rent." For other political activities, see TeBrake, "Irish

Peasant Women in Revolt," p. 70; for women stopping process servers, see Davitt, *The Fall of Feudalism*, pp. 316–17. Davitt ends his account with a typically sentimental touch; a young policeman is saved from the mob by a young girl who shields his body with her own, and though the two had never met before the incident, they ultimately married.

54 St. John Ervine, *Parnell* (London: Ernest Benn, 1925), pp. 158, 199, Innes, *Woman and Nation*, p. 113.

55 Tynan, *Reminiscences*, p. 82.

56 Tynan, *Reminiscences*, p. 82.

57 Quoted in Davitt, *Fall of Feudalism*, p. 451, n. 1.

58 Parnell, *The Tale of a Great Sham*, pp. 89–90. Katharine Tynan, who was present when Michael Davitt first proposed the LLL, declared in her memoirs that "I believe Mr. Parnell disliked the women's organisation from the beginning, and he certainly detested it in the end." Tynan, *Reminiscences*, p. 73.

59 Quoted in TeBrake, "Irish Peasant Women in Revolt," p. 71.

60 Quoted in Ward, "The Ladies' Land League," p. 31.

61 Quoted in F.S.L. Lyons, *Charles Stewart Parnell* (Bungay, Suffolk: Fontana/Collins, 1978), pp. 178–9.

62 Quoted in Lyons, *Parnell*, pp. 178–9.

63 James Daly in the *Connaught Telegraph*, February 12 1881, quoted in Niamh O'Sullivan, "The Iron Cage of Femininity: Visual Representation of Women in the 1880s Land Agitation," in *Ideology and Ireland in the Nineteenth Century*, ed. T. Foley and S. Ryder (Dublin: Four Courts Press, 1998), p. 195.

64 *The Times* (London), October 22 1881; January 5 1882.

65 Quoted in Ward, "The Ladies' Land League," pp. 31, 32.

66 Innes, *Woman and Nation*, p. 113.

67 In 1881, Parnell and his associates had issued a "No Rent Manifesto" from prison, calling on all Irish tenants to refuse to pay rent in order to force the government to change its repressive policies. Although the LLL thought this call was ill-advised, they agreed to support it; however, when the men changed their minds in early 1882 and told the women to abandon it, the LLL refused, arguing that this sudden reversal would do more harm than good. Ward, "Ladies' Land League," p. 32.

68 Maud Gonne, *The Autobiography of Maud Gonne: A Servant of the Queen*, ed. A. Norman Jeffares and Anna MacBride White (Chicago: University of Chicago Press, 1994), pp. 96–7. Despite ill-health, Gonne did undertake a great deal of nationalist work, including fundraising in Europe and America and founding Inghinidhe na hÉireann (Daughters of Ireland). She continued her nationalist activities through the 1920s, acting as a nurse during the fighting in 1920–1, and organizing a Prisoners' Defence League to assist republican prisoners. At her death in 1953, she was buried in the Republican Plot in Glasnevin cemetery, Dublin.

69 Davitt, *Fall of Feudalism*, p. 349. In her memoirs, Katharine Tynan declared that since Anna personally was so like Charles, it was understandable that the LLL "had taken a course of its own and one in many ways opposed to his wishes and policy." Tynan, *Reminiscences*, pp. 89–90.

70 In August 1882, Parnell wrote to a colleague about the LLL's unmanageability: "I have never heard that anybody could ever persuade a woman to do, or not to do, anything which she had made up her mind to do, no matter what the consequences to herself or others might be." Parnell to John Dillon, August 9, 1882,

quoted in Lyons, *Charles Stewart Parnell*, p. 228. However, Anna Parnell strongly denied that the LLL had any wish to continue their work, saying that they "cherished hopes of an early release from a long and uncongenial bondage," upon the men's release from gaol. Parnell, *The Tale of a Great Sham*, pp. 152–3.

71 Davitt, *Fall of Feudalism*, p. 356.

72 Parnell, *Tale of a Great Sham*, pp. 154–5.

73 Parnell, *The Tale of a Great Sham*, p. 173.

74 Quoted in Ward, "Ladies' Land League," p. 33.

75 Gonne, *Autobiography*, pp. 96–7.

76 Luddy, "Women & Politics in Nineteenth-Century Ireland," p. 102.

77 Edward W. Said, *Culture and Imperialism* (New York: Vintage Books, 1994), pp. 226–7.

78 Scott Hughes Myerly has shown that symbols reflecting the power and control of the dominant or oppressive culture can be so alluring that even the state's staunchest opponents might admire its imagery, even though these represent some of the most oppressive elements of the existing regime. See "Political Aesthetics: British Army Fashion, 1815–55," in *Splendidly Victorian: Essays in Nineteenth- and Twentieth-Century British History in Honour of Walter L. Arnstein*, ed. Michael H. Shirley and Todd E.A. Larson, (Aldershot: Ashgate, 2001), p. 46.

79 C.L. Innes argues that the frequent use of Deirdre, who is a focus of conflict between her father and her lover, and Cuchulain, the great male warrior who fights to the death for his people, exemplify the "extreme division between what are seen as male qualities of militarism and female qualities of passivity and submission." *Woman and Nation*, p. 34.

80 Patrick J. Keane's *Terrible Beauty: Yeats, Joyce, Ireland, and the Myth of the Devouring Female* (Columbia, MO: University of Missouri Press, 1988), discusses in detail the literary duality of Ireland as mother/lover and as the devourer/bringer of death.

81 See, for example, Louise Ryan, "A Question of Loyalty: War, Nation, and Feminism in Early Twentieth-Century Ireland," *Women's Studies International Forum* 20 (January/February 1997), pp. 21–32.

82 Mary Cullen, "How Radical was Irish Feminism between 1860 and 1920?" in *Radicals, Rebels, and Establishments*, ed. Patrick Corish (Belfast: Appletree Press, 1985), p. 193.

83 Rosemary Owens, " 'Votes for Ladies, Votes for Women' : Organised Labour and the Suffrage Movement, 1876–1922," *Saothar* 9 (1983), pp. 33–4.

84 Condren, "Sacrifice and Political Legitimation," p. 167. Karen A. Ray makes a similar point about Indian nationalists; see "Image and Reality: Indian Diaspora Women, Colonial & Post-Colonial Discourse on Empowerment and Victimology," Chapter 11.

85 She had been the secretary of the Fenian Ladies' Committee in the 1860s, which raised funds to support Fenian prisoners and their families, and later she traveled alone to America after her husband had been gaoled, supporting herself by "writing, public readings and giving lessons in elocution." William O'Brien and Desmond Ryan, eds. *Devoy's Post Bag, 1871–1928*. 2 vols. (Dublin: C.J. Fallon, Ltd., 1948, 1953), 1:401.

86 O'Brien and Ryan, *Devoy's Post Bag*, 2:482–3.

87 Condren, "Sacrifice and Political Legitimation," p. 180.

88 Maryann Gialanella Valiulis, "Power, Gender and Identity in the Irish Free State," *Journal of Women's History* 6/7 (Winter/Spring 1995), pp. 128–9.

Chapter 5 French Views of Native American Women in the Early Modern Era: The Tupinamba of Brazil

1 An earlier version of this essay appeared in *Terrae Incognitae* 26 (1994), pp. 9–25 and is reproduced with permission.
2 A good introduction to the topic is Hugh Honour, *The New Golden Land: European Images of America from the Discoveries to the Present Time* (New York: Pantheon Books, 1975). More detailed accounts may be found in *First Images of America: The Impact of the New World on the Old*, ed. Fredi Chiapelli, 2 vols. (Berkeley: University of California Press, 1976). See also Cornelius J. Jaenen, "Conceptual Frameworks for French Views of America and Amerindians," *French Colonial Studies* 7 (1978), pp. 1–22, for a summary of some of the dominant philosophical, literary and religious conceptions that influenced French portrayals of Native American society.
3 For a discussion of male bias in anthropology, see the introduction to *Women and Colonization: Anthropological Perspectives*, ed. Mona Etienne and Eleanor Leacock (New York: Praeger Publishers, 1980), pp. 1–6. Sharon W. Riffany and Kathleen J. Adams, *The Wild Woman: An Inquiry into the Anthropology of an Idea* (Rochester, VT: Schenkman Books, Inc., 1985), p. 2, assert that "anthropologists evaluate human behavior in a language that silences and dismisses women." William T. Divale, "Female Status and Cultural Evolution: A Study in Ethnographer Bias," *Behavior Science Research* 11 (1976), pp. 169–211, concludes that male anthropologists can overcome gender bias to a substantial degree by spending longer amounts of time in native societies and learning the language. However, female enthnographers provide more accurate reports about women, and more favorable assessment of their status than do their male colleagues.
4 Sally Slocum, "Woman the Gatherer: Male Bias in Anthropology," in *Toward an Anthropology of Women*, ed. Rayna R. Reiter (New York: Monthly Review Press, 1975), pp. 37–49; and Michelle Z. Rosaldo, "The Use and Abuse of Anthropology: Reflections on Feminism and Cross-Cultural Understanding," *Signs* 5 (1980), pp. 389–417, who argues that although men and women perform distinct roles in every culture, concepts of gender inequality are not innate, but rather are a social creation.
5 Carole Devens, *Countering Colonization: Native American Women and Great Lakes Missions, 1630–1900* (Berkeley: University of California Press, 1992), pp. 115–19. Throughout her study, Devens describes how Native American women resisted the efforts of Christian missionaries in order to maintain their traditional autonomy; conflict between native men and women occurred in the wake of colonization.
6 See Tiffany and Adams, *The Wild Woman*, pp. 61–96. Louis Montrose, "The Work of Gender in the Discourse of Discovery," in *New World Encounters*, ed. Stephen Greenblatt (Berkeley: University of California Press, 1993), p. 208, maintains that European man "represents territorial conquest as the enforced defloration and possession of a female body." For a discussion and sampling of visual representations of America as a female figure, see Honour, *The New Golden Land*, pp. 84–117. Contemporary French reactions towards the nudity and sexual conduct of Tupinamba women are discussed later in this essay.
7 Joan Kelly, "Early Feminist Theory and the *Querelles des Femmes*, 1400–1789," *Signs* 8 (1982), pp. 4–28, discusses the prevailing misogynist view and notes that some contemporary women did write to counter these ideas. Kelly also refers to the growth of the state as adversely affecting women's political position. See also Natalie Zemon Davis, "Women on Top" in her collection of essays, *Society and Culture in Early Modern France* (Stanford: Stanford University Press, 1975). Davis discusses the dominant

negative perception of women as unruly and disorderly, and sees the growing subjection of women to men in the patriarchal family as symbolic of the domination of all subjects by the increasing power of the state (pp. 124–8). Sarah Hanley, "Engendering the State: Family Formation and State Building in Early Modern France," *French Historical Studies* 16 (1989), pp. 4–27, likewise describes the deterioration of wives' legal status, and views this as a social model for expanding political authority of the monarchic state.

8 Alfred Métraux, "The Tupinamba," in *Handbook of South American Indians*, ed. Julian H. Steward, 7 vols. (Washington DC: U.S. Government Printing Office, 1948), 3:133, cites in his bibliography accounts written by the sixteenth- and seventeenth-century Frenchmen, Claude d'Abbeville, Jean de Léry, André Thevet, and Yves d'Evreux; see also his "Les Précurseurs de l'éthnologie en France du XVIe au XVIIIe siècle," *Cahiers d'histoire mondiale* 7 (1963), pp. 721–38.

9 Jean de Léry, *Histoire d'un Voyage Faict en la Terre du Brésil*, ed. Paul Gaffarel, 2 vols. (Paris, 1880); see the editor's "Preface," 1:i–xv. This text is a reproduction of Léry's second edition, originally published in Geneva in 1580. Janet Whatley has provided an English translation and introduction, *History of a Voyage to the Land of Brazil* (Berkeley: University of California Press, 1990). John Hemming, *Red Gold: The Conquest of the Brazilian Indians, 1500–1700* (Cambridge, MA: Harvard University Press, 1978), pp. 119–38, provides a history of this colonial venture, know as "Antarctic France." Frank Lestringant, *Le Huguenot et le Sauvage: L'Amérique et la controverse coloniale en France au temps des Guerres de Religion (1555–1589)* (Paris, 1990), pp. 69–70, emphasizes the twenty-year gap between Léry's actual experience in Brazil and his written reminiscence, which Lestringant claims is a highly idealized and sentimentalized version of events.

10 Léry, *Histoire d'un Voyage*, 1:75–6, 128, 134–5.

11 Léry, *Histoire d'un Voyage*, 1: 131, 136, 138–9.

12 Léry, *Histoire d'un Voyage*, 1: 139. Lestringant, *Le Huguenot et le Sauvage*, pp. 66–9, discusses Léry's unhappy and unsuccessful marriage as the source of his misogyny, and hence the idealization of his youthful experience in Brazil.

13 See Hemming, *Red Gold*, pp. 198–216.

14 Claude d'Abbeville, *Histoire de la Mission des Pères Capucins en l'Isle de Maragnan et terres circonvoisinces ou est traicté des singularitez admirables et des Meurs merveilleuses des Indiens habitans de ce pais* (Paris, 1614), pp. 267–9.

15 Abbeville, *Histoire de la Mission des Pères Capucins*, p. 270.

16 Abbeville, *Histoire de la Mission des Pères Capucins*, p. 271.

17 French travel writers of the early modern era often praised aspects of Native American life and culture as a means of commenting upon certain moral flaws of contemporary European society. See especially the two works of Gilbert Chinard, *L'Exotisme Américain dans la Littérature Française au XVIe Siècle* (Paris: Hachette, 1911; reprint edn, Geneva: Slatkine, 1970); and *L'Amerique et le Rève Exotique dans la Littérature Française au XVIIe et au XVIIIe Siècle* (Paris: Libraire E. Droz, 1934). Lestringant, *Le Huguenot et le Sauvage*, continually reminds the reader that portrayals of Native Americans as "noble savages" should be viewed solely within the realm of myth.

18 Abbeville, *Histoire de la Mission des Peres Capucins*, pp. 282–3.

19 Léry, *Histoire d'un Voyage*, 2: 89–90. Geoffroy Atkinson, *Les Relations de Voyages du XVIIe Siècle et L'Evolution des Idées* (Paris: Libraire E. droz, 1924: reprint edn, Geneva, Slatkine, 1972), asserts that travelers to the New World who reported about native mothers nursing their own babies greatly influenced the thought of social critics in eighteenth-century France, notably Jean-Jacques Rousseau, who encouraged

European women to adopt this practice. See also G. Pire, "Jean-Jacques Rousseau et les Relations de Voyages," *Revue d'Histoire Littéraire de la France* 56 (1956), pp. 355–8; and the two works of Chinard, *L'Exotisme Américain* and *L'Amérique et le Rève Exotique*.

20 André Thevet, *The New Found Worlde, or Antarctike*, trans. Thomas Hacket (London, 1568), p. 71. This text is a translation of Thevet's original 1558 edition. A modern edition has been prepared by Frank Lestringant, *Les Singularités de la France Antarctique* (Paris, 1983).

21 Yves d'Evreux, *Suitte de L'Histoirse des Choses plus Memorable Advenües en Maragnan* (Paris, 1615), pp. 89–93. This text is available in a modern edition, *Voyage au Nord du Brésil fait en 1613 et 1614*, présentation et notes d'Hélène Clastres (Paris: Payot, 1985). Analysis of artistic depictions of Native American women with hanging breasts reveals underlying European assumptions regarding the "fallen" nature of the native peoples of the New World. See Bernadette Bucher, *La sauvage aux seins pendants* (Paris: Hermann, 1977). Tiffany and Adams, *Wild Woman*, p. 7, note that nineteenth- and twentieth-century anthropologists continue to associate sexual promiscuity with women in non-Western cultures.

22 Evreux, *Suitte de L'Histoirse des Choses plus Memorable*, pp. 48, 76, 96, 98–100, 135, 300.

23 Evreux, *Suitte de L'Histoirse des Choses plus Memorable*, pp. 48, 72, 119, 299–300.

24 Davis, "Women on Top," pp. 124–5, notes that the typical view of women in the early modern era advanced the notion that females had a stronger sex drive than men, and more readily gave in to their physical desires.

25 Evreux, *Suitte de L'Histoirse des Choses plus Memorable*, pp. 341–2.

26 Evreux, *Suitte de L'Histoirse des Choses plus Memorable*, p. 69.

27 See Davis, "Women on Top," pp. 126–8 and Hanley, "Engendering the State," pp. 8–11.

28 Eleanor Burke Leacock, *Myths of Male Dominance* (New York: Monthly Review Press, 1981), pp. 32–5, 45–9 and Leacock, "Montagnais Women and the Jesuit Program for Colonization," in *Women and Colonization*, ed. Etienne and Leacock, pp. 25–42. Leacock stresses the egalitarian nature of gender relationships, and the autonomy experienced by women among the Montagnais of eastern Canada. French missionaries especially sought to restrict women's independence, and impose a male dominated monogamous family structure. Devens, *Countering Colonization*, p. 25, adds that the Jesuits were "shocked" by both the unrestricted sexual activity of Montagnais women, and the power that they exercised within the family.

29 Métraux, "The Tupinamba," pp. 111–12.

30 Evreux, *Suitte de L'Histoirse des Choses plus Memorable*, pp. 85, 89.

31 Evreux, *Suitte de L'Histoirse des Choses plus Memorable*, pp. 86–7, 113.

32 Léry, *Histoire d'un Voyage*, 2: 85–6, 92. Métraux, "The Tupinamba," p. 112, confirms that polygyny was a common practice and a native headman could have as many as thirty wives. However, Tupi women derived benefits from polygynous marriage as well. Women welcomed additional wives as helpers with whom they could share their work.

33 Thevet, *The New Found Worlde*, pp. 65–6. Margaret T. Hodgen, *Early Anthropology in the Sixteenth and Seventeenth Centuries* (Philadelphia: University of Pennsylvania Press, 1964), shows that travelers to the New World often utilized cultural categories and practices of Old World societies in order to interpret New World culture. See also J.H. Elliott, *The Old World and the New, 1492–1650* (Cambridge: Cambridge University Press, 1970), and more recently, Anthony Pagden, *The Fall of*

Natural Man: The American Indian and the Origins of Comparative Ethnology (Cambridge: Cambridge University Press, 1986), p. 11, who states that Europeans described the New World "by means of . . . analogy with the old."

34 Thevet, *The New Found Worlde*, pp. 65–6.

35 Abbeville, *Histoire de la Mission des Pères Capucins*, pp. 125–6, 278, 280. Establishing Christian marriage along with religious conversion was one of the prime goals of Jesuit missionaries to Canada. See Leacock, *Myths of Male Dominance*, p. 47 and "Montagnais Women," p. 28. Carol Devens, "Separate Confrontations: Gender as a Factor in Indian Adaption to European Colonization in New France," *American Quarterly* 38 (1986), pp. 461–80, points out that Montagnais women were especially resistant to the Jesuit program of religious conversion, since it also called for the introduction of Christian marriage, which gave more authority to the husband and reduced the wife's autonomy.

36 Abbeville, *Histoire de la Mission des Pères Capucins*, pp. 126, 279–81.

37 Evreux, *Suitte de L'Histoirse des Choses plus Memorable*, p. 90.

38 Métraux, "The Tupinamba," p. 99, asserts that farming constituted the major portion of Tupi subsistence, and this agricultural work was performed by women. For a discussion of the key economic role of women, and the accompanying status they enjoyed in other New World Societies, see the "Introduction," Robert Steven Grunet, "Sunksquaws, Shamans, and Tradeswomen: Middle Atlantic Coastal Algonkian Women during the Seventeenth and Eighteenth Centuries," pp. 43–62, and Elisa Buenaventura-Posso and Susan E. Brown, "Forced Transition from Egalitarianism to Male Dominance: The Bari of Columbia," pp. 109–33 in *Women and Colonization*, ed. Mona Etienne and Eleanor Leacock (New York: Praeger Publishers, 1980). Judith K. Brown, "Iroquois Women: An Ethnohistoric Note," in *Toward an Anthropology of Women*, ed. Rayna R. Reiter (New York: Monthly Review Press, 1975), pp. 235–51, attributes the power and status enjoyed by Iroquois women to their crucial economic role.

39 See David Herlihy, *Opera Muliebria: Women and Work in Medieval Europe* (New York: McGraw-Hill, 1990) and Merry E. Wiesner, "Spinning out Capital: Women's Work in the Early Modern Era," in *Becoming Visible: Women in European History*, ed. Renate Bridenthal, Glaudia Koonz, and Susan Stuard, 3rd edn (Boston: Houghton Mifflin, 1998), pp. 203–31. Both note the deterioration of women's economic status in the later middle ages due to growing guild restrictions, increased technological change, economic specialization, and the advent of capitalism.

40 Jesuit missionaries likewise failed to acknowledge the key economic contribution of Montagnais women. French emphasis on the fur trade disrupted the native economy and favored activities in which men were dominant. See Leacock, "Montagnais Women," pp. 29–30, 38–40 and *Myths of Male Dominance*, pp. 36–8, 40–1; Devens, "Separate Confrontations," pp. 462–4, 467, 471–3 and *Countering Colonization*, pp. 10–18. For a fuller exploration of the impact of this development on women in Canada and Mexico, see Verónica Vázquez Garcia, "Native Women and State Legislation in Mexico and Canada," Chapter 7. Even modern anthropologists express their own cultural bias by assuming men play a dominant role in primitive societies and denying the crucial economic role of women. See Reiter, "Introduction," pp. 11–19, and Slocum, "Women the Gatherer," pp. 36–50, both in *Towards an Anthropology of Women*.

41 Léry, *Histoire d'un Voyage*, 1: 141, 143, 148, 155; 2: 35, 87, 97–9.

42 Thevet, *The New Found Worlde*, pp. 60, 65.

43 Abbeville, *Histoire de la Mission des Peres Capucins*, pp. 266, 309.

44 Evreux, *Suitte de L'Histoirse des Choses plus Memorable*, pp. 21, 83, 90, 112–16.
45 Evreux, *Suitte de L'Histoirse des Choses plus Memorable*, p. 76.
46 Thevet, *The New Found Worlde*, p. 92.
47 Léry, *Histoire d'un Voyage*, 1:147.
48 Léry, *Histoire d'un Voyage*, 1:123.
49 Abbeville, *Histoire de la Mission des Pères Capucins*, pp. 297–9.
50 Thevet, *The New Found Worlde*, p. 65.
51 Ruth Kelso, *The Doctrine of the English Gentleman in the Sixteenth Century* (Urbana: University of Illinois Press, 1929; reprint, Gloucester, MA: P. Smith, 1964), p. 156. Nancy Lurie, "Indian Cultural Adjustment to European Civilization," in *Seventeenth Century America*, ed. James Morton Smith (Chapel Hill: University of North Carolina Press, 1959), p. 57, notes that Europeans misinterpreted the role of hunting and fishing in Native American societies.
52 Henri Baudet, *Paradise on Earth: Some Thoughts on European Images of Non-European Man* (New Haven: Yale University Press, 1965); Charles L. Sanford, *The Quest for Paradise: Europe and the American Moral Imagination* (Urbana: University of Illinois Press, 1961); and Henry S. Bausum, "Edenic Images of the Western World: A Reappraisal," *South Atlantic Quarterly* 67 (1968), pp. 672–87. These are but a sampling from a broad array of works on this topic.
53 The overworked Indian woman, and the lazy Indian man were prime components of the negative English interpretation of native North Americans. See David D. Smits, "The 'Squaw Drudge': A Prime Index of Savagism, " *Ethnohistory* 29 (1982), pp. 281–306. Leacock, *Myths of Male Dominance*, p. 45, notes that the Jesuits often viewed hard-working Montagnais women as "slaves." Devens, *Countering Colonization*, pp. 123–4, comments that pity for over-worked native women was an expression of the European stereotype that viewed females as the "weaker sex." The French observers of the Tupinamba discussed in this essay portrayed native women as busy, but generally did not view them as oppressed. However, Yves d'Evreux compared Tupinamba women to mules, because they followed after their husbands, carrying their belongings. See Evreux, *Suitte de L'Histoirse des Choses plus Memorable*, p. 90.
54 Léry, *Histoire d'un Voyage*, 1:35.
55 Thevet, "To the Reader," in *The New Found Worlde*, n.p.
56 Pagden, *Fall of Natural Man*, pp. 4–5, maintains that new information from America was "absorbed within existing paradigms," or even ignored, so as not to disrupt the dominant conceptual frameworks of the era.

Chapter 6 Indian Women as Symbols of Disorder in Early Rhode Island

1 I wish to thank Monique Bourque, Rachel Buff, Joanne Melish, Laura Micham, John E. Murray, and Karin A. Wulf for their helpful critiques of earlier versions of this essay.
2 The fifteen towns are Charlestown, Cumberland, East Greenwich, Exeter, Glocester, Hopkinton, Jamestown, Middletown, New Shoreham, Providence, Richmond, South Kingstown, Tiverton, Warren, and Warwick. These fairly represent the wealth, age, population, economic orientation and geographic location of Rhode Island's thirty towns at the time of the American Revolution.

3 See Ruth Wallis Herndon and Ella Wilcox Sekatau, "The Right to a Name: The Narragansett People and Rhode Island Officials in the Revolutionary Era," *Ethnohistory* 44:3 (Summer 1997), pp. 433–62. Discussion of this point follows below.

4 For a discussion of the term "mustee," see below.

5 For a more thorough discussion of the nature of communitarian patriarchy in eighteenth-century Rhode Island, see Ruth Wallis Herndon, "The Domestic Cost of Seafaring: Town Leaders and Seamen's Families in Rhode Island, 1750–1800," *Iron Men, Wooden Women: Gender and Seafaring in the Atlantic World, 1700–1920*, ed. Margaret S. Creighton and Lisa Norling (Baltimore: Johns Hopkins University Press, 1996), pp. 55–69.

6 See Ruth Wallis Herndon, "Governing the Affairs of the Town: Continuity and Change in Rhode Island, 1750–1800" (PhD Thesis, The American University, 1992), pp. 95–102, 183–206.

7 For the specific poor law regulations in eighteenth-century Rhode Island, see Acts and Laws of His Majesty's Colony of Rhode-Island and Providence Plantations (Newport: J. Franklin, 1745–52), pp. 48–51; Acts and Laws of the English Colony of Rhode-Island and Providence Plantations (Newport: Solomon Southwick, 1767), pp. 228–32; and The Public Laws of the State of Rhode-Island and Providence Plantations (Providence: Carter and Wilkinson, 1798), pp. 352–8.

8 For a full discussion of legal settlement and warning out, see Ruth Wallis Herndon, *Unwelcome Americans: Living on the Margin in Eighteenth-Century New England* (Philadelphia: University of Pennsylvania Press, forthcoming).

9 Of 1,924 heads of household warned out of Rhode Island towns between 1750 and 1800, 772 were identified racially. Of these 772, 169 (22 percent) were designated as people of color. According to contemporary estimates, in 1783, African Americans made up 4.5 percent of Rhode Island's population and Indians made up 1.9 percent (Evarts B. Greene and Virginia D. Harrington, *American Population before the Federal Census of 1790* [Gloucester, Mass.: Peter Smith, 1966], p. 67.) Lorenzo Greene believes that the estimate for blacks is too low; he figures blacks comprised 7.3 percent of Rhode Island's population in 1782 and 6.3 percent of the population in 1790. (*The Negro in Colonial New England* [New York: Atheneum, 1969], p. 87.) In either case, blacks and Indians together comprised less than 10 percent of the population towards the end of the eighteenth century.

10 In the towns under study, there were forty-eight instances of people described as "Indian" or "mustee" being warned out between 1750 and 1800; thirty-six were women (seventy-five percent) and twelve (twenty-five percent) were men. See Herndon and Seketau, "The Right to a Name," p. 442. There are many more warnouts of people described as "black," "mulatto," and "Negro" in the town records; and when all these cases are figured together, the disparity is not quite so pronounced: of 169 warnouts of people of color, 105 were women (62.1 percent) and sixty-four were men (37.9 percent).

11 TCM July 4 1759, Jamestown TCR 1:99.

12 TCM August 7 1786, Providence TCR 5:393.

13 TCM July 10 1787, Providence TCR 6:13.

14 TCM September 4 1779 and February 26 1780, East Greenwich TCR 3:198 and 3:201.

15 TM May 11 1757, Middletown TMR 1:63.

16 TCM 8 November 1800, Providence TCR 7:576. These local round-ups followed the lead of the colonial legislature which had passed laws earlier, banning people of

color from congregating at taverns or being out past nine o'clock in the evening without permission of their masters. See "An Act to prevent all Persons, within this Colony, from entertaining Indian, Negro or Mulatto Servants or Slaves," Acts and Laws of Rhode Island (1767), pp. 151–2.

17 When officials approached a man about taking on a child as an indentured servant, they were tacitly recruiting his wife as well, for women were essential to the administration of servitude in the domestic setting. While children technically "belonged" to men (fathers, masters, guardians, or "town fathers"), women were necessary partners in their care; and the patriarchal principle could not be satisfied without both. If a master's wife died, for example, young servants – especially female ones – would quickly be taken out of the home where there was no longer a "proper person" to raise them. See Ruth Wallis Herndon, "'Bastards,' Orphans, and Servants: 'Mulatto' and 'Mustee' Children in Early Rhode Island," paper presented at the annual conference of the Omohundro Institute for Early American History and Culture, Worcester, Massachusetts, 6 June 1998.

18 Of 765 indentures drawn up by Rhode Island town officials between 1750 and 1800, 176 (23.0 percent) involved children (and a few adults) explicitly designated as "Indian," "mustee," "mulatto," "Negro," or "black." For an analysis of public indentures of children in eighteenth-century Rhode Island, see Ruth Wallis Herndon, "'To live after the manner of an apprentice': Public Indenture and Social Control in Rhode Island, 1750–1800," paper presented at the Annual Meeting of the American Studies Association, Boston, Massachusetts, seven November 1993.

19 TCM May 13 1751, South Kingstown TCR 4:200.

20 TCM August 27 1754, Jamestown TCR 1:75–6.

21 TCM April 4 1755, New Shoreham TCR 3:323.

22 Of all 713 indentures of children in Rhode Island towns between 1750 and 1800, 460 (64.5 percent) were for boys, and 230 (32.3 percent) were for girls; in 23 cases the child's sex was not identified. Among non-white children the disparity was slightly larger than the statistics for all children. Of 172 indentures of children of color, 48 were for girls (27.9 percent) and 117 were for boys (68.0 percent); in seven cases the child's sex was not identified.

23 For a full discussion of how the poor relief system worked, see Ruth Wallis Herndon, "'Who died an expence to this town': Poor Relief in Eighteenth-Century Rhode Island," *Down and Out in Early America*, ed. Billy G. Smith (University Park: Penn State University Press, forthcoming).

24 See, for example, the complaint by the Charlestown town council that the reservation Indians were supposedly failing to care for their poor members who were living in the adjacent town. TCM April 7 1783, Charlestown TCR 3:132.

25 In the towns under study, there were thirty-five instances of people described as "Indian" or "mustee" receiving direct financial support between 1750 and 1800; 30 cases (eighty-six percent) involved women and five cases (fourteen percent) involved men. See Herndon and Seketau, "The Right to a Name," p. 440.

26 TCM July 16 1751, Jamestown TCR 1:44; TCM 13 May 1760, Exeter TCR 2:87.

27 Samuel Johnson's eighteenth-century English dictionary defines mulatto as "one begot between a white and a black," but provides no parallel definition of "mustee." See Samuel Johnson, *A Dictionary of the English Language*, 2 vols. (London, 1755). Jack D. Forbes has suggested that far more useful in determining meanings of these racial terms is a scrutiny of the primary data in which the terms appear. See Jack D. Forbes, *Africans and Native Americans: The Language of Race and the Evolution of Red-Black Peoples*, 2nd edn. (Urbana: University of Illinois Press, 1993), p. 3.

28 TCM August 29 1761, East Greenwich TCR 3:76; TCM March 27 1762, Jamestown TCR 1:143–4; TCM March 14 1764, Warwick TCR 2:241–2.

29 TCM 2nd Monday in September 1752, Jamestown TCR 1:54–5; TCM 4 January 1796 and 7 November 1796, Providence TCM 7:72, 7:116; TCM 13 and 20 April 1752, Warwick TCR 2:99–100. Elsewhere in the colonies, the definitions of "mulatto" and "mustee" were more explicitly written into law. In Virginia, for example, legislators in 1705 defined "mulatto" as including the children of Indians. See Kathleen M. Brown, *Good Wives, Nasty Wenches, and Anxious Patriarchs: Gender, Race, and Power in Colonial Virginia* (Chapel Hill: University of North Carolina Press, 1996), p. 215.

30 For a full discussion, see Herndon and Sekatau, "The Right to a Name." Similarly, Kathleen Brown has shown that in Virginia, non-white ancestry was more powerful than white ancestry as a determinant of a person's legal status and treatment. See *Good Wives, Nasty Wenches*, pp. 212–16.

31 Public Laws of Rhode-Island (1798), p. 483. This law was repealed in January 1881, a few months after the state legislature had officially declared the Narragansett Indian people to be extinct by virtue of their "dilution" through intermarriage with Negro and white people. See *Acts, Resolves and Reports of the General Assembly of the State of Rhode Island and Providence Plantations* (Providence: R.D. Freeman & Co., 1881), p. 108.

32 TCM May 2 1785, Providence TCR 5:313.

33 TCM May 14 1796, South Kingstown TCR 6:229–30.

34 TCM January 30 1790, East Greenwich TCR 4:110.

35 For a full analysis of the treatment of people of color in late eighteenth-century New England, see Joanne Pope Melish, *Disowning Slavery: Gradual Emancipation and "Race" in New England, 1780–1860* (Ithaca: Cornell University Press, 1998).

36 TCM March 20 1780, Providence TCR 5:169; PTP 5:39.

37 TCM June 30 1759, East Greenwich TCR 3:56.

38 TCM March 27 1762, Jamestown TCR 1:143.

39 TCM May 24 1763, May 15 1764, March 23 1767, and April 30 1768, Jamestown TCR, vol. 1; TCM July 18 1768, New Shoreham TCR 4:174.

40 TCM November 1 1758, Jamestown TCR 1:95.

41 For her birthdate and parentage, see the examination of Sarah Gardner, TCM March 20 1780, Providence TCR 5:168–9.

42 Examination of Sarah Gardner, TCM March 5 1770, Providence TCR 4:299.

43 Examination of Sarah Gardner, TCM March 20 1780, Providence TCR 5:168–9.

44 TCM June 14 1762, Warwick TCR 2:211.

45 TCM November 19 1762, Warwick TCR 2:218.

46 TCM December 13 1762, Warwick TCR 2:221–2.

47 Warwick town officials granted Gardner a settlement certificate so that she could live in the town of Smithfield (TCM March 19 1768, Warwick TCR 2:29). But Providence records show that Gardner left Smithfield for Providence within the year.

48 TCM March 5 1770, February 17 1772, March 20 1780, April 4 1780, September 2 1782, and October 1 1787, Providence TCR 4:299, 4:322, 5:168–9, 5:172, 5:215, and 6:23.

49 TCM April 4 1780, Providence TCR 5:172.

50 Letter from Deputy Governor Jabez Bowen to the Providence Town Council, July 23 1782, PTP 6:150; warrant to appear before the Providence Town Council, July 23 1782, PTP 6:150. The group warrant includes "Indian" woman "Elizabeth

Gardner," but I believe this is the clerk's slip, because all other documents of the incident indicate the clerk meant Sarah Gardner.

51 TCM March 20 1780 and October 1 1787, Providence TCR 5:169, 6:23. The original transcript of the 1780 examination contains Sarah Gardner's signature: a large, bold "X" – another sign of her self-possession before the town councilmen. PTP 5:40.

52 TCM October 1 1787, Providence TCR 6:23, PTP 10:148.

53 For a related discussion of the ways in which Indian women violated officials' sense of community order, see my "The Racialisation and Feminisation of Poverty in Early America: Indian Women as 'the Poor of the Town' in Eighteenth-century Rhode Island," in *Empire and Others: The British Encounter with Indigenous Peoples, 1600–1850*, ed. R. Halpern and M. J. Daunton (London: University College London Press, 1999), pp. 186–203.

54 Ruth Wallis Herndon, "On and Off the Record: Town Clerks as Interpreters of Rhode Island History," *Rhode Island History* 50:4 (November 1992), pp. 103–15.

55 TM October 19 1785, Jamestown TMR 1:98.

56 TCM December 1 1760 and February 1 1768, Tiverton TCR 2:162, 2:231; TCM April 9 1770, South Kingstown TCR 5:228.

57 TCM April 18 1750, Warwick TCR 2:110–11.

58 TCM October 14 1765, Warwick TCR 2:266.

59 TCM January 15 1754, Jamestown TCR 1:71–72.

Chapter 7 Native Women and State Legislation in Mexico and Canada: The Agrarian Law and the Indian Act

1 Eleanor Leacock, "Introduction" to F. Engels, *The Origin of the Family, Private Property and the State* (New York: International Publishers, 1972); Eleanor Leacock, "Women's Status in Egalitarian Society: Implications for Social Evolution," *Current Anthropology* 19 (1978); Judith Brown, "A Note on the Division of Labour by Sex," *American Anthropology* 72 (1970); Diane Bell, *Daughters of the Dreaming* (Melbourne: McPhee Gribble, 1983).

2 Henrietta Moore, *Feminism and Anthropology* (Minneapolis: University of Minneapolis Press, 1988); Karen Sacks, *Sisters and Wives: The Past and Future of Sexual Equality* (Westport: Greenwood Press, 1979).

3 See Suellen Huntingdon, "Issues in Women's Role in Economic Development: Critique and Alternatives," *Journal of Marriage and the Family* 37 (1975); Simi Afonja, "Changing Modes of Production and the Sexual Division of Labor among the Yoruba," *Signs* 7 (1981): 299–313.

4 Fiona Wilson, "Women and Agricultural Change in Latin America: Some Concepts Guiding Research", *World Development* 13 (1985).

5 See Lourdes Arizpe, *La mujer en el desarrollo de México y de América Latina* (Mexico: UNAM-CRIM, 1989); GIMPTRAP, *Las mujeres en la pobreza* (Mexico: GIMTRAP-COLMEX, 1994); Soledad González Montes and Vania Salles, *Relaciones de género y transformaciones agrarias* (Mexico: COLMEX, 1995); Pilar Alberti and Emma Zapata, *Estrategias de sobrevivencia de mujeres campesinas e indígenas ante la crisis económica* (Mexico: Colegio de Postgraduados, 1997).

6 José Luis de Rojas, *México Tenochtitlan: Economía y Sociedad en el Siglo XVI* (Mexico: Fondo de Cultura Económica, 1986), p. 101.

7 G. McBride, *The Land Systems of Mexico* (New York: American Geographical Society, 1923), p. 117.

8 Anna-Britta Hellbom, *La participación cultural de las mujeres indias y mestizas en el México precortesiano y postrevolucionario* (Stockholm: The Ethnographical Museum, 1967), pp. 235–6; S. Cline, *Colonial Culhuacan, 1580–1600. A Social History of an Aztec Town* (Albuquerque: University of New Mexico Press, 1986), p. 112; María de Jesús Rodríguez, *La mujer azteca* (Toluca: Universidad Autónoma del Estado de México, n.d.), p. 99.
9 Susan Kellogg, "Kinship and Social Organization in Early Colonial Tenochtitlan," in *Handbook of Middle American Indians* (Austin: University of Austin Press, 1986), 4:105.
10 Cline, *Colonial Culhuacan.*
11 Kellogg, "Kinship and Social Organization," p. 117.
12 See Susan Kellogg, "Aztec Women in Early Colonial Courts: Structure and Strategy in a Legal Context," in *Five Centuries of Law and Politics in Central Mexico*, ed. R. Spores and R. Hassing (Nashville: Vanderbilt Publications, 1984) for examples on native women's land claims in colonial courts.
13 The *hacienda-latifundios* were large estates owned by one family (typically of Spanish origin) where landless peasants had access to a small plot of land to cultivate for self-consumption in exchange of free labor.
14 Deborah Kanter, "Hijos del pueblo: Family, Gender and Community in Rural Mexico, the Toluca Region, 1733–1849" (PhD Thesis, Department of History, University of Virginia, 1993).
15 A widow's rights were usually specified as "use rights" during the course of her lifetime. Wills stated that she should use the inherited property to fulfil her obligations as a parent vis-à-vis her children and that the property should be transferred to them at the time of her death or when children reached adulthood. See Margarita Loera y Chávez, *Calimaya y Tepamaxalco. Tenencia y transmisión hereditaria de la tierra en dos communidades indígenas. Epoca colonial* (Mexico City: Instituto Nacional de Antropología e Historia, 1977).
16 Enrique Florescano Mayet, *Origen y desarrollo de los problemas agrarios en México* (Mexico City: ERA, 1984), p. 24.
17 Mercedes Olivera, "The Barrios of San Andrés Cholula," in *Essays on Mexican Kinship*, ed. H. Nutini, P. Carrasco, and J. Taggart (Pittsburgh: University of Pittsburgh Press, 1976), p. 72; Florence Mallon, "The Conflictual Construction of Community: Gender, Ethnicity and Hegemony in the Sierra Norte de Puebla" (unpublished manuscript, 1990).
18 Kanter, *Hijos del pueblo.*
19 Soledad González Montes and Pilar Iracheta, "La violencia en la vida de las mujeres campesinas: el distrito de Tenango, 1880–1910," in *Presencia y transparencia. La mujer en la historia de México* (Mexico: COLMEX, 1987), p. 123.
20 Jacques M. Chevalier and Daniel Buckles, *A Land without Gods. Process Theory, Maldevelopment and the Mexican Nahuas* (London: Zed Books, 1995), p. 31.
21 Lourdes Arizpe and Carlota Botey, "Mexican Agricultural Development Policy and Its Impact on Rural Women," in *Rural Women and State Policy in Latin America*, ed. Carmen Diana Deere and Magdalena León de Leal (Colorado: Westview Press, 1987), p. 70.
22 Shirlene Soto, *Emergence of the Modern Mexican Woman. Her Participation in Revolution and Struggle for Equality* (Denver: Arden Press, 1990), pp. 109–10.
23 Esperanza Tuñón Pablos, *Mujeres que se Organizan. El FUPDM, 1935–1938* (Mexico City: UNAM-Porrúa, 1992).
24 Arizpe and Botey, "Mexican Agricultural Development," pp. 70–1.

25 Arizpe and Botey, "Mexican Agricultural Development," p. 71.
26 For more details, see Verónica Vázquez García, "Gender and Capitalist Development: The Nahuas of Pajapan, Veracruz" (PhD Thesis, Department of Sociology and Anthropology, Carleton University, 1995).
27 Rocío Esparza Salinas, *Las mujeres campesinas ante las reformas al Artículo 27 de la Constitución* (Mexico: GIMTRAP, 1996), p. 25.
28 Kathleen Jamieson, *Indian Women and the Law in Canada: Citizen Minus* (Ottawa: Minister of Supply Services, 1978), p. 113.
29 J.R. Miller, *Skyscrapers Hide the Heavens. A History of Indian–White Relations in Canada* (Toronto: University of Toronto Press, 1989), p. 9.
30 Olive Dickason, *Canada's First Nations* (Toronto: McClelland and Stewart, 1992), p. 71.
31 Carol Devens, "Separate Confrontations: Gender as a Factor in Indian Adaptation to European Colonization in New France," *American Quarterly* 38 (1986), p. 464; Eleanor Leacock, "Montagnais Women and the Jesuit Program of Colonization," in *Rethinking Canada. The Promise of Women's History*, ed. V. Strong-Boag and A. C. Fellman, (Toronto: Copp Clark Pitman, 1991), pp. 11–27.
32 Quoted in Donna Kahenrakwas Goodleaf, "Under Military Occupation. Indigenous Women, State Violence and Community Resistance," in *And Still We Rise. Feminist Political Mobilizing in Contemporary Canada*, ed. L. Carty (Canada: Women's Press, 1993), p. 227.
33 Devens, "Separate Confrontations," p. 472.
34 Jennifer Brown, "A Demographic Transition in the Fur Trade Country: Family Sizes and Fertility of Company Officers and Country Wives, Ca. 1759–1850," *The Western Canadian Journal of Anthropology* 6 (1976), p. 68; Silvia Van Kirk, "Women in the Fur Trade," *The Beaver* (Winter, 1972), p. 21.
35 Kathleen Jamieson, "Sex Discrimination in the Indian Act," in *Arduous Journey. Canadian Indians and Decolonization*, ed. J.R. Ponting (Toronto: McClelland and Stewart, 1986), p. 116.
36 Quoted in Jamieson, "Sex Discrimination, " p. 117.
37 *Indian Acts and Amendments, 1868–1950* (Canada: Treaties and Historical Research Centre and Department of Indian and Northern Affairs Canada, 2nd edition, 1981).
38 Indeed, the Indian Act of 1876 states that native women did not have to be educated or "civilized" to prove that they could survive in the white world, since the responsibility for them was transferred from the government to their husbands.
39 Miller, *Scyscrapers*, pp. 220–2.
40 Jamieson, "Sex Discrimination," p. 125.
41 Jamieson, "Sex Discrimination," p. 126.
42 Sally Weaver, "First Nations Women and Government Policy, 1970–1972: Discrimination and Conflict," in *Changing Patterns. Women in Canada*, ed. S. Burt, L. Code and L. Dorney (Toronto: McClelland and Stewart, 1993), p. 116.
43 Jamieson, "Sex Discrimination," p. 131; Weaver, "First Nations Women," p. 121.
44 Jamieson, "Sex Discrimination," p. 132; Weaver, "First Nations Women," pp. 122–3.
45 Weaver, "First Nations Women," p. 137; Wendy Dudley, "Native Rights. Bill C-31 has Indians battling each other," *Calgary Herald* (August 17 1993).
46 Weaver, "First Nations Women," p. 137; Dudley, "Native Rights."
47 Jamieson, *Indian Women and the Law*.

Chapter 8 The 'Male City' of Havanna: The Coexisting Logics of Colonialism, Slavery, and Patriarchy in Nineteenth-Century Cuba

* This chapter stems from research for my book *Fighting Slavery in the Caribbean: The Life and Times of a British Family in Nineteenth-Century Havana* (Armonk, NY: M.E. Sharpe, 1998). Earlier versions were presented at the Twenty-Fifth Annual Meeting of the Association of Caribbean Historians, Mona, Jamaica, March 1993, and the Seventeenth Annual Conference of the Society for Caribbean Studies, Oxford, UK, July 1993. It was first published in a slightly different version as "Life in a 'Male City': Native and Foreign Elite Women in Nineteenth-Century Havana," in *Cuban Studies* 25, ed. Louis A. Pérez, Jr., © 1995. Reprinted by permission of the University of Pittsburgh Press. I am grateful to Mary Moran, Faye Dudden, Roslyn Turborg-Penn, Lizabeth Paravisini-Gebert, and to the editors of this volume for reading earlier versions of the essay and for providing numerous suggestions for improvement.

1 There is an ample and rich body of nineteenth-century travel accounts by US and European visitors to Cuba. For a partial listing, see: Louis A. Pérez, Jr., *Cuba: An Annotated Bibliography* (New York: Greenwood Press, 1988), pp. 19–28. Also see Harold F. Smith, "A Bibliography of American Travellers' Books about Cuba Published before 1900," *The Americas* 22:4 (April 1966), pp. 404–12. In a recently published compilation: *Slaves, Sugar, & Colonial Society: Travel Accounts of Cuba, 1801–1899* (Wilmington, DE: Scholarly Resources, Inc., 1992), Louis A. Pérez, Jr. reproduces excerpts from several of these travelogues. Quotes from Antonio C. N. Gallenga, *The Pearl of the Antilles* (London: Chapman and Hall, 1873; reprint, New York: Negro Universities Press, 1970) pp. 36, 29.

2 Nicolás Tanco Armero, "La Isla de Cuba," in *La isla de Cuba en el siglo xix vista por los extranjeros*, ed. Juan Pérez de la Riva (Havana: Editorial de Ciencias Sociales, 1981), p. 112.

3 [John George F. Wurdemann], *Notes on Cuba* (Boston: J. Munro and Co., 1844), p. 40.

4 Census of 1861, reproduced in Cuba, Instituto de Investigaciones Estadísticas, *Los censos de población y viviendas en Cuba*, one vol. to date (Havana: Instituto de Investigaciones Estadísticas, 1988), 1:111–13.

5 The sex imbalance among rural slaves aged 12–60 was, at mid-century, 136,000 males to 69,256 females; there were instances of plantations having all-male work forces. Among urban slaves of the same age group, however, the imbalance was inverted and much lighter: 22,891 men to 25,232 women. John S. Thrasher, "Preliminary Essay," to Alexander Humboldt, *The Island of Cuba* (New York: Derby & Jackson, 1856), p. 75; Richard Robert Madden, *The Island of Cuba: Its Resources, Progress and Prospects* (London: Partridge & Oakey, 1853), p. 4; José García de Arboleya, *Manual de la isla de Cuba*, 2nd edn (Havana: Imprenta El Tiempo, 1859), p. 116.

6 Verena Martínez-Alier, *Marriage, Class and Colour in Nineteenth-Century Cuba* (Ann Arbor, MI: University of Michigan Press, 1989), p. 57.

7 Census of 1861 in Cuba, *Censos*, 1:111–13; most of these demographic shifts were nineteenth-century developments related to the dramatic social and economic transformations brought about by the sugar revolution. As late as 1810 the population of Havana was sexually balanced, in fact, it was closer to the typical Latin American metropolitan center with a slight female majority (48,470 women to 47,644 men). Census of 1810, cited in Humboldt, *Island of Cuba*. For demographic information on Mexico City, see Silvia Arróm, *The Women of Mexico City* (Stanford, CA: Stanford University Press, 1985), p. 106.

8 It is true that other societies in the hemisphere had similar social structures. Several factors, however, explain why restrictions on female behavior were not as severe in other parts of Latin America. For one, the prolonged wars of independence and the republican legislation that followed their success disturbed traditional morality codes and allowed greater freedom for the women of post-independence Latin America. In Brazil, with a slave-based social structure similar to that of Cuba, the arrival of the Portuguese court in 1808 also allowed for a greater degree of freedom for the women of Rio de Janeiro and other coastal cities. See Johanna S.R. Mendelson, "The Feminine Press: The View of Women in Colonial Journals of Spanish America, 1790–1810," and June E. Hahner, "The Nineteenth-Century Feminist Press and Women's Rights in Brazil," both in Asunción Lavrin, ed., *Latin American Women: Historical Perspectives* (Westport, CT: Greenwood Press, 1978). Many of the restrictions on female behavior in Havana were not enforced in neighboring San Juan, Puerto Rico, where slavery was less important, the social structure was more fluid, and the correlation between color and class was not as strong. Antonio de las Barras y Prado, *Memorias, La Habana a mediados del siglo xix* (Madrid: Ciudad Lineal, 1925), p. 178.
9 Martínez-Alier, *Marriage*, pp. 109, xiii.
10 Editors of *La Verdad, Cuestión negrera de la isla de Cuba* (New York: La Verdad, 1851), p. 8.
11 Demoticus Philalethes, *Yankee Travels through the Island of Cuba* (New York: Appleton, 1856), p. 11. Italics in the original.
12 Thrasher, "Preliminary Essay," pp. 69–71.
13 Political governor of Havana to the captain-general of Cuba, March 3 1855, Archivo Nacional de Cuba, Gobierno Superior Civil, legajo 1373, expediente 53615.
14 Philalethes, *Yankee Travels*, p. 11.
15 Quote from [Mercedes de Santa Cruz y Montalvo] Condesa de Merlín, *Viaje a La Habana* (Havana: Editorial de Arte y Literatura, 1974), p. 107; for other sources on seclusion, see Gallenga, *Pearl*, p. 29; de las Barras y Prado, *Memorias*, p. 178; Benjamin Moore Norman, *Rambles by Land and Water, or Notes to Travel in Cuba and Mexico* (New York: Paine & Burguess, 1845), pp. 28–9; Robert Wilson Gibbes, *Cuba for Invalids* (New York: W.A. Townsend & Co., 1860), p. 11. According to Julia Louisa M. Woodruff (W.M.L. Jay, pseud.), the social etiquette in Matanzas was "less rigid in this particular than that of Havana, allows ladies to alight from their volantes, if they like." [Julia Louisa M. Woodruff] W.M.L. Jay, *My Winter in Cuba* (New York, E.P. Dutton, 1871), p. 123.
16 Philalethes, *Yankee Travels*, p. 11.
17 [William Henry Hurlbert], *Gan-Eden: or Pictures of Cuba* (Boston: J. P. Jewett and Company, 1854), p. 12; Richard Henry Dana, Jr., *To Cuba and Back* (Carbondale, IL: Southern Illinois University Press, 1966), p. 10. Interestingly, these restrictions included prostitutes; according to one traveler, street walking was not permitted in Havana and "these women are allowed to 'ply their vocation' from the windows of their houses." Samuel Hazard, *Cuba with Pen and Pencil* (Hartford, CT: Hartford Publishing Co., 1871), p. 199.
18 [Santa Cruz y Montalvo], *Viaje*, p. 107.
19 Quote from Gallenga, *Pearl*, p. 28; John Mark, *Diary of My Trip to America and Havana* (Manchester: J.E. Cornish, 1885), p. 66; Henry Tudor, *Narrative of a Tour in North America, Comprising Mexico, the Mines of Real del Monte, the United States, and the British Colonies with an Excursion to the Island of Cuba*, 2 vols. (London: James Duncan, 1834), 2:120; de las Barras y Prado, *Memorias*, pp. 116–17; Fredrika Bremer, *The Homes of the New World; Impressions of America*, 2 vols. (New York: Harper and Brothers, 1854), 2:376.

20 José María Gómez Colón, *Memoria sobre la utilidad del trabajo de la muger pobre en la isla de Cuba y medios para conseguirlo* (Havana: Imprenta de Manuel Soler, 1857), pp. 49–50.
21 Gallenga, *Pearl*, p. 29.
22 Norman, *Rambles*, p. 29.
23 George Augustus Henry Sala, *Under the Sun; Essays Mainly Written in Hot Countries* (London: Tinsley Brothers, 1872), p. 142.
24 Julia Ward Howe, *A Trip to Cuba* (Boston: Ticknor and Fields, 1860; reprint, New York: Negro Universities Press, 1969), p. 43.
25 Norman, *Rambles*, p. 29.
26 Maturin Murray Ballou, *Due South; or Cuba Past and Present* (Boston: Houghton, Mifflin and Co., 1885; reprint, New York: Young People's Missionary Movement, 1910), p. 175.
27 Ballou, *Due South*, p. 175.
28 Dana, *To Cuba and Back*, p. 17.
29 Tanco Armero, "Isla de Cuba," p. 135.
30 Philalethes, *Yankee Travels*, pp. 16–19.
31 [Hurlbert], *Gan-Eden*, p. 42; also see: Hazard, *Cuba*, p. 161.
32 James O'Kelly, *The Mambí Land* (Philadelphia: J. B. Lippincott, 1874), p. 26; also see: Wurdemann, *Notes on Cuba*, p. 42; Gallenga, *Pearl*, p. 36.
33 [Woodruff], *My Winter*, pp. 204, 294.
34 Bremer, *Homes*, 2:281.
35 James William Steele, *Cuban Sketches* (New York: Putnam's Sons, 1981), p. 214.
36 Howe, *Trip*, p. 43.
37 Howe, *Trip*, pp. 44, 85.
38 Rachel Wilson Moore, *Journal of Rachel Moore, Kept during a Tour to the West Indies and South America, in 1863–64* (Philadelphia: T. E. Zell, 1867), p. 37.
39 [Woodruff], *My Winter*, pp. 70–1.
40 Howe, *Trip*, pp. 44–5; other sources on volantas: Richard J. Levis, *Diary of a Spring Holiday in Cuba* (Philadelphia: Porter and Coates, 1872), p. 25; Ballou, *Due South*, pp. 219–21; Anthony Trollope, *The West Indies and the Spanish Main* (London: Frank Cass, 1968), p. 144.
41 [Santa Cruz y Montalvo], *Viaje*, p. 210; Hazard, *Cuba*, pp. 176–7; [Woodruff], *My Winter*, p. 48.
42 Hazard, *Cuba*, p. 158.
43 [Woodruff], *My Winter*, pp. 204, 294.
44 Henry Anthony Murray, *Lands of the Slave and the Free: Or Cuba, the United States, and Canada*, 2 vols. (London: J.W. Parker and Son, 1855), 1:281–83; [Woodruff], *My Winter*, pp. 28–9; Hazard, *Cuba*, pp. 176–7.
45 Ballou, *Due South*, pp. 219–29; Frances Erskine Calderón de la Barca, *Life in Mexico* (London: J.M. Dent and Sons, 18—), p. 10; Murray, *Lands*, 1:283; Bremer, *Homes*, 2:266.
46 [Hurlbert], *Gan-Eden*, pp. 10–11.
47 Sala, *Under the Sun*, p. 147.
48 John Stevens Cabot Abbott, *South and North; or, Impressions Received During a Trip to Cuba and the South* (New York: Abbey & Abbot, 1860), p. 44; [Woodruff], *My Winter*, pp. 20–8; Phillippo, *United States*, pp. 433, 31.
49 [Santa Cruz y Montalvo], *Viaje*, pp. 101–7; Carlton H. Rogers, *Incidents of Travel in the Southern States and Cuba* (New York: R. Craighead, 1862), p. 81.
50 Sala, *Under the Sun*, p. 141.

51 Reau Campbell, *Around the Corner to Cuba* (New York: C. G. Crawford, 1889), p. 9.
52 Hazard, *Cuba*, pp. 160–77; also see: Levis, *Diary*, p. 25, and [Santa Cruz y Montalvo], *Viaje*, p. 210.
53 Trollope, *West Indies*, pp. 144–50.
54 Tanco Armero, "Isla de Cuba," p. 131; Gibbes, *Cuba for Invalids*, p. 11.
55 Ballou, *Due South*, p. 159; Phillippo, *United States*, p. 432.
56 [Woodruff], *My Winter*, pp. 26–7.
57 Tudor, *Narrative*, 2:116–17.
58 Philalethes, *Yankee Travels*, pp. 189–90; Bryant, *Letters*, 3:27–8; Wurdemann, *Notes on Cuba*, p. 42; Campbell, *Around the Corner*, p. 28; [Woodruff], *My Winter*, p. 70.
59 Amelia Matilda Murray, *Letters from the United States, Cuba and Canada*, 2 vols. (London: J.W. Parker and Son, 1856), 2:55.
60 Hazard, *Cuba*, p. 157; [Woodruff], *My Winter*, pp. 30, 70; Howe, *Trip*, p. 45.
61 Hazard, *Cuba*, p. 431; Wurdemann, *Notes on Cuba*, p. 22.
62 Arróm, *Women*, pp. 65–6.
63 Captain-General Valentín Cañedo to the president of the Council of Ministers, July 5, 1853 Archivo Histórico Nacional, Madrid, Ultramar, legajo 1683, expediente 28.
64 [Santa Cruz y Montalvo], *Viaje*, p. 145.
65 Bryant, *Letters*, 3:31; Wurdemann, *Notes on Cuba*, p. 22; George W. Williams, *Sketches of Travel in the Old and New World* (Charleston: Walker, Evans, and Cogswell, 1871), p. 13.
66 [Woodruff], *My Winter*, p. 167.
67 Ballou, *Due South*, p. 139.
68 Richard Burleigh Kimball, *Cuba and the Cubans* (New York: Samuel Hureton, 1850), p. 153.
69 Rogers, *Incidents*, p. 88.
70 [Woodruff], *My Winter*, p. 58.
71 Curate of the Church of Monserrate to the captain-general of Cuba, September 1 1868; and superior civilian governor of Cuba to the chief of police of Havana, Sept. 3, 1868, Archivo Nacional de Cuba, Gobierno Superior Civil, legajo 743, expediente 25436.
72 Hazard, *Cuba*, p. 127; Rogers, *Incidents*, p. 89.
73 Wurdemann, *Notes on Cuba*, p. 22; [Woodruff], *My Winter*, p. 58; Calderón de la Barca, *Life in Mexico*, p. 13.
74 Norman, *Rambles*, p. 101.
75 [Woodruff], *My Winter*, p. 191.
76 Norman, *Rambles*, p. 38.
77 Quotes from: Hazard, *Cuba*, p. 130, and Rogers, *Incidents*, p. 89.
78 Steele, *Cuban Sketches*, p. 175.
79 Kimball, *Cuba*, p. 153.
80 Dana, *To Cuba*, p. 28–9.
81 Hazard, *Cuba*, p. 184; Steele, *Cuban Sketches*, p. 147.
82 [Santa Cruz y Montalvo], *Viaje*, p. 208; Ballou, *Due South*, p. 136; Rogers, *Incidents*, p. 147.
83 Ballou, *Due South*, pp. 135–6; Wurdemann, *Notes on Cuba*, pp. 82–3; Rogers, *Incidents*, p. 85; Philalethes, *Yankee Travels*, p. 201; Gibbes, *Cuba for Invalids*, p. 39; William Cullen Bryant, *Letters of William Cullen Bryant*, 4 vols. (New York: Fordham University Press, 1975–84), 3:28; de las Cuevas, *Tipo de las habaneras*, pp. 9–10; Mark, *Diary*, p. 66; James Mursell Phillippo, *The United States and Cuba* (London: Pewtress & Co., 1857), p. 430.

84 Hazard, *Cuba*, p. 404.
85 J.T. O'Neil, "Porto Rico," in Richard S. Fisher, ed., *The Spanish West Indies* (New York: J. H. Colton, 1861), p. 153; Philalethes, *Yankee Travels*, p. 18; Murray, *Lands*, 1:289; Steele, *Cuban Sketches*, pp. 58–9; Kimball, *Cuba and the Cubans*, p. 147: de las Barras y Prado, *Memorias*, p. 91; Ballou, *Due South*, p. 128.
86 De la Barras y Prado, *Memorias*, p. 91.
87 Hazard, *Cuba*, pp. 420–1.
88 "Edades de la mujer y del hombre simbolizadas por las aves," *El Avisador* (Ponce, Puerto Rico), January 14 1875; Virgilio Biaggi, *Las aves de Puerto Rico* (Río Piedras: Editorial Universitaria, 1970).
89 Hazard, *Cuba*, p. 300.
90 Ballou, *Due South*, p. 136.
91 [Woodruff], *My Winter*, p. 82.
92 Hazard, *Cuba*, p. 300.
93 Beth K. Miller, "Avellaneda, Nineteenth-Century Feminist," *Revista/Review Interamericana* 4 (Summer 1974), pp. 177–83.
94 Rogers, *Incidents*, p. 85; Henry Ashworth, *A Tour in the United States, Cuba, and Canada* (London: A.W. Bennett, 1861), p. 50.
95 García de Arboleya, *Manual*, p. 176.
96 Howe, *Trip*, p. 146.
97 [Woodruff], *My Winter*, p. 208; Tudor, *Narrative*, 2:121.
98 Martínez-Alier, *Marriage*, pp. 71–99; Gómez Colón, *Memoria*, pp. 49–50; de las Barras y Prado, *Memorias*, pp. 115.
99 See Margaret Zoller Booth, "Education for Liberation or Domestication: Female Education in Colonial Swaziland" in this volume for a discussion on a parallel system of education that discriminated against women.
100 Jorge Domínguez, *Insurrection or Loyalty* (Cambridge, MA: Harvard University Press, 1980), p. 19; García de Arboleya, *Manual*, p. 304.
101 Howe, *Trip*, p. 202; Steele, *Cuban Sketches*, p. 141; Ballou, *Due South*, p. 128.
102 Steele, *Cuban Sketches*, p. 139.
103 Howe, *Trip*, p. 83.
104 Steele, *Cuban Sketches*, p. 63.

Chapter 9 Imperial Eyes, Gendered Views: Concepción Gimeno Re-writes the Aztecs at the End of the Nineteenth Century

1 I want to thank the Program for Cultural Exchange between the Spanish Ministry of Education and the American Universities for a 1995 travel grant which supported my initial research in Spain on Concepción Gimeno.
2 *Inmigración y exilio, reflexiones sobre el caso español* ed. Clara E. Lida (Mexico: Siglo XXI, 1997); *Una inmigración privilegiada: comerciantes, empresarios y profesionales españoles en Mexico en los siglos XIX y XX* ed. Clara E. Lida (Madrid: Alianza Editorial 1994). Manuel Grijalba Miño, et al., *Tres aspectos de la presencia española en Mexico durante el Porfiriato* (Mexico: El Colegio de Mexico 1981). The influence of these clubs and societies went well beyond what Sara Mills calls the role of travel texts as reinforcers of the colonial rule
3 Mary Louise Pratt, *Imperial Eyes: Travel Writing and Transculturation* (London and New York: Routledge, 1992), p. 4.
4 For a general overview of European visions of America, see David Brading, *The First America: The Spanish Monarchy, Creole Patriots and the Liberal State 1492–1867*

(Cambridge: Cambridge University Press, 1991). Antonello Gerbi, *The Dispute of the New World, The History of a Polemic 1750–1900* [La dispute del Nuovo Monde, scoria Di Una polemic 1750–1900 (Milano: 1955)], trans. Jeremy Mole, rev. ed. (Pittsburgh: University of Pittsburgh Press, 1973); Edmund O'Gorman, *La intension de America* (Mexico: FACE 1962).

5 Women and imperialism, the travel writing they produced, and the specifics of their gendered texts is a growing field of historical and literary inquiry which has produced outstanding, pathbreaking works of revisionism. See *Women and Colonialism: Anthropological Perspectives*, ed. Mona Etienne and Eleanor Leacock (New York: Praeger, 1980); Anne McClintock, *Imperial Leather: Race Gender and Sexuality in the Colonial Context* (New York and London: Routledge, 1995); Sarah Mills, *Discourses of Difference* (London: Routledge, 1993); *Western Women and Imperialism*, ed. Nupur Chauduri and Margaret Strobel (Bloomington: Indiana University Press, 1992); Laura E. Donaldson, *Decolonizing Feminism: Race, Gender and Empire Building* (Chapel Hill: Indiana University Press, 1992), and Mary Louise Pratt, *Imperial Eyes: Travel Writing and Transculturation* (London and New York: Routledge, 1992).

6 The tendency to view indigenous Americans as "the Other" is a tradition that is reflected in the numerous works published in Europe since the conquest, in which continental and British travelers refashioned American cultures and peoples as a part of the construction of a new reality, an imaginary space into which they often projected their own fantasies. This process is well described by Benedict Anderson in *Imagined Communities: Reflections on the Origins and Spread of Nationalism*, rev. edn (London: Verso, 1991). More often than not, these accounts viewed the indigenous people of the Americas through the perspective of an imperialistic discourse which Mary Louise Pratt has called "Imperial Eyes." Pratt, *Imperial Eyes*. I want to thank Professor Pratt, a visiting scholar at the Centra de Investigations y Escudos Superiores en Anthropology Social in Guadalajara, Mexico in the 1998–9 academic year, for her comments on a previous version of this article.

7 This is even more confusing because she claimed 1860 was her birthday. However, in a rare autobiographical article in *El Album Hispanoamericano* (July 7 1902) she states that she published her first novel at 23. *Vicotrina o el heroism el corazón* appeared in 1873, which means that if she had indeed been born in 1860, she would have then been 13 years old! See Maryellen Bieder, "Concepción Gimeno de Flaquer (1852–1919)," in *Spanish Women Writers, a Biographical Source Book*, ed. Linda Gould Levine, Ellen Engelson Marson and Gloria Feiman Waldman, (Westport: Greenwood Press, 1990), p. 219.

8 Concepción Gimeno, "A los impugnadores del bello sexo," in *El Trovador del Ebro* (Zaagoza, 1869).

9 Gómez Aurora Rivere, *La educación de la mujer en el Madrid de Isabel II* (Madrid: Direción General de la Mujer, 1993), p. 90.

10 Antonio Espina, *Las tertulias de Madrid* (Madrid: Alianza Tres, 1995).

11 This was the only one of her novels to appear in that Spanish journal in the typical serialized formal so fashionable at the time. Bieder, "Concepción Gimerno de Flaquer," p. 220.

12 Gimeno de Flaquer's bibliography is quite abundant; she wrote an average of one article a week for the journals she edited, *El Album de la mujer* and *El Album Iberoamericano*. Her published novels are *Victorina o el heroismo del corazon*, Prologue by Ramon Ortega y Frias, 2 vols. (Madrid: Asociacion del Arte de Imprimir, 1873); *Madres de hombres célebres* (México: Tipografía de la Escuela Industrial de Huerfanos Tecpan de Santiago, 1884); *Culpa o Expiacion*. 4th edn (Mexico: Oficina Tipografica

de la Sria de Fomento, 1890); *Mujeres de la Revolucion Francesa* (Madrid: A Alonso, 1891); *La mujer juzgada por una mujer* (Barcelona: L Tasso, 1892); *Mujeres, Vidas Paralelas* (Madrid: A Alonso, 1893); *Ventajas para instruir a la mujer y sus aptitudes para instruirse* Disertacion leida por su autora, en el Ateneo de Madrid en la noche del 6 de mayo de 1895 (Madrid: Imprenta de Francisco G. Pérez, 1896), and *La mujer intelectual* (Madrid: Asilo de Huerfanos, 1908).

13 See Gertrude Himmelfarb, *Marriage and Morals among the Victorians* (New York: Alfred Knopf, 1986).

14 Similar contradictions appear in the Cuban case, as noted in this volume by Luis Martínez-Fernández in "The Male City of Havana," Chapter 8. Mills *Discourses of Difference*, p. 61.

15 *Escritoras romanticas espanolas*, ed. Majoral Marna (Madrid: Fundacion Banco Exterior, 1990). Enrique Pineiro, *The Romantics of Spain*, trans. E Allison Piers (Liverpool: Institute of Hispanic Studies, 1934).

16 Mills, *Discourses of Difference*, p. 40.

17 See: Frances Calderon de la Barca, *La Vida en Mexico* (Mexico, Porrua, 1963). Pratt, *Imperial Eyes*, pp. 144–71.

18 Inga Clendinnen, *Aztecs, an Interpretation* (Cambridge: Cambridge University Press, 1991). George Valliant, *Aztecs of Mexico: Origin, Rise and Fall of the Aztec Nation* (Baltimore: Penguin Books, 1972). Jacques Soustelle, *Daily Life of the Aztecs on the Eve of the Spanish Conquest* (Stanford, California: 1970).

19 See Alfonso Caso, *El pueblo del sol* (Mexico: Fondo de Cultura Economica, 1962). Miguel Leon Portilla *Los antiguos mexicanos a traves de sus crónicas y cantares* (Mexico: Fondo de Cultura Económica, 1961). Fernandez Justino, *Coatlicue, estetica del arte indígena*, Prologo de Samuel Ramos (Centra de Escudos: Filosóficos, UNAM, 1954).

20 Concepción Gimeno. "La diosa y la mujer en los antiguos mexicanos," in *El Album Iberoamericano* (December 22 1904), p. 554.

21 Gimeno de Flaquer, "Malintzin, la inspiradora de Hernan Cortes," *El Album de la Mujer* (September 11 1881).

22 Gimeno de Flaquer, "La consejera de Hernan Cortes," in *El Album Iberoamericano* (January 7 1902), p. 3. The deep economic and social changes in Aztec Society has been treated in the pioneering work of Charles Gibson, *The Aztecs under the Spanish Rule: A History of the Indians in the Valley of Mexico 1519–1810* (Stanford, California: Stanford University Press, 1964). For Aztec women, see Susan Kellogg, "Aztec Woman in Early Colonial Courts: Structure, and Strategy in a Legal Context," in *Five Centuries of Law and Politics in Mexico*, ed. Ronald Spores and Ross Hassings (Nashville, Tennessee: Vanderbilt Publications, 1984).

23 Gimeno de Flaquer, "La consejera de Hernan Cortes," p. 3.

24 After she left Mexico and resettled in Madrid, she published *El Album hisopanoamericano*, which often included news about Mexican cultural and political life as well as published Mexican literary authors and historians.

25 I use the term "border culture" in the same way that Renato Rosaldo uses it in reference to Hispanic culture in contemporary USA. See "Ideology, Place and People without Culture," in *Cultural Anthropology* 3 (February 1988), p. 85. This concept is comparable to Mary Louise Pratt's notion of the "Contact zone." The idea of Latin America as a space of cultural confrontation is well exemplified in Faustino Sarmiento's *Civilización y Barbarie*. (Coleccion Nuestra America: Mexico, UNAM, 1965).

Chapter 10 The Indian Other: Reactions of Two Anglo-Indian Women Travel Writers, Eliza Fay and A.U.

1 Here I am using the term "Anglo-Indian" in its nineteenth-century sense – a Briton in India and not a Eurasian.

2 Carmen Ramos-Escandon, "Imperial Eyes, Gendered Views: Concepción Gimeno Re-writes the Aztecs at the End of the Nineteenth Century," Chapter 9; and Katherine Fleming, "Greece in Chains: Philhellenism to the Rescue of a Damsel in Distress," Chapter 3.

3 Shirley Foster, *Across New Worlds: Nineteenth-Century Women Travellers and Their Writings* (London: Harvester Wheatsheaf, 1990), p. viii.

4 Mary Louise Pratt, *Imperial Eyes: Travel Writing and Transculturation* (London: Routledge, 1992); Sara Mills, *Discourses of Difference: Women's Travel Writing and Colonialism* (London: Routledge, 1991); Sara Mills, "Knowledge, Gender, and Empire," in *Writing Women and Space: Colonial and Postcolonial Geographies*, ed. Alison Blunt and Gillian Rose (London: Guilford Press, 1994); Susan Morgan, *Place Matters: Gendered Geography in Victorian Women's Travel Books about Southeast Asia* (New Brunswick: Rutgers University Press, 1996); Inderpal Grewal, *Home and Harem: Nation, Gender, Empire, and the Cultures of Travel* (Durham NC: Duke University Press, 1996); Susan L. Blake, "A Woman's Trek: What Difference Does Gender Make?" in *Western Women and Imperialism: Complicity and Resistance*, ed. Nupur Chaudhuri and Margaret Strobel (Bloomington: Indiana University Press, 1992).

5 Mills, *Discourses of Difference*, p. 86.

6 Mrs. Eliza Fay, *Original Letters from India: 1779–1815*, intro. E.M. Forster, new intro. M.M. Kaye (1817; reprint, London: The Hogarth Press, 1986), p. 200.

7 Forster, "Introductory Notes," in Fay, *Original Letters*, p. 11. It is not clear whether the mother of this child was an Indian, European, or mixed-race woman.

8 Fay, *Original Letters*, p. 201.

9 This was as close to a divorce that Eliza Fay could hope to achieve, since she could not pursue the very expensive and public course of obtaining a divorce through parliamentary decree (the only way to obtain a divorce then). Since Eliza Fay was the wronged party, there were no grounds for a divorce; Parliament only granted such petitions if there was clear evidence of a wife's adultery – adultery in a husband was in no way illegal, and mere incompatibility of temper was insufficient grounds for a divorce or separation. See Lawrence Stone, *Road to Divorce, England 1530–1987* (Oxford and New York: Oxford University Press, 1995), pp. 158–9, 322–3. Nevertheless, separation on any basis was not a step a woman would take lightly; while men who were separated were rarely criticized for taking mistresses, the actions of women separated from their husbands were often under great scrutiny, in part because their husbands hoped to find a reason to end support payments. Stone, *Road to Divorce*, p. 169. However, Eliza Fay refers to a "secret" connected to her husband, and she implies that he will not interfere with her because of his fear that she will disclose it; this was probably because he had fathered an illegitimate child.

10 See Ramos Escandon "Imperial Eyes, Gendered Views," p. 6.

11 Background information on the Fays can be found in Forster, "Introduction," in Fay, *Original Letters*, pp. 11–12.

12 Rashna B. Singh, *The Imperishable Empire: A Study of British Fiction on India* (Washington, DC: Three Continents Press, 1988), p. 30.

13 Singh, *Imperishable Empire*, p. 30 points out that since few single women chose to make this arduous journey, many English men took Indian mistresses or even wives, and some adopted the customs of prosperous Indian gentlemen.

14 According to Philip Lawson, these changes brought about the transformation of the English from traders to professional administrators; the "welcome reform" that placed an emphasis on "pride and incorruptibility as ideals in service to the [East India] Company." *The East India Company: A History* (London and New York: Longman, 1993), p. 129.

15 C.F. Andrews, *India and Britain* (London, 1935), pp. 15–16, declared that while few Britons actually knew – or cared – about India at this time, for those who did think of it, "A gold lust, unequalled since the hysteria that took hold of the Spaniards of Cortes' and Pizarro's age, filled the English mind." Quoted in Singh, *Imperishable Empire*, p. 30.

16 Fay, *Original Letters*, p. 179.

17 Fay, *Original Letters*, p. 120.

18 C.A. Bayly, *Indian Society and the Making of the British Empire* (Cambridge: Cambridge University Press, 1988), pp. 68–9. According to Bayly, although Calcutta, Madras, and Bombay were the most important bases for British rule in India during the late eighteenth century, the English residents had relatively little impact on the urban design or local governance of these cities until the nineteenth century, so Eliza Fay's Calcutta would have shown little impact from English rule.

19 Fay, *Original Letters*, p. 207.

20 Fay, *Original Letters*, pp. 206–7. It is clear that some, if not most, of her information on marriage comes from her banian, since immediately after this quote she goes on to report what her banian told her about his own marriage and that of his friends. p. 207.

21 C.A. Bayly notes that *sati* never had the sanction of Hindu scriptures and that by the early nineteenth century, it bore "all the hallmarks of a 'reinvented tradition' which spread among the newly respectable commercial people of the Calcutta region." Nevertheless, he goes on to make the astonishing statement that *sati* was "more a symbolic issue than a major social problem" since there were "fewer than 1,000 widows burned each year during the 1820's according to official figures." *Indian Society*, p. 122.

22 Fay, *Original Letters*, p. 202.

23 Some scholars have argued that European women writers observed people and wrote about their customs and manners because women were supposed to avoid any abstract intellectual topics. Although Fay seemed to have felt that this was true enough to guide her writings, this passage shows that she reflected considerably upon the position of Indian women in their own society. Joanna Trollope, *Britannia's Daughters: Women of the British Empire* (London: Hutchinson, 1983), p. 156; Mary Russell, *The Blessings of a Good Thick Skirt: Women Travellers and Their World* (London: Collins, 1986), p. 213.

24 Fay, *Original Letters*, p. 203. It seems likely that some of Fay's bitterness towards her own marriage is reflected in this description, which was written little more than a month after she separated from her husband.

25 Fay, *Original Letters*, p. 203. The list of burdens borne by the heroine Fay describes suggests that she had her own situation in mind when she wrote these words.

26 Felicity A. Nussbaum, *Torrid Zones: Maternity, Sexuality, and Empire in Eighteenth-Century English Narratives* (Baltimore: Johns Hopkins University, 1995), p. 187.

27 Fay, *Original Letters*, p. 204.

28 Benita Parry, *Delusions and Discoveries: Studies in India and the British Imagination, 1880–1930* (Berkeley and Los Angeles: University of California Press, 1972), p. 18. Though Parry's observation covers a much later period, I believe that this feeling of racial superiority of the Anglo-Indians began much earlier and existed throughout the British Raj.

29 This disdain helped to create the social gulf that existed between Britons and Indians by the late nineteenth century, and various scholars have pointed out that women played a vital role in this separation. Nevertheless, not all Europeans approved of the introduction of strict adherence to English social norms in the colonies, and more than one Anglo-Indian accused English women of being responsible for the ultimate loss of the colonies. See Margaret Strobel, *European Women and the Second British Empire* (Bloomington: Indiana University Press, 1991), especially Chapter 1, "Sexuality and Society: The Myth of the Destructive Female," pp. 1–15.

30 Nancy Miller, "Women's Autobiography in France: For a Dialectics of Identification," in *Women and Language in Literature and Society*, ed. S. McConnell-Ginet (New York: Praeger, 1980), p. 266; Mills, *Discourses of Difference*, p. 41

31 A.U., *Overland, Inland and Upland*, p. 123.

32 A.U., *Overland, Inland, and Upland*, p. 123.

33 A.U., *Overland, Inland and Upland*, pp. 123–4.

34 In this volume, see Margaret Zoller Booth, "Education for Liberation and Domestication: Female Education in Colonial Swaziland," Chapter 14, and Micheline R. Lessard, "Civilizing Women: French Colonial Perceptions of Vietnamese Womanhood and Motherhood," Chapter 12.

35 A.U., *Overland, Inland and Upland*, p. 124.

36 For a general description of British women's attitude toward Indian women, see, Janaki Nair, "Uncovering the Zenana: Visions of Indian Womanhood in Englishwomen's Writings, 1813–1940," in *Expanding the Boundaries of Women's History: Essays on Women in the Third World*, ed. Cheryl Johnson-Odim and Margaret Strobel (Bloomington: Indiana University Press, 1992), pp. 26–50.

37 Bernard S. Cohn, "Cloth, Clothes, and Colonialism in India: India in the Nineteenth Century," in *Cloth and Human Experience*, ed. Annette B. Weiner and Jane Schneider (Washington and London: Smithsonian Institution Press, 1989), p. 331.

38 A.U., *Overland, Inland and Upland*, p. 49.

39 See P. Mason, *Prospero's Magic: Some Thoughts on Class and Race* (London: Oxford University Press. 1962); J. Walvin, *Black and White: the Negro and English Society, 1555–1945* (London: Allen Lane Penguin, 1973); C. Knapman, *White Women in Fiji: 1835–1930: The Ruin of Empire?* (Sidney: Allen & Unwin, 1986); M. Ferguson, *Subject to Others: British Women Writers and Colonial Slavery, 1670–1834* (London, New York: Routledge, 1992). For the development of a binary racial view in eighteenth-century New England, see Ruth Wallis Herndon, "Women as Symbols of Disorder in Early Rhode Island," Chapter 6.

40 For further discussion on this topic see, Martínez-Fernández, "The 'Male City' of Havana: The Coexisting Logics of Colonialism, Slavery and Patriarchy in Nineteenth-century Cuba," Chapter 8.

41 A.U., *Overland, Inland and Upland*, p. 125.

42 Here I am using "supporting cast" in the same sense as Kathryn Castle used it in her *Britannia's Children: Reading Colonialism through Children's Books and Magazines* (Manchester: Manchester University Press, 1996), p. 6.

43 Stephen Greenblat, "Invisible Bullets: Renaissance Authority and Its Subversion, Henry IV and Henry V," in *Political Shakespeare: New Essays in Cultural Materialism*, ed. Jonathan Dollimore and Alan Sinfield (Ithaca: Cornell University Press, 1985), p. 27; Deirdre David, *Rule Britannia: Women, Empire, and Victorian Writing* (Ithaca: Cornell University Press, 1995), p. 4.
44 A.U., *Overland, Inland, and Upland*, p. 52.
45 Mills, *Discourses of Difference*, p. 86.
46 Lisa Lowe, *Critical Terrains: French and British Orientalisms* (Ithaca: Cornell University Press, 1991), p. 109.

Chapter 11 Image and Reality: Indian Diaspora Women, Colonial and Post-colonial Discourse on Empowerment and Victimology

1 Research for this chapter was made possible by a Research Grant and Release Time Stipend from the Social Sciences and Humanities Research Council of Canada, a Senior Fellowship from the Shastri Indo-Canadian Institute, by McGill University where Michael Maxwell shared seed money, and by a leave grant from Marianopolis College, Montreal.

Abbreviations used in this paper: CUL – Cambridge University Library; IOR – India Office Library and Records, London; NAI – National Archives of India, New Delhi; PP – Parliamentary Papers; PRO – Public Record Office, London; SNN – Selections from the Vernacular Press of India (also styled, Selections from Native Newspapers in NAI and IOL); TNA – Tamil Nadu State Archives, Madras.
2 In this volume, Tamara L. Hunt, Micheline R. Lessard, and Jiweon Shin, all suggest that similar developments took place in Ireland, Vietnam, and Korea, respectively. See "Wild Irish Women: Gender, Politics, and Colonialism in the Nineteenth Century," Chapter 4; "Civilizing Women: French Colonial Perceptions of Vietnamese Motherhood," Chapter 12; "Social Construction of Ideal Images of Women in Colonial Korea: 'New Woman' versus 'Motherhood'," Chapter 13.
3 See, for instance, Reeta Chowdhari and Prema Kumtakar, "Governance and Representation: A Study of Women and Local Self-Government," pp. 454–66.
4 All statements in italics are taken directly from the attestations of the women. Quotation marks within the italicized section denote direct English translations of the testimony.
5 Testimony of "Minnu" contained in the Memorial from the Marwari Association, Calcutta, praying for the abolition of indentured emigration from India to the Colonies, to the Secretary to the Government of India, Department of Commerce and Industry, Delhi, through the Government of Bengal, February 7 1916, Department of Commerce and Industry, Emigration, B Files, April, 1916, Nos. 30–33, File No. 24, S. No. 1–4 NAI. (Hereafter, Marwari Memorial, NAI)
6 The abolitionist literature used the word *thug*, from *thugna*, to deceive.
7 Marwari Memorial, NAI.
8 For instance Hugh Tinker, *A New System of Slavery* (Oxford: Institute of Race Relations, 1974). Lord John Russell coined the phrase "new system of slavery." See also Karen Ray, "Kunti, Lakshmibhai and the 'Ladies': Women's Labour and the Abolition of Indentured Emigration from India," *Labour, Capital and Society* 1–2 (1996), pp. 137–59.
9 A survey of indentured and other Indian emigration and the position of Indians overseas is provided in Tinker's trilogy, *A New System of Slavery, Separate and Unequal:*

India and the Indians in the British Commonwealth, 1920–1950 (London: C. Hurst, 1976) and *The Banyan Tree: Overseas Emigrants from India, Pakistan and Bangladesh* (Oxford: Oxford University Press, 1977). For an incisive survey of indenture, see K.O. Laurence, *A Question of Labour: Indentured Immigration into Trinidad and British Guiana, 1875–1917* (New York: St. Martin's Press, 1994).

10 See for instance David W. Galenson, *White Servitude in Colonial America* (Cambridge: Cambridge University Press, 1981).

11 Report from the Select Committee on the Practicability and Expediency of supplying the West India Colonies with Free Labourers from the East, PP 1810 II (225), p. 409; "Mr Geohagen's 'Report on Coolie Emigration from India'," India Office, 1874, in PP 1874 XLVII (314) also cited as John Geoghegan, *Report on Coolie Emigration from India* (India Office, 1874), with notations, IOL.

12 "Report of the Committee on Emigration from India to the Crown Colonies and Protectorates," PP 1910, Cd. 5192, XXVII (1) p. 18.

13 Elizabeth Whitcombe, *Agrarian Conditions in Northern India* (Berkeley: University of California Press, 1972), 1:274–5, also 160–205; presents the first and still best documented argument that peasant agriculture in the Bhojpuri and other regions from which the emigrants came had never been self-sustaining and that seasonal labour migration was essential; Shahid Amin, "Small Peasant Commodity Production and Rural Indebtedness: The Culture of Sugarcane in Eastern U.P., c. 1880–1920," *Subaltern Studies I: Writings on South Asian History and Society*, ed. Ranajit Guha (Delhi and Oxford: Oxford University Press, 1982), pp. 39–87.

14 John Geohagen's Report, IOL.

15 *Kuli Pratha: Biswi Shatavdi ki Gulami* (Cawnpore: Shiv Narayan Misra at the Pratap Karyyalay, 1915).

16 S.G. Checkland, *The Gladstones; A Family Biography, 1764–1851* (Cambridge: Cambridge University Press, 1971), p. 318; quoted in Tinker, *New System of Slavery*, p. 63.

17 Report of the Committee on Emigration, 1910, p. 88. In fact, most never returned, and were lost to their villages and families during their most productive years.

18 John Geohagen's Report, IOL.

19 Karen Ray, "Gandhi Comes to the Congress: the Indenture Issue in Indian Politics," *The Congress and Indian Nationalism*, ed. John Hill (London: Curzon Press, 1991), pp. 259–86 and Ray, "Women's Labour and Abolition."

20 The ratio changed from time to time and colony to colony.

21 Henry Saloman Leon Polak, *The Indians of South Africa* (Bombay, Madras: G.A. Natesan, 1909), p. 24. H.S.L. Polak, b. 1882; lawyer and journalist; lieutenant of Gandhi's 1904–14; editor of *Indian Opinion*; returned to England after Gandhi left South Africa.

22 C.F. Andrews and W.W. Pearson, "Report on Indentured Labour in Fiji," *Modern Review* 19 (March–June 1916), pp. 333–9, 392–402, 514–25, 615–24; C.F. Andrews Papers, Benarsidas Chaturvedi Collection, NAI, pp. 32–9.

23 Report to the Government of India on the Conditions of Indian Immigrants in four British Colonies and Surinam, by Messrs, James McNeil and Chinian Lal [*sic*]; Part I: Trinidad and British Guiana, PP 1914–16, XLVII (Cd. 7744); Part II: Surinam, Jamaica, Fiji and General Remarks, PP 1914–16, XLVII (Cd. 7745), p. 319 (hereafter McNeil Report). For the decade prior to the investigation, the suicide rate for Indians indentured in British colonies ranged from 1 in every 10,000 population (twice the rate in India) for British Guiana, to the one suicide for every thousand

indentured immigrants recorded in Fiji. During 1912, the last year recorded for Fiji, the suicide rate rose to 1 in 859 labourers, or 26 times the rate in Madras, the province from which most Fijian immigrants then came. The report, in explaining this situation, comments that in Fiji there is "no tendency to minimise the number of cases," leaving the reader in some doubt about the reliability of the other colonies' reporting.

24 McNeil Report, p. 314.

25 Testimony in the Sanderson Committee Report, Part II, Evidence; testimony of women in the Marwari petition, NAI.

26 Personal Interviews, Port of Spain, St Augustine, and Point Cumana, Trinidad, August, 1995.

27 Sanderson Report; Evidence.

28 *Satyagraha.*

29 Ray, "Gandhi Comes to the Congress," pp. 259–86.

30 Both quotations, Polak, *Indians of South Africa*, p. 21.

31 Polak, *Indians of South Africa*, p. 22.

32 The Protector of Emigrants was a position mandated in every colony. He was supposed to hear any complaints against plantation owners, in addition to keeping the records of indentures.

33 Polak, *Indians of South Africa*, p. 40.

34 January 13 1910, *Advocate* (Lucknow), published in English, twice weekly, circulation 1033, ed. Ganga Prasad Varma, long-time Congressist and Moderate politician, SNN, U.P., 1910, p. 37; January 16 1910, *Leader* (Allahabad), SNN, U.P., 1910, p. 57; January 21 1910, *Oudh Akbar* (Lucknow), Urdu, daily, circ, 327, ed. Jalpa Prasad, January 29 1910, *Swarajya* (Allahabad), Hindi, SNN, U.P., 1910, pp. 57 and 103; March 28 1910, *Madras Mail*, SNN, Madras, 1910.

35 Ray, "Women's Labour and Abolition."

36 Selig Harrison, *India: The Most Dangerous Decades* (Princeton: Princeton University Press, 1960), p. 114. Dipesh Chakrabarty, "Conditions for Knowledge of Working-Class Conditions: Employers, Government and the Jute Workers of Calcutta, 1890–1940," *Subaltern Studies II* (Delhi and Oxford: Oxford University Press, 1983), pp. 259–310. Thomas A. Timberg, *The Marwaris, from Traders to Industrialists* (New Delhi: Vikas, 1978); Thomas A. Timberg, "Speculative Gains and Primitive Accumulation: A Way into Industry." Paper presented at the Association for Asian Studies, New York, 1972, p. 4 and "The Origins of Marwari Industrialists." (PhD Thesis, Harvard, 1973).

37 Census of India, 1911, Calcutta, Superintendent of Government Printing, 1913, United Provinces XV and India I.

38 James Donald, Secretary to Govt. of Bengal, Financial Dept. to Govt. of India, Commerce and Industry, October 14 1915, Govt. of India, C&I, Emigration, A Proceedings 43–54, December 1914, NAI.

39 Statement of Shankar Rao in the Calcutta Police Court, November 11 1912. Statement of Panchkouri Shao, A Halwai Bania, in the Calcutta Police Court, November 14 1912. Govt. of India, C&I, Emigration, B Proceedings 30–33, April 1916, NAI.

40 Statement of woman identified only as Lakshmi, included in Memorial from the Marwari Association, Calcutta to the Govt. of India, February 7 1916. A slightly different account is give in Andrews and Pearson, *Report on Indentured Labour in Fiji*, p. 17, and in some newspaper stories, but this seems the original and most accurate version.

41 It was not an unknown practice to set up the kidnapping by recruiters of an inconveniently inquiring employer or even an importuning paramour. Lakshimi may well have fit in both categories.
42 Lakshmi's statement, Memorial from the Marwali Association, NAI.
43 The Honorary Secretary, Marwari Association, Calcutta to the Sec'y to the Govt. of India, Commerce and Industry, February 7 1916, Govt. of India, C&I, Emigration, B Proceedings 33–30, April 1916, NAI.
44 Marwari Association to the Govt. of India, February 7 1916.
45 Marwari Association to the Govt. of India, February 7 1916.
46 Statement of a Brahmin woman of the family of Parikh priests of Khandela (registered by the recruiters as Mahatab), quoted in Marwari Association to the Govt. of India, February 7 1916.
47 Marwari Association to the Govt. of India, February 7 1916.
48 Marwari Association to the Govt. of India, February 7 1916.
49 Order by S. Bhattacharjee, Magistrate First Class, October 10 1913.
50 *Escape from Deceivers*, Broadside printed at Narayan Press, Muzaffarpur, No. 68-6-6-15; 20,000 printed.
51 See, for instance, the report of James McNeil and Chimman Lal, cited above.
52 Note initialled by Hardinge, to Crewe, attached to C. F. Andrews to Viceroy, 27 September 1915, Hardinge Papers, Vol. 116, CUL.
53 *Hindustani*, February 11 and 15 enclosed in "Note to H.M.," presumably from the Secretary to Government, June 11 1915, Madras Public, Ordinary Series, G.O. 1331, September 13 1915, TNA.
54 *Mahratta*, January 21 1917, Government of India, SNN Bombay 1917, p. 11.
55 *New India*, January 17 in Madras, Public, Ordinary Series, G.O. No. 1331, September 13 1915, TNA.
56 "Declaration of Jal Chamar", paragraph 29.
57 *Fiji Dweep me Mere Ikkis Varsh* (Firozabad, Agra: Bharati Bhawan, 1916).
58 Note 1151, C.I.D., U.P. April 20 1915, in U.P. Govt. to Madras Govt., Madras Public, Ordinary Series, G. O. No. 1331, September 13 1915. TNA (Despite the frequent and frenzied requests of the Madras Government, the book was never translated into English).
59 *Kuli Pratha*, Publicity surrounding indentured women and Australian overseers was later credited with halting a plan to place Fiji under the control of the Australian government.
60 Examples, especially from *New India* (May 28 1915 and June 3 1915) are preserved in Madras, Public, Ordinary Series, G.O. No. 1331, September 13 1915, TNA.
61 "Note to H.M."
62 "Note to H.M."
63 *Hitkarini*, February 4 1917, SNN, Madras, 1917a, p. 458.
64 Decisions about the system were ultimately made at cabinet level, since both the India Office and the Colonial Office were involved.
65 Nupur Chaudhuri, "The Indian Other: Reactions of Two Anglo-Indian Travel Writers," Chapter 10.
66 Tinker, *New System of Slavery*, pp. 116–35.
67 Tinker, "Prologue: Helots in the Empire," *Separate and Unequal*, pp. 21–42.
68 Hugh Tinker, *The Ordeal of Love: C. F. Andrews and India* (Delhi and Oxford: Oxford University Press, 1979).
69 Laurence, *A Question of Labour*, especially, pp. 46 and 551, endnote 46.

70 P.C. Emmer, "The Meek Hindu: The Recruitment of Indian Labourers for Service Overseas, 1870–1916," P.C. Emmer, ed., *Colonialism and Migration; Indentured Labour before and after Slavery*, series: Comparative Studies in Overseas History (Dordrecht: M. Nijhoff, 1986), pp. 187–207.
71 "Memo on Questions Likely to Arise at the End of the War," 1916, Hardinge Papers: Papers of Lord Hardinge of Penshurst, Viceroy of India, 1910–1916, CUL.
72 C.G. Todhunter, Acting Sec'y to the Govt. of Madras, Public Department to the Sec'y to Government, Commerce and Industry Department, September 3 1915, Madras, Public, G.O. 1296.
73 Kalpana Kannabiran, "Mapping Migration, Gender, Culture and Politics in the Indian Diaspora: Commemorating Indian Arrival in Trinidad," *Economic and Political Weekly* (October 31 1998), WS-53-57.
74 Kannabiran, "Mapping Migration."
75 *Hindu Nesan* (February 27 1917), SNN, Madras, 1917a.
76 Tinker's word used in a chapter title.
77 Kannabiran, "Mapping Migration."

Chapter 12 Civilizing Women: French Colonial Perceptions of Vietnamese Motherhood

* The research conducted for this chapter was made possible with the help of a number of institutions, organizations, and individuals. I would like to thank the Association for Asian Studies for its Southeast Asia Council Grant of 1995, Carthage College for its Faculty Research and Development Grant of 1997, and AsiaNetwork for the Freeman Foundation Student-Faculty Fellowship of 1999. I am most grateful also to Dr. David K. Wyatt and to Dr. David H. Krause for the many letters they wrote on my behalf and which no doubt greatly contributed to the acquisition of these grants and fellowships. Finally, thanks also to Dr. Kurt Piepenburg and to Dr. David Steege for their help in administrating and allocating these funds.
1 Rachel G. Fuchs, "France in a Comparative Perspective," in *Gender and the Politics of Social Reform in France, 1870–1914*, ed. Elinor A. Accampo, Rachel G. Fuchs, and Mary Lynn Stewart (Baltimore: Johns Hopkins University Press, 1995), p. 180.
2 Micheline R. Lessard, "Tradition for Rebellion: Vietnamese Students and Teachers and Anticolonial Resistance, 1888–1931" (Ph D Thesis: Cornell University, 1995), p. 46.
3 John M. Merriman, *The Margins of City Life. Explorations on the French Urban Frontier, 1815–1851* (New York: New York University Press, 1991), p. 14.
4 Merriman, *Margins of City Life*, p. 14.
5 Fuchs, "France in a Comparative Perspective," p. 181.
6 Judith F. Stone, "The Republican Brotherhood," in *Gender and the Politics of Social Reform in France, 1870–1914,* ed. Elinor A. Accompo, Rachel G. Fuchs, and Mary Lynn Stewart (Baltimore: Johns Hopkins Press, 1995), p. 48.
7 Fuchs, "France in a Comparative Perspective," p. 173.
8 Accampo, "Gender, Social Policy," p. 8.
9 Marylynn Salmon, "The Cultural Significance of Breastfeeding and Infant Care in Early Modern England and America," *Journal of Social History* 6 (Winter 1994), p. 251.
10 Judith F. Stone, "The Republican Brotherhood," in *Gender and the Politics of Social Reform in France, 1870–1914*, ed. Elinor A. Accampo, Rachel G. Fuchs, and Mary Lynn Stewart (Baltimore: Johns Hopkins University Press, 1995), p. 33.

11 Joshua Cole, "'A Sudden and Terrible Revelation:' Motherhood and Infant Mortality in France, 1858–1874," *Journal of Family History* 21 (October 1996), p. 419.
12 Cole, " 'A Sudden and Terrible Revelation'," p. 428.
13 Cole, " 'A Sudden and Terrible Revelation'," p. 432.
14 Cole, " 'A Sudden and Terrible Revelation'," p. 428.
15 Cole, " 'A Sudden and Terrible Revelation'," p. 421.
16 Cole, " 'A Sudden and Terrible Revelation,", p. 428.
17 Barbara Ehrenreich and Deirdre English, *For her Own Good. 150 Years of Experts' Advice to Women* (New York: Doubleday Press, 1978), p. 75.
18 Jean Louis Flandrin, *Le Sexe et l'occident* (Paris: Editions du Seuil, 1981), p. 205.
19 Miriam Cohen and Michael Hanagan, "The Politics of Gender and the Making of the Welfare State, 1900–1940: A Comparative Perspective," *Journal of Social History* 3 (Spring 1991), p. 475.
20 *Journal officiel de l'Indochine française* (January 28 1889).
21 *La revue du Pacifique*, 2 (1923), p. 207. All translations in this essay by the author.
22 AOM, Commission Guernut, Carton 24, BD 1937.
23 Jules Michelet, "Le peuple," quoted in Raoul Girardet, in *Le Nationalisme Français* (Paris: Editions du Seuil, 1983), p. 14.
24 Edouard Marquis, "L'Enseignement en Cochinchine," *Revue du Pacifique* (May 7 1935).
25 *Avenir du Tonkin* (April 10 1926).
26 *Echo Annamite* (July 15 1927).
27 *Echo Annamite* (July 15 1927).
28 Archives Outre-mer (hereafter cited as AOM), Fonds des Amiraux (hereafter FA), Dossier 2674.
29 *L'Annam Scolaire* (August 5 1927), AOM, SLOTFOM V, Dossier 35.
30 Mai Thi Thu and Le Thi Nham Tuyet, *Women in Vietnam* (Hanoi: Foreign Language Publishing House, 1978), p. 45.
31 The *Dong Kinh Nghia Thuc* (Tonkin Free School) had been created by a number of Vietnamese reformers and nationalists. The school opened in 1907, but was shut down in 1908 by French colonial authorities who claimed its leadership, curriculum and activities were anti-French and anti-colonial.
32 David G. Marr, *Vietnamese Tradition on Trial, 1920–1945* (Berkeley: University of California Press, 1981), p. 210.
33 AOM Indochine Nouveaux Fonds, Carton 325, Dossier 2634.
34 *L'Etudiant indochinois* (May 1928).
35 *L'Annam Scolaire* (August 5 1927). The Trung Sisters are revered figures in Vietnamese history. As army generals, they are said to have defeated and expelled Chinese colonizers between 40 BCE and 43 BCE. They are often invoked to rally Vietnamese women in patriotic and nationalist causes.
36 *Nam Phong*, 1926–27.
37 *Trung Bac Tan Van* (June 16 1931).
38 *Phu Nu Thoi Dam*, 1931.
39 This interpretation was drawn from a survey of the *Bulletin général de l'instruction publique* in the 1920s and 1930s. It was also drawn from a number of other archival sources such as the Fonds des Amiraux.
40 AOM, CG Carton 24, BD 1937.
41 AOM, CG Carton 24, BD 1937.
42 AOM Résidence Supérieure du Tonkin (hereafter RST), Dossier 20479.
43 AOM Résidence Supérieure du Tonkin (hereafter RST), Dossier 20479.

44 AOM, FA Dossier 2674.
45 Laurence Monnais-Rousselot, *Médecine et colonisation, l'aventure indochinoise, 1860–1939* (Paris: CNRS Editions, 1999), p. 57.
46 Monnais-Rousselot, *Médecine et colonisation*, p. 25.
47 Monnais-Rousselot, *Médecine et colonisation*, p. 167.
48 Tran Nguyen Hanh, "Coutumes et constitution de la famille annamite," *Bulletin de la société académique indochinoise* (1882–83), p. 147.
49 *Bulletin général de l'instruction publique*, March 1923.
50 Mai Thi Thu and Le Thi Nham Tuyet, *Women in Vietnam*, p. 100.
51 Ann Stoler, "Making Empire Respectable: The Politics of Race and Sexual Morality in Twentieth Century Colonial Cultures," *American Ethnologist* 16 (November 1989), p. 647.
52 Stoler, "Making Empire Respectable," p. 640.
53 *Rapport sur l'enseignement à distribuer au Lycée de Hanoi*, AOM, RST Dossier 36311.
54 Stoler, "Making Empire Respectable," p. 638.
55 Ann Stoler, "Sexual Affronts and Racial Frontiers: European Identities and the Cultural politics of Exclusion in Colonial Southeast Asia," *Comparative Studies in Society and History* 34 (July 1992), p. 528.
56 *Echo Annamite* (July 15 1927).

Chapter 13 Social Construction of Idealized Images of Women in Colonial Korea: "New Woman" versus "Motherhood"

1 Research for this chapter stemmed from numerous discussions with Professor Kazue Muta of Konan Women's University, Japan. I would like to thank Professor Theda Skocpol, Professor Merry White (both at Harvard University) and Professor Yasemin Soysal (University of Essex) for their encouragement and support on my research. Comments from the editors of this book, Professor Tamara Hunt and Professor Micheline R. Lessard, are greatly appreciated, and were especially helpful. Dr. Kyeongjae Cho helped me to clarify my arguments by reading earlier versions of this chapter and giving editorial advice. Earlier versions of this chapter were presented at the following conferences/seminars: "The New Image of Motherhood in Korea, 1920s–1930s," The Annual Meetings of the Association for Asian Studies, Chicago, March 13–16 1997; "Images of Motherhood and Womanhood Reconstructed, Korea 1920s–1930s" Presentation at "A Thousand Modernities," An Interdisciplinary Round Table on Women and the Modern, The Beatrice M. Bain Research Group on Women and Gender and the East Asian Languages Department, UC Berkeley, April 16 1998;" 'New Woman' and the Construction of Modern Motherhood in the 1930s' Korea," International Convention of Asia Scholars, Leiden, June 25–28 1998. All translations from Korean are by the author unless otherwise noted. Chizuko Ueno, "Collapse of 'Japanese Mothers'," *U.S. – Japan Women's Journal*, English Supplement No. 10 (1996), pp. 3–5.
2 Masami Ohinata, "The Mystique of Motherhood," in *Japanese Women*, ed. Fujimura-Fanselow and Kameda (New York: The Feminist Press, 1995), p. 205.
3 Edward Shorter, *The Making of Modern Family* (New York: Basic Books, Inc., 1975), p. 168.
4 See: Chizuko Ueno "Collapse of 'Japanese Mothers'," pp. 3–19 and "Genesis of the Urban Housewife," *Japan Quarterly* 34 (1987), pp. 130–42, Robert J. Smith, "Making Village Women into 'Good Wives and Wise Mothers' in Prewar Japan," *Journal of Family History* 8 (1983), pp. 70–84; Shizuko Koyama, "The 'Good Wife and Wise

Mother' Ideology in Post-World War I Japan," *U.S.–Japan Women's Journal*, English Supplement No. 7 (1994), pp. 31–52; Kazue Muta, "Images of Family in Meiji Periodicals: The Paradox Underlying the Emergence of the 'Home'," *U.S.–Japan Women's Journal*, English Supplement No. 7 (1994), pp. 53–71; Akiko Niwa, "The Formation of the Myth of Motherhood in Japan," *U.S.–Japan Women's Journal*, English Supplement No. 4 (1993), pp. 70–82; Ruth H. Bloch, "American Feminine Ideals in Transition: The Rise of the Moral Mother, 1785–1815," *Feminist Studies* 4 (1978), pp. 101–26; and Marilyn Helterline "The Emergence of Modern Motherhood: Motherhood in England 1899 to 1959, " *International Journal of Women's Studies* 3 (1980), pp. 590–614.

5 Educating women to be good mothers was a widespread concern at the end of the nineteenth century and the beginning of the twentieth century, and was often taken up by colonial powers as part of their "native" policies. See Margaret Zoller Booth, "Education for Liberation or Domestication? Female Education in Colonial Swaziland," Chapter 14, and Micheline R. Lessard, "Civilizing Women: French Colonial Perceptions of Vietnamese Womanhood and Motherhood," Chapter 12.

6 The three major journals used for this article are: *Kajong Chapji* (Home Journal), 6/25/1906-1/25/1907, 7/25/1907-8/25/1908; *Shin Yosong* (New Woman) 9/1/1923-4/4/1934, and *Shin Kajong* (New Home), 1/1/1933-9/1/1936. These were selected on the basis of their social impact. Writers include eminent intellectuals, including scholars, teachers, artists, musicians, poets, novelists, and social activists. Secondary journals utilized include *Nyoja Chinam* (4/25/1908), *Chason Puinhoe Chapji* (8/5/1908), *Shin Yoja* (3/10-5/20/1920), *Shin Saenghwal* (3/11-9/5/1922) and *Samchon'li* (6/12/1929-11/1/1941) Newspaper editorials are included from *Tongnip Shinmun* (*The Independent*, 4/7/1896) *Chosun Ilbo* (*Chosun Daily* 3/5/1920), and *Tong'a Ilbo* (*Tonga Daily*, 4/1/1920).

7 The impact and significance of the March First Movement on Japanese colonial policy is explained below.

8 Keun-su Kim, *Hankuk Chapji-sa Yonku* [*History of Journals in Korea*] (Seoul: Hankookhak Yonkuso, 1992).

9 Wol-mi Park, "1920-nyondae Yosong Haebang Uishik'kwa Chiwi Byunwhae Kwanhan Yonku" [A Study on Women's Liberation and Status Change in the 1920s], (MA Thesis: Seoul: Yonsei University, 1984); Bonnie Oh, "From Three Obediences to Patriotism and Nationalism," *Korea Journal* 22 (1982), pp. 37–55; Yung-chung Kim, "Women's Movement in Modern Korea," in *Challenges for Women*, (Seoul: Ewha Women's University Press), 1986, pp. 77–8.

10 Y. Kim, "Women's Movement in Modern Korea," pp. 77–8.

11 Editorial, *Tongnip Shinmun (The Independent)* (December 13 1898), cited in Y. Kim, "Women's Movement in Modern Korea," p. 81; Oh, "From Three Obediences to Patriotism and Nationalism," pp. 41–3.

12 Editorial, *Tongnip Shinmun* (*The Independent*) (April 21, 1896), cited in Oh, "From Three Obediences to Patriotism and Nationalism," pp. 42–3. Considering the existing educational policies in Korea 1896, it seems likely that this plea was actually aimed at Korean men, rather than the largely illiterate Korean women.

13 The first private school for women was founded in 1886.

14 *Kajong Chapji* 1/3 (1906).

15 *Kajong Chapji*, 1/4 (1906).

16 Oh, "From Three Obediences to Patriotism and Nationalism."

17 As Korean studies scholars point out, the pervasive social, economic, and cultural change carried out by the Japanese colonial government to the benefit of the

Japanese state throughout the ruling period left lasting influence on every aspect of Korean society and its people by 1945, when the colonial period finally ended with the surrender of Japan. The loss of sovereignty had influenced the direction of Korean nationalism, and the vigilant colonial control policy intensified the internal conflicts among the national leaders; the cultural/educational policy aimed to assimilate the Korean people, to make them obedient colonial subjects, and to skew their cultural development and distort national identity. For the process of colonization, change and trends in Japanese colonial policy, formation and directions of nationalistic reactions/movements, and the Japanese colonial legacy in Korea, see Carter J. Eckert *et al.*, *Korea Old and New: A History* (Seoul: Ilchokak Publishers, 1990), pp. 199–333; Ki-baik Lee, *A New History of Korea*, trans. Edward W. Wagner with Edward J. Shultz (Cambridge MA: Harvard University Press, 1984), pp. 267–372; and Bruce Cumings, "The Legacy of Japanese Colonialism in Korea," in *The Japanese Colonial Empire, 1895–1945*, ed. Ramon H. Meyers and Mark R. Peattie (Princeton: Princeton University Press, 1984), pp. 478–96.

18 Eckert, *Korea Old and New.*

19 Eckert, *Korea Old and New.*

20 Having realized that direct confrontation was self-destructive, cultural nationalists decided to take a gradual approach to independence by concentrating efforts on quiet educational and political campaigns. They reasoned that ultimately, this approach would pave the way for a stronger nationalism and eventually, independence. Eckert, *Korea Old and New*; Lee, *A New History of Korea.*

21 *Shin Yosong* (November 1923), pp. 30–1.

22 *Shin Yosong* (November 1923), pp. 2–3.

23 Myung-ho Kim, "Inner Revolution Required for Women," *Shin Yosong* (September 1926), pp. 7–9.

24 Myung-ho Kim, "The Future of Women's Fate," *Shin Yosong* (March 1926), pp. 13–16.

25 Myung-ho Kim, "Directions for Modern Women," *Shin Yosong* (July 1926), pp. 17–18.

26 Kim, "Directions for Modern Women," pp. 19–21.

27 "The Social Status of Choson [Korean] Women," *Shin Yosong* (October 1925), pp. 2–5.

28 *Shin Yosong* (June/July 1925), pp. 7–13.

29 "Three Conditions of Marriage," *Shin Yosong* (May 1924), pp. 15–16.

30 "Three Conditions of Marriage," p. 16.

31 "The Streams of Feminist Movement," *Shin Yosong* (February 1925), p. 7.

32 Wol-mi Park, *1920-nyondae Yosong Haebang Uishik'kwa Chiwi Byunwhae Kwanhan Yonku* [*A Study on Women's Liberation and Status Change in the 1920s*], pp. 46–7.

33 Yo-sup Chu, "How to Manage a Marriage Life," *Shin Yosong* (May 1924), pp. 22–9.

34 Kim Maria, *Shin Kajong*, (April 1933).

35 Tamara L. Hunt describes a similar situation in Ireland, when early twentieth-century Irish feminists were labeled "unpatriotic." See "Wild Irish Women: Gender, Politics, and Colonialism in the Nineteenth Century," Chapter 4.

36 Cha-young Noh, "Maternal Love and Eternal Stars," *Shin Kajong* (March 1934), p. 127.

37 *Shin Kajong* (February 1936), p. 108.

38 *Shin Kajong* (April 1933), p. 155.

39 *Shin Kajong* (May 1933), pp. 12–14.

40 *Shin Kajong* (December 1933), pp. 26–44.

41 Kwang-su Lee, "Mother," *Shin Kajong* (April 1933), p. 155.
42 Kwang-su Lee, "Lovely Wife," *Shin Kajong* (April 1933), p. 155.
43 Oh, "From Three Obediences to Patriotism and Nationalism," pp. 37–55.
44 Chizuko Ueno, "Collapse of 'Japanese Mothers'," p. 18.

Chapter 14 Education for Liberation or Domestication? Female Education in Colonial Swaziland

1 See Elizabeth Schmidt, *Peasants, Traders, and Wives: Shona Women in the History of Zimbabwe, 1870–1939* (Portsmouth, NH: Heinemann, 1992); Nakanyike B. Musisi, "Colonial and Missionary Education: Women and Domesticity in Uganda, 1900–1945," in *African Encounters with Domesticity*, ed. K.T. Hansen (New Brunswick, NJ: Rutgers University Press, 1992); Deborah Gaitskell, "At Home with Hegemony? Coercion and Consent in African Girls' Education for Domesticity in South Africa Before 1910," in *Contesting Colonial Hegemony: State and Society in Africa and India*, ed. Dagmar Engels and Shula Marks (London: British Academic Press, 1994).
2 Women and Law in Southern Africa Research Trust, *Family in Transition: the Experience of Swaziland* (Manzini: Ruswanda Pub. Bureau, 1998), p. 5.
3 Hilda Kuper, *The Uniform of Colour: A Study of White-Black Relationships in Swaziland* (Johannesburg: Witwatersrand University Press, 1947), p. 152. Kuper dominated the anthropological study of the Swazi from the 1930s until her death in 1991.
4 Hilda Kuper, *The Swazi: A South African Kingdom*, 2nd edn. (New York: Holt, Rinehart and Winston, 1986); and *An African Aristocracy Rank among the Swazi of Bechuanaland* (London and New York: International African Institute, Oxford University Press, 1947).
5 Kuper, *African Aristocracy*, p. 130.
6 Kuper, *African Aristocracy*, p. 117.
7 Some recent analyses include Unesco, *The Educational Process and Historiography in Africa* (n.p.: Vendome, 1985); John Karefa Marah, "Educational Adaptation and Pan-Africanism: Developmental Trends in Africa," *Journal of Black Studies* 17 (1987), pp. 460–81; Kilemi Mwiria, "Education for Subordination: African Education in Colonial Kenya," *History of Education* 20 (1991), pp. 261–73; Clive Whitehead, "Education for Subordination? Some Reflections on Kilemi Mwiria's Account of African Education in Colonial Kenya," *History of Education* 22 (1993), pp. 85–93.
8 Richard Corby, "Educating Africans for Inferiority under British Rule: Bo School in Sierra Leone," *Comparative Education Review* 34 (1990), pp. 314–49. See also Bob White, "Talk About School: Education and the Colonial Project in French and British Africa (1860–1960)," *Comparative Education* 32 (1996), pp. 9–25.
9 "Missionary Work," *The Times of Swaziland* (February 2 1907). Hereafter *TOS*.
10 *TOS* (February 2 1907), pp. 7–8.
11 Great Britain, Colonial Office, Advisory Committee on Education in the Colonies, *Mass Education in African Society* (London: HMSO, 1944), p. 18.
12 Dickson A. Mungazi and L. Kay Walker, *Educational Reform and the Transformation of Southern Africa* (Westport, Connecticut: Praeger, 1997), p. 34.
13 Schmidt, *Peasants, Traders, and Wives*, p. 127.
14 Rev. Christopher. C. Watts, "Enclosure to Resident Commissioner's Despatch Swaziland No. 357 of 15 November 1924." Saint Marks Coloured School, Mbabane, Swaziland. September 17 1924, (SNA).

15 Swaziland Government, Education Department, *African Primary School Syllabus 1934* (Bremersdorp, Swaziland, 1934).

16 For some of the recent literature on this topic, see Nakanyike B. Musisi, "Colonial and Missionary Education: Women and Domesticity in Uganda, 1900–1945," in *African Encounters with Domesticity*, ed. K.T. Hansen (New Brunswick, NJ: Rutgers University Press, 1992); Schmidt, *Peasants, Traders, and Wives*, p. 141; Dagmar Engels and Shula Marks, "Introduction: Hegemony in a Colonial Context" and Gaitskell, "At Home With Hegemony?" in Engels and Marks, eds., *Contesting Colonial Hegemony*; Geiger, *TANU Women: Gender and Culture in the Making of Tanganyikan Nationalism, 1955–1965* (Portsmouth, NH: Heinemann, 1997); White, "Talk about School"; Great Britain, Colonial Office, *Mass Education in African Society*, p. 6; *Colonial Office Summer Conference on African Administration*, 2nd Session, August 19–September 2 1948 at King's College, Cambridge, p. 53, SNA, File 774II.

17 Only Lesotho and Botswana historically have revealed similar gender patterns. The two reasons consistently given for boys having such low school enrollment rates in these three countries (Botswana, Lesotho and Swaziland) are: strict gender rules regarding the practice of herding cattle, and early adolescent motivation to follow the path of a migrant-labor father who makes adequate wages in South African mines. See John E. Bardill and James H. Cobbe, *Lesotho: Dilemmas of Dependence in Southern Africa* (Boulder, CO: Westview Press, 1985), p. 105. Also see P.T. Mgadla, "Missionary Wives, Women and Education: The Development of Literacy among the Botswana 1840–1937," *Pula: Botswana Journal of African Studies* 11 (1997), pp. 70–81. And Richard P. Stevens, *Lesotho, Botswana, and Swaziland: The Former High Commission Territories in Southern Africa* (New York: Praeger, 1967).

18 Alan R. Booth, *Swaziland: Tradition and Change in a Southern African Kingdom* (Boulder, CO: Westview Press, 1983), p. 34.

19 Booth, *Swaziland*, p. 34.

20 Confidential interviews, Malindza, Mafutseni, Hlatikhulu, Croydon, Ezulwini Valley, and Steki, Swaziland. June, July 1998.

21 Musisi, *Colonial and Missionary Education*; Schmidt, *Peasants, Traders, and Wives*.

22 Schmidt, *Peasants, Traders, and Wives*, p. 129.

23 For examples of these disputes see "Swaziland Missionary Conference," *TOS*, January 14 1934; "Native Education," *TOS*, February 1 1934, and "Swaziland in the Making," *TOS*, April 12 1945.

24 Phelps-Stokes Fund, *Education in East Africa* (New York: 1925), p. 347. Also see, L.J. Lewis, *Phelps-Stokes Reports on Education in Africa*, abridged, with an introduction by L.J. Lewis (London: 1962). The Phelps-Stokes Reports were utilized by the British as one of the major guiding documents for much of the twentieth-century colonial education policy guidelines.

25 Phelps-Stokes Fund, *Education in East Africa*, p. 340.

26 Phelps-Stokes Fund, *Education in East Africa*, p. 340.

27 Phelps-Stokes Fund, *Education in East Africa*, p. 341.

28 Phelps-Stokes Fund, *Education in East Africa*, p. 283.

29 Phelps-Stokes Fund, *Education in East Africa*, p. 351.

30 Phelps-Stokes Fund, *Education in East Africa*, p. 342.

31 "Letter from C.C. Watts to government Secretary, attached to *Native Schools Report*, 1924, p. 3 (SNA, File 137).

32 *Report on Education in Swaziland, 1931*.

33 *Board of Advice on Native Education, 1931*.

34 *Board of Advice on Native Education*, p. 221.
35 Swaziland Government, Education Department, *African Primary School Syllabus, 1934.*
36 Paramount Chief Sobhuza II, "Memorandum Upon Native Education" (March 1933), SNA, RCS 3328/33, p. 1.
37 Swaziland Government, Department of Education *Annual Report on Education in Swaziland for the year 1941*.
38 Schmidt, *Peasants, Traders, and Wives*.
39 *Swaziland Annual Report, 1955*. The Director of Education. Ohio University Microfiche collection.
40 *Swaziland Annual Report, 1955*, The Director of Education. Ohio University Microfiche collection. p. 12
41 Great Britain, Colonial Office, *Colonial Office Summer Conference*, p. 53.
42 Gaitskell, "At Home with Hegemony?".
43 Miranda Miles, *Missing Women: A Study of Swazi Female Migration to the Witwatersrand, 1920–1970* (MA Thesis, Kingston, Ontario: Queen's University, 1991), p. 68.
44 Schmidt, *Peasants, Traders, and Wives*, p. 122.
45 Phelps-Stokes Fund, *Education in East Africa*, p. 341.
46 "Mission Work in Swaziland," *TOS* (10 December 1931).
47 Great Britain, Colonial Office, *Swaziland Annual Report, 1953* Report of the Director of Education, pp. 18–22.
48 Great Britain, Colonial Office, *Swaziland Annual Report, 1955* Report of the Director of Education.
49 Miles, "Missing Women."
50 "The Native Education Advisory Board" and "The Ibuto System," *TOS* (21 December 1933), pp. 2–3.
51 "Advisory Board on Native Education," *TOS* (8 December, 1932), p. 2.
52 J. Lukele, "Bantu Customs and White Man's Law," Letter to the Editor, *TOS* (March 30 1933).
53 Kuper, *The Swazi*, p. 59.
54 Confidential interviews, Malindza, Mafutseni, Hlatikhulu, Croydon, Ezulwini Valley, and Steki, Swaziland. June, July 1998.
55 Phelps-Stokes Fund, *Education in East Africa*, p. 341.
56 Schmidt, *Peasants, Traders, and Wives*, p. 122.
57 Miles, "Missing Women." See also Kuper, *A Uniform of Colour*, p. 19. The South African Railways and Harbours Transport Service began running busses in Swaziland in 1927. The busses ran to Breyten, Transvaal, where passengers enbarked on the train to Johannesburg and elsewhere.
58 "Advisory Board on Native Education," *TOS* (18 December 1932).
59 Kuper, *A Uniform of Colour*, p. 19.
60 "The Swazis and Indirect Rule," *TOS* (20 November 1941), p. 2.
61 Alan Booth, " 'European Courts Protect Women and Witches': Colonial Law Courts as Redistributors of Power in Swaziland 1920–1950," *Journal of Southern African Studies* 18 (1992), pp. 253–75.
62 Musisi, "Colonial and Missionary Education," p. 185.
63 Phelps-Stokes Fund, *Education in East Africa*, p. 347.
64 Phelps-Stokes Fund, *Education in East Africa*, p. 347.
65 Roland Oliver and Anthony Atmore, *Africa Since 1800*, 3rd edn. (Cambridge: Cambridge University Press, 1981).

Chapter 15 Women, Gender History, and Imperial Ethiopia

1 "Greece in Chains: Philhellenism to the Rescue of a Damsel in Distress," Chapter 3 above.

2 D. Crummey, "Society, Stage and Nationality in the Recent Historiography of Ethiopia", *Journal of African History* 31 (1990), pp. 103–19.

3 H. Marcus, *A History of Ethiopia* (Berkeley, Los Angeles, London: University of California Press, 1994); Bahru Zewde, *A History of Modern Ethiopia, 1855–1974* (London: James Currey; Athens: Ohio University Press; Addis Ababa: Addis Ababa University Press, 1991); Teshale Tibebu, *The Making of Modern Ethiopia: 1896–1974* (Lawrenceville, NJ: Red Sea Press, 1995); C. Prouty and E. Rosenfeld, *Historical Dictionary of Ethiopia and Eritrea* (Mutuchen, N.J. and London: Scarecrow Press, 1993). For work on Islam and developments in archaeology: Hussein Ahmed, "Islam and Islamic Discourse in Ethiopia (1973–1993)" and D.W. Phillipson, "The 1993 Excavations at Aksum," in *New Trends in Ethiopian Studies, Papers of the 12th International Conference of Ethiopian Studies, Vol. 1, Humanities and Human Resources* ed. H. Marcus (Lawrenceville, N.J.: Red Sea Press, 1994), pp. 84–96 and 775–801.

4 K. Fukui and J. Markakis, *Ethnicity and Conflict in the Horn of Africa* (Athens: Ohio University Press, 1994) and J. Sorenson, *Imagining Ethiopia: Struggles for History and Identity in the Horn of Africa* (New Brunswick, N.J.: Rutgers University Press, 1993). Almaz Eshete talks of "restoring women's identity" in her "Issues of Gender and Sexuality in the Context of Cross-Cultural Dynamics of Ethiopia – Challenging Traditional Pervasives," in *Ethiopia in Broader Perspective, Vol. 1*, ed. K. Fukui, E. Kurimoto, and M. Shigeta (Kyoto: Shokado, 1997), pp. 569–76.

5 For the best of past collaborative work between anthropologists and historians, see for instance, D. Donham and W. James, *The Southern Marches of Imperial Ethiopia: Essays in History and Social Anthropology* (Cambridge: Cambridge University Press, 1986). For the current regime's commitment to equality between the sexes, see the aspirations of the 1994 Constitution as depicted by M.P. Porter, "Law in Conflict: the Status of Women in the Constitution and Laws of Ethiopia," in Fukui, Kurimoto, and Shigeta, *Ethiopia in Broader Perspective, II1*, pp. 585–99.

6 Crummey, "Society, State and Nationality," p. 118.

7 Anna Fernyhough, "The Traditional Role and Status of Women in Imperial Ethiopia," *Journal of the Steward Anthropological Society* 13 (1982), pp. 69–81.

8 Helen Pankhurst, *Gender, Development and Identity: An Ethiopian Study* (London: Zed Books, 1992), p. 6.

9 S. Comhaire Sylvain, "Higher Education and Professional Training of Women in Ethiopia," *Proceedings of the Third International Conference of Ethiopian Studies, Addis Ababa 1966, III* (Addis Ababa: Institute of Ethiopian Studies, Addis Ababa University, 1970), pp. 197–202.

10 Danile Haile, *Law and the Status of Women in Ethiopia* (UN Economic Commission for Africa, 1979, 1980); Salome Gebre Egziabher, "The Changing Position of Women in Ethiopia," *Zeitschrift für Kulturaustasch* (Sonderausgabe, 1973), pp. 112–15; J. Olmstead, "Women and Work in Two Southern Ethiopian Communities," *African Studies Review* 8 (1975), pp. 85–98, and "Ethiopia's Artful Weavers," *National Geographic* 143 (1973), pp. 125–41; Laketch Dirasse, "The Socio-Economic Position of Women in Addis Ababa: the Case of Prostitution" (PhD Thesis: Boston University, 1978).

11 Hirut Tefere and Lakew Woldetekle, "Study of the Situation of Women in Ethiopia," *Research Report 23* (Addis Ababa: Institute of Development Research, 1986); Anne

Cassiers, "Mercha: An Ethiopian Woman Speaks of Her Life," in P. Romero, *Life Histories of African Women* (London: Ashfield, 1988); Hanna Kebede, "Gender Relations in Mobilizing Human Resources," in *Ethiopia: Options for Rural Development*, ed. S. Pausewang *et al.* (London: Zed Books, 1990), pp. 59–68; Addis Tiruneh, "Gender Issues in Agroforestry," addendum to *Land Tenure and Land Policy in Ethiopia after the Derg, Proceedings of the Second Workshop of the Land Tenure Project* (Addis Ababa: Institute of Development Research, Addis Ababa University; University of Trondheim Centre for Environment and Development, 1994).

12 Tsehai Berhane-Selassie, *Gender Issues in Ethiopia* (Addis Ababa: Institute of Ethiopian Studies, Addis Ababa University, 1991). Papers in this collection include: Gennet Zewdie, "Women in Primary and Secondary Education"; Seyoum Teferra, "The Participation of Girls in Higher Education in Ethiopia"; Atsede Wondimagegnehu, "Women in Science and Technology in Ethiopia"; Adanech Kidanemariam, "The Role and Status of Women in Traditional Health Care Services in Ethiopia"; Mekonnen Bishaw, "Ethiopian Women and the Media"; Almaz Eshete, "Perspectives on Gender and Development"; Dessalegn Rahmato, "Rural Women in Ethiopia: Problems and Prospects."

13 In Tsehai Berhane-Selassie, *Gender Issues* see the editor's piece "Gender and Occupational Potters in Wolayta," and Getachaw Kassa, "A Change in the Role and Status of Pastoral Women in two Garri Villages."

14 Helen Pankhurst does not use the term *conjoncture*, but in this part of her book she clearly enters the *monde Braudellien*. For discussion of *conjonture*, a term very difficult to render accurately in English, see J. Hexter, "Fernand Braudel and the *Monde Braudellien*," *Journal of Modern History* 44 (1972), pp. 481–539, especially, pp. 498–512.

15 H. Pankhurst, *Gender, Development and Identity*, see especially Chapters 6–8. Almaz, "Issues of Gender and Sexuality," and "Perspectives on Gender and Development."

16 Serihun Asfaw, "Women in the Works of Ethiopian Short Story Writers," *Ethiopia in Broader Perspective, Vol. III*, pp. 118–27, see especially the introduction and conclusion.

17 E. Biasio, "The Burden of Women – Women Artists in Ethiopia," in *New Trends in Ethiopian Studies, Vol. 1, Humanities and Human Resources*, ed. H. Marcus (Lawrenceville: Red Sea Press, 1994), pp. 304–34.

18 Richard Pankhurst, "The Role of Women in Ethiopian Economic, Social and Cultural Life: from the Middle Ages to the Times of Tewodros," in *Proceedings of the First National Conference of Ethiopian Studies*, ed. R. Pankhurst, Ahmed Zekaria and Taddesse Beyene (Addis Ababa: Institute of Ethiopian Studies, Ababa University, 1990), pp. 345–63, and "The History of Prostitution in Ethiopia," *Journal of Ethiopian Studies* 12 (1974), pp. 159–78.

19 Bairu Tafla, "Marriage as a Political Device: An Appraisal of a Socio-Political Aspect of the Menilek Period, 1889–1916," *Journal of Ethiopian Studies* 10 (January 1972), pp. 13–22; R. Pankhurst, "Dynastic Inter-Marriage in Medieval and Post-Medieval Ethiopia," in Fukui, Kurimoto, and Shigeta, *Ethiopia in Broader Perspective, Vol. 1*, pp. 206–20.

20 C. Prouty, "Empress T'aitu Bitoul, 'Lioness of Judah'," H. Marcus, *Proceedings of the First U.S. Conference on Ethiopian Studies, 1973* (East Lansing: Michigan State University African Studies Center, 1975), pp. 117–13 and her "Eight Ethiopian Women of the Zemene Mesafint, 1769–1855," *Northeast African Studies* 1 (1979), pp. 63–85.

21 C. Prouty, *Empress Taytu and Menilek II: Ethiopia, 1883–1910* (Trenton, N.J.: Red Sea Press, and London: Ravens Educational and Development Services, 1986).

22 D. Crummey, "Women and Landed Property in Gondarine Ethiopia," *International Journal of African Historical Studies* 14 (1981), pp. 444–65; *idem.*, "Women, Property and Litigation Among the Bagemder Amhara, 1750s to 1850s," in *African Women and the Law: Historical Perspectives*, ed. J. Hay and M. Wright (Boston: Boston University Papers on Africa, VII, 1982). Subsequent page references to these two papers are to pre-publication drafts. See also Crummey's "Family and Property among the Amhara Nobility," *Journal of African History* 24 (1983), pp. 207–20.

23 Almaz, "Issues of Gender and Sexuality," p. 569.

24 The phrase, re-used by Bock (see next footnote), derives from G. Lerna, *The Majority Finds Its Past: Placing Women in History* (Oxford; Oxford University Press, 1979).

25 Gisela Bock pursues this theme, with an even longer list, in her "Women's History and Gender History: Aspects of an International Debate," originally published in *Gender and History* 1 (1989, but usefully reprinted in R. Shoemaker and M. Vincent, *Gender and History in Western Europe* (London: Arnold, 1998), pp. 25–42, and see especially, pp. 34–7.

26 For an explicit rejection of gender history conducted from the perspective of social scientists, see J.W. Scott, "Gender: A Useful Category of Historical Analysis," *American Historical Review* 91 (1986), also reprinted in Shoemaker and Vincent, *Gender and History*, pp. 42–65. The editors' introduction to this collection, on which we draw here, provides a succinct introduction to the historiography of gender, pp. 1–20.

27 For that new interest in African women and the shift in topical focus, see *Women in Africa: Studies in Social and Economic Change*, ed. N.J. Hafkin and E. G. Bay (Stanford; Stanford University Press, 1976); J.M. Due and R. Summary, "Constraints on Women and Development in Africa," *Journal of Modern African Studies* 20 (1983), pp. 155–66.

28 Verónica Vázquez García, "Native Women and State Legislation in Mexico and Canada: The Agrarian Law and the Indian Act," Chapter 7 above.

29 E. Evans-Pritchard, *The Nuer* (Oxford: Clarendon Press, 1947), *The Position of Women in Primitive Societies and Other Essays in Social Anthropology* (New York: Free Press, 1965), and his *Man and Woman among the Azande* (New York: Free Press, 1974); A.R. Radcliffe-Brown, *Structure and Function in Primitive Society* (New York: Free Press, 1952); M. Fortes, "The Structure of Unilineal Descent Groups," *American Anthropologist* 55 (1953), pp. 17–41, "Descent, Filiation and Affinity: A Rejoinder to Dr. Leach," *Man* 59 (1959), pp. 193–7, 206–12; "Ritual and Office in Tribal Society," in M. Gluckman, *Essays on the Ritual of Social Relations* (Manchester: Manchester University Press, 1962). Fortes elucidated his views in his *Kinship and the Social Order* (Chicago: Aldine, 1969). In most of Africa, membership in a corporate group and property rights are determined through a single line of ancestry, through unilineal descent (patrilineal or matrilineal). Distinctively in Ethiopia, the ideology of descent was ambilineal or cognatic. Individuals, men and women, claimed descent and property rights bilaterally through both intermediate male and female links.

30 R. Firth, "A Note on Descent Groups in Polynesia," *Man* 57 (1957), pp. 4–8; D.M. Schneider, "Some Muddles in the Models: or, How the System Really Works," in *The Relevance of Models for Social Anthropology*, ed. M. Banton (London: Tavistock, 1968), and see especially Part 3 of Schneider's book, *A Critique of the Study of Kinship* (Anna Arbor: University of Michigan Press, 1984); H.W. Scheffler, "Ancestor Worship in

Anthropology: or, Observations on Descent and Descent Groups," *Cultural Anthropology* 7 (1966), pp. 541–51.

31 H.W. Scheffler, "Filiation and Affiliation," *Man* 20 (1985), pp. 1–21, see especially, pp. 9–10, but note also Scheffler's revisionist auto-critique of his own advocacy of the concept of the "cognatic descent group."

32 Fernyhough, "Traditional Role", focuses on the inadequacies of the "unilineal model," pp. 69–70.

33 The following two paragraphs draw particularly on issues delineated and discussed in Helen Pankhurst's introduction, pp. *Gender, Development and Identity*, pp. 3–7.

34 H. Baumann, "The Division of Work according to Sex in African Hoe Culture," *Africa* 1 (1928), pp. 289–319. For Baumann's significance see J. Guyer, "Naturalism in Models in African Production", *Man* 19, 3 (1984), pp. 371–88.

35 E. Boserup, *Woman's Role in Economic Development* (London and New York: St. Martin's Press, 1970).

36 Guyer, "Naturalism in Models in African Production," p. 373. To substantiate the point see also Guyer, "Female Farming and the Evolution of Food Production Patterns among the Beti of South-Central Cameroun," *Africa* 50 (1980), pp. 341–56, and her "Food, Cocoa, and the Division of Labour by Sex in Two West African Societies", *Comparative Studies in Society and History* 22 (1980), pp. 355–73.

37 H. Pankhurst, *Gender, Development and Identity*, p. 6.

38 J. Goody, *Technology, Tradition and the State in Africa* (London: Hutchinson, 1980), pp. 21–33, and see also his *Production and Reproduction. A Comparative Study of the Domestic Domain* (Cambridge: Cambridge University Press, 1976), pp. 110–11.

39 As Crummey remarks in, "Women and Landed Property," p. 6.

40 There is a rich literature on land, state, and society in Ethiopia, and debate about the utility of feudal concepts, see for instance: J.M. Cohen, "Ethiopia: A Survey on the Existence of a Feudal Peasantry," *Journal of Modern African Studies* 12 (1974), pp. 665–72; G. Ellis, "The Feudal Paradigm as a Hindrance to Understanding Ethiopia," *Journal of Modern African Studies* 14 (1976), pp. 275–95; D. Crummey, "Abyssinian Feudalism," *Past and Present* 89 (1980), pp. 115–38, and D. Donham, "Old Abyssinia and the New Ethiopian Empire," in Donham and James, *Southern Marches*, pp. 3–48.

41 As Helen Pankhurst comments in *Gender, Development and Identity*, p. 5, agricultural surplus could sustain only a shifting capital for most of Ethiopia's history. She argues that the political and social hierarchy was "not solely or even primarily" based on agricultural production, and highlights the importance of elite control over long-distance trade. In our view, and despite the occasionally intense competition to control trade routes (most clearly between Menilek of Shawa and Takla-Haymanot of Gojjam in the 1870s and 1880s) Ethiopia was an overwhelmingly agrarian society in which the ruling classes rested firmly and primarily on the peasantry.

42 Crummey, "Abyssinian Feudalism," p. 127.

43 H. Pankhurst, *Gender, Development and Identity*, p. 6.

44 As shown by Margaret Booth's essay, "Education for Liberation or Domestication? Female Education in Colonial Swaziland," (Chapter 14 of the current volume) the women she interviewed had different views about their education than those stated by either colonial officials or Swazi leaders. She rightly implies that using only male sources of information can provide a misleading view of African societies, since male leaders, as well as colonial officials, have political or social agendas which may not adequately reflect the realities of female life.

45 D. Levine, *Wax and Gold. Tradition and Innovation in Ethiopian Culture* (London and Chicago: University of Chicago Press, 1965), p. 79.
46 D. Levine, *Greater Ethiopia. The Evolution of a Multiethnic Society* (London and Chicago: University of Chicago Press, 1974), p. 54.
47 Hanna Kebede, "Gender Relations," p. 59; Almaz, "Issues of Gender and Sexuality," pp. 570–1.
48 M. Meshesha, *Ethiopian Refugees: Beyond the Famine and the War* (Massachusetts: Newton International Press, 1994), pp. 49–50.
49 In the language of colonialism, Orientalism, and gender, this could be compared to the "binary" view of self/Other as discussed in several essays in this collection. In such instances, the colonial gaze viewed all native peoples as the same, making no differentiation between them despite wide variations in social structure, ethnicity, culture, religion or language. In this volume, for discussions of the "binary" view, see Ruth Wallis Herndon, "Women as Symbols of Disorder in Early Rhode Island," Chapter 6, Carmen Ramos-Escandon, "Imperial Eyes, Gendered Views: Concepción Gimeno Re-Writes the Aztecs at the End of the Nineteenth Century," Chapter 9, and Nupur Chaudhuri, "The Indian Other: Reactions of Two Anglo-Indian Women Travel Writers, Eliza Fay and A.U.," Chapter 10.
50 Levine, *Greater Ethiopia*, pp. 54–5.
51 Hirut Tefere, "Gender and Cross Cultural Dynamics in Ethiopia with Particular Reference to Property Rights, and the Role and Status of Women," in Fukui, Kurimoto, and Shigeta, *Ethiopia in Broader Perspective, Vol. III*, pp. 541–68, and especially, pp. 555–6.
52 Tefere, "Gender and Cross Cultural Dynamics in Ethiopia," p. 568.
53 Prouty, *Empress Taytu*, pp. 76–99, 155–61, 305–32.
54 Bahru, *History of Modern Ethiopia*, p. 128 for "political innocuousness."
55 Marcus, *History of Ethiopia*, p. 117.
56 See Marcus, *History of Ethiopia*, pp. 46–7. Mentewab's husband was Bakaffa (r. 1721–30), her son Iyasu II (r. 1730–55), her grandson, Iyoas (r. 1755–69).
57 R. Pankhurst, "Role of Women," pp. 345–6.
58 Tadesse Tamrat, *Church and State in Ethiopia, 1270–1527* (Oxford: Clarendon Press, 1972), pp. 287–90.
59 Chartism is characterized in much the same way by Anna Clark; see her *The Struggle for the Breeches: Gender and the Making of the British Working Class* (London: Rivers Oram Press, 1995).
60 Salome, "Changing Position of Women," p. 113.
61 There are similarities between Ethiopian women's land rights and the pre-colonial land rights of Mexican women as discussed in Vázquez García, "Native Women and State Legislation in Mexico and Canada," Chapter 7 above.
62 D.F. Bauer, *Household and Society in Ethiopia: An Economic and Social Analysis of Tigray Social Principles and Household Organization* (East Lansing: Michigan State University African Studies Center, 1977), pp. 240–2.
63 A. Hoben, *Land Tenure among the Amhara of Ethiopia: The Dynamics of Cognatic Descent* (Chicago: University of Chicago Press, 1973), p. 61.
64 See Wolfgang Weisleder, "The Political Ecology of Amhara Domination" (PhD Thesis: University of Chicago, 1965).
65 This paragraph draws heavily on Hoben, *Land Tenure*, pp. 1–28.
66 Salome, "Changing Position of Women," pp. 112–13.
67 Crummey, "Women and Landed Property," p. 18.

68 Yared Amare, "Women's Access to Resources in Amhara Households in Wogda, Northern Shewa," in Fukui, Kurimoto, and Shigeta, *Ethiopia in Broader Perspective, Vol. III*, pp. 753–7. See in similar vein, H. Pankhurst, *Gender, Development and Identity*, pp. 24–5.

69 Crummey, "Women and Landed Property," p. 31.

70 J.C. McCann, *People of the Plow: An Agricultural History of Ethiopia, 1800–1990* (Madison and London: University of Wisconsin Press, 1995), especially, pp. 72–7. H. Pankhurst, *Gender, Development and Identity*, especially Part 2, "Women's Work and Women's Lives."

71 In addition to the references in the previous footnote, see also Yared on the deference shown by peasant women to their spouses in Wogda. The spouse washes her husband's feet on his return from work, and always serves him first with food and drink; see her "Women's Access to Resources," p. 750.

72 Helen Pankhurst offers the most detailed discussion for of the broad range of peasant women's work activities in near-contemporary Ethiopia (in Menz), see her *Gender, Development and Identity*, pp. 75–100. Walter Plowden, the first British Consul to Ethiopia, comments on the broad range of women's domestic labour in nineteenth Ethiopia, see his *Travels in Abyssinia and the Galla Country with an Account of a Mission to Ras Ali in 1848* (London: Longmans, Green and Co., 1868), pp. 146–7. For specific tasks see (for grinding) M. de Almeida, *Some Records of Ethiopia, 1593–1646* (trans. and ed. C.F. Buckingham and G.W.B. Huntingford, London: Hakluyt Society 1954), p. 81, cited in McCann, *People of the Plow*, p. 75, and C. Johnston, *Travels in Southern Abyssinia*, 2 vols. (London: Madden and Co., 1844) 2: 27–8; (for cooking), M. Parkyns, *Life in Abyssinia: Being Notes collected during a Three Years' Residence and Travels in that Country* (London: 1868), pp. 195–6 and N. Pearce, *Life and Adventures of Nathaniel Pearce*, 2 vols. (London: Colburn and Bentley, 1831), 1:347–8. For further historical examples, including a number of those cited above see, R. Pankhurst, "Role of Women," pp. 346, 350–3.

73 H. Pankhurst, *Gender, Development and Identity*, pp. 96–9.

74 H. Pankhurst, *Gender, Development and Identity*, p. 83 for the "dirty work" in animal care, and for women in agriculture, pp. 78–82.

75 McCann, *People of the Plow*, p. 75, for "blurred gender roles"; Guyer, "Naturalism," p. 373.

76 Pankhurst remarks of the Menz region that "Men ploughed and . . . it was unheard of for a woman to do so," see her *Gender, Development and Identity*, p. 78. McCann comments that "Nowhere in the historical or contemporary experience of farmers I have interviewed is there evidence of women plowing."

77 McCann, *People of the Plow*, p. 74; Yared, "Women's Access to Resources," pp. 754–6, and note especially her comment that "cutting and piling hay and grain stalks" are as much men's work as plowing, but see also Pankhurst, note 69 above.

78 For "historically ubiquitous," see McCann, *People of the Plow*, p. 75, who puts the percentage of female-headed households in Denki district of Shawa at fifteen percent. In Gragn district of Menz, Helen Pankhurst approximated the percentage of apparently independent women at twenty-three percent. However, she notes the figure of single women registered as heads of household as actually nearer fifteen percent; see her *Gender, Development and Identity*, pp. 120–1.

79 Yared, "Women's Access to Resources," p. 750. McCann also records how one peasant woman from Ada district, southeast of Addis Ababa, asserted that if her husband tried to use all their land for *teff* (the fine grain grown only in Ethiopia and the main ingredient of *enjara*), she would intervene to ensure that he reserved a "corner

of land" for wheat and other cereals to provide bread for their children, see his *People of the Plow*, p. 77.

80 J. McCann, *From Poverty to Famine in Northeast Ethiopia. A Rural History, 1900–1935* (Philadelphia: University of Pennsylvania Press, 1987), pp. 51–2.

81 Helen Pankhurst depicts six kinds of monogamous marriage in Menz and other parts of the northern highlands in her *Gender, Development and Identity*, pp. 102–7 (and also describes cases of polygyny and extra-marital relationships). Types of marriage included *serg* (ceremonial first marriage organised by parents with endowment of resources), *qurban* (religious marriage, often for priests and their spouses), *semanya* (civil marriage, which may overlap other forms), *qot'assir* (arranged marriage, marked by provision of labor, with a young groom often working in the household of his future wife, and by the youth of the bride), *garad* or *demoz* (contractual marriage involving payments to the bride, favored in the past by traders and soldiers away from home), and *t'iff* (kidnapping, with varying degrees of parental and bridal knowledge and cooperation, often a precursor to *serg* or *semanya*). For further discussion of these and forms of marriage in other parts of Ethiopia, see E. Lvova, "Forms of Marriage and the Status of Women in Ethiopia," in Fukui, Kurimoto, and Shigeta, *Ethiopia in Broader Perspective, Vol. III*, pp. 577–84. Judith Olmstead notes the cooperation of the "kidnapped" bride among the Dorze of southern Ethiopia in "Ethiopia's Artful Weavers," pp. 125–41.

82 Pankhurst, *Gender, Development and Identity*, p. 50, 53–4, and see also McCann's *People of the Plow*, pp. 73–4. Note both sources also for average number of marriages, 2–3 for women in Shawa, 3–4 perhaps in Wallo. This paragraph also draws on Yared, "Women's Access to Resources," pp. 752–3, especially for detailed discussion of divorce settlements. Relatively uncommon uxorilocal marriages, where the husband joined the bride's parents' homestead, providing his labour (*qot'assir*), required the man to leave the marital home on divorce.

83 H. Pankhurst, *Gender, Development and Identity*, p. 114; McCann, *People of the Plow*, p. 53.

84 For Menz, H. Pankhurst, *Gender, Development and Identity*, p. 115. In the same chapter she also questions why in the very religious society of Christian Abyssinia the church played so small a role in marriage, concluding that the "only credible explanation is that marriages are too unstable for the Church to wish to be involved, or for the population to wish to sanctify unions," p. 119. For Wallo see McCann, *People of the Plow*, p. 54.

85 According to Helen Pankhurst and Yared Amare, women's reasons for initiating divorce included wasting money or decline of the household's finances, lack of personal and sexual attraction, physical and sexual abuse, adultery, excessive demands for labor, poor relations with mothers-in-law, illness, barren unions, homesickness, and age difference between spouses, see *Gender, Development and Identity*, p. 116, and "Women's Access to Resources," p. 751.

86 H. Pankhurst, *Gender, Development and Identity*, p. 117–18. Pankhurst dismisses Reminick's view of the contradiction between egalitarian marriage and hierarchical society in Ethiopia, see R. Reminick, "The Manze Amhara of Ethiopia: A Study of Authority, Masculinity and Sociality" (Ph.D. Thesis, University of Chicago, 1973).

87 See Yared's comments in her "Women's Access to Resources," p. 756.

88 "Careering through Marriage" is the title of Helen Pankhurst's incisive chapter on marriage and divorce, see *Gender, Development and Identity*, pp. 102–26.

89 Pankhurst, *Gender, Development and Identity*, pp. 127–41; Almaz, "Issues of Gender and Sexuality," pp. 572. Almaz also discusses such "oppressive practices" as the

insertion of lip plates among peoples of the southwest, and of female genital mutilation, common in many parts of Ethiopia (pp. 573–4). She makes the forceful argument that in trying to force women to adhere to prevailing notions of beauty and decency, such accepted customs "challenge their humanity" and enforce their subordination.

90 H. Pankhurst, *Gender, Development and Identity*, pp. 148–67, and p. 157 for "the opportunity for expression" and "sphere of power."

91 R. Pankhurst, *Role of Women*, p. 345, and *passim* for the following list of women and their occupations.

92 Almaz, "Issues of Gender and Sexuality," p. 570.

93 To adapt Elizabeth Fox-Genovese's comment, originally made in her "Placing Women's History in History," *New Left Review* 133 (1982), pp. 5–29, and cited in the introduction by Shoemaker and Vincent to their *Gender and History*, see p. 2.

94 The comment about patriarchy reflects Shoemaker and Vincent's observations, see *Gender and History*, p. 4, but see also J. Tosh, "What Should Historians do with Masculinity? Reflections on Nineteenth-Century Britain," first published in *History Workshop Journal* 38 (1994), reprinted in *Gender and History*, see especially, p. 81.

95 While we have reservations about the utility of deconstructionist analysis used in isolation, Donald Levine and Helen Pankhurst have, from different perspectives, highlighted the construction of meaning through language. Pankhurst, in particular, has demonstrated how in Menz gender distinctions in language reinforced male domination, whilst gender reversal subverted male hegemony. See Levine *Wax and Gold*, pp. 5–9, and Pankhurst, *Gender, Development and Identity*, pp. 169–71. For an introduction to the vigorous debate about history, gender history, and postmodernism, see Shoemaker and Vincent, *Gender and History*, pp. 8–10 and 18, notes 31–2.

Index